A
THEORY
OF
MUSICAL
SEMIOTICS

Advances in Semiotics

Thomas A. Sebeok, *General Editor*

EERO TARASTI

A
THEORY
OF
MUSICAL
SEMIOTICS

INDIANA UNIVERSITY PRESS
Bloomington and Indianapolis

Library of Congress Cataloging-in-Publication Data

Tarasti, Eero.
    A theory of musical semiotics / Eero Tarasti.
       p. cm. — (Advances in semiotics)
    Includes bibliographical references.
    ISBN 0-253-35649-0 (cloth)
    1. Music—Semiotics.   2. Music—Theory.   3. Musical analysis.
I. Title. II. Series.
ML3845.T35   1994
781' .1—dc20   93-47889

1 2 3 4 5 99 98 97 96 95 94   MN

To Eila

CONTENTS

Part One: Theoretical Background

I. In Search of a Theory

II. Musical Time

III. Musical Space

IV. Musical Actors

Part Two: Analyses

V. Semiosis of the Classical Style: Beethoven's "Waldstein"

VI. Narrativity in Chopin

FOREWORD

Thomas A. Sebeok

The flourishing series Advances in Semiotics, in which Eero Tarasti's uncommonly thoughtful and inspired treatise now appears, was launched in 1976 with Umberto Eco's *A Theory of Semiotics*. From the beginning, the most salient characteristic of the series was—as it has remained in the intervening eighteen years—its distinctly global cast. Of course, this adjective resonates in several of its abundantly polysemous senses, one being "international," some possibly pejorative antonyms of which can be "provincial" and, more tellingly, "parochial." The Lausanne linguist Mortéza Mahmoudian introduced of late the vaguely menacing expression "semiotic omnipotence" as a synonym for universality. In this respect, my view of semiotic inquiry has been guided by a gentler phrase I adapted after a line in Wallace Stevens's "Anecdote of the Jar": "it took dominion everywhere." By "global semiotics," I mean first of all an intricate piece of political negotiation, one which spins a network or, to use another familiar image, a web. But while I believe in devising all-encompassing scenarios, I reckon it wise to act on them locally.

Accordingly, we endeavored to capture both the singular theoretical canons on display from Classical times, through the age of Vico, up to this very day, and applications thereof by the same or by a host of other eminent contributors to the doctrine of signs to quite diverse domains as developed or developing in both United States and foreign workshops. In addition to more than half a dozen books written, edited, or co-edited by Eco, the series has been the principal outlet, among home-grown colleagues, for three fundamental treatises by Floyd Merrell and several basic books by John Deely. Here belongs, too, Milton Singer's fascinating *Man's Glassy Essence*, with its Peircean resonances—as befits the list of a university press that has heavily invested its limited resources in works of, about, or shaped by America's foremost framer of modern semiotics, Charles Sanders Peirce: for example, in linguistics, by Michael Shapiro; in literature, by the Danish scholar Jørgen Dines Johansen; and, in the urgent arena of biography, the pioneering, spine-chilling story of Peirce's difficult life by the historian Joseph Brent.

Among European scholars (as I had spelled out in my Foreword to Cesare Segre's *Introduction to the Analysis of the Literary Text*), the series has no doubt leaned toward the rich harvest of Italian scholarship, recently adding, on the one hand, such classics as Giorgio Fano's *The Origins and Nature of Language,* and, on the other, fresh books by younger semioticians, including Giovanni Manetti (on the history of Western semiotics in Antiquity) and Marco De Marinis (on performance semiotics).

But Indiana University Press has by no means neglected works in various facets of worldwide semiotic inquiry and practice by Australians (Horst Ruthrof), Belgians (André Helbo), our Canadian neighbors on both sides of their language boundary (Paul Bouissac, Marcel Danesi, Marike Finlay, Fernande Saint-Martin, Lorraine Weir), Germans (Winfried Nöth, Erika Fischer-Lichte), French (Geneviève Calbris, Jean-Claude Gardin, A. J. Greimas and J. Courtés), and quondam Soviets (the late Yuri M. Lotman, Sebastian Shaumyan).

There are several specialties in respect to which, in the aggregate, the series stands virtually unique, one such area being the semiotics of the theatre and kindred areas of performance: here belong books by Bouissac, Marvin Carlson, De Marinis, Fischer-Lichte, Helbo (the last-mentioned also incorporating inputs from several of the aforementioned and from Patrice Pavis and Anne Ubersfeld), Laura Oswald, and Marcello Pagnini.

A while ago, I suggested to Indiana University Press that we embark upon yet another, tangentially related, coherent cluster of materials: to wit, in musical semiotics. The first pertinent book in the series was the American Robert S. Hatten's *Musical Meaning in Beethoven: Markedness, Correlation, and Interpretation*, which, with a Foreword by the noted Canadian musicologist David Lidov, appeared not long ago. Eero Tarasti's *A Theory of Musical Semiotics* is our second book in this subspecialty, but it is the first from the studio of a Finnish colleague.

In his Preface, Tarasti modestly characterizes himself as a synthesizer of "semiotic theories and specifically musicology" who, having taken as his starting point the semiotic scheme of A. J. Greimas, proceeded to apply some radical notions of Yuri Lotman, and is now productively utilizing the classic concepts of C. S. Peirce. However, Tarasti's work is in the end—as it ought to be—empirically driven, moving from concrete detail (the behavior of "real" composers, like Beethoven and Debussy, their performers, and audiences) to abstract idea, in what Tarasti refers to as "the conceptual jungle of semiotics."

In 1981, Tarasti was appointed to a Professorship in Arts Education at the University of Jyväskylä, a town in an area of Finland generally perceived as midway between the North and the South. In the same year, he founded the Semiotic Society of Finland (which now has about 270 members), and visited Indiana University for the first time. He has returned to the Bloomington campus (and the Peirce Edition Project, located on our Indianapolis sister-campus) frequently, most recently as a Fellow in our Institute for Advanced Study. In 1984, he was called to the University of Helsinki to occupy the Chair of Musicology. In the latter 1980s, he organized a series of Conferences on Musical Signification, now sustained by an international core group of some one hundred musicologists and semioticians.

It has been a fascinating experience for me to observe since 1946, firsthand, if intermittently, the emergence (especially after 1981), rapid consolidation, and dramatic growth of semiotic studies in Finland. At least since gaining independence and becoming the Republic of Finland in 1917, the people tend to view their country, Suomen Tasavalta, as anchored in a mediating position between a mythical "East" and a comparably chimerical "West." In semiosis, the pivotal operative notion is always the Sign, which occupies, as it were, a mediating position between a hypothetical entity called an "Object"—but which in truth is another sign, or, more accurately, a limitless array of other—and another putative, somewhat cryptic entity Peirce called an "Interpretant"—but which in verity is yet another sign, or, more exactly, an unending chain of other signs. The Finnish preoccupation (some would call it an obsession) with a perpetual, complex dialectic between Center ("inclusion") and Periphery ("exclusion") is played and replayed in various forums of their cultural, social, and political life; not surprisingly, it has surfaced even as an explicit topic selected for discussion in several of their annual conferences dedicated to semiotics. (The first volume of the series Acta Semiotica Fennica was subtitled *Center and Periphery in Representations and Institutions* [1990].) Finland today has itself become a mazelike Supersign poised amidst a dense profusion of other signs, relegated to the margins.

Thanks to Tarasti's personal as well as scholarly initiatives and hard work, Finnish semiotics has bloomed at the confluence of Baltic semiotics and Nordic semiotics. The two most-celebrated figures of Baltic semiotics, even posthumously, are the above-mentioned magnetic Russian indweller of Tartu, Yuri Lotman, and the acclaimed Lithuanian resident of Paris, A. J. Greimas. Notwithstanding that these personages, or, in the wider sense, the so-called Moscow-Tartu School and the L'école de Paris, have palpably affected Finnish semiotics, its intrinsic contour—further enriched by Eco's thought and, increasingly so, directly by the mighty river of the Peirce's doctrine of signs— abides as conspicuously separate and original, sometimes to the point of unashamed idiosyncrasy. Finland continues, however, in its customary generous ecumenical embrace, to reach out to the young semioticians of abutting Estonia, Latvia, and Lithuania. And, on yet another neighborly front, in 1989, in Imatra, Finland was one of the founding members of the Nordic Association for Semiotic Studies (also comprising Denmark, Iceland, Norway, and Sweden), of which Tarasti is currently president.

But where is Imatra? The answer to this question depends on whether one defines it geopolitically or semiotically. If, from a Eurocentric standpoint, Finland does in some sense lie "at the Periphery," then, from an internal Finnish standpoint, the City of Imatra is situated at the Periphery of that Periphery. This small Karelian industrial community is located at the easternmost edge of Lake Saimaa, near the Russian border. It is popular among tourists for Alvar Aalto's Church of the Three Crosses and for the Vuoksi River rapids, which (when switched on) roar down through its "center."

More to the point, however, Imatra is legendary among semioticians of the world since 1988 for being the site (when switched on, as is currently the case, both during the academic year and in midsummer) of the International Semiotics Institute. This Institute is in a sense comparable only with, although it is also dissimilar in important respects from, Urbino's Centro internazionale di Semiotica e Linguistica. The most conspicuous difference lies in the fact that the Centro is nested within a large, established Italian Università degli Studi, with a faculty and a student body, augmented by supporting facilities, including a vast dormitory system with food services. ISI, by contrast, lacks a permanent faculty and has no home-grown students or physical plant of its own (except, significantly, for its excellent reference library, with a steady acquisitions program for important semiotics books published around the world).

Tarasti, as ISI's *spiritus movens*, has achieved a creative, if on the face of it unlikely, synthesis between the Center, which is Helsinki, and the Periphery, which was in Imatra, transforming the latter into an incorporeal Epicenter, a semiotic Mecca. How was this accomplished? Administered in a combined effort with the University of Helsinki, ISI's operations are financed from the Center by the Finnish Ministry of Education and the Academy of Finland, and, at the same time, from the Periphery by the City of Imatra itself and the provincial government, abetted by the support of several enlightened local companies. Finland's international program dedicated to the Doctrine of Signs—emphasizing semiotics of music, medicine, philosophy, and sociology and applications to literature, film, and art history—entitles students at the University of Helsinki to participate in lectures and seminars offered by ISI in Imatra, but they may also sit for examinations in semiotics at the University of Vaasa and the Helsinki School of Economics and Business Administration.

In the early 1990s, Finland, like much of Europe, was in the midst of a recession, and its many universities were threatened by "downsizing." But a wise government, knowing that the future of the country rests in those hands, shelters and educates its youth. The symbolic transposition, on the wings of a subject such as semiotics, of Imatra from the country's cultural Periphery to its Center of gravity, a move fraught with political meaning, may lead to the establishment of a Chair in Semiotics at the University of Helsinki. In this Foreword, speaking for myself as well as for the global semiotics community, I salute and thank this administration for its trust and foresight, and Eero Tarasti, its Professor of Musicology, for his proficiency and sagacity.

BLOOMINGTON, INDIANA

PREFACE

It is impossible for me to say exactly when the idea of writing a theory of musical semiotics ripened into a firm decision. This volume is the product of at least fifteen years' work. During that time I have appeared in the roles of both musicologist and semiotician, so whenever more traditional-minded music scholars worried about losing their way in the conceptual jungle of semiotics, I could tell them that I also do "normal" musicology. This end-product reflects my attempt to synthesize semiotic theories and specifically musical problems. As a student of A. J. Greimas in Paris in the early 1970s, then later as a researcher in Brazil and the United States, I deliberately set out to explore theoretical and practical problems in semiotics. Yet right from the beginning I considered it important that, at the same time as I built up a theory, I must also account for its applicability to music—in a word, for its musicality. Quite early on I adopted as my starting point the semiotic theory of Lithuanian-born scholar A. J. Greimas. I then completed my investigation, piece by piece, until I felt the theory was "ready."

My work, especially in recent years, has developed in a strongly empirical direction. This was certainly influenced by my time at Indiana University, Bloomington, at the Research Center for Language and Semiotic Studies, directed by Thomas A. Sebeok and Jean Umiker-Sebeok, and at that university's famous School of Music. I further recall the criticism I received at Gilbert Rouget's ethnomusicological seminar at the Musée de l'Homme in Paris: "We want analyses, concrete illustrations of a theory, not just structuralist speculations!" This book consequently offers an abundance of analyses from different style periods of Western art music. There could have perhaps been more, particularly of contemporary music. I also remember a symposium, chaired by Joseph Ujfalussy at the University of Budapest, at which my colleague Daniel Charles said: "You semioticians might be kings of nineteenth-century music, but are your categories and grammars still valid for the music of our own time?" At the end of this treatise I open the door somewhat in that direction, but leave to another inquiry a full answer to Charles's question.

This almost never-ending project has advantages and disadvantages. On the positive side, theoretical reflection and analyses have been able to ripen together, and at a relatively tranquil tempo. At first, for instance, I did not realize how important the discovery of modalities in music would become. Likewise the idea of a generative model grew stronger over time, though my own view of it differs from the most rigorous computer applications. Over the years the theoretical "monism" of my study has also been mitigated by the theories of Charles S. Peirce and Juri Lotman, just as I have also been influenced by new, purely musicological findings, such as recent scholarship on Ernst Kurth and the work of Lerdahl and Jackendoff, Cogan and Escot, and others. A negative side to this kind of long-term project is that by the time it is completed, its foundations have become outdated. Yet I do not believe that a pure theory, like that of Greimas, can get "old" when viewed in the historical perspective of 2,000 years of Western semiotic. Indeed, I believe that relying on one, almost axiomatic theory can be balanced by adapting the theory to the empirical data.

As a scholar I consider myself the "idoneist" described by Swiss mathematician and philosopher Ferdinand Gonseth, that is, a researcher who takes into account the circumstances and context in which the examination proceeds. Even as a Greimasian semiotician and in my usage of Peirce, I have given priority to the musical reality itself, and if the theory has not fit the facts, it has been corrected and changed.

Some semioticians might therefore accuse me of eclecticism. At the annual meeting of the American Semiotic Society, in Buffalo, New York, a Canadian colleague was astonished at the subject of my paper— "Peirce and Greimas in music semiotics"—and said it was like putting fire and water into the same vessel. In response, I should first like to state, echoing Juri Lotman, that the whole dispute over whether the structure of the sign is binary or ternary is outdated, since what is essential is not the inner organization of the sign but its functioning as a part of the semiosphere, a continuum of signs. Second, I believe that all rigorous conceptual systems, such as Greimas's, are directed in their usage by a kind of higher-level logic. Oddly enough, the nature of this higher logic has not received much semiotic attention. Though I might not be able to make this logic completely explicit—for example, by justifying *why* I have chosen certain concepts and levels from the Greimasian generative trajectory and *how* I in fact use them—I do not think that my analytic method thus becomes arbitrary in nature.

There exist nowadays several strict mathematico-logical systems whose rules are quite explicit, automatically given by their grammars. Sad to say, those systems often produce rather trivial results. Yet their adherents almost always say: "Naturally, this is *still* fairly rudimentary, because we are dealing with a new method, with which we are experimenting for the first time. But just wait for the method to develop; then you'll see how it can resolve more complicated problems and situations!" Most often such a moment never arrives.

That is to say, I have always tried to avoid building a musical semiotic theory that might be completely coherent, systematic, and logical as a theory—in the words of Louis Hjelmslev, exhaustive, noncontradictory, and economical—*but* that can be applied only in extremely primitive musical situations. I mean, for instance, very simple, stereotypical music genres, brief fragments of musical texts, or, in the worst case, merely brief sections of melody or even single notes. I want the theory to relate to the musical reality in all its complexity, the reality in which both researcher and listener live. After all, most significant compositions display a relatively high degree of sophistication and complexity.

Theory must elucidate those works and the behavior of real composers, performers, and listeners, not of "laboratory mice."

Some might consider my aspirations too high, but I am nevertheless aiming at a method that makes sense in terms of the object itself, i.e., the special qualitative nature of the music under examination. The reader will notice that, in spite of the unifying theory, each of my analyses differs slightly from the others. There must be room for change in any theory or method, to avoid the shortcoming in which the analytic result is always the same, whatever the object analyzed (as in some cases of Schenkerism). Thus the analyses in Part Two make free use of some aspects of the model and leave others aside, according to what the music demands.

Why have I chosen to analyze just these pieces from Beethoven to Debussy and not others? There are many reasons. First, as a music semiotician I rarely start to analyze a piece that I do not know well in advance, and in a purely musical sense. My theory grew out of deep intimacy, as both performer and listener, with the pieces analyzed. Yet some true "findings" have resulted from the analytical process itself, during which I became familiar with and came to like a work only by analyzing it. Such is the case with the Debussy study, written for the European Congress of Music Analysis in 1989, and the Sibelius essay, whose context was the 125th anniversary of the composer's birth.

I have arranged the present analyses in chronological order, not according to theoretical criteria, thereby hoping to emphasize that musical semiotics is not always so far removed from traditional historical approaches, and that it perhaps lies somewhere between German systematic and historical musicology. The historical "urge" was so strong that in the final phase of my work I noticed that this book might equally well be entitled "Music History in the Light of Semiotics." Nevertheless, my colleague from Edinburgh, Raymond Monelle, finally persuaded me that the work we semioticians of music were undertaking was rather of a theoretical nature.

The ideal reader of this book has some familiarity with semiotics, in its Saussurean incarnation as "semiology" and its Peircean form as "semiotic," with structuralism, and with narratology, especially that of A. J. Greimas. Even if this is not the case, in the theoretical speculations of Part One and the analyses of Part Two, terms and concepts should clarify themselves by the context in which they occur. To that end, a Glossary has been added that further explains and provides background for technical terms.

My analyses aim for theoretical rigor and formalization, while in the background lie my own musical intuition and competence. Regardless of the formal-logical notation in which my analyses are couched, their roots run to the listening, performing, and experiencing of music. I dare say this even at the risk of being misunderstood and accused of subjectivity. Yet, in the end, theories of music are often only rationalizations of a scholar's own musical experiences, at a certain historical moment and in a certain community. I have been astonished by some recent methods of music analysis that claim to make explicit "the intuitions of a competent music listener," and all the while the person disguised in the abstract concept of listener is none other than the writer him- or herself. Of course, the semiotical approach, too, in whatever form it emerges in any era, will itself constitute such an "ideological" product.

Terms and Symbols Used in the Text

Octave registers conform to those of the American Acoustical Society: middle C = C4; one octave below middle C = C3; C one octave above middle C = C5; etc. Scale degrees are designated with carats; e.g., $\hat{3}$ = scale degree 3. The modalities are denoted with single quotes; e.g., 'being'. Because the original French terms for modalities include a wider range of connotations than their English counterparts, in many cases the French terms appear along with the English (e.g., *être* = 'being').

ACKNOWLEDGMENTS

I owe debts of gratitude to so many people that it is not possible to mention all of them. First of all, I want to thank, for constant and patient encouragement, Professor Thomas A. Sebeok of Indiana University. Next, I am grateful to my assistant editors, Richard Littlefield and Paul Forsell, for invaluable help in revising and editing my book into its final form. Robert S. Hatten read the manuscript and gave me several good ideas for improvement.

Naturally, I want to include in this list of thanks all the members of the Musical Signification project, as well as my colleagues, students, and friends in musicology and semiotics, both in Finland and abroad.

My wife, Eila, has been my support in everything during these years, and I dedicate this volume to her.

I

Theoretical Background

I

IN SEARCH OF A THEORY

1.1 A Brief Critical History of Musical Semiotics

An implicit starting point for the study of all cultural phenomena is the fact that we live quite literally surrounded by various signs and significations, at the intersection of messages coming from everywhere. This universe of signs includes musical signs and messages. Not only are all stylistic periods of musical history simultaneously present in our time, but also our musical consciousness has expanded in an anthropological dimension, as Westerners are increasingly exposed to the different values and realities of non-Western cultures. Against this background it seems natural that musicologists, too, should join the search for theories and models that can explain, more effectively than before, the total heterogeneity of musical reality. Partly because of these circumstances, an entirely new branch of research—musical semiotics—has emerged; and interest in this type of research has also increased considerably among scholars representing "traditional" musicology. The dispersion of our musical reality justifies the question whether there exist any common features in all human uses and practices of music, i.e., musical universals, categories of the human mind that form a basis for any and all musical activity.

The problem can be put another way: Is it possible to construct a theory, a musicological metalanguage, to deal with and describe these universals? More particularly, can musical semiotics serve as this kind of integrating method? The first problem encountered, considered crucial by Charles Seeger, concerns the gap between two kinds of knowledge about music (1960: 225). According to him there is a conflict between the inner knowledge of music (felt immediately by producers and receivers of music) and the knowledge conveyed verbally, "outside" the musical process. Seeger viewed the relation between the inner universals of music and the speech universals of its observation from the "outside" as the basic problem of musicology. How can musicology, which is verbal activity, bring knowledge of the inner logic of music?

This question can be answered in three ways. First, one may assume that the two sets of universals overlap, that there is no basic difference between them, and that language can express the most essential aspects of music. This viewpoint is an oversimplification, for if verbal and tonal languages were parallel phenomena, we could not explain why musical expression has developed so far and formed a specific discourse in almost all cultures. The second viewpoint is supported by many musicians, who claim that musical and verbal knowledge are mutually exclusive. Someone may have a wide verbal knowledge of music without any idea of how music sounds or is made to sound. To speak about music is useless, suffice to play it. This attitude ignores facts of music history, since musical tradition is essentially transmitted with the support of verbal expressions, and no sign system in any culture functions separately from other modeling systems. Therefore, the third and most reasonable alternative would be to take a mediating position, from which we can say something true about music while accepting that some aspects of music cannot be depicted verbally, though some aestheticians paradoxically have written whole books about music and the ineffable (e.g., Jankélévitch 1961). Consequently, musicology must consider its place among different ways of speaking about music and the relation of its metalanguage to musical phenomena, and such consideration must include semiotical observations concerning the nature of the musical sign system.

Sign systems can be classified according to their physical channels or modes: whether their expressions belong to the visual sense (gestures, mime, writing, plastic arts, etc.), the auditory sense (spoken language, music, etc.), or the tactile sense (the language of the blind). We should note that musical reality is not limited to aural expressions. As Ingmar Bengtsson has suggested (1977: 17), the concept of tone can refer to notation (*tone n*), or to a physically measurable frequency (*tone ph*), or to an experienced, aural and phenomenal entity (*tone ϕ*). To complete the paradigm, "tone" may also exist in a tactile mode, when the performer transforms the score into a gestural language of musculatory movements and touches. We might call this case *tone g*, with *g* meaning gesture (according to one French school, piano playing is a science of gestures). This classification reveals that, in some of its modes of existence, music comes very close to nonverbal sign systems, not only to verbal ones (which appeal to that faded metaphor, "the language of music"). Thomas A. Sebeok has suggested that we call the basic units of all nonverbal sign systems "g-Signs" (1976: 161–62). In music one might also speak of "technemes" (Baudrillard 1968: 12), since music involves technical, concrete realization.[1]

Because musical reality manifests itself in various ways, we have to ask what the relation is between expression and content (signifier and signified) in each mode (tactile, visual, physical, phenomenal) and whether the different musical modes can be translated into each other, thus making possible the continuity of the musical process. The first "translation" occurs in the composer's mind, with the transformation of his or her musical idea into visual notation. Next, the performer translates the score into gestural language and body techniques. Then the listener translates sound phenomena into the "language" of inner experience. Finally, the most radical translation is made by those who set out to describe in words some of these modes of expression.

In the next two sections I shall survey what might be called "semiotical" ways of speaking about music. This does not imply an unambiguous solution based on safe application of an established method. Musical semiotics is a discipline in flux, a science under construction. The theories and methods of musical semiotics can nevertheless be roughly classified into two main types. On the one hand are theories proceeding from surface level toward deep structures. I call this method "structuralist," in that it represents reductionism, a reduction of sensory reality to a small number of categories. On the other hand are methods that are basically antireductionist, whose proponents argue that one should not reduce music to abstract categories that function outside the musical process, but that the significance of music is "iconic," based strictly on itself. This view emphasizes the gestural nature of music as something sensory, as a process.

Structuralist Approaches to Music

Besides the search for deep levels, the structuralist method is characterized by study of the smallest significant units of a sign system. Especially during the first phase of musical semiotics, in the 1960s, semiotics was dominated by structuralism and the direct borrowing of linguistic methods. It was thought that in music also one might distinguish the units of the first articulation (meaningful items, musical "words") and the second articulation (musical "phonemes," meaningless items). Through a sort of *ars combinatoria*, musical semioticians tried to build units of signification from these small atoms. All sign systems, even music, were assumed to operate like language. In this sense we may understand the argument of Lévi-Strauss in his introduction to his *Mythologiques* (1964: 26–30), namely, that nonfigurative painting and atonal music are not languages since they lack the level of the first articulation— meaningful and recognizable figures in painting, tonal functions in music. Accordingly, Lévi-Strauss's critique of avant-garde art has to be seen in relation to problems inherent in semiotics of the 1960s, when even composers like Pierre Boulez (1971) and Luciano Berio (1974) became interested in linguistics and structuralism. A great number of structuralist analyses inspired by linguistics appeared at that time, among them studies by Mâche (1971: 75–91), Chiarucci (1973), Boiles (1973: 81–99), Ruwet (1972), and Nattiez (1976). Later, I too applied structuralist methodology to the aesthetics of music in the Romantic era, by distinguishing a particular network of mythical semes, the smallest items of mythical meaning in music, as constituting an operational reading model of certain musical texts (Tarasti 1979).

There are also structuralist methods of music analysis that have nothing to do with linguistics. Such is the case with Heinrich Schenker's theory, which we might call a structuralism before structuralism. Schenker's theory is based on "triple articulation" since he distinguishes three levels: *Vordergrund, Mittelgrund,* and *Hintergrund* (1956; see also 1954). The first of these represents the audible musical surface, while the last level is that to which the surface can be reduced. The phases through which this reduction occurs are called *Mittelgrund*. According to Schenker there exists only one deep structure, the *Ursatz*, which he claims is based on the overtone series of nature. The natural (major) triad, or "Chord of Nature," manifests itself contrapuntally; it consists of an upper, descending part, called the *Urlinie*, and the basic harmonic progression, called the *Grundbrechung*.

Schenker's theory, with its most passionate defenders and representatives in the United States, has been developed further as well as criticized. Eugene Narmour, among others, has called attention to the fact that Schenkerians always proceed from an axiom, from a preestablished structure, and everything in a musical work which is incompatible with that structure is excluded (1977: 83–86, 167–88). Thus Schenkerian analysis is restricted to *langue* but is totally unable to explain the changes of musical *langue* in a given period because new *paroles,*—new "idiolects" or personal styles—emerge which start to realize elements that are implicated by the *Ursatz* but are left out in concrete manifestations of *langue*. Nevertheless, Schenker's theory, like other structuralist inventions, retains its heuristic value. For example, Schenker's attempt to define the *Ursatz* is an effort to explain the coherence of a musical work. Musical events that take place in a work at distant temporal intervals can be understood as belonging together because they form starting and ending points of an extensive *Urlinie* development which Schenker called "composing out" (*Auskomponierung*).

What Schenker tried to make explicit with his concept of *Ursatz* was later paralleled by A. J. Greimas's borrowing of the term "isotopy" from physics. Isotopy designates a set of semantic categories whose redundancy guarantees the coherence and analyzability of any text or sign complex (Greimas 1980: 86–87, 112–20). In music, isotopies mean the principles that articulate musical discourse into coherent sections. If Schenker assumes that there exists only one isotopy for music, the *Ursatz,* we might argue that, on the contrary, there are in fact several isotopies on different levels. Further, several overlapping isotopies can function simultaneously, in which case we speak of complex isotopies. For example, two rhythmic isotopies overlap in the Menuetto of J. S. Bach's Partita in G major (Ex. 1.1),where the rhythmic groups can be perceived as either 2 x 3 or 3 x 2, terminating in a triple rhythm at the end of each phrase. Or one may speak of harmonically complex isotopies, as in the *Todes-*

Example 1.1. J. S. Bach, Partita in G major, Menuetto, mm. 1–4.

motive of Wagner's *Valkyrie* (Ex. 1.2). The first chord, D–F–A, is not really a D minor triad, since F should be interpreted enharmonically as E♯ and the other tones as upper and lower neighboring tones to a seventh chord on C♯.

Example 1.2. Wagner, *Die Valkyrie, Todesmotive.*

Complex isotopies are also exemplified by bitonal and polyrhythmic passages, and by even larger formal units, for example, the so-called telescoping technique in sonata: A particular passage belongs at the same time to two different formal sections or isotopies; what is involved is a section that leads from development into repetition. This can be illustrated by the sections between the development and recapitulation in the first movements of Beethoven's Piano Sonatas in C major, Op. 2 no. 3, and G major, Op. 14 no. 2. Complex isotopies are also used in modern music as a deliberate stylistic device, as in Charles Ives's symphonies.

In sum, the concept of isotopy is one of the most fruitful structuralist ideas, and it remains valuable for semiotical analysis of music. Of all the semiotical and structural approaches in France in the 1960s and 70s, Greimasian theory was the only one that preserved the structuralist heritage of the isotopy concept; Greimasian theory also renewed it, even to the extent that references to the "third semiotic revolution" seem fully justified. The concept of isotopy in music will be defined in more detail before we proceed to iconic analyses of music.

Mere analysis of the musical signifier can never explain the factors that hold together musical form and guarantee its coherence. Music as such may be fragmentary; for example, long pauses may separate different sections of a musical text. Yet these sections are experienced as belonging together. Rudolph Réti called this factor the "thematic process." In his opinion there are two form-creating forces in music. One is external and is based on the segmentation and grouping of units on the manifest level of music; the other is internal and covers so-called thematic phenomena in music (Réti 1951: 138). The dramatic course, the "plot," of a work can be conceived only on this latter level. What Réti understands by the thematic level can be redefined in terms of Greimas's concept of isotopy, producing at least five interpretations of what we mean by musical isotopy:

1. Isotopy can be a more or less achronic and abstract deep structure, such as the *Ursatz* in Schenker or the semiotic square in Greimas. As we relate

music to such deep structures, we experience it as "making sense" (Lidov 1980). Of interest is not the mere fact that this type of structure looms in the background, but the way it manifests itself temporally in the course of a musical work. For example, given a semiotic square as in Fig. 1.1, we are interested in what order and exactly how its terms emerge during the work. What is the direction and what are the dynamics of the thematic structuring of a composition? Do we proceed from s1 to s2 and further to non-s2 and to non-s1? Or do we start with non-s2 and only at the end come to the positive term of s1? What are the dynamics of this unfolding? Is the tensional quality hesitating, expiring, retarding, accelerating, beginning, ending?[2] These questions cannot be answered without consideration of music's temporal unfolding.

Figure 1.1. The semiotic square.

According to Greimas (1979), there are three temporal categories: inchoativity, durativity, terminativity. Also, his category of perfectivity/imperfectivity describes the relation of the temporal process to the initial problem of the composition. The "problem" does not necessarily refer to any initial "lack" in a narrative, or "conflict" in a mythical sense. Rather, what is involved is that every tone heard after the first puts the balance of the work in question and creates a demand for the return of that balance; it would be difficult to imagine a musical universe lacking all tensions caused by durativity. In chapter 2 the fundamental problems of temporality in music will be examined in the light of semiotics.

2. What Réti meant by *thematicity* can form an isotopy of music. For example, Beethoven's Piano Sonata in E major, Op. 109, consists of three movements whose interpretation is problematic, since they break the normal alternation of fast and slow movements in a sonata. First comes a movement where *vivace* and *adagio* alternate, then a fast middle movement in *prestissimo*, and at the end a large variation section built on a *lied*-type theme (Ex. 1.3). The structure of the sonata becomes clear when we notice that the whole musical substance of the first two movements has been inferred from the *lied* theme of the last movement. All that is heard in the work before the emergence of this theme belongs to the "not yet."

3. Musical *genre* features can serve as an isotopy. French philosopher Vladimir Jankélévitch claims that the ear cannot discern sonata form without a retrospective view of the path that has been traveled. Nevertheless some genres or form types (sonata, chaconne, fugue, and the like) can function as "ready-made" contexts, which filter an immediate musical experience into a

form and offer a self-evident isotopy for sound events. Only when listening to avant-garde music and music of exotic cultures are we no longer able to use the genre features stored in our memory as an isotopy for music. Thus the *lied* theme in Beethoven's Op. 109 (Ex. 1.3) is no ordinary *lied*, but follows rather

Example 1.3. Beethoven, Op. 109, mvt. III, mm. 1–2, related to mvt. I, opening.

strictly the rhythmic pattern of a sarabande.[3] And we listen to the *lied* theme in a different way if we take sarabande rhythms as its isotopy (see Ex. 1.4).

Example 1.4. Sarabande rhythm patterns.

4. The type of *texture* can function as an isotopy; this is one of the simplest ways for isotopies to appear in music. This kind of isotopy is usually experienced only when it changes. For example, in the middle section of Chopin's F minor Ballade (Ex. 1.5), there is a very surprising strict polyphonic development of the main theme, followed by a sudden return to the initial melody-accompaniment texture. Despite the identical thematic material, one senses a quick shift to another isotopy. Beethoven was the first composer to create for every theme its own timbral isotopy (think, for example, of the variations of the slow movement of the Fifth Symphony), thus isotopy can sometimes function in music as a sort of milieu, a musical landscape in which the theme-actant moves and acts.

Example 1.5. Chopin, F minor Ballade, mm. 144–47.

5. Finally, one may speak of *text strategy* as an isotopy. In music the same theme or thematic idea can be presented in a different light. It can lead to a different result, for example, to a dramatic solution; or it can lead to the achievement or unfulfillment of the action, to perfectivity or imperfectivity (in Greimas's terms). For example, in Chopin's G minor Ballade (analyzed in Chap. 6.2), the main theme, reminiscent of a slow waltz, changes unexpectedly in the development into a tense and durative section, which modulates to E major, into a euphoric emotional state. But at the end of the work, the main theme brings about its own opposition, the dysphoric G minor, thereby reinforcing the piece's elegiac and tragic final solution.

In the analyses of Part Two we shall further apply these concepts of musical isotopy. Now we move on to our second main category of musical semiotics, that of iconicity.

Iconic Approaches to Music

Here we consider theories that differ from the above structuralist views in that they do not attempt to reduce music to categories and abstract schemes external to music, but seek musical universals in the actual sound patterns of music. A well-known mediating position in this change of research strategy is that of the so-called paradigmatic method developed by Nicolas Ruwet and Jean-Jacques Nattiez. This method relies on the inner iconicity of music, that is, on the idea that the concrete musical expression, the "neutral level" (Nattiez 1975: 50–62), contains all the information necessary for analysis of musical content. Musical semantics is thereby reduced to syntactics, which can be investigated through application of generative procedures.

In order to understand iconicity in music, one has to take into account the way Ferdinand de Saussure divided the very concept of the sign into two aspects: signifier and signified, or to use Hjelmslev's terms (1961), expression and content. In music the relationship between these two sides differs essentially from that in verbal language. Any concept or proposition can be phonetically conveyed in many ways, since the meaning to be transmitted is not bound to the concrete phonemes or graphemes. This situation is due to the arbitrary relation between the signifier and signified of a verbal sign. In music, however, this relation is not arbitrary: expression and content are inseparably connected with each other. The slightest change on the level of expression produces a change of content as well. For example, it is hard to imagine how the minuet movement of a Mozart symphony might be translated into some other system (such as gamelan music based on a *slendro* scale) without also changing the content. Consequently, the relation between signifier and signified in music should be viewed as iconic.

From the iconicity of musical signs, musicologists have drawn various conclusions. Some believe that on the basis of iconicity it is possible to construct a universal musical lexicon: two iconically similar musical signs are also identical in content, though they might originally have belonged to entirely different systems. The futility of such efforts, such as Deryck Cooke's dictionary of musical words (1959), is immediately evident: iconic relations can be valid in the context of one work, style, or tradition, but irrelevant outside that context.

Another false conclusion was that drawn in the 1960s by Nicolas Ruwet, who argued that the musical signified can only be grasped through the most accurate analysis of signifiers. Yet in order to investigate musical semiosis, one must consider not only elements and relations *in praesentia* but also latent potentials for development. These potentials may remain in the background of a composition but still influence events on the surface, that is, the music as actually heard. Relations *in absentia* are inferred on the basis of signifiers (surface phenomena) as well as the musical competence of listener and analyst, and are at least as important as relations *in praesentia* on the syntactic level.

The iconic concept can also lead to a demand for musical description that maintains the original iconicity of music, i.e., that does not fragment music's primarily functional unity. This view is particularly held by theories that emphasize the kinetic, energetic, and processual nature of music, theories which add the demand of functionality to the search for musical universals. Swiss musicologist Ernst Kurth is a typical representative of this approach. In his opinion, music psychology should analyze "the psychic functions in the basic phenomena of music," and he further supposes "that these basic psychic functions are objective in nature" (1947: 57). In Chap. 4.1 we shall closely examine Kurth's position in the tradition of musical semiotics.

The question remains of how to make explicit these functions and properties. Some scholars see music as a gestural language, and in this way come near to viewing music as the result of an action performed by an "organism," as regards not only its production but also its content. One might even apply the theory of action of Charles Morris (1956) and George Herbert Mead (1948) to musical organisms. One could similarly speak of musical gestures when referring to the action and conduct of this "organism" in a composition. Wilson Coker (1972) identifies "motif" or "pattern" with musical gesture. Like all signs, gestures can assume three functions in communication: semantic, syntactic, and pragmatic. Gino Stefani has analyzed the use of a rhythmic gesture (/, /, ///) in both classical and popular music. This pattern occurs particularly often in political slogans and songs, and Stefani calls it *scanzione incitativa*. It appears in a song like "Bella ciao" as well as in Mozart's *Eine kleine Nachtmusik* and at the beginning of a Beethoven sonata (Stefani 1976: 104–21). Musical gestures function as what speech-act theory calls "performatives"—events complete in themselves. Rather than making "statements" *about* something, performatives, musical or otherwise, *do* something (they belong to Peirce's category of Firstness), and that is why they have direct affective impact. From this perspective, Susanne Langer's (1951) opinion that music is not a symptom of feelings, but their logical expression, would be questionable.

Musical iconicity has also been studied empirically. One effort to examine experimentally the basic psychic functions in music is the "sentics" of Manfred Clynes (1978), who studied emotional responses to music and painting by measuring physiological reactions. During the test, the inner pulse of music was gauged by a machine that registered reactions through the pressure of a finger tip. The person tested was asked to imagine a certain piece of music and to "conduct" it, with finger pressures substituting for arm movements. The inner pulse, measured from an average of fifty pulses in a given piece, was taken to be a sentic graph of the composer in question (see Fig. 1.2).

Whatever validity Clynes's research might have, it holds a certain interest for musical semiotics, as an effort to reveal musical *Ursatzen* on an entirely experimental basis. These experiments suggest that the Schenkerian concepts of *Urlinie* and *Ursatz* could be extended by assuming that every composer has a personal *Urlinie*, just as Clynes claims that each composer has a personal sentics graph. These graphs do not exhibit stylistic affinities; for example, Mozart and Haydn, Debussy and Ravel, had entirely different sentics graphs. Rather, Clynes's theory relates to the iconicity of music: the inner musical pulse is projected into a tactile sign system and described by a visual graph; i.e., translation occurs between the auditive and tactile modes of music.

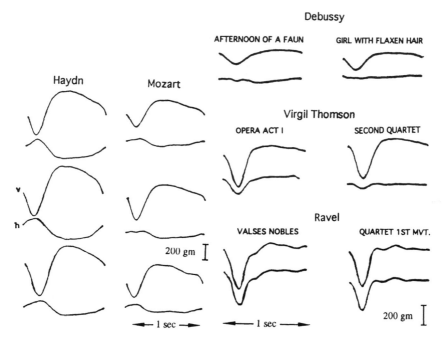

Figure 1.2. Sentics graphs (after Clynes 1978).

The issue of iconic translation was also pondered by French aesthetician Etienne Souriau, who compared melodic line to an ornament and claimed that this comparison was based on a physical disposition that yields morphological affinities between two different arts (1969: 223–35). In his opinion, music can be described by graph lines that serve as iconic signs of musical motion. Such graphs eventually might lead to a new notation that would be more effective than traditional staves (see Fig. 1.3).

Another parallel to Clynes's theory is the musical aesthetics of Roland Barthes (1978), especially in his analysis of Robert Schumann's *Kreisleriana*. In Barthes's view, music is based more on inner movements of the body than on states of mind. The accents in music are crucial. In music the body starts to "speak,"[4] as suggested by the quasiparlando directive so often used by Schumann. The human voice is referred to as a gesture which, particularly in Romantic music, was internalized into instrumental pieces as well (even Hugo Riemann believed that song was the origin of all music). Thus music

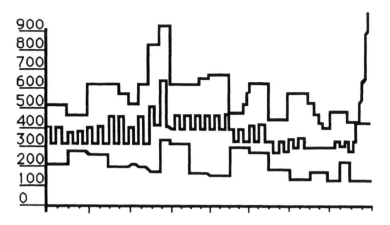

Figure 1.3. Graph of musical motion.

might be analyzed through its accents and pulses, whose basic units Barthes called "somathemes" (after *soma*, Greek for "body"). Though Barthes's analysis could easily be neglected if placed in the category of nonscientific descriptions of music, it could have a certain heuristic value in other contexts—applied to other musical cultures, for example, or to the study of musical therapy, where the immediate physiological impact of music is so important.

Gestural theories of music have drawn criticism, however, as when Adorno (1952: 32), referring to Wagnerian *leitmotifs*, argued that gestures cannot be developed but only repeated. Nevertheless, Coker considers gesture a formal unit of musical discourse and lists ten techniques for transforming musical gestures, techniques which necessarily overlap with traditional principles of thematic elaboration in counterpoint, such as inversion, augmentation, diminution, and so on (1972: 83–84). David Osmond-Smith (1975) had recourse to the same devices for depicting iconic transformation techniques in music.

The most suspect point in iconic musical theories concerns ways of using them as tools for music analysis. This practical problem troubles Charles Seeger's theoretical essay "On the Moods of a Music-Logic" (1960). Seeger attempts to describe music iconically and on this basis to make a systematic analysis of all musical parameters. Discussing musical deductions and inferences, he also touches on the problem of the development of iconic signs in music. According to Seeger, any musical motif can be transformed into any other motif. He takes as an example the motivic chain that leads from the main theme of Schubert's C major Symphony to Richard Strauss's *Till Eulenspiegel*. Ex. 1.6 represents iconic development in music and at the same time the destruction of iconicity: the chain proceeds so far from the starting point that the last member no longer shares any iconic feature with the first. Motivic development in Sibelius's symphonies could also be compared to this process, where one cell of the theme at a time is replaced by another, finally resulting in a theme that has no cell in common with the first: abcd, abch, abgh, afgh, efgh (Gray and Jalas 1945: 87).[5]

Example 1.6. Motivic transformation of main theme of Schubert's Ninth Symphony, mvt. I, into that of Strauss's *Till Eulenspiegel.*

Further, Seeger presents a theoretical outline of music analysis in terms of its smallest units, which he calls "moods." He describes them systematically, finding a symbolic formalization for them in each musical parameter. Thus for melodic movement he borrows symbols from Gregorian neumatic notation which can be combined in various ways. The problem remains of how to use his theoretical diagrams in actual music analysis, even though Seeger takes into account the tensions of musical movements: increase in tension is depicted by +, decrease by –. Seeger supposes that an increase in tension mostly occurs together with a rising melodic line. In some cases this is true, as in Mozart's "Jupiter" Symphony, where in the fugue of the Finale the melodic lines rise and the tension increases. But the reverse can also be true, as in the Prelude to Wagner's *Lohengrin,* where the music gradually descends from the brightest register of the orchestra while the tension noticeably increases, relaxing at the end, when the music returns to the upper register. Or, using Seeger's system, how could we describe such complex movements as the intersecting, "diagonal" lines in Ravel's *Une barque sur l'océan?* It seems that functional unity based on tension/release cannot be easily inferred from iconic aspects of music.

With Seeger we have reached the extremes of iconic method. Used alone, it is no more capable of describing music as a process than is the structuralist method, if by such a process we mean the inner, form-building forces that are inextricably bound to the nature of music as a specifically temporal art.

1.2 Reflections on the Logic of Musical Discourse

After these explorations in the history of musical semiotics, I now take a step toward the construction of my own theory. First, I shall try to determine the position of musical discourse in relation to the models that guide and influence its formation, while considering how these models affect the internal structure of music. Second, I shall try to outline a "new" starting point for musical semiotics, by emphasizing the processual, functional nature of music and by applying to musical discourse the modal logic of Finnish philosopher Georg Henrik von Wright (1963).

Musical Discourse

The nature of musical discourse can be articulated with a model that is semiotic in two senses: first, because it accounts for the external conditions of musical communication, not only the creation of a musical work but also the communicative factors manifested in a composition itself; second, because it seeks to perceive musical reality in depth, and thus distinguishes between manifest and immanent levels. This model focuses on what we shall call "musical discourse."

American semiotician Charles Morris made an exhaustive list of various discourses (1971: 203-32), to which musical discourse could be added with good reason, as a subclass of artistic discourses. The term "discourse" should be understood in a rather broad sense, because it contains all the different modes of music, not only notation, but also tonal realization (musical "intonations," according to Asafiev 1977). Together, notation and tonal realization form various modes of existence in musical discourse, which takes its place in the whole chain of musical communication, shown in Fig. 1.4.

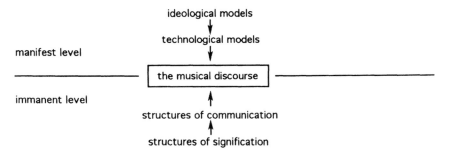

Figure 1.4. Musical communication.

Musical discourse is in turn ruled by two models, the *ideological* and the *technological.* Here "ideological" is understood in opposition to the "technical" aspect of music, and is formed by models of thought which determine all symbolism related to music. In musical societies there are conceptions and norms that evaluate music according to the norms and tastes of that society. On the other hand, there also exist rules that regulate and guide the production of musical discourse. In Western art music, ideological models are represented by musical aesthetics and are evident in tracts, essays, pamphlets, critiques, and manifestos of schools of composing. Consider, for example, Eduard Hanslick's famous essay *Vom Musikalisch-schönen,* Wagner's *Oper und Drama,* Busoni's writings about young classicality, or Stravinsky's musical poetics. In so-called folk or traditional music cultures, ideological models are often mythical in nature.

In our own musical culture, technological models are represented by all manner of textbooks dealing with harmony, counterpoint, and composition, from Fux's *Gradus ad Parnassum,* to Schoenberg's *Harmonielehre.* In traditional music cultures, technological knowledge is transmitted orally. Such is the case in our own music tradition with regard to musical interpretation and teaching. The models guiding these activities can be regarded as special means of manipulation or modes of persuasion.

Just as in musical discourse one finds various connections between the semiotic level and the symbolisms of the semantic level, in music itself the same semiotic network can articulate different symbolisms; the technological and ideological models can cooperate in several different ways. Sometimes the technological model also serves as an ideological model: the history of Gregorian plainchant shows the importance the Middle Ages attached to implanting orthodox methods of singing in various parts of Europe. Or to take an individual composer, Anton Bruckner's daily exercises in Palestrina counterpoint also had a certain ideological meaning for his Catholic-mystical world view.

Ideological and technological models can also develop independently of each other. For example, the controversy of nineteenth-century aesthetics between absolute and program music consisted of a conflict between ideological models, and this conflict did not always affect technical aspects of music. For example, one can easily find Wagnerian traits in Brahms, and Brahmsian features in Bruckner. There are also technological models of music that limit their sphere of influence to the level of musical "craftsmanship" and technique. In his *Harmonielehre,* Schoenberg himself said that by rules one does not learn to produce aesthetically beautiful compositions, but only their groundwork: "eine gute Handwerkslehre" might well represent "eine schlechte Aesthetik." An essential question in musical aesthetics is how musical discourse is formed under the influence of these two models, the ideological and the technological.[6] A musical style usually results from the cooperation of these two models. On the other hand, technological models can develop independently of aesthetic theories. The fact that composers have been able to manipulate musical structure as a pure sign system has been a precondition for the whole development of Western art music, beginning with the first tentative efforts at polyphonic writing during the early Middle Ages.

Perhaps the most interesting problem from the viewpoint of musical semiotics is the way the influence of these models is felt in the musical discourse itself, in the very structures of music. The impact of these models on music appears above all in the domain called the *structures of communication.* To this domain belong all those musical mechanisms that a composer uses to communicate musical ideas. The structures of communication are thus represented by stylistic structures insofar as a composer follows certain "automatisms" of stylistic norms. If one thinks of a musical process as a causal chain of choices realized by a composer, then one may presume that the influence of aesthetic and technological models is manifested precisely during those moments when a choice is made between several alternatives in the music. Accordingly, the impact of these two models can be considered mainly as normative: they restrict the choices of a composer by offering ready solutions in situations of choice.

Does a composer, while composing, function exclusively according to the ideological and technological models of the time? If this were so, hardly any aesthetically significant works would emerge; a composer's production would be redundant, too socialized a speech (*parole*), with mannerisms and clichés unable to serve an aesthetic function. Thus a composition cannot be identified solely with its structures of communication. Rather, in a musical work the structures of communication provide the area in which the composer's fantasy can move in a relatively free manner and thereby produce some unique signification. This area forms a musical work's *structures of signification,* and here the true aesthetic moment of music is to be found. The structures of communication and a particular signification might conflict with each other, in which case the aesthetic value of the work is experienced precisely as a break in norms, as Umberto Eco has noted (1971). The same distinction has also been clearly defined by Eugene Narmour (1977), who speaks of musical style as the point where structure (structure of communication) and idiostructure (structure of signification) emerge.

We now consider how to distinguish between these two kinds of structure in musical discourse. Such a distinction is relevant to music analysis, especially insofar as music is conceived in its original processual meaning as a kinetic event that unfolds in time.[7] Until recently the main task of musical semiotics has been to distinguish the smallest significant units. At the same time, study of *connections* among these units has been neglected; the integrating forces of musical discourse have not been taken into account. Almost all theories of musical semiotics have aimed at transforming the moving character of music to a static one, continuity to discontinuity, *temps de durée* to *temps d'espace.*

In view of the fundamentally processive nature of music, musical logic cannot be based on the logic of a static world, where phenomena are either this or that, but on a logic that depicts the constant changes of phenomena from one state to another. Consequently, musical signification should be based on the continuous becoming and changing of musical figures. On the other hand, analyzing musical discourse with methods originally developed for analysis of other sign systems, without regard for the "musicality" of music, will lead to an atomization of music, to its dissolution into mechanical units and their conglomerates. Such atomization does not correspond to the spontaneous phenomenal observation of music and would certainly not represent semiotics in Saussure's sense of the term. Thus, if the paradigmatic method—the method on which the concept of style is based—can be applied to music (mainly on the principle of repetition), then one should keep in mind that, because of music's kinetic nature, paradigmatic signifying units cannot be projected onto only one chart (as, for example, in traditional motive charts or in *leitmotif* collections of Wagner's operas). For one musical work several paradigms are needed, sometimes an infinite number, since the emergence of each new element in the musical process changes the relations among preceding elements in the paradigm. The smaller the units observed, the more evident it becomes that still more paradigms exist.

Still, we can assume that in the course of the music some points are more decisive than others because they more radically affect the paradigm that takes shape in the listener's consciousness. Therefore, one should somehow attempt to describe those paradigms that are reconstructed in the mind of a listener participating in the musical semiosis. Only in that way can one arrive at the musical signification as it is really articulated. It is precisely at these "changing points" of a paradigm that the influence of the above-mentioned structures of communication emerge. Through these points, ideological and technological models grasp the course of the musical process and direct it to certain channels. The structures of communication are those models of decision which a composer can experience as either "possible" or "permitted," "recommended" or "necessary," in which case they correspondingly exclude other alternatives as "forbidden" or "not recommended." Such a viewpoint offers an interesting opportunity to apply concepts and methods of modal logic to the analysis of musical discourse. A. J. Greimas has presented a typology of various rules (1976: 97). This typology can be transferred to the domain of music in order to describe the effect of the structures of communication on a composer's activity (see Fig. 1.5).

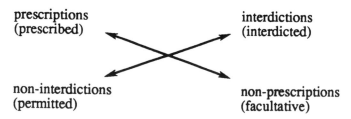

Figure 1.5. Constraints of structures of communication on composer's activity.

Every style period of music contains implicit instructions as to which musical expressions are grammatical (obey stylistic norms) and which are nongrammatical (do not follow norms). In the semiotic square of Fig. 1.5, these instructions correspond to positive and negative injunctions, i.e., prescriptions and interdictions. But the situation is not so simple that a composer can always choose between a single correct expression and a wrong one. If this were so, hardly any room would remain for individual creativity.ʰ There are also rules that do not manifest themselves as explicit instructions, i.e., cases where a choice is either forbidden or permitted. Sometimes there are facultative solutions, for which there are no special instructions.

In Western art music all musical innovations on the technological level probably first belonged to the level of facultative solutions, which the ideological models thereafter hastened to legitimate on the level of music aesthetics. For example, at the beginning of Wagner's *Tristan*, the customary prominence of dissonances increases to such an extent that their usage moves from the domain of facultative solutions to the sphere of permission and further to the stylistic features assumed by the whole of late Romanticism, i.e., to the level of prescriptions. At the same time, the emotive value (aesthetic signification) of dissonances changes, as Adorno, among others, has noted (1974: 62).

Modal Logic

In the field of modal logic, efforts have been made at formalizations that would apply the aforementioned modal rules to given series of events. One of the most famous is Georg Henrik von Wright's theory on the logic of change, as presented in his *Norm and Action* (1963). The basic operation in this logic is the simple scheme pTq, which denotes a transition from a state p to a state q (von Wright 1963: 17–34). If musical discourse is approached from the kinetic viewpoint and is primarily conceived as a process, one might try to formalize it with the tools of von Wright's logic. The expression pTq would simply mean that a motif or section p is followed by a motif/section q; but since the musical process is above all supported by expectations, the mere symbol T (or →), expressing the transition, will not suffice. An additional symbol is needed just to point to an expected change: for example, pTTq or p→→q; i.e., "after p, q is expected and q follows." Should something contrary to expectation happen, the situation might be expressed with the scheme pTT(q)x, which would mean: "after p, q is expected, but x follows."

Constant becoming is not the only characteristic of musical semiosis; in addition, a paradigm based on memory is shaped in the mind of the listener. This paradigm consists of all the earlier choices and changes along the process of the composition. Memory is an essential factor in music. The memory presupposed by a text, thus also the distance between tensions in syntactic structures of music, is a variable that changes from one composer to another: the internal memory of a Bruckner symphony differs from that in a work by Webern. Along with repetition, another factor in music helps the functioning of memory, namely, the double articulation. If the first level of articulation is "known" (e.g., all the stylistic norms of Viennese Classical music), then the listener's memory will be free to receive individual features of a work and composer. (Here again one finds an illustration of the distinction between structures of communication and signification.)

Resting upon memory, a very subtle network of references functions in every musical work, even the simplest, and this network forms a contrary force against the dynamically moving nature of music and attempts to reduce that dynamism to "stasis." Such a reference to something previous can be denoted by parentheses or by an arrow pointing in the opposite direction. However, the motif or section to which the arrow refers does not belong to the same level as the actual members of the musical chain, but occurs *in absentia*. That is, pTTq (1) means: "after p one expects q, which follows and refers to an earlier element 1." There is good reason to suppose that the elements *in absentia* are at least as important as, if not more important than, the elements *in praesentia*. This should be remembered especially in connection with Ruwet's theories, which seem to contain an iconic conception of musical signification according to which the musical signifieds (*signifiés*) can be analyzed only insofar as they manifest themselves in signifiers (*signifiants*) (Nattiez 1975: 134). Such a method can easily lead to exclusion of relations *in absentia* and accordingly to disregard of the depth dimension. The same argument concerns other iconic theories as well, such as Barthes's somatheme-analysis of Schumann's musical universe (1975), Coker's gestural-meaning theory (1972), or Seeger's moods of music logic (1960: 64–101).

A teleological musical process should therefore be presented with the schema pTTq(p); that is, q is a musical unit that is at the same time expected and refers to the element preceding it; it is perceived as if it were the objective of the process (like the occurrence of a theme in its definitive form at the conclusion of a composition). Such a musical system might be considered a predetermined process. But of course music can also proceed without any predetermined direction; this is often the case in traditional music cultures, with monodies having no distinctive beginning or end (Asafiev 1977), but which in the manner of ornaments in decorative art can, in principle, continue endlessly. On the other hand, there are also multileveled musical processes in which some level proceeds as a teleological process and another as a causal one; i.e., the determinism of the various levels is of different degrees. Examples are easily found in modern music, but the case can also be illustrated by cadential sections of traditional solo concertos; such sections form a sphere of entropy in the otherwise regular structure of a composition.

In addition to the progression and retrospection of musical process, a third essential factor should be considered: the paradigm of all possible choices in a certain moment of transition. This can be formalized with brackets. Consequently, if after p, q is expected but r occurs, and after p, q, r, or s is possible, one can write: pTT(q)r [q, r, s]. In this way one might determine the tensions of the musical situation in question and the ways that paradigms differ from one another in the various phases of musical process. Such a description preserves the primal energetic nature of music.

The smallest musical action is consequently the syntagm, a temporal continuum consisting of two hierarchically different musical elements. Mere repetition of similar elements does not form a musical event and does not move us from the 'being' of music to its 'doing'. This could be formalized simply as F (x, y), or pTq if we use symbols from von Wright's logic of change. This logic can be further enriched by examining all that is contained in the symbol T. One can in that way develop a particular logic of temporality. In turn, if we presume that the elements x and y connected by these operators are hierarchically different, and if we investigate their logical relations, we are placed at the spatial level, which has not yet been temporalized and brought into the narrative process (soon to be discussed): these elements can be of different pitches or of different dynamic strength. Accordingly, two different branches of musical logic can be developed: one deals with the process of change symbolized by T, moving in time, and the other with the events themselves (x and y) in this flow of time.

A third branch of musical logic opens with the entrance of a subject, which connects modal elements to a fundamental narrative formula like xTy. In this formula, x is hierarchically more important than y, and, accordingly, x *modalizes* y by its 'will' as we go from x to y in the musical process. The same situation can be expressed through Greimas's symbolic notation: Fm (x, y), where m means the modality, which in the above case is that of willingness. Hence this logical formula fulfills the minimal conditions for any musical event or action: the three categories of temporalization, spatialization, and actorialization. If we want to interpret in semiotic terms, say, "tension"—a notion crucial in current music theory as well as in general semiotics but having not yet attained satisfactory formulation—the joint cooperation of all three categories is needed. The temporal dimension alone, no more than the spatial (structure of hierarchic subordination) or actorial (the tension exclusively due to modalization effectuated by a subject), will not suffice to explain "tension." Furthermore, one may ask whether these three branches of musical logic can be developed separately, and, if so, how far from each other independently.

We shall have more to say about these three categories and the logic of change in the analyses of Part Two. Now I must enter an area that is closely related to and sometimes identified with semiotic theory, namely, *narrativity* in music.

1.3 The Problem of Narrativity in Music

Musical narration can be seen as a musico-historical problem if one assumes that, particularly in the Classical and Romantic periods, a strong cognitive model organized, and still organizes, not only musical discourse itself (musical works) but discourse *about* music as well.[9] We have already seen the structures and mechanisms that, in general, make possible the emergence of narrativity in music. Now we must examine more closely what narrativity in music is, and how one can argue that some music is narrative even though it has no explicit connection with a verbal, gestural, or pictorial language that can provide a "plot." The problem is simply whether music as such can be narrative.

Let us first make some general observations about musical narration. To start, one may consider the idea of narrativity in music as a superstructure, a "secondary modeling system," to use the term of the Tartu School, which presupposes the existence of a primary modeling system as a substructure. Not every musico-syntactic structure is a narrative structure, otherwise all music would be "narrative." An undeniable fact of musical experience is that when we listen to, say, the first measures of Scriabin's First Symphony, we might sigh and say: "How narrative!" (as Ricardo Muti reportedly exclaimed upon hearing this work). On the other hand, much music evidently does not try to tell a story. Our first task is to determine the distinctive features of narrativity in music. One view of it is as a latent trait that only emerges through certain modalizations, that is, when a musical work is interpreted, played, or performed in a given way. It seems that some artists have the ability to perform music in a narrative way (a point pondered in Chap. 7.2, below). Some pianists or violinists are said to possess a narrative touch or sound. This alternative seems quite possible, since we generally have to distinguish between two cases in musical semantics: first, a musical utterance, under certain conditions, always has a given semantic content; second, a musical utterance can be pronounced in a way that imbues it with semantic significance. French semioticians would say that narrativity should be investigated on the level of musical utterance (*énoncé musical*) as well as that of musical performance (*énonciation musicale*). Accordingly, there is a type of narrativity that only emerges in the act (*énonciation*) of utterance, when the performer or listener connects an element from the *intonational store* to a musical structure. Such narrativity cannot be analyzed without accounting for the interaction between musical subject and object in the process of musical communication. It is impossible to analyze it merely at the "neutral" level of musical structure (utterance).

One might try another path, in an attempt to show that narrative structures do exist at the level of musical utterance. For example, Fred Lerdahl and Ray Jackendoff, in their generative theory of tonal music (1985), have determined a Strong Reduction Hypothesis. It states that all the pitches of a tonal work can be organized to form a structure based on hierarchic relations of subordination, which constitute the basis for musical tensions that bring about musical "energetic" movement. In other words, the pitch hierarchy yields a psychological sense effect that is experienced as a "tension," or to use Greimas's and Schopenhauer's terminology, as 'will' (*vouloir*) and 'must' (*devoir*) among the tones. In this way the narrative movement of a musical work, the arch of tension between beginning and end (Greimas's inchoativity/durativity/terminativity), manifests itself at a purely structural level.

Finally, narrativity can be understood in the very common sense as a general category of the human mind, a competency that involves putting temporal events into a certain order, a syntagmatic continuum. This continuum has a beginning, development, and end; and the order created in this way is called, under given circumstances, a narration. With this view, the logic of narration appears to be very abstract and of a fairly general level. It turns out to be a certain tension between the beginning and the end, a sort of arch progression. Even a traditional musicologist like Arnold Salop (1971: 33–34) describes narrativity in this way:

> The narrative composer . . . works somewhat as follows. First, he organizes some particular musical elements (like harmony, melodic line, or intensity) into an easily perceived and reasonably simple pattern of trends. Second, some time after the initial trend gets under way, he may introduce either a reversal of its direction, or an abrupt change to a quality quite different from that which has been reached. Either of these would be introduced, furthermore, before the trend has gone so far as to acquire a sense of contrived, mechanical motion. Third, the composer would continue and culminate the program to which his choice of digression has committed him. I do not mean to imply that these should be considered rigid commitments; there are many fine shadings of timing as well as of degrees of contrast, all of which would influence the expectations concerning what is to follow. In addition, there are many situations where several different moves would seem equally plausible. Nevertheless, there is a range of possibilities beyond which the composer could not well go without causing the narrative sense to break down. . . . By proceeding through a process of this kind it is possible to get some idea of how far a composer carried his narrative organization, and, by inference, of how much he depended upon it to produce appeal. Knowledge of this kind can reveal something of the intellectual substance behind a style, as well as provide some valuable information concerning interpretation.

Nevertheless, as both Greimas and Schenker assume, there is often some entirely achronic structure in the background of the linear unfolding of a work: with the former, the semiotic square and its logical interrelations; with the latter, a tonic triad. According to these theorists, the narrative-generative process is revealed through a gradual expansion or "composing out" of this achronic fundamental structure. When analyzing the nuclear narrative structure of a text or its surface, one proceeds in reverse, through phases Greimas calls "reductions" or "conversions" and Schenker calls "diminutions." Basically it is true that Schenkerian analysis is concerned with musical space (registral and tonal organization) and not with temporal organization: "There is no rhythm in the *Hintergrund*" (Schenker, in Lerdahl and Jackendoff 1985: 142). Yet Schenker's model could easily be developed into a method of narrative analysis of music. Its basic premise—that a musical work is a totality created by a structure wherein all events relate to a basic model and the tension it provides—corresponds well to the syntagmatic demand of narrativity.

Since our study aims expressly at the analysis of narrativity in "abstract," nonprogrammatic music, we may justifiably refer to "classic" musicological texts. Ferruccio Busoni, for example, scrutinized "absolute" music in his famous *Entwurf einer neuen Aesthetik der Tonkunst* (1916). His remarks lead us to the threshold of a certain narrativity:

> Absolute music! What the lawgivers understand by it is perhaps the most remote from the Absolute in music. "Absolute music" is a play with forms without poetic program, whereby form gives up its central role. Yet it is precisely form, which works against absolute music, which has adopted the godlike advantage of being free from material conditions. . . . Is it not peculiar that originality is required above all from a composer and that he is offered it just in form? What a wonder that when he then is really original, he is accused of formlessness. Mozart! That searcher and finder, the great man with a childish heart, we admire him and depend on him, but not on his tonics and dominants, his developments and codas.
>
> Such a will-to-freedom also filled Beethoven, the Romantic-revolution man, in the sense that he took a small step in the reduction of music to its highest nature: a small step in the great task, a big step in its own way. He never entirely reached absolute music, but in special moments he anticipated it, as in the introduction to the Fugue of the *Hammerklavier* sonata. In general, composers came closest to the true nature of music in opening and middle movements (preludes and transitions), since there they believed that they were permitted to neglect symmetrical relationships and seemed to breathe unselfconsciously. Even such a lesser composer as Schumann is at such moments taken by something of the unlimited nature of the all-art [*Pan-Kunst*]—one need only think of the transition to the last movement of the D minor symphony—and the same can be said of Brahms and the introduction to the Finale of his First Symphony. However, as soon as they return to the main movement, their attitude becomes stiff again, like that of a man entering his office.

Busoni's prophetic passage corresponds closely to the distinction made in Chap. 1.2, between structures of signification and communication. For example, sonata form with its spheres of tonic and dominant, its developments, etc., constitutes precisely what is to be understood by structures of communication: a composer must use them in order to transmit his or her message to the listener. Hence structures of communication are there only to carry the true aesthetic content of music. This is why, according to Busoni, only in those passages that do not fall into any ready scheme of communicative structure does the original and deepest spirit of music come to the fore. He evidently considers symmetry and architectonic construction as typical structures of communication, as revealed by the examples he chooses as ideals of absolute music and in which no architectonic form is recognizable.[10] In this regard Busoni comes very close to the conception of form by Kurth and Asafiev, which is opposed to the "tectonic" as well as to the "geometric" view of the musical form.

How then are narrative structures situated in this conceptual context? Does narrativity in music belong to structures of communication or those of signification? If we think of some "semiotical," linguistics-inspired methods of analysis (say, the generative theories of Schenker and of Lerdahl and Jackendoff), might they be accused of analyzing, in the end, merely the music's syntactical structures of communication, without grasping music's proper structures of signification? If a semantic dimension were added to these generative models, in what phase would it emerge?

Perhaps we should distinguish between two types of narrative program: programs of surface structure (structures of communication) and programs of deep structure (structures of signification). For example, the "topics" of the Classical style (Ratner 1980)—dance, march, hunting signals, and so on— originated in the outer conditions of musical communication, from which they were internalized into the discourse of music. Such topics typify structures of communication in music. Certainly a competent music listener at the end of the eighteenth century could recognize these topics and was delighted to find them (for example, in various parts of a symphony), and this discovery produced a low-level aesthetic pleasure (see Ex. 1.7).

Example 1.7. Topics in Mozart, Fantasy in C minor, K. 396, mm. 1–5.

Likewise, the rhetorical figures of the Baroque period were narrative techniques situated in the structures of communication (or perhaps elements of technique, since by narrativity one has to understand only the syntagm, the temporally ordered continuum consisting of these elements). The narrativity of the deep level "grasps" passages having a ready-made signification and weaves a narrative texture using them as material.

Does a narrative texture always need a prefabricated network of definite meanings, such as topics and rhetorical figures? Or can narrative do without them? If we answer the second question in the affirmative, we come to the Busonian category of absolute music, thus accepting the thesis that even "pure" music can be narrative in character. Again, recall that in our theory narrativity is understood in a very broad sense. As Greimas says:

> In the semiotical project that is ours, generalized narrativity—freed from its restricted sense which was bound with the figurative forms of narration—is to be considered as the organizing principle of the whole discourse. All semiotics can be treated either as system or process, and hence the narrative structures can be defined as constituents of the deep level of the semiotical process. [1979: 249–250]

Thus we return to our original question of how we might uncover the hidden narrativity in absolute music.

Let us now modify the critical remark presented above, that some generative models account only for the superficial structures of communication in music and not its deeper, "absolute" structures of signification. This does not hold true in the sense that those generative models do have surface and deep levels: they aim at reducing the surface to a wholly achronic structure. For Greimas this achronic deep structure is already a structure of signification, but in Schenkerian analysis the deepest structure is a single tonic chord to which it is difficult to join any hidden meaning. Therefore, if we still wish to consider music as a process of signification, in which phase can we bring in structures of signification as we articulate the tonal pitch structure? Do structures of musical signification form a generative process parallel to syntactical structures in music?

We also have to take seriously the possibility that significations come into music, in a deeper sense, not from external functions of social communication but through *modalizations*. The subject brings "sense" to abstract, moving sound forms only in the process of listening to music, by modalizing a musical structure in the same way that a speaker modalizes speech with wishes, will, belief, and emotions (more precise definition of modalities will follow, in Chap. 1.4). Even in this case music would be a process of signification, for analogously to language, even the simplest musical utterance can be presented as a modal utterance or interpreted as such; in the same sense, for example, as the phrase "It is raining today" could be transformed into the form "I am afraid that it is raining today" or "It seems to me that it is raining today." Then it is the performer who by interpretation shifts music from the level of a purely descriptive statement to that of modal utterance, providing it with his or her own subjective dynamics of will: "It seems to me that . . .," "I am convinced that . . .," etc. Thus music always becomes persuasive communication while it is performed, even in cases where composers deny their attempts to make the listeners communicate with them. Such is the reasoning of Steve Reich, who says, "The pleasure I feel while playing is not the pleasure of self-expression, but that of subordinating myself to the music and having a sentiment of ecstasy due to my fusion with it" (1974: 11). In other words, Reich does not want to modalize his music, but to become modalized *by* it.

We can also presume that modalization emerges gradually in the generative course of music, not only when music has reached its final form at the surface level. In this case, one might think that modalizing structures of signification would be parallel to the syntactic structures, and that the structures in the *Hintergrund* and *Mittelgrund*, as well as in the *Vordergrund*, might be interpreted as carrying modal contents. In fact, by "energeticism" Ernst Kurth and Boris Asafiev undoubtedly meant precisely this kind of analysis but were unable to develop their theories in a systematic form and derive any coherent method of analysis from their principles.

Lerdahl and Jackendoff base their "tree model" on the assumption that all events in a musical work constitute a hierarchic system, in which relations of subordination/domination are experienced as tension-and-release. One could further reason that these tensions yield modal processes in music in such a way that, say, the modality of 'will' (*vouloir*) would mean dominance, the subordination of any other musical element (pitch or rhythm); while from the point of view of the subordinated unit, the modal process involves obligation or 'must' (*devoir*). When the subordinating unit precedes the subordinated one, we say that its 'will' dominates the latter; while in the case of a subordinated element preceding its subordinator (an appoggiatura chord preceding its resolution, a weak beat preceding a stronger beat, etc.), we have an instance of willingness (*vouloir*). Since cadences are crucial to transforming tonal music into a goal-directed process, one could argue that the 'must' (*devoir*) of the musical process comes under the rule of a narrative arch whose structural beginning and ending tones lead toward a goal, i.e., to the dominant-tonic cadential progression. Correspondingly, with regard to musical events situated at different points of this arch, the whole appears to represent the kinetic energy and will of those events. One consequence of this insight is that we obtain almost gratuitously from Lerdahl and Jackendoff's theory a notational procedure that suits our semiotical description and by which we can depict the relations of subordination (Fig. 1.6).

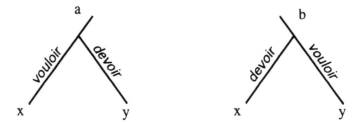

Figure 1.6. Modal relations of subordination/domination
(after Lerdahl and Jackendoff 1985).

The basic modal categories of music, 'being' and 'doing', also find their counterparts in the theory of Lerdahl and Jackendoff. The structure of hierarchical subordination corresponds to the 'being' of tones, while the fact that these tones with various degrees of existence are placed in a syntagmatic (linear) order constitutes the 'doing' of tones (musical action). Musical events and actions in tonal music thus rely precisely on such an *a priori* hierarchy of tonal elements, i.e., a paradigm from which elements are picked for the musical discourse so as to form its temporal continuum. The paradigmatic hierarchies, in turn, could easily be presented as oppositional relations such as contrary, contradictory, and implicational relations, and as a model comprising those relations. This involves a spatial distinction, i.e., a hierarchy of pitches which has nothing to do with the temporal structure of music. Does the temporality emerge only as a result of musical action as the originally achronic hierarchies are made narrative? Evidently, yes. So in order to have a musical event we must presuppose that the elements in a musical syntagm are *a priori* of different values: I is stronger than V, and so on.

Lerdahl and Jackendoff admit the possibility of this kind of parallel modal description. Discussing the beginning of the first part of Mozart's much-analyzed A major Piano Sonata, K. 331, they state: "One might say that the phrase begins in relative repose, increases in tension . . . stretches the tension in a kind of dynamic reversal to the opening, and then relaxes the tension. . . . It would be highly desirable for a reduction to express this kind of musical ebb and flow" (1985: 122). In other words, in music there is a spatial-temporal-actorial isotopy which causes us to "read" the text as a coherent whole rather than as discrete fragments.

Paul Ricoeur (1980) has commented on Greimas's generative-narrative course. He calls attention to the fact that, to derive everything from an achronic fundamental structure, care must be taken that, while shifting from level to level (in Schenker from *Hintergrund* toward *Vordergrund*), one does not bring from outside presuppositions that are not included in the all-generating basic model. Otherwise there would be no generative system; rather, the generative course would be guided by external factors. From this point of view, it is important that the semantic processes are included in the fundamental structure and that they do not appear at just any phase from the outside.

It seems possible to create a parallel terminology for Greimas's generative course, a terminology that would enable one to define the moment of musical tension (kinetic energy). This problem prevails in any musico-semiotical research: how to connect the level of content to that of expression, how to join musical concepts and meanings to syntactical features of music. In order to assert that music is a semiotical process and that musical semiotics is possible, we have to believe that it has at least those two levels of signification. There are music analyses that are syntactically correct but not semiotical, in the sense that they convincingly show how music signifies and conveys content. Likewise, there are analyses that on the level of content take into account the moment of tension in music, its modal character, but fail to demonstrate how these contents are manifested in the musical syntax.

Models that try to manage with only one level of signification, such as Hanslick's theory and Schopenhauer's philosophy, are not semiotical. Yet even in extreme cases of formalist music analysis we catch glimpses of both these levels; hence such analysis is at least momentarily semiotical, when uniting the levels of content and expression. Few formal analyses of music are so formal that they could do without any references to the level of content, i.e., to that which is usually hinted in discourse about the aesthetics of a composition. There are intuitive factors shaping music which are probably irreducible to Gestalt theoretical laws but which nonetheless entail elements of signification (in other words, there are isotopies in music).

From the preceding discussions we may conclude that there are points in the musical discourse in which structures of communication dominate, and points where structures of signification come into the foreground. This statement almost coincides with the structuralist thesis, according to which discourse balances between *langue* and *parole*. Discourse needs both, but it is in danger of becoming either conventional clichés entirely ruled by *langue* (Busoni's norms of lawgivers, tonic-dominant relations, developments and codas) or an idiolect dominated by *parole*, which communicates nothing. The latter case inclines toward the "absolute" music of Busoni, although he does not recognize the risk hidden in a complete fulfillment of the ideal of absolute music, *Pan-* or *Ur-Musik*, a music that nobody would be able to receive or understand.[11] In such music, how do the principles of narrativity appear? Or do such works belong entirely outside the area of narrativity? Or do they represent "pure" narrativity in the most common sense of the term, since in them one breaks free of the excessive influence of structures of communication?

It might seem too equivocal a position to presuppose that music divides itself into sections in which structures of communication and signification alternately prevail. Yet it is impossible to believe that when a composer uses sonata form, Baroque dances, fugal techniques, or other structures of communication, the content of music entirely disappears at these moments and emerges from their shadow only momentarily, in sections of a "freer" nature. Rather, Charles Rosen's remark about sonata form holds true: "In a sonata exposition, modulation must not only be done, it must be seen to be done" (1976: 24). In other words, the purely syntactical operation, the shift from tonic to dominant, though not a structure of signification, becomes one only when this change is supported by other levels in music: "The move to the dominant in the first half of a sonata form is not merely confirmed by a full cadence on V at the end, but is marked by a decisive change of texture at a point between one-fourth to three-fourths of the length of the exposition" (Rosen 1976: 229). A musical event presented in this way becomes a narrative element.

From this we might draw the conclusion that narrativity in music is based on an immanent process of signification, that is, on modal structures which are tensions hidden in the syntactical structures; but for narrativity to arise, the modal (and other) structures must be foregrounded. They must be made pertinent, in the sense similar to markedness values in linguistics. In music, it is certainly difficult to distinguish between primary structures of signification and "secondary modeling systems" such as narrativity.

Narrative structures can emerge particularly when, as a stylistic device, syntactical structures are deliberately broken. For example, the two chords at the beginning of the Prélude to Debussy's *Pelléas et Mélisande*, the triads, with omitted third, and C form a movement of parallel fifths. Louis Laloy, in his famous analysis (which has been praised by Henri Bergson), considers it necessary to explain away this parallelism by depicting the latter chord as an inversion of a minor dominant triad (see Ex. 1.8). What is involved is a movement from the D minor tonic to the dominant. In Laloy's opinion, music is made not only for the ear but also for the spirit—this seems to reject the Gestalt-theoretical view and to affirm the signifying aspect of music!—and "series of notes or chords, even harmonious, were nothing but agreeable noise for us, if the order of their succession seemed arbitrary to us" (1974: 117). In this case, the analyst considers it his task to reduce the new structure of signification of music into structures of communication, that is, into familiar and accepted tonal figures. Debussy's narrative device, the parallel fifths, escapes his attention.

Example 1.8. Debussy, *Pelléas et Mélisande*,
Prelude, opening chords.

Let us now return to the notion of isotopy, a central concept in the analysis of musical signification. Isotopies are levels of signification, but they are not static units. Rather, they are moving, growing, diminishing, dynamic entities by which the inner tensions and narrative utterances of a musical work can be depicted.

As stated above, the smallest narrative utterance in music, F (x, y), presupposes the existence of at least two contrary elements. In addition one may suppose that these minimal units are dissonant with each other because of their dissimilitude. We need not limit the size of these elements to small dimensions, such as two phrases or two tones; the symbols x and y may represent sections of any size. So, for example, an essential innovation of sonata form, as compared to the binary and basically stable formal structures of Baroque music, was, according to Rosen (1980: 25) "a new and radically heightened conception of dissonance raised from the level of the interval and the phrase to that of the whole structure." As its consequence, "all the material played in the dominant is conceived as dissonant, i.e., requiring resolution by a later transposition to the tonic." The fact that this technique of "dissonant isotopies" was invented during the Classical period supports our previous hypothesis about the formation of the narrative model at just that time and the latter's elevation to a dominant "thought-of" model (discussed in Chap. 2.2, below). It seems that the concept of isotopy is not based on Gestalt psychological factors.[12] When an isotopy takes shape, a dimension of signification is always already involved. The mere existence of two spatial isotopies of "tonal space" does not form a narrative structure. Only when the spatial dissonance formed by those isotopies is temporalized—a paradigmatic relation is moved to a syntagm, a relation is transformed into an operation—only then does a narrative musical structure arise.[13]

When a dominant musical element is chosen for a certain section, then one is in the narrative process of the achronic, hierarchic relation of opposition, which lies so close to the surface of the discourse and to the latter's more or less anthropomorphic configurations, that a new actorial isotopy enters: a theme identifiable as a musical actant. On the other hand, a musical actant or theme is a concept that does not necessarily coincide with that of isotopy. According to "rule" built into the aesthetics of Western art music, a theme-actant must appear in the environment to which it belongs, in its proper isotopy. In other words, a proper accompaniment and a sonorous harmonic and rhythmic background must be created for a theme. In order to meet this requirement, Classical style in particular developed a special technique in which theme and accompaniment were derived from the same motivic material. Despite this rule, one may well imagine a theme situated, either deliberately or by error, in a "wrong" isotopy, in a musical environment alien to it. As a conscious narrative device this technique is very effective, as proven by numerous examples of premature or "false" recapitulation, i.e., a return to the main theme in the course of the development but in a wrong spatial isotopy, a wrong (not tonic) key. A good example is the end of the development section in Beethoven's Piano Sonata, Op. 2, in C major, where the main theme returns in V/V.

If one thinks of, say, narration in dramatic works or novels, usually at some point the protagonist is brought into a "wrong isotopy," an environment to which he does not belong in a social, temporal, or local sense and from which he eventually returns to his own isotopy. Entire stories are based upon the idea of a "wrong" isotopy: the strangers in Wild West stories, Siegfried in the court of the Gibichungs, the ugly duckling in Andersen's tale, etc. This holds true for musical narration as well.

On the other hand, there are examples in the field of music of unconscious choices of wrong isotopies. The early history of ethnomusicology is full of such choices, made during the phase in which that discipline was still bound to traditional historical musicology. The latter considered the only correct isotopy to be the tonal structures of Western art music in its Classical-Romantic period, and it saw all other forms and styles of music as "primitive." For example, in the first volume of music history by Ambros (1887), which was devoted to the music of ancient Greece and the Orient, music of the Far East is introduced with many music examples. Along with some joyful songs, Ambros gives an example of the so-called Djungel-Tuppah song, which he has harmonized, i.e., joined to the isotopies of Western music (see Ex. 1.9). In his view this tune contains deep melancholy, aroused particularly by the augmented second between scale degrees $\hat{6}$ and $\hat{7}$ in the minor mode. Ambros describes this impression with the title "Mondnacht am Ganges" (Moonlight on the Ganges).

Example 1.9. Ambros's harmonization of the Djungel-Tuppah song.

Especially noteworthy is Ambros's total conviction that the melody has been placed in the most appropriate isotopy: "Here, as in all other samples of Indian melody, I have added the harmonization. This shows to what extent these melodies have been composed in the European style; they not only allow a rich harmonic elaboration, but almost demand it" (Ambros 1887: 237).

We end our speculations in this section by concluding that the generative course of music does not place the three basic categories of isotopies (spatial, temporal, and actorial) only at the final surface level. Instead, the achronic fundamental structure of music is first spatial at a deeper level (at least two opposed pitches, or if we go still deeper, a tonic triad in its basic position, from which the Schenkerian generative course starts). At the next level, when music starts to get "narrativized," this hierarchic relation is made temporal. Finally, at the figurative, surface level, the actorial category enters as identifiable complexes of motifs and theme-actants, which through modalizations make this the "anthropomorphic" level of music.[14] At this surface level, music is experienced like human speech, *Klangrede*, since most people identify compositions by themes, characteristic rhythmic figures, or timbres. When music moves from this surface level of our generative model to form a part of human musical consciousness it has already passed through a long process that enables us to experience it as a phenomenon capable of carrying and yielding significations.

1.4 Toward the Definition of Modalities: Signs in Opera

We have made only brief mention of an important concept which is in fact a cornerstone of our whole theory of musical semiotics, namely, the notion of *modality* and *modalization*. We shall now examine the concept of modalities more closely, by situating them in a field that at first might seem quite distant from these philosophical-linguistic entities. I mean the theory of opera, or rather the fact that, so far, it seems there exists *no* theory of opera.

For a semiotician, the operatic art is a particularly fascinating and challenging subject of study, providing tasks for scholars in almost all areas of semiotics. Yet nobody can claim to have attained the ultimate synthesis of all the sign processes involved in opera, which by nature is a polydiscursive, intertextual totality of signs. Every operatic performance depends on the collective effect of numerous sign systems, none of which can be absent, because the receiver of an operatic utterance expects to experience a simultaneity of tones, colors, words, and gestures. The first question one would expect an opera researcher to pose is: What makes an opera's polydiscursive wholeness cohere? Producers of operatic performances must also answer this question through their own practical semiotic activity.

This problem was dealt with by many opera researchers at the turn of the twentieth century. Their thoughts are worth noting today, since many of them were artists and were consequently able to form an intuitive vision of the matter based on artistic practice itself.[15] Two representative art theorists of that period were: Adolphe Appia, author of *Die Musik und die Inszenierung* (1899), and the French composer Vincent d'Indy, whose *Cours de composition musicale* (1897–1900) is well known. Both Appia and d'Indy theorize from artistic intuition, and both works appeared in the golden age of Wagnerism; accordingly, the aesthetic experience they absolutized into a theory is undoubtedly the Wagnerian *Gesamtkunstwerk*. Nonetheless their ideas are of interest other than as documents in the history of Wagnerism. Both men attempted to construct a model of all the sign systems that participate in opera (although d'Indy emphasizes music). Thus their main theoretical concern follows the same path as that of contemporary semioticians. Appia and d'Indy may even be considered protosemioticians in their own field, if they were not both given to unnecessary speculations that led to premature generalizations and to metaphysics.

On the other hand, their theories are not mere taxonomies of various operatic sign systems, such as Noske's (1977) list of operatic signs. Their theories also take into account the force that holds opera together. Appia's main objective is to clarify why a work of art is experienced as a harmonic unity: "In every work of art we must feel unconsciously the harmonic unity between its content, the means of conveying it, and the message itself" (1899: 1). In Appia's view, the more elements in a work of art the more important this unity becomes, particularly in operatic art. Appia places music in the dominant position over other sign systems in opera (see Fig. 1.7). He regards music as both expression (*Ausdruck*) and form (*Gestalt*), which are united by the fact that music expresses the inner life and emotions. These in turn provide the music with a form: "Unser Seelenleben gibt also der Musik die Form, in welcher die Musik unser Seelenleben zum Ausdruck bringt" (1899: 6). This statement, hardly astonishing in its novelty, will later acquire new substance, when we discuss the semiotics of opera from the viewpoint of Greimas's theory.

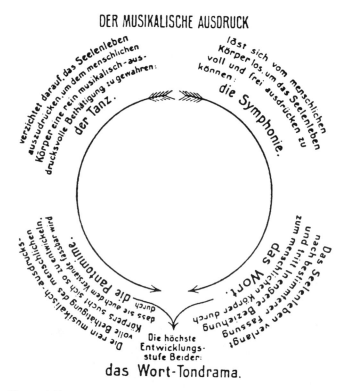

Figure 1.7. Appia's conception of the word-tonedrama (1899: 23).

Appia proceeds from musical expression to "word-tonedrama" through four categories: dance, symphony, pantomime, and word. These elements he compiles into a diagram showing that word-tonedrama results from two different developmental tendencies. 1. Combination of music with gesture and word: musical expression makes dance emerge as a purely musico-expressive activity of the human body, and as pantomime, in which this activity becomes comprehensible. 2. Musical expression may also try to escape the human body in order to convey forms of spiritual life with complete freedom, the result of which is so-called abstract music, or Appia's category of symphony. When word is added to absolute music, the musical expression returns to its starting point, the human body. The result of these two tendencies is the word-tonedrama. Accordingly, in Appia's diagram, absolute music becomes more concrete through word, while dance assumes greater abstraction through pantomime, until both meet each other and merge with the operatic whole (1899: 23).

There is a similarity between d'Indy's classification of symphonic forms (Fig. 1.8) and Appia's diagram. Behind the two trends, symphonic and dramatic music, loom the sign systems of gesture (*geste*) and speech (*parole*). According to d'Indy, there are two form-building principles in music: the rhythm of speech, which leads to recited or sung speech (*parole recitée ou chantée*); and the rhythm of gesture, from which emerge body movements, mime, and dance (1897–1900: 6–7). Thus d'Indy comes rather close to Appia's categories. These categories may seem rudimentary when compared to more recent semiotic taxonomies of dramatic art (e.g., Kowzan 1975). They nonetheless have a certain value as we start to ponder the factors that unify operatic discourse.

One integrating element of opera on the level of large syntagmatic units is naturally the plot. As Claude Brémond notes (1973), we perceive colors, tones, gestures, and words, but through them all we follow a story. Perhaps the simplest method of analyzing an opera is that developed by Vladimir Propp (1968) for the analysis of folktales. First, divide the story into functions, the actions of the protagonists. At this point one can see the opera's mythical model of basic actants (subject, object, receiver, sender, helper, and opponent) and define the actions and dramatic situations in which these actants meet, as Propp did with terms such as Departure, Battle, Recognition, Victory, Return, Wedding, and Death. This approach might prove useful, particularly when dealing with a large corpus of operas, such as all Verdi operas or all Finnish operas, in determining whether the former group manifests some personal myth of the composer, or if the latter reveals elementary models of actants (reflecting ultimately the semiotics of Finnish culture).

The fragmentation of opera into functions and their sequences, however, will only account for operatic unity on the macrolevel. The execution of a function onstage may last an entire act (for example, the function of Recognition and Seduction takes up the whole first act of Wagner's *Valkyrie*). Yet function alone cannot explain the unity of opera on the microlevel, that is, the force which

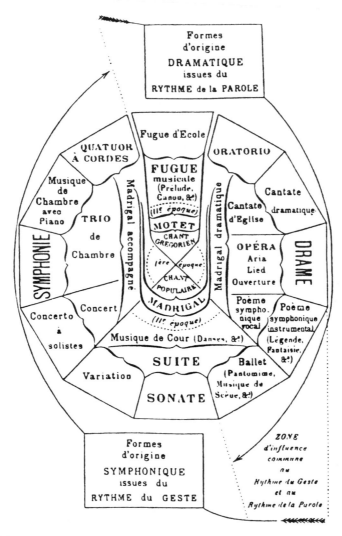

Figure 1.8. D'Indy's classification of symphonic forms (1897–1900: 6).

animates every cell of the polydiscursive organism of opera. For smaller units in the narrative program of opera one needs other concepts. If opera is, according to Osolsobe's apt definition (1980), communication that represents communication, one may extend the reasoning by asking which factors of "ordinary" communication does operatic communication choose to present. Opera does not represent only speech communication, situations in which somebody says (sings) something to someone else, for there may be long sections where the presentation unfolds only through gestures, pantomime, and music. Which factor of human communication do mere gestures represent (for example, in the opening scene between Siegmund and Sieglinde in *Die Valkyrie*)? Furthermore, in opera, music alone often advances the plot. What then is communicated?

Both Appia and d'Indy discuss the role of gesture and speech in musical expression, and still other theories have focused solely on the gestural nature of music. For example, Kurth (1947) alludes to gesture in his discussions of the kinetic energy of musical movement. In musical semiotics this view has also been developed by Coker (1972). Barthes (1975), in his short essay on Schumann, suggests that music be analyzed according to the physiological sensations it arouses in the performer and the listener. He calls these sensations "somathemes." The concept could easily be transferred to the field of opera to facilitate analysis of cases where gesture and tone form an inseparable cluster. This observation suggests that music swallows and absorbs features from other sign systems to such an extent that the enjoyment of those operagoers who close their eyes during the performance and "only" listen to the music seems justified. Music is essentially a dramatic art; it is intimately related to drama since in a certain sense each melody is like an act, as Brelet has remarked: "La mélodie est expressive dans la mesure où elle exprime l'acte de la voix" (1949: 414).

If each melody, theme, and motif is an act, what are the consequences? It follows that if musical logic obeys the logic of an act, then musical semiosis is shaped according to norms and intentions similar to those governing ordinary pragmatic acts. Thus the role of music in opera would be quite clear: music mirrors the actions of the protagonists, musical themes function as actants, and one can distinguish among subject-themes, object-themes, helper-themes, opponent-themes, etc., and the whole universe of opera would be contained exclusively in music. Yet operatic music does not consist entirely of gesture and dramatic action, but also of symphonic-formal principles. Does this make music an autonomous element? Does the realization of abstract musical forms in opera bring about a state in which music leads its own life, without being greatly concerned about the fates of the protagonists, the flesh-and-blood actants on the stage? Berg's *Wozzeck* and Ginastera's *Don Rodrigo*, two of the twentieth century's most rigorously structural operas, prove that this is not necessarily the case.

The Modalities

Behind music, speech, and gesture lies an unknown factor that is not reducible to the mere syntax of music or speech, or to the external, measurable movements of gesture. In the semiotic theory of Greimas it is called *modalities* (Greimas and Courtés 1979: 230–32). Modalities denote all the intentions by which the person who voices (*énonciateur*) an utterance may color his or her "speech"; i.e., modalities convey evaluative attitudes (such as will, belief, wishes) toward the content of an utterance. Larousse's French dictionary defines modality as:

Psychic activity that the speaker projects into what he is saying. A thought is not content with a simple presentation, but demands active participation by the thinking subject, activity which in the expression forms the soul of the sentence; without it the sentence does not exist. This activity can be (a) a statement concerning the truth of the utterance, when the modality is *affirmative*; (b) a question related to the utterance, when the modality is *interrogative*; (c) an expression of the will related to the utterance, when the modality is *volitive*; (d) an emotion, when the modality is *exclamative*.

Displacing mere structural analysis, the invention of modalities in the 1970s radically transformed semiotic study in the Greimasian school and brought to light the dynamic aspects of human communication. Modal articulations also can be considered the proper form-building elements of art, if form is construed as the living tensions inside the external manifestation.

The theory of modalities was anticipated by d'Indy's *Cours*. Speaking of the starting point of melody, the accent, d'Indy distinguishes two cases: *accent tonique* (or *logique*) and *accent expressif* (or *pathétique*). The first affects words alone, the latter whole sentences; and both accents also occur in musical "words" and "phrases." As an example d'Indy (1897–1900: 30) gives three ways of accentuating the phrase "Il a quitté la ville" (He left the city): 1. It can be pronounced in a neutral way which follows only the inner accents of words (*accent tonique*) and without any expression of emotion, as shown in Ex. 1.10a. 2. It can be pronounced in an interrogative way (Ex. 1.10b), when the tempo accelerates toward the end and the word *ville* receives a pathetic accent. 3. The sentence can be uttered affirmatively (Ex. 1.10c) when the main accent goes to the word *quitté* and the tempo slows toward the end. From this d'Indy concludes: "Accordingly, under the influence of various emotions, this originally very neutral and shapeless sentence, in which hardly any rhythm was discernible, becomes animated and receives its own accents. . . . The syllables seem, so to speak, to become musicalized" (1897–1900: 31). With this statement he comes close to a definition of musical modalities.

Other scholars (Barthes, Kurth, and Brelet) have explored the area of gesture in their search for the integrating factor of music. Yet even gestures can be reduced to modal contents. For example, an orchestra conductor does not concentrate on gestures as such, but rather on the modal content of a musical work. Just as the proper "musicalization" depends on the conductor, so it also depends on the musicians' ability to discover (interpret) the modal components. Composers often assume that musicians have the ability to modalize (musicalize) and do not indicate this important element of music in the scores. (For example, we know that Chopin hardly ever played a work the same way twice, but always modalized it in a new manner.) The performer can greatly affect the essence of a musical message.

Now we can answer the question as to what is the most important integrating factor of the various sign systems in opera. The answer is: the modal dimension. This dimension becomes manifest, for example, in those scenes in Wagner's operas where music gives way to gestures, where the symphonic

Example 1.10. D'Indy's three means of accentuation:
a. *accent logique*; b. *accent tonique*; c. *accent pathétique*.

a.

Il   a   quit - té   la   ville

Deux accents logiques. -- Pas d'accent pathétique

b.

Il   a '   quit - té   la   ville ?...

(Accent tonique.)   (Accent pathétique.)

c.

Il   a   quit - té   la   ville

(Accent pathétique.)   (Accent tonique.)

continuity of music changes into the discontinuity of gestural language. In such scenes, two actors meet and are gradually linked to the same modal dimension, as occurs in the first meeting of Senta and Daland in the *Flying Dutchman* or the awakening of Brünnhilde in the last act of *Siegfried*.[16]

What are the modalities of music, and how can they be analyzed? Are they simply different emotions and passions? In that case the semiotics of opera would change into the semiotics of passions; and Appia's observation, according to which music gives a special form to our spiritual life, would find its exact meaning. It is evidently futile to try to isolate modalities from musical discourse exclusively through induction, that is, by gathering together all examples of modal utterances in music. If on the other hand a deductive approach is chosen, do the same modal categories present in language also apply to music?

Let us begin to answer this question by returning to the most advanced theory of modalities, that of Greimas. He divides the modalities into three groups: virtualizing, actualizing, and realizing (Fig. 1.9). Each group comprises *exotaxic* modalities, which presuppose two different subjects, and *endotaxic* modalities, which are realized within one and the same subject. From these categories, interesting things follow for musical semiotics. For the semiotics of opera, the most important is to prove the validity of modalities as regards music, since for drama their efficiency has already been tested (Salosaari 1989).

	Modalities *virtualizing*	*actualizing*	*realizing*
exotaxic	to be obliged to	to be able to	to do
endotaxic	to want	to know	to be

Figure 1.9. Greimas's categories of modality.

First of all, what do the categories of 'doing' (*faire*) and 'being' (*être*) mean in music? Is music's 'being' its sound or its being in the score? If music's 'being' is its being in the consciousness of the intonation's receiver, then 'doing' would be the same as causing an intonation to sound, or that which makes music be. If music is construed as an organism in which movement and progression form the 'doing' of this organism, then the activity that impels the organism to move and on which its life depends is by nature factitive (*faire-faire*). Hence the three basic coordinates of musical communication as regards musical enunciation (performance) are composer, performer, and listener. Each has individual endotaxic modalities of 'will', 'know', and 'be'; and the interrelations of these three coordinates represent exotaxic modalities of 'must', 'can', and 'do'.

These modalities might first be examined within the musical organism itself (as utterance, *énoncé*), inasmuch as musical themes and motifs can be considered as symbolically functioning entities, as actants. Let us assume that musical themes can be modalized both endo- and exotaxically, like human actants. Then, endotaxically, one could speak (with Kurth 1947) of a theme's or motif's inner 'will' or kinetic energy. A theme's 'know' (*savoir*) would mean the information it transmits: a theme's (sounding) rhythmic, melodic, and harmonic elements. In other words, 'know' would mean the musical substance apart from its function in a musical work. Taken together, 'will' and 'know' form the 'being' of a musical theme.

What are the exotaxic modalities of a musical utterance, i.e., the action among musical themes? In the simplest relation between two successive themes (for example, the main and subordinate themes in a sonata, or two successive motifs in an opera), the first theme's 'will', its kinetic energy and developmental potential, greatly influences the kinetic energy of the second theme. The impact of the former theme on the latter is in a certain sense normative, in that it modalizes the latter theme. From the perspective of the second theme, a relation of 'must' is involved. One must also consider the first theme's 'can' (*pouvoir*), that is, its ability to change and influence the nature of the second theme. In the same way, the second theme can affect subsequent events in the music, which thus form the sphere of its 'being able to do something'. For the subsequent musical material this 'can' once again appears as obligation ('must') within the limitations set for it. Finally, the inner energies of themes can contradict each other: their tensions of 'can', 'will', and 'must' may lead in contrary directions, and only later in a composition (say, the development section of a sonata) are they allowed to blend together or are their contrasts sharpened.

There remain the categories of 'doing' and 'being' within the music itself (utterance). It is intuitively clear that in music there must exist a certain balance between doing (event) and being (state). A composition that only 'is' (for example, endless repetitions of the same motif) might bore the listener. Conversely, a musical work with a maximum of events and entropy might perplex the listener. Such utterances cannot by themselves form a musical narrative program (*programme narratif*, abbreviated as PN), since they realize only one modality (for example, the sadness which permeates Sibelius's *Valse triste*). A musical utterance that only 'is' can be called qualificative.

On the other hand, functional utterances also can be discerned in music, when the emphasis goes to 'doing', to events. What is involved is a situation in which a theme or motif S1 acts in such a way that a succeeding motif S2 is heard as different, and this difference is perceived as caused by S1. (See, for example the middle section of *Valse triste*; the faster tempo and more joyful flavor contrast with the slow, elegiac waltz at the beginning and end). Motif/section S2 can thus be said to be modalized by motif/section S1.

A musical work consisting only of qualificative utterances which stress 'being' can be described by the expression $E(m)\{S1 \to S1' \ldots S1n\}$, where $E = être$ ('being') and m = modality (for example, sadness). Correspondingly, a functional musical utterance, in which something—a musical action—really happens might be represented by $F(m)\{S1 \to S2\}$, where $F = faire$ ('doing') and m = modality (for example, sad turns to joyful).

For *Valse triste* we get the following expression as the PN (narrative program) of the work:

$$PN1: E(m)[S1 \to PN2: F(m)\{S1 \to S2\} \to S1]$$

This grammar is rudimentary and forms only the first step of formalization. It nevertheless seems that the modal categories of Greimas's general semiotic theory do apply to musical discourse. Of course there remains the problem of conceptually refining and denominating various musical events and states; music contains much that is ineffable, and one may always argue about what is in fact sad or joyful music. Despite this problem, the meaningful effects produced by all the modal operations of music constitute a valid, though very complex, phenomenal field. One might even find that music has modalities that do not exist in other discourses.

The fact that Greimasian modalities can be applied to music is significant for the semiotics of opera. Both the music and the whole intertextuality of opera are dominated by a complex and subtle network of modalities which guarantees the continuity of the operatic discourse on all its levels and forms the cohesive force of the operatic text. The modalities provide a descriptive language by which the inner semiotic processes of opera can be grasped simultaneously with their relation to outer reality: the "natural world" of the spectators, which opera seeks to affect.

As regards this "natural world," Greimas's modality of 'believing', explored at length in Chap. 1.5, plays a central role. An opera performance transforms the epistemic units of culture in the same way as, for example, a circus performance serves as a melting pot of cultural elements (as Bouissac 1976 has shown). If articulated according to the categories 'to be', 'to appear', 'not to appear', 'not to be', with their equivalent epistemic units of truth, untruth, secret, and lie, the modality of believing could be applied to opera as well. Often that which in the natural world belongs to the category of 'hidden' (secret or lie) can be transformed in the operatic world into its opposite: When Wotan, at the end of *Rheingold*, gives up his ring and thus denies the modality of will or his will to power, he exhibits a value model that runs contrary to the ideological reality of the society of Wagner's time, a society in which the truth of the natural world—the will to power—is revealed as untruth in the world of opera. Sheer music has the ability to manifest the hidden epistemic contents of the libretto. In this sense opera must be considered a unit of cultural semiotics, a unit that refers to the possible world of its community and in that community forms a sphere of "otherness."

1.5 On the Truth in Music
(Or What Schoenberg and Asafiev Said about the Modality of 'Believing')

> Die Wahrhaftigkeit ist vielleicht auch ein
> mathematisch Ausdrückbares, vielleicht sogar
> eher als die Schönheit.

In Chap. 1.4 we arrived at 'believing', the last of the modalities in Greimas's theory, but by no means the least. In fact, the functioning of other modalities may aim for a global effect of belief, persuasion, and convincingness. This effect is important not only to the semiotics of spectacles but to any musical communication.

We probably cannot explain the changes and crises in music without considering this modality and its influence on music history. As Michel Foucault says of epistemes, certain units and principles of the epistemological level can direct the whole of cultural development. And insofar as the ultimate reason for stylistic change is based on the transformation of aesthetic concepts, the replacement of the concept of "the beautiful" by that of "the truthful" links music to the epistemological network of an entire culture, such a network being that which in each era is considered true or untrue, and what qualifies as reality. It is difficult to imagine that people would fight passionately merely for the sake of beauty; but it is highly credible that if art mirrors the epistemes of truth/untruth, aesthetic issues may become so vital as to cause crises and catastrophes in the history of music.

A consistent formulation of this point of view can be found in Arnold Schoenberg's *Harmonielehre*, in the chapter on nonharmonic tones (*harmoniefremde Töne*). Schoenberg suggests that one should appeal to the concept of the truthful rather than the beautiful. Accordingly, he identifies aesthetics with epistemology. For example, aestheticians have always balked at the use of dissonant chords because they are not beautiful. Yet in Schoenberg's opinion beauty exists only from the moment in which uncreative people start to measure it. It does not exist previously, since artists do not need beauty: for them it suffices to express themselves truthfully (*wahrhaftig*), to "say" what has to be said. Beauty bound to fixed rules and static forms is sought only by the uncreative. To an artist, beauty exists without its having been wanted or expected. Schoenberg thus connects the aesthetic quality of music only to its receiver and draws the following conclusion concerning creative and uncreative people:

> And beauty is in the world only by virtue of one thing: by virtue of the congenial excitement in the nature of the nongenius, by virtue of the ability to suffer, to sympathize with what greatness experiences. As an accompaniment of that great capacity for sympathy that arouses the average person, as a by-product of the accomplishment of those necessary tasks that the genius performs in his penetration of nature—as such beauty may very well exist.[17]

For this reason, Schoenberg rejects the whole concept of beauty, and insists that the notion of truthfulness best conveys the relation of artist to work.

A similar view of the epistemology of music is found in the intonation theory of Russian musicologist Boris Asafiev. He differs from Schoenberg in his emphasis on the receiver, construed as a collective musical consciousness. For Asafiev music arises directly from epistemic changes in a culture. For example, every reform in opera, from Gluck to Wagner to Musorgsky, started with "a feeling of the inopportuneness, the obsolescence, and the deadening of intonations even in compositions still considered as image-bearing" (Asafiev 1977: 715). Unlike Schoenberg, who sees it as the relationship between composer and composition, Asafiev views truth as interaction between intonations and their receivers: "when intonations and rhythms correspond to the content of ideas and the inclination of feelings of the ruling strata of the people, then perception in turn becomes natural and unrestrained; music is heard as true 'speech' and felt as reality, as truth" (1977: 710).

At least two weaknesses can be found in Asafiev's theory. First, it does not explain completely the process by which a composer's feelings and thoughts are transformed into intonations, or how states of consciousness are changed into sound phenomena. The very concept of intonation is rather loose, since by it Asafiev means not only the actually performed and heard music, but also music that sounds "internally," that is, the imaginary or "hummed" material of the collective musical memory. Consequently, intonations are at the same time manifest as well as immanent units (which brings the notion of intonation closer to the semiotical theories of Hjelmslev and Greimas).

Another weakness of Asafiev's theory lies in its normative conservatism. If all new intonations must pass through the censorship of the people whom Schoenberg called "uncreative," how can new intonations ever penetrate the store of dominant intonations? For the invention and breakthrough of every new intonation already means a small crisis in the present intonational culture and renders previous musical values questionable, just as Schoenberg declared that every new tone in a musical work raises a problem and demands continuation in order to restore the initial balance of the work.

Despite its shortcomings, Asafiev's theory may lead us to reevaluate the notion of music history. Is "written" music history the history of only those intonations that have won a permanent place in people's memory? Does music history attend to only those intonations that, at the moment of writing, correspond to the epistemic units of the period? Asafiev speaks of intonational crisis as a change involving an entire culture, thus obliging people to search for new types of intonations. Yet he does not mention those battles among intonations which are being waged ceaselessly in every music culture and which show that the idea of stable balance in musical culture is highly illusory.

We may now semiotically interpret the problem of a musical "truth" or correct interpretation as the relation between the store of intonations *and* a composition or its performance. Here one can apply Greimas's veridictory square, as shown in Fig. 1.10. The veridictory square shows that music's 'being' means its existence in the store of intonations, while music's 'appearing' is its aural manifestation in a composition. 'Not to be' signifies absence from the store of intonations, while 'not to appear' refers to music that is not played, but is deprived of any sound manifestation and remains so-called paper music. Consequently, music that 'is' (is in the store of intonations) but which is not played belongs to the category of 'secret' (something concealed) in the veridictory square; while music that is only played, but which has no equivalent in the store of intonations, goes in the category of 'lie'. In turn, music that both 'is' and 'appears' belongs to the store of intonations and gets performed; this music corresponds to the category of 'truth'. It follows that music that neither exists in the store of intonations nor gets played belongs in the category of 'untruth'.

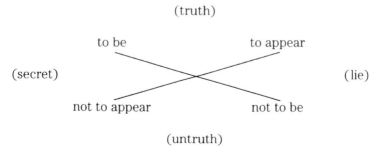

Figure 1.10. Veridictory square (after Greimas).

The definitions just given allow us to approach the theory of the truth of a musical utterance, as well as the question of how to estimate its truth value. Terms such as 'truth', 'lie', 'untruth', and 'secret' seem applicable to music, at least intuitively; but the interpretation of these categories demands further reflection, especially on what we mean by 'true' music, that which both 'is' and 'appears' (sounds).

What relation exists between the aural intonation and the intonation stored in the consciousness of listeners? Is it a relation of equivalence, in which the only true musical utterance would be one that has existed in the collective musical memory? This could mean several things, such as the fact that all possible sound structures exist, so to speak, in the human brain, as potentialities; the composer finds and reveals them to the listener, in which case one only listens to oneself through music.[18] This philosophical reflection does not necessarily give us, from a pragmatic point of view, a useful answer to the original question of how to distinguish between a 'true' and an 'untrue' musical utterance. It is nonetheless evident that a true utterance cannot mean a mere relation of equivalency. If this were so, how could any new music have been created? And yet Western classical music has certainly developed during the past centuries.

Instead, what is involved is a relation between the modalities of 'will' (*vouloir*) and 'must' (*devoir*). Every new composition, theme, and motif has its own 'will' or kinetic energy, an energy that aims to realize its inner growth and development, but whose life is limited by normative obligations ('must') determined by the dominant intonations.[19] This 'will' explains, among other things, the phenomenon of redundancy in music: music that unambiguously corresponds to certain intonations and in which no independent 'will' appears is always redundant for the listener. The listener to Western art music does not expect to hear maximally redundant music (save pop music), which merely repeats the store of intonations. Our aesthetics views such music as inadequate in form and content, not offering us the effect of psychological surprise and admiration which we demand of an aesthetic experience. Rather, we expect a certain difference between the 'being' (inner intonation) and the 'appearing' (aural manifestation) of music. It is precisely this process of comparing a musical intonation with the store of intonations that may be called a sort of interpretation.[20]

Opinions vary greatly as to what is "true" interpretation in the aforementioned sense. Some think that music should be in a relation of contrast and negation to the store of intonations; others hold that it should be in a relation of affirmation. This problem is also a modal one: before one can deny or affirm the dominant musical immanency in a piece, one must be able to (*pouvoir*), know (*savoir*), want to (*vouloir*), and even be obliged to (*devoir*) deny or affirm. What does it mean that one 'can' deny or affirm? A composer must possess the technical means for denying or affirming.[21] What does it mean to 'know' how to deny/affirm intonations? A composer must know tradition, the culture of intonations in which she or he lives. Finally we have to consider 'will' as a precondition of denial or affirmation. 'Will' joined with 'can' brings about what John Ruskin called "ideas of power," which refer to the physical and psychic efforts required to create a work of art. From this one may infer, for example, that there is less power in Mozart than in Beethoven, since the former composer's music expresses no struggle between means and ends, but emerges "spontaneously" and without much elaboration.

The composer might store in her or his works an energy of will that runs contrary to the dominant culture of intonations. In this case the normative pressure of existing intonations is broken by the power of a new composition, which in turn permits the emergence of new intonations. In order to penetrate the intonational store, these new intonations must possess a certain power and 'will'. In some cases this process is embedded in the structure of a composition; for example, Chopin's mazurkas, waltzes, and polonaises are far superior to the mazurka, waltz, and polonaise intonations of the salon music of his time. Chopin may even depict the battle between new and old intonations as, for example, in his *Polonaise-Fantaisie,* Op. 61 (analyzed in Chap. 6.1). The force of a theme, its will and power, can be greater than that of another theme, which is thus subordinated to it. In fact, a composition's main theme is that in which the modalities of *pouvoir, savoir*, and *vouloir* are more abundant than in other themes. Finally, the internal energy of themes can also break conventional formal molds and thereby intrude into a culture's dominant intonations.

1.6 The Theory Itself in an Abridged Form

Now it is time to put together the ideas dealt with in the previous sections. I shall present "the theory itself" as a two-part form. One part deals with the main branch of the theory: adaptation of Greimas's generative trajectory. The other part, as a kind of "second theme" of this treatise, relies on Peirce.

Greimas's Generative Course as Applied to Music

What I understand by generativism is not quite the same as the Chomskyan tree models elaborated by many "computer musicologists."[22] The difference between Greimas's generative course (*parcours génératif*) and the Chomskyan model is clear: Chomsky's grammar has nothing to do with significations, whereas Greimas expressly takes into account significations, while progressing gradually from deep level (semio-narrative structures) toward the surface (discursive structures) of a text. In what follows I shall use Greimas's model (Fig. 1.11) only as a starting point and source of inspiration, and shall quite freely outline my own model of generation of musical meaning.

PARCOURS GÉNÉRATIF			
		composante syntaxique	composante sémantique
Structures sémio- narratives	niveau profond	SYNTAXE FONDAMENTALE	SÉMANTIQUE FONDAMENTALE
	niveau de surface	SYNTAXE NARRATIVE DE SURFACE	SÉMANTIQUE NARRATIVE
Structures discursives		SYNTAXE DISCURSIVE Discursivisation actorialisation temporalisation spatialisation	SÉMANTIQUE DISCURSIVE Thématisation Figurativisation

Figure 1.11. Greimas's generative course.

The very idea of "generation" must be understood here in a less rigorous way than in the most formalized grammars. Still, my aim is to move *toward* formalization, though I have perhaps attained it only in some of the analyses in Part Two. Some might consider this lack of formalization as a deficiency. To these critics my response is that often I have purposely stopped the formalization on some level, because it is assumed that some music reveals its true essence better in a "softer," more philosophical-hermeneutical discourse. If I am classified outside the group of "hard" semioticians of music, then so be it. The levels I adopt from Greimas now follow.

1. Isotopies: levels of meaning of a text. Isotopies serve as criteria for the first segmentation of a text under analysis.

2. Spatiality, Temporality, and Actoriality: these categories form respectively articulation of tonal space, temporal organization, and thematic or actorial elements, in which engagement/disengagement (centripetal/centrifugal motion) and extero-/interoceptivity (*outer* vs. *inner*) play a central role. *Spatial* articulation in the inner sense means the distinguishing of tonal centers or tonality/ atonality; in the outer sense it means which registers music occupies in the sound space. *Temporal* articulation in the inner sense means a kind of comparison of the elements in a musical syntagm (see Chap. 2.1, on musical micro-time), in the outer sense, it means a rhythmic and metric analysis. *Actorial* articulation signifies, besides distinction of theme-actors, the distribution of actoriality in the form of thematics or other "anthropomorphic" elements of the text.

3. Modalities: the level of modalities emerges from the preceding spatial, temporal, and actorial articulations; modalities are therefore not arbitrary, subjective interpretations imposed on the text. The basic modalities are 'being'

(*être*): state of rest, stability, consonance; and 'doing' (*faire*): musical action, event, dynamism, dissonance. In addition one can distinguish 'becoming' (*devenir*), which refers to the "normal" temporal process of music.

There are other modalities. 'Will' (*vouloir*): the so-called kinetic energy of music, the tendency to move toward something, musical direction; the volitive logic of music. 'Know' (*savoir*): musical information, the cognitive moment of music. 'Can' (*pouvoir*): the power and efficiency of music, its technical resources, particularly in performance (performance techniques, idiomatic writing, virtuosity, etc.). 'Must' (*devoir*): aspects of genre and formal type (sonata, fugue, rondo, chaconne, etc.); the relation of a musical work to stylistic and normative categories which can originate from the store of intonations that exist outside of a musical work, or which can be established by the work itself; the deontic logic of music. 'Believe' (*croire*): the epistemic values of music, its persuasiveness in reception, the distribution of epistemic values like truth/untruth, lie/secret, in various phases of the text according to its narrative program(s).

4. **Phemes/Semes; Figures:** the minimal units of the musical substance on the levels of signifier (phemes) and of signified (semes); together with modalities, phemes and semes form musical figures. Figures are musical situations, such as Struggle and Victory, that recur in a certain musical corpus (e.g., Beethoven sonatas, Chopin ballades, Sibelius symphonies) and which are generated by all the previous phases. In figures, for instance, various modalities and spatial-temporal-actorial categories occur in a certain hierarchy or order of pertinence; i.e., at some point in a musical text the spatial dominates the temporal aspect; in some other, 'will' rules 'know'; etc. This last phase of generation accounts for the question left open by, among others, so-called paradigmatic analysis, namely, how a composer in the context of one work varies paradigmatic criteria. Such variation can be explained precisely by the inner organization of figures.

The above scheme presents the main features of the generative trajectory in music. Since a good deal of its concepts originate from French, I have also given original terms here and sometimes later in this volume. In addition, there are many other semiotic tools which can be used on any level of generation. They include the semiotic square, the Peircean notions of icon, index, symbol etc., Juri Lotman's concept of "semiosphere" (which we paraphrase here as "tonosphere," the continuum of musical signs which enables the functioning of any particular musical sign), the actantial model of Greimas (see particularly Greimas and Courtés 1979 and 1986). An essential difference between earlier music-semiotical analysis and our own lies in the fact that here the segmentation of a musical piece takes place only as a consequence of all the aforementioned operations. Musical form is thus viewed as a process and not as an external scheme.

The generation of musical texts does not initiate from conventional distinctions like melody, rhythm, harmony, timbre, and growth (LaRue 1970). Taking one of these parameters, say, the timbre of an orchestration, one notices that it operates simultaneously on many levels of generation. Orchestration influences both inner and outer time, spatial effects from the interaction of external space (interaction between concert hall and orchestra, seating arrangement of musicians, their number) and internal space of music. Orchestration manifests also in the actorial category, since different instruments are already actors of musical uttering (*énonciation*), by which a composer can emphasize actors (such as themes) of musical utterances (*énoncés*) by setting instruments into dialogue with each other. Moreover, orchestration can express musical modalization in many different ways.

My semiotical-generative system also means a new configuration of musical knowledge, while in some phases it comes close to traditional methods of analysis. The system also strives to be a model independent of musical style period. It can thus be applied to many kinds of musical texts. How can one verify the correctness of the results of the method? Is the definition of modalities basically a subjective activity depending on its interpreter? Should one conduct experiments with various listener groups, for example, to decide whether the modalities of a piece have been correctly determined? In no way diminishing the significance of experimental research in the quest for cognitive processes in music, I consider this requirement irrelevant in this context. (Has anyone chastised Lévi-Strauss for not conducting experiments with the Bororo Indians, to verify if he had interpreted their myths correctly? Has anyone demanded that Carl Dahlhaus empirically test his musical-aesthetic concepts?) The problem is that we are faced here with two different but complementary goals: the elucidation of basic structures of musical cognition and the interpretation of remarkably complex musical texts. The verification of knowledge in these cases is realized in various ways. My own model, which requires the notion of a competent listener, is naturally closer to the latter approach.

Before introducing our "second theme"—my theory based on Charles S. Peirce—I must offer further observations on the modalities. The modal phase of my generative trajectory and method of analysis is perhaps the most crucial level, and it crystallizes most of the previously discussed philosophical principles concerning musical time, process, and energy. I have already briefly explained what each modality in music means; for example, 'know', the degree of information in a music, by which I mean all that is new or innovative. But how can one describe with precision the *amount* of each modality in any moment of a musical work? To do so we shall employ the Greimasian aspectual semes sufficient/insufficient, excessive/inexcessive, and they might be digitalized so that the value ++ means excessive, + sufficient, 0 neutral, - insufficient, and - - deficient. The composer's art consists in creating a balanced whole and apportioning modalities correctly. As Jean Cocteau says (in *Le coq et l'arlequin*), one has to know "jusqu'où on peut aller trop loin."

It is intuitively clear that the modalities are interdependent. Greimas has also pondered compatibilities and incompatibilities of various modalities on a logical-semiotic level, but inferences about compatibilities of musical modalities can probably be drawn only after empirical analysis of individual texts. For example, we often declare that a piece by a novice composer projects a true 'will' of creation, an "inner necessity," but that the composer lacks the tools, the technique to convey it. In modal terms, 'will' receives the value ++ whereas 'can' and 'know' lie between 0 and -. Some music follows norms of a genre or style tradition but becomes "stiff" when the composer follows strict academic rules without creative inspiration. Such a case involves a high value of 'must', + or even ++, while the value of 'will' is on the minus side. Or a composer may write music that is correct, according to the rules, but has not been able to provide that music with technical-instrumental effectiveness; in this case, 'know' and 'will' are sufficient, sometimes almost excessive, but 'can' is 0 or -.

Modal analysis involves not only the examination of a musical utterance but also, for the performance, the act of uttering. The performer has to pay attention to the modal organization of a piece and perhaps fill its "lack" with her or his own modalizations. By positive (+) values of 'can' and 'know', an excellent performance can compensate for the minus values of the original text (utterance). In some cases the interpreter modalizes excessively, giving the musical text more modalities than it truly contains. If by "authentic" interpretation we mean a performance whose modalizations come as close as possible to the inner modalities of the original text, it follows that authentic interpretation must be based on detailed knowledge of the musical utterance itself.

In the age of Romanticism, performers emphasized the difference between the modal insufficiency of the original text and the all-mighty, self-legitimating excessiveness of the interpretation. Busoni's arrangements of Bach illustrate such remodalization, with + values in almost all musical parameters. Yet despite their differences, both the "authenticity" movement and Romanticism are phenomena of a musical culture that aims to establish the relationship between composer and performer, utterance and act of uttering, *modalities* (qualities of musical utterance) and *modalizations* (qualities of musical uttering) .

Fig. 1.12 compares two different modalizations of Chopin's first Nocturne in B♭ minor, in the form of recordings by Artur Rubinstein and Samson François. The juxtaposition of these two performances reveals two entirely different aesthetics, two opposed musical cultures. This inventory reveals two attitudes, one "objective" almost to the point of insensitivity, the other "subjective," bordering on overinterpretation.

Though we touched on the issue in Chap. 1.5, we have not yet carefully investigated the modality of 'believing', or rather of 'making to believe', which appears as the intention of a composer in a musical text. This modality concerns the global meaning-effect of a text, an effect based on other modalities, and mappable on the veridictory square as being/appearing, as the categories truth/untruth/secret/lie, and epistemically as modal operations of affirm/deny and admit/doubt (see Fig. 1.13). Claude Zilberberg (1985) has studied this structure, supposing that 'to make to believe' is based on a situation in which 'appearing' modalizes 'being' (m = make; a = appear; b = be). It would represent different cases of 'believe' as seen from the point of view of the composer or sender of the message; i.e., the verbs in Fig. 1.13 depict the way a composer operates in order to persuade the listener.

Rubinstein:	François:
- tends to transform tempo into fast-slow-fast	- transforms tempo into slow-fast-slow
- melody and accompaniment synchronized	- melody and accompaniment not synchronized
- melody interpreted as written; without pathetic accent	- speech-like melody; pathetic accents
- redundancy; uniform and invariable sound surfaces	- entropy and surprise; avoids mechanical repetition
- unvaried touch; "nocturne" sonority; mechanistic	- varied touch; makes "polyphony" out of monophonic texture; polysemic
- "nocturne" genre as basis, emphasizing *langue*	- piece's "message" as basis, emphasizing *parole*
- minimal interpretation; sostenuto on first note the only stylistic device; follows old cembalist school	- maximal interpretation, often contrary to score
- uniform tempo; tends to accelerate slow time-values, slow down faster time-values	- erratic tempo, unequal pulse; accelerates fast time-values, slows down small time-values; much rubato

Figure 1.12. Summary of two modalizations of Chopin, Nocturne in B♭ minor.

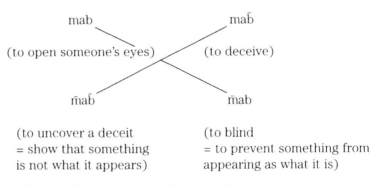

(to uncover a deceit = show that something is not what it appears)

(to blind = to prevent something from appearing as what it is)

Figure 1.13. Epistemic modalities according to the composer.

From the listener's or receiver's perspective, one might think that 'believing' in the proper sense would represent a situation in which 'being' modalizes 'appearing': 'make-be-appear'. This is logical if one thinks that a composer prepares a musical message ('make appear') that is based on the common store of intonations ('be') of composer and listener. Instead, the 'being' (musical competence) of a listener modalizes the musical 'appearance', the sounding manifestation (performance) of a piece, so that we arrive at the diagram in Fig. 1.14.

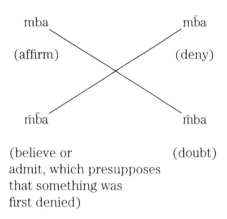

Figure 1.14. Epistemic modalities according to the listener.

Greimas (1983) argues that the modality of believing is by nature gradual between the cases 'b' vs. 'not-b'. For him, graduality manifests itself in the categories of little or much of something, or as a corresponding aspectual seme. We have either little or much of the three main operations of discursivization: actorialization (some), temporalization (early/late), spatialization (near/far). Accordingly, we can have either too much or too little of all these categories. For example, insufficiency can appear as something which is either "almost" or "too." In other words, the tensional quality—our main concern— appears according to the semiotic square shown in Fig. 1.15. These aspects of 'believe' are distributed throughout the discourse, not only in the actorial-temporal-spatial articulations, but also in other modalities, of which there can then be either too much or too little. The credibility of a musical discourse emerges as their joint result. This means that, from the point of view of a composer, he or she strives to convince, i.e., exercises a persuasive activity. The listener, in turn, interprets a composition either as true or untrue, lie or secret, or affirms/denies, admits/doubts the content of a musical message. Consequently, the modality of 'believe' contains a considerable amount of semiotic operations and content.

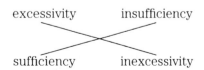

Figure 1.15. Aspectual semes in Greimas's semiotics.

The second phase of the generation of a musical text describes the degree of disengagement/engagement (see the analysis of Beethoven's "Waldstein" Sonata in Chap. 5). One must then evaluate the *significance* of the amount of disengagement/engagement regarding the global effect and meaning of the text. Has a spatial disengagement, for example, deviated too far from the tonal center (tonic) or from the original register? Has one returned early enough or perhaps too late to the right tonal center? Are there too many thematic elements or actors in a composition, a sufficient amount, or perhaps too few?

"Traditional" musical aesthetics operates with such terms when judging the aesthetic value of a composition. An aesthetic judgment takes place with these modal articulations of 'believing' and more particularly with the aspectual articulation of something being excessive/inexcessive, sufficient/insufficient. To be convinced of this, take any collection of musical criticism and analyze its texts with the aforementioned terms: "The performance was technically lacking" (= there was not enough 'can'). "The composition showed no clear will of expression" (= there was insufficient 'will'). "The orchestration was excessive in relation to the musical substance" (= there was too much 'can' in relation to 'knowing'); and so on. Musical aesthetics thus finds a place in our generative trajectory, but it can only be interpreted as a joint effect of complex actorial-spatial-temporal categories and various modalities and modalizations.

Peirce's Method

Next we outline a model of music analysis based on the sign categories of Charles S. Peirce: signs in themselves (*legisign, sinsign, qualisign*), signs in relation to object (*symbol, index, icon*), and signs in relation to their interpretants (*rheme, dicent, argument*). Musical semiotics has not yet determined what the musical counterparts of these sign categories are. Most suggestions have concerned only the best-known category of signs in relation to objects (see Coker 1972 and Karbusicky 1986 in particular). The most extensive discussion and sharp analysis of these concepts can be found in Monelle 1992.

According to Karbusicky—and in what follows I shall take his definition as my starting point—*index* refers to the state of the object. It includes all that belongs to the area of musical expression; for example, tone color displaying subtle nuances of emotion, spiritual state, or mood. In principle, indexes stand in a relation of contiguity with their objects. So, a military or radio signal would be a typical musical index in the traditional sense. An example of an index in everyday life is the famous "nightingale floor" in the *shogun* palace near Osaka, Japan. It forms an indexical sound system by means of mechanism that causes the wooden planks of the main hall to sound like a nightingale in order to warn the chief of approaching enemies.

Icons function on the basis of isomorphism. Hence their counterparts in music are imitations of natural sounds like bird song, wind, the murmur of a forest, raindrops, thunder, and so on. The range of iconic isomorphism in music is very large, and there are several subclasses of slightly transformed iconicity. The aria from Bach's *St. Matthew Passion* in which Peter's cry is imitated would thus be both an index (expressing an emotional state) and an icon (the melodic curves are reminiscent of crying). Even the qualities of musical performance by a certain instrument or voice can be reflected in the form of a musical sign itself. This is true of the so-called *Spielfiguren* or instrumental figures (see Besseler 1957 and Mäkelä 1989). A certain musical figure may fit well, say, with the position of a hand on a keyboard; consequently, the composer might choose that figure over another simply because it is more convenient for the player. A typical *Spielfigur*, a motif based on open strings of the violin, occurs at the beginning of Alban Berg's famous Violin Concerto. Another, a chord consisting of the pitches of a guitar's open strings, is found in the work of Alberto Ginastera.

Symbols in music are signs that, through certain conventions of a musical tradition, convey some meaning, even abstract meanings like beliefs and values. National anthems provide a good illustration. For example, the Finnish national anthem *Maamme* (Our Country) was written by the German-born composer Fredrik Pacius. As a mazurka-type German *lied*, it has no iconic relations with Finland; neither is there anything "Finnish" in the *Finlandia* hymn by Jean Sibelius. Only later, through subsequent conventions stemming from certain historical events, did these melodies assume their positions as national symbols.

Peirce's other sign categories have not been much used in musical semiotics. However, one could say that, in music, signs in relation to their interpretants concern those sign processes that take place in the mind of the listener, whereby he or she interprets the musical experience. Signs in themselves form a dimension of musical creation in the proper sense: musical signs take form on the basis of other, previously known sign complexes, and thus serve as a rule (or legisign) for the production of subsequent signs (sinsigns or single signs) and again for qualisigns. Thus we see how musical signification is generated through these three sign relations, which together constitute the Three-Dimensional Model of Music Analysis, shown in Figure 1.16. In the lowest musical dimension (that of a musical work), a composition consists in a chain of icons, indexes, and symbols which may alternate in any possible order. Similarly, any musical unit or member in the syntagm has its own legisigns, which have served as models or types for its creation, for its particular shape as a sinsign, and for its qualisign, i.e., its concrete, aural qualities (which depend in large part on how the piece is performed). These sign relations serve as the organs of a musical "being," the feelers or tentacles with which it orients itself and reacts to its environment. It receives "nourishment" through them. Without these "tentacles" a musical work would fade away and die. Sign relations are the real sources of musical semantics; these relations form a bridge between an autonomous musical work and the reality outside it.

Now, if this were the whole business of analyzing musical works semiotically, the task would be easy. It would suffice to list all the icons, indexes, and

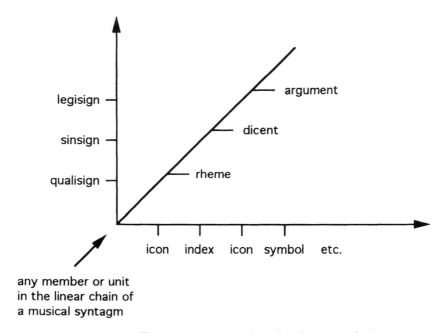

Figure 1.16. The three-dimensional model of music analysis.

symbols in a piece, search for their possible legisigns and stylistic models, describe their concrete musical articulation as sinsigns, and finally scrutinize their qualities in performance. Thereafter one would simply study the reception (listener) and examine the rhemes, dicents, and arguments, in a certain context, tradition, or culture, that might apply to any unit of the musical syntagm.

A musical work also constitutes an autonomous whole, however, following its own inner rules of organization. Many music theoreticians deny that there can be any correspondence between music and external reality. Defenders of *tönend bewegte Formen* theories believe that only the inner musical structure (which they consider a distinctive feature of a good musical work) deserves study. Yet even in abstract serial music, the inner network based on a row often does not suffice, but needs outer references as well; e.g., the main theme of Berg's Violin Concerto, or the *leitmotif* rows in Dallapiccola's opera *Il Prigioniero* (the rows of Hope, Freedom, etc.).

On the other hand, it is also true that even music can become "communication of communication" (Osolsobe 1980). This means that all the Peircean sign categories, with all nine subclasses, can be internalized into the musical discourse. Then one might study icons, indexes, symbols, rhemes, arguments, etc. *within* a musical work.[23] Internalized, signs start to form a purely inner network, their own "language game," in which the outer reality little by little loses importance.

Iconicity would thus simply mean similarity throughout the piece, i.e., the principle of repetition in the broadest sense (see Osmond-Smith 1975). Any relation of, say, a theme to its variations would enact the iconic principle. Indexicality would refer to the coherence of a musical piece, its moving and passing from one section or motif to another. The more its indexicality the more music is experienced as a flowing forward. The most agitated, indexical sections often are accompanied by a *crescendo* or *accelerando*, which are concrete signs of continuity and compelling direction. When something in music is heard as a result of what occurred before it, then indexical sign processes are operating. In the largest sense, any resolution of a dominant to its tonic represents a sort of indexicality in music. We should, however, note the contrary case: music may also accrue to one point, with the tension accumulating and building toward the final resolution, rather than diminishing. Such a passage displays the functioning of *anti-indexes*, which obstruct the music rather than driving it forward. The simplest case of the anti-index in music is the pause.

Inner and outer sign relations, in the sense used here, often appear to be quite contradictory. One might formulate the following hypothesis (the validity of which has yet to be proven): the more music functions as an outer sign the less we experience its functioning as an inner sign. I will call *exteroceptive* those signs that direct our attention to the relation between the music and the external world; inner signs, which refer to relations within the musical work, will be called *interoceptive* (see Greimas and Courtés 1979: 141, 191).

We must consider how these two cases, inner and outer, relate to each other. How is the exteroceptive icon related to the interoceptive icon? How is the exteroceptive index related to the interoceptive index? Does it reinforce, emphasize, or weaken its original sign character? If some motif is undeniably an index of, say, a passionate emotion—for instance, the recitativo octave theme in the third section of Liszt's *Vallée d'Obermann* (see Chap. 7.1)—then how is this index influenced by the fact that this passionate figure later either continues in the same fashion or changes and ultimately leads to another kind of index?

In general, the paradigmatic aspect of music represents interoceptive iconicity, while the syntagmatic aspect corresponds to a kind of interoceptive indexicality. The *topoi*, or topics (kinds of isotopy), of the Classical style in particular should be considered exteroceptive icons (see Grabócz 1985: 324–32). These topics can be analyzed and reduced to icons, indexes, and symbols in the exteroceptive sense, because they originally functioned musically as a part of human sociocultural practices; for example, in Mozart the topics of waltzes, marches, hunting calls, galant style, *Empfindsamkeit*, etc., discussed in Chap. 1.3. When a composer repeats these topics at various points throughout a composition (to produce certain musical *effets de sens*), often following some narrative program in his or her mind, they cross into the area of interoceptive iconicity, which mitigates the exteroceptive iconicity. If the same topic is repeated frequently, it no longer influences the listener through its exteroceptive quality. Instead it assumes an interoceptive function in the global structure of the work. A composer may use this device quite deliberately to ensure that the exteroceptive and interoceptive semiotic networks support each other. This also explains why music that exploits only exteroceptivity and neglects inner structural implications does not create a lasting effect, and remains program music in the pejorative sense of the term.

Finally, one must ask what an interoceptive symbol means in music. What does it mean to say that some musical element or passage stands in a symbolic (conventional, arbitrary, representational) relation to some element or passage heard earlier in the work? The matter is complicated by the fact that sign categories often intermingle, thereby making it difficult to distinguish a pure symbol in the inner sense. For example, are the final chords in Liszt's B minor Sonata a symbol for the whole piece, like the final statement in the *Vallée d'Obermann*, or the last ascending outburst of the main motif at the end of the Adagio movement of Sibelius's Fourth Symphony? Such sections seem to condense into a single phrase the essential structural content of the piece or movement. One might also consider as an interoceptive symbol the way certain musical situations are resolved throughout a piece. A certain musical situation, rather than any particular musical substance, can constitute an interoceptive symbol of what happened earlier in the piece. Interoceptive symbols are certainly much more difficult to define verbally than exteroceptive ones.

We can now summarize our discussion of the interoceptive sign categories of Peirce as applied to music. Here we dare to develop Peirce's theory a little further, in order to make it fit better with musical facts: 1. Interoceptive iconicity in music means similarity within a musical piece–the principle of repetition and identity. 2. Interoceptive indexicality gives music its continuity, its compelling direction: the more indexicality in the music the more tension the listener experiences. 3. Interoceptive symbolicity in music occurs through abstract sign relations that allude to certain musical situations and their resolutions rather than to musical substance itself.

After this presentation of the model, some considerations remain as to the nature of musical temporality, spatiality, and actoriality. A chapter on each category follows, and many fundamental issues of the semiotic approach will be clarified through these reflections. There is nothing new in this triple categorization, since a great quantity of musicological literature already exists on time and space in music. Yet I believe that this will only emphasize the novelty and specificity of some *semiotic* interpretations of these phenomena. The next three chapters will also introduce more concrete evidence as empirical support for my theory. Without the "mediation" of these chapters, I might not have had the courage to write the analyses that form Part Two of this volume.

II

MUSICAL TIME

2.1 Music in Micro-Time: The Role of Memory

Music is a phenomenon that takes place in time. In the same way as the fundamental axiological model of human life is anchored on temporality, every musical work is, temporally, like the model of human life. All cultures try to control time; spatial time, the physically measurable *temps d'espace* of Bergson, is not just an idea of Western culture. Lewis Rowell (1979: 98), comparing different terms linked with time in the cultures of India, China, and ancient Greece, has shown that a remarkable unity exists in the way they conceive time as "regular, dependable, seasonal, repetitive, objective, irreversible clock-time," in which case we are dealing with "the time of being." Time can also be considered as generative, with particular moments like destiny and death; this is subjective time, which represents time as "becoming." Of all the symbolic means by which a culture controls time, music is certainly the subtlest. Its mystery is based on the paradox that music functions not only "as a machine to stop time," as Lévi-Strauss wrote, but equally as an accelerator of time. Nevertheless, musical time also has, as its essential quality, the 'becoming' (*devenir, Werden*) which no culture can control. Therefore music functions in its temporality as a border and transition between nature and culture. To listen to music brings us the illusion of ruling over time, just as at each moment it reminds us of time's irreversibility and irrevocability, and of our fate in the course of time.

Temporality in music is not a parameter that can be regulated deliberately, as pitch, timbre, and dynamics can be; it constitutes a more fundamental element of music. Neither can temporality be reduced to simple rhythmic or metric schemes. What is involved here is a deeper category, for which rhythmic phenomena are but surface prolongations. Because of temporality, musical semiotics must be one of continuous, not discontinuous, processes.

Vladimir Jankélévitch (1974), on the Bergsonian philosophical basis, offers an interesting starting point for the study of temporality, including that of music. Temporality, particularly in the form of 'becoming', is neither 'being' nor 'not-being', but something between the two, an "almost-nothing" (*presque-rien*). Time can never be grasped like an object placed in front of us; time, which is implicated in the most intimate mechanisms of our thinking, cannot even be thought of save temporally. Therefore, if time, as simple 'becoming', covers everything, it has to appear in the musical discourse as something central *par excellence*, even if it is precisely through music that we learn how time can be slowed or accelerated. Entire stylistic periods can lean toward one or another form of temporality: Romanticism is the period of *rallentando* and *ritardando*, of a turn to the background. We take as illustration the first measures of Beethoven's Piano Sonata in E♭ Major, Op. 31 no. 3 (Ex. 2.1).

Example 2.1. Beethoven, Op. 31 no. 3, mm. 1–7.

In music of the early twentieth century there appears a phobia concerning *rallentando*; e.g., the works of Poulenc and Prokofiev push dynamically forward. Moreover, a style period can aim at negation of both these kinds of time, a negation which Jankélévitch finds in the serial school (1974: 43–44):

> Also this equal speed of time, this speed neither rapid nor slow, this non-speed, infinite time, has certainly something inhuman about it. . . . It is no longer only the *rallentando* which is prohibited . . . the repetitions . . . are chased off, forbidden and excluded. . . . Orpheus will no longer turn around. . . . This time no longer has anything rhapsodic about it, because it is devoid of all inflections of passion.

Nevertheless, as Jankélévitch ultimately concludes, in time there is a certain core we can neither reverse nor accelerate nor slow down. We simply call it 'becoming' and reflect upon the consequences of adopting this category for musical semiotics. This pure time as 'becoming' is by nature *qualitative*: its "when-ness" is essential.

We recall that Greimas's system of modalities is based on two fundamental categories: 'being' and 'doing'. The effect of these categories upon 'becoming' manifests as a supra- or *surmodalization*, one with added modal layers. The impact of 'being' appears as a retardation; the influence of 'doing' activates the musical pulse. Now, surmodalization by 'being' does not necessarily mean a resolution of tension and negation of 'becoming'. Neither does surmodalization by 'doing' automatically lead to increase of tension. Rather, it is contrast that leads to musical tension, because very often the tempo slows just before a culmination point; on the other hand, the tempo can get faster as a result of a decrease of tension caused by smaller time units.

'Being', carried to extremes, naturally forms a pause, which can serve many functions in a musical discourse. Yet 'being' manifested as a pause often varies in tension: think of the long pauses in Bruckner's symphonies, or his long culminating passages (*Steigerungsanlagen*, as Kurth called them), which, after a while, stop with exhaustion and lead to nothing. In the cadence of an overture to an oratorio, or in a concerto grosso, or a choral scene in Handel, a pause must dramatically prolong the tension in the cadential progression of I 6/4–V–I. Such a pause contains much tension. As shown in Fig. 2.1, if 'being' and 'doing' represent the first surmodalization upon 'becoming', then the other modalities, from 'will' to 'must', represent the second surmodalization.

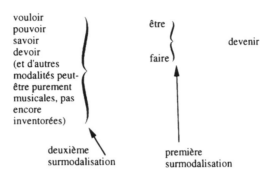

Figure 2.1. Surmodalizations.

When studying musical semiosis, we also have to account for enunciation (performance), in which the relation between subject and object plays a central role. The musical object, as a micro-universe progressing in its own time, is also situated inside the macro-universe of a subjective and individual musical consciousness. It is impossible to neglect the sounding reality of music, since music does not exist at all as an aural art before the act of intoning. Therefore, music lies on two axes of different temporalities: the axis of the *intonator* and *intonatee*, and the axis of that which is *intoned*. The musical subject and object are thus subordinated to temporality, somewhat as in the metaphor of Bergson, who speaks of two trains going the same speed, on two parallel lines. This image evokes the relation between a music listener and music itself: both are moving, but when the listener abandons himself to the magic power of musical process, he feels his own temporality accelerated or slowed because of the time of the musical work itself (according to the order encoded in the composer's narrative program).

The form and syntagmatic course of a musical work are typically described with a chain of letters that symbolize the segmented units, such as ABA CDC ABA. This chain does not sufficiently capture the temporal becoming of a composition. The units are there, true, in a temporally linear order; but chains of letters cannot describe music as an intonation, as a reality of temporally unfolding sound forms (Asafiev 1977: 720–27). One of the basic properties of the temporal course of music is its irreversibility. Because of this fact there is no symmetrical repetition in music at all, and even in simple ABA form, the second A differs from the first. A "second time" does not exist for the receiver of a musical intonation. This irreversibility is particularly manifest at highly dramatic moments of music. Events that transform the pure 'becoming' of music threaten to annul the "normal," unnoticed irreversibility of musical time, its primal temporal character. Accordingly, what follows will be an effort to describe the pure 'becoming' of musical discourse.

In Jankélévitch's music philosophy, another category is added to that of irreversibility: unpredictability (1974: 42). Combining these categories and their positive and negative articulations, we get a conceptual network which can be projected onto the semiotic square of Fig. 2.2.

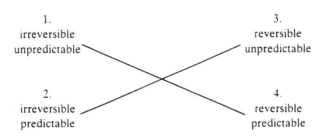

Figure 2.2. Irreversibility and unpredictability as projected on the semiotic square.

What kinds of musical universes could occur in this square? The first would be a universe of "first times," in which nothing really returns and nothing can be predicted; it would represent a moment-to-moment, punctual consciousness, a negation of all durativity. Since prediction of the future relies to some extent on memory, a complete loss of memory would dominate in this musical universe. No musical event would be retained in the mind, and hence the future would be experienced as a continuous surprise. Isn't such an apotheosis of uniqueness exactly like the aesthetics of certain schools of avant-garde music?

In universe 2 one can predict what will follow, but at the moment it happens, it is forgotten. It is difficult to imagine this (admittedly hypothetical) musical universe. It in fact represents a certain performance by a musical subject, either composer or performer: a syntagmatic talent that creates or performs without obeying the constraint of the global form, forgetting, for example, when writing/playing a sonata, whether he or she is in the development or the recapitulation.

Universe 3 presents a case in which the receiver of the intonation perceives it for the first time (for example, our first hearing of a symphony). Every moment, every event in the stream of music is new and unique and kept in the memory, while the global form is conceptualized only after the last bars of the piece have sounded. In Universe 4, one is oriented to both past and future. Every event is anticipated and also recalls an earlier one. The return of a theme is at least similar to its first occurrence. At the same time, a certain freshness of invention is maintained because of the continuous 'becoming'. This last case will be scrutinized more closely below.

We noted above that the description of musical form as a linear chain of symbols does not correspond to the sound reality. With mechanical repetition of one and the same element, the 'becoming' provides each occurrence of that element with its own *presque-rien*, its temporal *différance* (Derrida 1982), which changes the signification of each element not only in the unconscious shaping process of the receiver of the intonation but also on the level of quite manifest *effets de sens*. For example, a suite of songs for baritone, piano, and typewriter, by Finnish avant-garde composer Olli Kortekangas, begins with simple arpeggiations of the C major tonic, undulating over the keys of the piano. A listener who had read the concert program, and thus knew to place the work in the context of avant-garde music, would be surprised by such a conventional beginning. A conservative listener, close to Adorno's "culture consumer," would be enchanted and experience the music as "beautiful." But the composition continues in the same way, and suddenly the redundancy changes the beautiful into the "comical." All at once the work becomes *too* beautiful and then ridiculous. As the arpeggios continue, a third change of signification takes place: continuously repeated, the comical effect disappears and finally becomes banal. Thus by mere mechanical repetition the music, because of its pure becoming, makes listeners experience three aesthetic categories: the beautiful, the comical, and the banal. The speed at which these significations alternate in the minds of the listeners correlates directly with their musical competence. Where the conservative listener needs ten repetitions, the connoisseur is satisfied with three or four.

The effect of 'becoming' on musical semiosis has to be seen as a cumulative process, based upon the fact that earlier musical events are stored in the listener's memory and thus continuously influence the experience of any event heard in the "now" moment. Beside the conventional linear chain depicting the phases of music, one should therefore place another paradigm, that of memory, which enlarges continuously until the end of the work (see Fig. 2.3). At any given moment, the comparison, which may occur very quickly and unconsciously, between the sounding members of a musical chain and preceding elements is essential. Against this model one might argue that human memory will not carry very far, even in the context of one work or section of a work. In fact, the comparison is always made between the nearest preceding musical elements (according to the principle of contiguity or indexicality) and repeated elements (according to the principle of similarity or iconicity). Furthermore, the phase at which the elements of the paradigm of memory start to fall away is largely determined by the existence of musical isotopies. When a new isotopy is introduced into a piece, bringing with it an entirely new field of signification, a change also occurs in the paradigm of memory, and the accumulation of elements begins again, right from the beginning. Naturally, if the preceding isotopy comes back, the element of its paradigm of memory will also return.

The situation gets more complicated when we realize that memory is not only repetitive but also creative. Consequently, if in a musical piece we hear at moment T1 the semes a, b, c, d, at moment T2 the semes d, e, f, g, and at moment T3 the semes a, b, c, d, in situation T1 we do not yet know which semes are pertinent and which are not. Only at T3, when the semes return and it has been possible to compare them with the semes at T2 (d, e, f, g), do we know their real significance. Only then do we notice what was implicitly at T1 the rank order of semes a, b, c, and d: a, b, d, and c, with d having more pertinence than c, since it occurs three times, and c only twice. This is of course a rather rudimentary situation, where pertinence is decided by simply counting the number of occurrences of semes. In fact, the situation is much more complicated, since even at T2 the preceding paradigm of semes is compared with that which is heard now, and in the light of the new experience the memory reevaluates them.

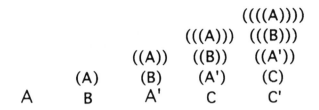

			(((((A))))
		(((A)))	(((B)))
	((A))	((B))	((A'))
(A)	(B)	(A')	(C)
A	B	A'	C	C'

Figure 2.3. Paradigm of memory: retention of musical events.

Besides memory, a second and entirely different type of paradigm arises, that of expectations. Two kinds of expectation occur in music. In the first there prevails a strong feeling of expectation, of becoming, though the listener does not know what will follow; for example, the drum-pedal transition to the Finale of Beethoven's Fifth Symphony, or the transition to the fugue in César Franck's Prelude, Chorale, and Fugue (Ex. 2.2). The second kind of expectation involves passages where the listener has a strong presentiment of, yet passionately anticipates, what will follow. For example, in the transition before the final climax in the Franck work, the arpeggio figure of the Prelude returns simultaneously with the interlaced Chorale theme (Ex. 2.3).

Example 2.2. César Franck, Prelude, Chorale, and Fugue, mm. 128–30.

Thus on the basis of expectations an entirely different paradigm is formed in music, that of the possible musical elements at each moment. Whereas the paradigm of memory has a continuous tendency to grow, the paradigm of expectations continuously decreases as the work proceeds and the available choices diminish. Of course, the ability to see possibilities in a musical work depends on the competence of the listener. Musical competence not only restricts the number of choices from fortuitous to pertinent ones but also enables one to see the limits of the given elements in the context of a given style. For example, in the style of a Beethoven sonata, whole-tone scales are almost impossible and thus would not belong to the paradigm of expectations.

Example 2.3. Franck, Prelude, Chorale, and Fugue, mm. 388–16.

Finally, the paradigms of both memory and expectation are determined by the store of intonations, i.e., the collective musical memory of a given tradition, style, or musical community. If a musical element is recognized as identical or similar to one found in the store of intonations present in the listener, that element is maintained more easily in the memory and thus strongly influences the conception of the work on the basis of the paradigm of memory. The paradigm of the possible musical elements never originates solely from the context of the work itself; such elements mostly come from the store of intonations. We know to expect something, we experience something as possible, precisely because what we expect occurs in a paradigm external to the work and has been internalized even before our listening to the piece.

Taking into account the paradigms of memory and expectation, musical semiotics may gradually proceed toward more extensive and deeper models in order to explain the nature of musical semiosis. A structural semantics of music could emerge which does not subjugate musical discourse to categories out of keeping with its character of 'becoming'. Musical semiotics would thus meet the challenge of the whole tradition of musicology, whose problems could be reinterpreted and elucidated by an approach that is highly aware of its concepts and metalanguage and whose basic assumptions are perhaps more explicit than they often are in more traditional approaches.

For example, in terms of the temporal paradigms of memory and expectations, one could clarify Alfred Einstein's concept of *Verdichtung*, which refers to the density or conceptual "thickness" of music. *Verdichtung* distinguishes genius from mere talent and is manifested in music animated by energy and expression: "Was Bach mit seinen Vorlagen anfang, war nichts anderes als Verdichtung, stärkere Belebung mit musikalischer Energie und Expression" (Einstein 1951: 119). It is precisely *Verdichtung* that distinguishes, for example, Mozart's operas from the Italian operas of his time, Beethoven from Cherubini, and so forth.

It would be erroneous to imagine that the musical density is always the same as the number of musical events or semes. In that case, maximally complicated music would also be the most dense. But silence, too, can be experienced as an extremely dense and meaningful event. The musical density can be much greater in an aphoristic string quartet by Webern than in a lushly orchestrated symphonic poem by Richard Strauss. The density of music does not stem from the number of musical semes heard at the "now" moment, but from the special meeting of the paradigms of memory and expectations which occurs at culmination points of great music. There is *Verdichtung* in music when the paradigm of memory extends as far as possible, and when the paradigm of expectations puts us in the unbearably exciting situation where we do not yet know the "solution," that is, which of all possible choices the composer has made.

2.2 Music in Macro-Time: Music Models through the Ages

In Chapter 2.1 we considered micro-temporal, work-bound aspects of music in terms of modalities, musical time as 'becoming', and the effects of that 'becoming' on paradigms of memory and expectation. The present section will look at music in macro-time, through the course of history, and the models that we construct to account for that history.

What is music history? Is it a typical "thought-of model" (Lévi-Strauss 1958: 347–48), constructed by researchers and writers of music history in order to create continuity and coherence for a series of events and musical phenomena which would otherwise seem detached, incoherent, and discontinuous? Or is it really a "lived-in" model, based on the experience of musical subjects and aimed at shaping different coordinates (sender, performer, receiver) of musical communication?

In the latter case one might speak of music history as a particular experience, emerging at given moments in musical communication, as when the style changes abruptly, denying the intonations of a previous movement; or when there is a conscious return to an older style, such as the influence of Bach and Handel on Mozart and Beethoven, or Stravinsky's Neoclassicism. The issue here is whether the view of music history as experience is too limiting. Are we justified in speaking of music "history" only at moments when we feel the presence of history, say, when *Musik über Musik* is composed, or when we believe that we have heard an epoch-making work or, in the worst case, have recognized a work as faded, having historical interest, but with nothing to say to modern times? It seems that music history as an experience might easily become degraded into a subcategory of musical-aesthetic experience, a category that does not fully realize where the aesthetic *Gegenwärtigkeit* lies (Dahlhaus 1977: 13). According to Carl Dahlhaus, the essential tension between music history and aesthetics arises from the fact that although a musical work that belongs to history forms a document from a previous age, as an aesthetic phenomenon it is experienced by a listener as fresh, expressive, and meaningful in the present. Music history as an experience would merge into its exact opposite (aesthetics) and would consequently lose its own inherent characteristics. The conclusion to be drawn is that the notion of music history as only a lived-in model seems too restricted.

Evidently, music history is also a thought-of model, an interpretative scheme by which we organize the events of our musical past according to certain criteria. This case presents new types of problems: are there data in music-historical events that correspond to something like "development"? Does the concept of progress, used by Charles Burney (1789), have any empirical justification? Or is this notion of progress always and exclusively a function of an organizing consciousness; i.e., do we always bring this order with us? If so, music history is something rather arbitrary and depends on the musical model that each era uses to articulate its musical past. There would exist no music history in an objective sense. Accordingly, when we read music history written by Sir John Hawkins, Fétis, or Ambros, what we in fact read are only certain interpretations and aesthetic views, views which, by disguising their discourse as an objective and impartial narrative of historical data, try to legitimate composers and their music.

A basic human need is undoubtedly to create continuity and predictability in life, to replace the unsure state of entropy with redundancy. As defense against this chaotic view of music history, even elementary schoolbooks provide neat distinctions into periods, with characteristic features "found" in all the arts. Other means have also been used to find the underlying thread of music history. Jacques Chailley, for example, reasons that the history of Western art music follows the adoption of the intervals of the overtone series, in the order in which they emerge in the series (1977: 23): The age of octave and fifth lasted thousands of years. The third was accepted as a consonance and a proper element of music only at the end of the Middle Ages. The minor seventh came into usage a hundred years later. Atonal music meant the acceptance of minor seconds and major sevenths, and now composers experiment with micro-intervals produced by synthesizers. Interestingly, the farther one goes in the overtone series, the shorter the historical periods become. If this continuously accelerating progress were followed to its end, we would already have inevitably arrived at the end of all musical development. Chailley's is one way to make music history rational. His model involves a natural physical principle which musical systems of various ages, apparently unconsciously, have followed in their development. Yet it is as useless to try to prove this model right as it is to determine whether or not tonality is a perceptual, biologically rooted principle that is common to all human beings. Music, in all its modes of existence, is a remarkably more complicated and subtle phenomenon.

Is there a rationality, common to all periods, all musical experiences and practices, that would help us compare historically different musical works, composers, whole musical cultures and societies? Can one conceptualize the bases of a universal music model, perhaps not realized to its full extent in any concrete case, but forming an ideal type or paradigm whereby the diachrony of music history could be interpreted as a synchrony? Our question can be further specified: if such a rationality exists, is it based merely on the way in which a music historiographer organizes his or her discourse about musical data? Perhaps the existence of music history is only due to the phenomenon that Dahlhaus calls *Erzählbarkeit* (1977: 80), but which we shall call *narrativity*.

The narrative model is one of the strongest in Western thinking and art, and it is by nature both a thought-of and a lived-in model. Our music, as well as our talk about music, often follows narrative principles that were generalized during the Classical period and that persist even in the twentieth century. The whole of twentieth-century modernism has sought to sweep the narrative model from our consciousness, but without convincing success. Indeed, if modernism has any common denominator, it is undoubtedly anti-narrativity (called "anti-illusionism" by Brecht, *ostranenie* or "making strange" by the Russian Formalists).

The narrative model also carries over into any musical research that declares itself to be an "objective" science dealing only with facts. One has to remember that scientific discourse, which claims to be objective and universal, is itself based on the usage of certain discourse mechanisms (Greimas 1967: 153–54). By these mechanisms science creates an illusion of realism, the fiction of a language telling us about reality, "just as it is." Obviously, the way in which a discourse pretends to be objective corresponds to deep epistemes of our cultural era. Structuralists teach that we are guided by systems of thinking which rule over all our actions, oblige us to say certain things according to certain codes, and determine what reality is. For example, Juri Lotman argues that Freud did not "discover" the unconscious, but that the unconscious is a creation of our own culture, not a discovery in the sense of finding and charting some new continent, island, or planet (in Uspenski et al. 1973: 3–4).

All this holds true for music. When Hildesheimer (1980) claims to reveal the real Mozart, and when his views are transmitted to millions of theatre- and cinema-goers via Schaffer's and Forman's *Amadeus*, he appeals to Freud as his scientific authority, without noticing the interpretational nature of psychoanalytic doctrine (this is not to be understood as an objection to Freud-inspired art theories as such). In fact, Hildesheimer organizes Mozart's life according to classical narrative principles, so that it follows the actantial model developed by the Russian Formalists at the beginning of the twentieth century. It was later reformulated by Greimas as having six factors: sender/receiver, subject/object, helper/opponent. How naively well this model fits Schaffer's interpretation of Mozart's life: Leopold Mozart (sender), humanity (receiver), Amadeus (subject) music (object), Baron van Swieten (helper), Salieri (opponent). It is very difficult to get rid of the narrative model!

Nor is it possible to find a satisfactory continuity for music history by pointing out genetic relations between different works by the same composer, or works of different composers. This only follows a new variant of the narrative model, particularly regarding the relationship of sender/subject. For example, Tawaststjerna's biography of Sibelius tells of the composer's strong emotional reaction to a Vienna performance of Bruckner's Third Symphony. Moreover, there is an evident structural connection between the main themes of the *Kullervo* Symphony and Bruckner's Third (Tawaststjerna 1976: 110). Does this mean that there is a genetic relation between these two works? Or to return to Mozart: the small Fantasy in D minor for piano, K. 397, is almost like the whole of *Don Giovanni* in a nutshell. We may well hear the immobility of the Stone Guest in the chromatically descending chorale passage in the middle section, or the frivolous carelessness of Don Giovanni in the *allegro* at the end. According to Charles Rosen (1976: 296), Mozart's instrumental music often follows the dramatic development of his operas, and the expressiveness of his instrumental pieces is in fact a sort of drama-like dialogue of opera personages. Even so, we would hardly say that the small D minor Fantasy influenced the creation of *Don Giovanni*. Rather, this phenomenon exhibits "autocommunication," a semiotic term for the internal dialogue (or monologue) of a composer's consciousness.

A search for the "rationality" of music history might begin by comparing different aesthetical-theoretical models of music created at different times. Yet before we can start to confront the enormously varied sources and music models, we must already have in our minds a universal model for all music, a model of what music ultimately is. The empiricist might argue here that it would be reasonable to form such a general model only after we have gathered enough evidence from different musical practices. To counter this argument we must note that music history constitutes an endless and unarticulated storehouse, where we can find something only if we know what we are searching for. Another counterargument would be: doesn't the separation of musical ideas and models from their original historical contexts, from their complex ties with the epistemes of the age, its social and cultural history, easily lead to false conclusions? For example, the concept of *Affekt* of the Baroque era cannot be equated with the sentimentality of Romanticism. To this we reply: we shall not proceed in that way. Instead, we shall lay the groundwork for a reading model by which we can interpret musical thinkers of various ages. Accordingly, our hypothetically universal music model is not an empirical (lived-in) model but a theoretical construct, with a metalanguage and discourse of its own. In this regard my epistemological choice is the same as that of the Greimasian school of semiotics:

> This kind of discourse cannot appear, like empirical discourse, as an objective discourse, as a "pure" description of facts, since the aim is to form a model of the object of study, to project this model onto its object and again back to the discourse of the research. This procedure is based upon the idea that the reference of the study is not the relation to a reality conceived as being outside the discourse, but the relation to the model which the study has of its object. [Ahonen 1984: 155]

On the other hand, it is essential for all semiotical study that research make explicit its implicit biases and presuppositions, as Nattiez (1985: 89–106) has correctly emphasized. This is necessary so that the way in which the research forms its own referential illusion is not concealed, thereby acquiring ideological and dogmatic features. The theoretical model must therefore be set face to face with music models under examination, so that it can be corrected if need be.

On this level of examination, our "universal model" does not yet need to include the whole generative process of music but may concentrate on some level of it. Greimas (1979) distinguishes, in every formation of meaning, three processual phases: virtual, actual, and real. He supposes that the direction of the process goes from the virtual to the real, from the immanent to the manifest. This can be taken as a background for what we understand by music. Dahlhaus's ideas about musical-historical facts may also be interpreted in this light. Dahlhaus asks, What do we mean when we say that "a work" is a music-historical fact? Where do we ultimately find its historical character? In the intention of the composer, which the historiographer attempts to reconstruct? Or in the musical structure of a work, which is then analyzed by formal and genre-historical criteria? Or in the consciousness of the contemporary audience of a musical work, for whom the work was an "event," a consciousness which cannot be grasped in its individuality and uniqueness, but only in its general features and determined as a period, generation, or social class with all its characteristic traits (Dahlhaus 1977: 58–59)?

In other words, perhaps music does not begin, no more than it ends, in notation or in acoustic (played or sung) form. Music exists before it crystallizes (in the composer's mind) into a work, and it exists after it has been performed:

music continues to live in the consciousness of the receiver as an intonation (see Chap. 2.1). In fact, if we are to seek for the moment of continuity in music history, it will be found in the processes that occur before and after a work. The very category of a "work," as an identifiable and perhaps unique composition, is the factor that makes music history discontinuous. How, then, can we describe what happens before and after a musical work?

The Greimasian model, with its three phases going from the virtual through the actual to the real, can certainly describe what happens before the work, i.e., the process that leads to the outcome of a work. Can Greimas's model also sufficiently describe the reception of a work, the life of music in the collective memory of the society of receivers, which in turn forms a starting point for the creation of new musical works and thus brings us back to the very beginning of the generative process?

We may of course examine how some musical idea develops on the axes of virtuality, actuality, and reality (see Fig. 2.4). A musical structure first ripens, as it were, in its virtual mode of existence during one era, until at some later time it emerges as a concrete composition, only to disappear later, without perhaps vanishing altogether, but awaiting its next manifestation in some more favorable era. The horizontal lines in Figure 2.4 represent certain thresholds of repression, implying that not all virtual compositional-technical innovations, ideas, and structures are realized and attain the "real" level, since the musical-conceptual ability of the receiving audience places restrictions on them.

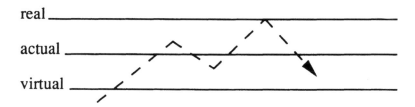

Figure 2.4. Development of a musical idea.

Greimas also describes each level in terms of its proper modalities: virtual modalities are represented by 'will' and 'know', actual modalities by 'can' and 'must', real modalities by 'being' and 'doing'. The crystallization of music into an intonation is produced through these modalities: the upward direction in Fig. 2.4 represents the 'will' of the sender/composer, the downward direction the 'will' of the receiver/listener, which appears to a composer as certain norms, obligations, and aesthetic judgments. Also, music can remain on the virtual level alone; i.e., the generative course can stop on any level. For example, in the Middle Ages the most appreciated part of music was *musica speculativa*, the pure thinking of theoreticians, 'know' without 'will', which need not result in actual sounding music.

Yet inasmuch as it aims at the level of manifest realization and communication, music always encounters expectations and aesthetic evaluations projected onto it by the receiver, all of which obstruct creativity, the free fulfillment of ideas, and the generative process. If aesthetics proceeds by either approving or rejecting musical intonations, we need another term (say, "anti-aesthetics") to depict the contrary direction, that is, the energy that flows from the virtual toward the real. Aesthetics, as a science and art of 'must', moves from the real to the actual and virtual; while for an artist, everything is possible, and the paradigm is open (in theory). Still, as soon as the artist starts to consider possibilities in a given situation of communication, he or she applies an implicit and inverse aesthetics, an internalized 'must', an obligation or artistic will.

We spoke earlier of the modalities as general attitudes by which a subject evaluates and humanizes an object. Comparison of different music models should attend precisely to the modal, not so much to the acoustic or syntactic, properties of music. If we can say that music "starts" from anything, then it evidently starts just from these modalities. The generative course of music (toward sound realization) can be reduced to modalities, but so can the contrary course—the life of music within the consciousness and memory of a listener. When we say that modalization is a process that humanizes and anthropomorphizes music (unites it with the sphere of human values), we are not referring to any concrete, semantic content, which also can be attached to various levels of music. The symbolic and referential dimensions of music remain totally outside modalization, although they are linked (both being modalizations) to other semiotic mechanisms that enable music to describe and represent extramusical events, personages, acts, choices, and the like.

One could thus depict the creation of music as follows: first, we meet the level of modalities ('will', 'know', 'can', 'must'), which combine into different *passions*. By "passion" we mean a certain constellation of modalities, their articulation, and the resulting virtual-actual state, which, accordingly, is already determined by the modalities it consists of, and can be conceived as a distinct emotion. For example, Fontanille (1980) has analyzed Despair by reducing it to various modalities; Greimas (1981) himself finds certain fundamental modalities within Anger; Herman Parret (1982) and Greimas and Fontanille (1991) have done several similar studies.

In music one might analyze, say, the Despair of the beginning of Liszt's *Dante* Sonata by using purely modal concepts. One might also examine the modalizations of different composers, modalizations which perhaps seem unique, but which rely on a common network of fundamental modalities. Take, for example, Scriabin's idiolectal modalizations, which appear on the verbal level as special linguistic (mostly French) performance indications, so many indications that a special dictionary of them has been compiled in Russian. If this dictionary were analyzed, one could cut down the number of entries by reducing the performance instructions to a few modalities.

This reduction of passions to modalities is a very similar procedure to that presented by Descartes, in his treatise *Les passions de l'âme*, where he first listed a great many passions (among them, *l'estime, le mépris, la générosité, l'orgueil, l'humilité, la bassesse, la vénération, le dédain, l'espérance, la crainte, la jalousie*), which he then reduced to six fundamental passions:

> But the number of those which are simple and primitive is not very great. Since while reviewing all those which I have listed, one may easily remark that there are only six of this category, namely, Admiration, Love, Hatred, Desire, Joy, and Sadness, and all the others have been composed of some of these six or are their subspecies. In order not to embarrass the reader by their multitude, I shall deal here separately with the six primitives. Then I shall make clear in which way all the others originate from them. [Descartes 1970: 115–16]

When reducing the passions to modalities we are doing a similar type of analysis. On the other hand, music evidently does not consist of presenting only one passion, one state of mind: music in particular is a temporal continuum of several passions, and a composition may contain several passions successively and even in a precisely planned order. Where ordering of passions occurs—where the listener is led to experience a given series of emotional states—we are approaching a still more complex series of events, which we might call narrativity. A musical work becomes in this case the realization of a certain narrative program (see Fig. 2.5).

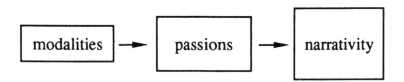

Figure 2.5. From modalities to narrativity.

Much music does not attain the narrative level, since to exist this level requires three kinds of structures and processes, i.e., three areas open to engagement/disengagement (Greimas 1979: 119–21): the operation of temporal, spatial, and actorial categories in musical discourse. For example, Liszt's *Dante* Sonata represents music where the narrative model functions: Despair and the powers of hell at the beginning are later replaced by Hope and the light of paradise. This simple narrative program in music could be described using the categories mentioned above: The actorial category of "personage" appears in the way that Liszt's theme serves as a musical fictive subject, a musical actant, a personage and hero with which the listener can identify. The temporal category contributes to the shape of this actant-theme; at first in the restless, jerking, and panting alternation of pairs of sixteenth notes in the Despair section, and particularly in the absence of clearly marked verse boundary (no clear-cut melodic or songlike structure, but a theme that goes against such clarity, with articulations left to the performer), and later in the rhythmic expansion that expresses Hope. The spatial category is manifested by the way the Despair motif dwells in a low register, changing back and forth chromatically, with minor-mode harmonies; in the Hope motif the music moves into a luminous upper register and major key.

The way musical narrativity emerges precisely from a series of emotions (caused by the music itself) forms a principle used in practical applications of music, such as musical therapy. According to the state of mind and level of musical culture of the person in therapy, a series of works or passages from works are selected that lead him or her through certain emotional states, according to a certain program (Guilhot et al. 1979: 48). In this case, the music is organized in accordance with the narrative principle, in exactly the same process as that used in many compositions based on narrativity. If one asks, for example, why Beethoven did not use the *Andante favori* originally planned as the slow movement of his "Waldstein" Sonata, but composed a new movement entitled "Introduzione," the answer surely is that he attempted to subordinate the whole sonata to one narrative program, which necessarily required a bridge between the rhythmically energetic character of the first movement and the *Klangfarben* theme, with its pedal effects, in the last movement. The influence of a similar type of integrating narrative principle is felt also in Schubert's "Wanderer" Fantasy, where different movements are articulated, it is true, according to Classical musical-syntactical genres such as sonata, variation, scherzo, and fugue but where the movements are temporally united under one dominant narrative program in such a way that the boundaries of the movements are weakened and actantially there is only one main theme.

D'Alembert remarked that the purely instrumental music of his time was on the threshold of narrativity when it expressed certain emotional series. Discussing Clementi's sonata, *Didone abbandonata*, he says:

> All that purely instrumental music without form and object does not speak to the spirit nor to the soul, and well deserves to be faced with Fontanelle's question: Sonata, what do you want of me? Composers of instrumental music produce only useless noise when they do not have in their minds, as the famous Tartini had, some action or expression to be painted. Some sonatas, but very few, do possess this desirable ability, which is so important in order to please people of good taste. We only mention one of them, entitled *Didone abbandonata*. It is a very beautiful monologue; one perceives there how pain, hope and despair follow one another quickly and distinctly in all their degrees and nuances; one might even use it for a very lively and pathetic scene on the stage. But such pieces are rarities. [d'Alembert 1821: 554][1]

We may say, then, that the narrative model is indeed one of the strongest models developed during the history of Western art music and of the other arts as well.

We might even wonder whether musical narrativity was born together with tonality. In the Renaissance any chord could still be followed by any other chord, while in the early Baroque period chords were given a certain direction, an order of succession, i.e., a program. Thus it would seem that the basic scheme of tonality (I→V, V→I) is that basic syntactic scheme to which the fundamental syntax of the narrative deep level could particularly well be linked (the fundamental narrative syntax which Greimas describes by his semiotic square as s1-s2, s̄2-s̄1), and which at the level of narrative surface syntax would appear as a process in which subject seeks object. In this case, the move from tonic to dominant would mean giving up the value-object (Greimas 1979: 124–25; Morris's "moving away," 1956), i.e., the disjunction of subject and object (S ∨ O); and the return from dominant to tonic would signify regaining the object or conjunction (S ∧ O), and is in fact the basic movement of all tonal music, i.e., "toward" something. Further, all movements taking place contrary to this scheme would represent movements against something.

On the other hand, the basic schemes of narrativity may also settle on other kinds of musical-syntactic structures, and the generative process of music may stop at some level. Consequently, the formation of narrativity may remain either at the level of passions or even at the level of modalizations preceding passions. Moreover, and taking into consideration all the modes of music, narrativity is a model which is difficult to situate exclusively at the level of a work. Within a musical work it has occurred most clearly in the compositions of the Romantic age (Beethoven, Schubert, Liszt) as a certain psychological conception of music in the syntagmatic and figurative form of Wandering (Nielsen and Sloth 1984: 222–23). In that age, even the development of a style was seen as a narrative process—as the development, rise, flourishing, decline, and destruction of some musical genre. Similarly, the lives of composers as they were depicted in biographies and finally the whole of music history were considered as narrativity.

Following from the above discussion, we can divide music models into two main classes: *narrative* and *non-narrative*, where non-narrative models are those in which the generative course has stopped at some phase or where various elements of the course are negated or annulled, which results in anti-narrativity (as represented, e.g., by Brecht's reaction to "culinary" opera and by John Cage's philosophy of silence). The term *non-narrative* is really not sufficient for these models, since what is involved is precisely an anti-narrative phenomenon.

In all music models, roughly speaking, two different levels can be distinguished: 1. the level of the signifier—the music to be listened to, the physical stimuli, musical material; and 2. the level of the signified—the concepts, thoughts, and emotions aroused by music; the content, whether it be the level described above of modal processes prior to music, or the level of its decoding and demodalizations, that is, the articulation of emotional content by the listener after a musical event. Music models can give value to and emphasize either signifier or signified, and in extreme cases they can entirely deny the existence of both. On the other hand, in the same way as composers search for

new ideas, new contents for their music to express, so journeys toward the unknown can be made by seeking for new signifiers, by enlarging the musical
material. Then music models determine what, at the level of the material, is
music, what is anti-music, and what is not music at all (Fig. 2.6).[2]

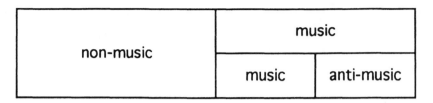

Figure 2.6. Music/non-music.

III

MUSICAL SPACE

In Chap. 2.1 we came to the conclusion that musical time cannot be studied apart from musical space. What Richard Wagner said in *Parsifal*— "Zum Raum wird hier die Zeit"—finds its theoretical justification precisely in musical semiotics, as I shall try to show in what follows.

What does it mean to speak of musical space? Certainly it has to be understood in a somewhat metaphorical sense. For isn't music primarily something to be *heard* and not seen?[1] If so, then musical space is a fictional "Third World" entity (in the sense of Karl Popper), and if any spatiality exists in music, it can be only of an imaginary nature. This view of musical space has had the support of various aesthetic experiences throughout the history of our culture. For example, Benoist-Méchin says in *La musique et l'immortalité dans l'oeuvre de Marcel Proust*: "Each musician of genius receives as an innate gift a kind of inner realm which is constantly recognizable, and whose rapidity or slowness opens up to him a universe of form marked by what can properly be called 'his originality'" (1926: 94). In this case, spatiality in music would always be of an internal nature.

At the same time, entire studies have focused on musical space, not as inner and metaphorical but as geometrical, with properties similar to those of any visual-spatial text. Cogan and Escot (1976) and Boulez (1971) have produced such studies. Conversely, space has often been interpreted in musical terms. These two views of musical space, the metaphorical and the geometrical, give us some hints about which direction to take. I shall give two illustrations.

The first is the poetic idea presented by British author Bruce Chatwin in his novel *The Songlines* (1988), which deals with the anthropology of Australian aborigines. Their mythology speaks of "dream time," when legendary totemic creatures wandered the continent and sang a name for everything they met— beasts, plants, stones, ponds—thus singing the world into life. For the natives the land did not exist before they saw and sung it. They believed that a land that was not sung was a dead land, since if the songs were forgotten, the land itself would die. To allow this to happen would be the worst of all possible crimes. In theory, all of Australia could be read like a score. The song lines of this "score" might be imagined as a congeries of *Iliad*s and *Odysseys*, in which each episode could be read "geologically." At any place one could thus point out a detail in a landscape and ask a native, "What story is there?" Or, "Who is that?" He might answer either "kangaroo" or "budgerigar," depending on which name his forefather had given it.

We need not be Heideggerians, believing that a work of art is like a house, to claim that Chatwin's idea applies to many things, music included. What else does a musical composition offer us but song lines, paths, routes we take through musical space? The concept of song line might even give us a key to the problem of space in music: the notation is a graphic presentation of an inner cognitive map which opens to us as we listen to or perform a musical piece. Listening to a composition is like journeying through this imaginary space. Each listener has personal inner maps or song lines which can follow entirely different courses within a musical work. Like Australian aborigines, listeners can mark quite different points in compositions as "sacred" places. This interpretation brings us close to the view that a musical space is something purely spiritual or imaginary. Just as only the natives could "see" their own invisible ways, it is likewise impossible to demonstrate by experiment the existence of these inner musical spaces to someone who does not "hear" (experience) them.[2] Most problems related to meaning, sense, and signification have to admit the fact of internal experience, which also holds true for musical signs and their contents.

Our next illustration comes from the "music" of architecture. We do not need to believe in Le Corbusier's "modulors" in order to admit, with Finnish architect Juhani Pallasmaa (1989), that more important than the abstract, logical structure of a building is the feeling it awakens. In this view, an intense experience of architecture is like subconscious touching and bodily identification—a form of actorialization. The structure of a building is felt as muscular tensions and movements, the space as an intensified experience of gravity and one's own existence, its lighting as a stream of time or deep, slow breathing. Very soon, in Pallasmaa's view, a building becomes an experienced reality, a thing which can be walked around, in which one can move, and whose acoustic properties one can listen to. Every house has its own recognizable voice, just as human beings do.

These two examples, one by a writer and the other by an architect, show that even space is often interpreted in terms of non-space, e.g., as kinetics, musicality, invisible feelings. Why not do the same with music, that is, stop interpreting it in purely "musical" terms and see it as a particular kind of space? In what follows I shall demonstrate that such an interpretation need not lead us outside music and into an intertextual field, but that the analysis of musical space concerns the innermost nature of music itself.

Preliminary Orientations

Let us first distinguish between "real" and "fictive" (metaphorical) spatiality in music.[3] Real spatiality can be understood as the pitch structure of music, which can be interpreted in either the inner or the outer sense: *Inner* spatiality is realized through the category of center/periphery, that is, the centripetal/centrifugal tendencies within a musical text. Some place in a musical universe or space can be chosen as center, in relation to which other places are more or less peripheral. As we have pointed out, in Greimasian semiotics, the concept of *débrayage/embrayage* points out movement from (*débrayage*) and return to (*embrayage*) a center.[1]

The most convenient illustration of inner space are key relations in Western tonal music, both learned and popular. But even in modern music these categories are useful. In Berio's *Omaggio a Joyce*, the center of the text, the starting point for all *débrayage*, is the reading of the original text with its "normal" prosody. The piece consists of a synthetic elaboration of basic phonetic material, with a continuous centripetal pull back to this basic "type," whose "tokens" are the electronic transformations. The return to the "model" functions structurally in precisely the same way as the *Tema con variazioni* movement in Beethoven sonatas (see Op. 109 and Op. 111).

Outer musical space refers to different registers in music; all the acoustic musical material can be measured in relation to the registers it occupies. Visual spatializations of music are usually based only on this kind of outer musical space. To this type of spatiality belong all those charts and diagrams, provided by computers and oscillographs, which depict the course of melodic lines on graph paper.

Outer space can also be understood in a more concrete sense, like the placement of musicians in a concert hall or theatre. We wait for the offstage trumpet fanfare in Beethoven's Leonore Overture (announcing the liberation of the prisoners in *Fidelio*), and we also recall the polychoral music of the seventeenth-century Venetian school, written for the Cathedral of St. Marco, where various groups of musicians performed from different sides of the hall. Likewise the gestural language of a conductor forms an externalization of the inner spatiality of music, its transformation into a physically perceptible, visual shape (see Rector 1985). Also, the whole art of orchestration includes, as one of its aims, the creation of spatial effects in concrete outer space. Throughout the history of orchestral performance conductors have experimented with different seating arrangements for the musicians. The location of performers has become very important in the musical theatre of the avant-garde (e.g., in Boulez's *Explosions*, Milhaud's *L'homme et son désir*, and Magnus Lindberg's *Kraft*). Finally, singers often imagine their voice as moving in a space. For example, scales are not sung from up to down and back, but from near to far and from far to near. Singing, like all performing arts, is quite literally *eine darstellende Kunst*, an art that presents, that sets something before the audience.

These examples suggest that musical space, both outer and inner, can be articulated according to the following dimensions: horizontal (before/after), vertical (up/down), and depth (in front of/behind). We should add a fourth dimension which is important in the semiotics of musical space: the distinction of center/periphery, in the sense that something in music can be *surrounded by* something else. By this I mean the Greimasian categories of surrounded/surrounding. Some musical element, say, a theme (musical actor), pushes itself to the fore, while the rest of the texture "surrounds" or envelops it.

These spatial dimensions may create an impression analogous to perspective in painting: one object is in the foreground and the rest remains as background, perhaps in a *claire obscure*, as a reflection of the main object. This *claire obscure* effect is typical of music in which the theme consists of the same material as its "accompaniment," as in the transition to the coda in Chopin's C♯ minor Scherzo, or at the beginning of Schumann's C major Fantasy. Sometimes the theme-actor is surrounded by other parts or instruments which twine around it, such as the folklike theme in the Canzona of Tchaikovsky's Fourth Symphony; the main idea of the piece is to transfer the theme to different timbral and textural "landscapes." What Robert S. Hatten means in his theory of "markedness" in music (1987b) also comes close to this conception. In musical space, some places stand out as marked against the background of nonmarked elements. Even the tones of a scale form a markedness system, as do chords.[5]

The illusion of foreground and background (surrounded/surrounding) often occurs through dynamics and accentuation of musical enunciation (performance). When performing a Bach fugue, for example, one can emphasize a particular strand of the polyphonic texture, just as in his Passions a chorale theme can be made to project from a thick texture. In fact, a good deal of impressive performance relies on this technique, which was magnificently utilized by Busoni in his historic recording of a Bach chorale arrangement in D major.

To conclude this section, which started with a distinction between outer and inner musical space, let us look at some concrete examples. Is there anything like spatial music, in which the spatiality would be manifest as the "gesture" of a piece, as a First in the Peircean sense? Indeed, some musical motifs are of a purely spatial nature, such as the main theme in the Scherzo of Beethoven's Pastoral Sonata (Ex. 3.1). Likewise, entire pieces can be of a spatial character. Listening to them, we feel as if we are moving in space, as in György Ligeti's *Atmosphères*. Typically, in such cases, the two other important categories of musical semiosis (temporality and actoriality) are absent.

Example 3.1. Beethoven, Op. 28, Scherzo, mm. 1–12.

How can we portray distinctions between outer and inner space in music, if everything in music is subordinated to the temporal principle of 'becoming'? Let us look at some examples: 1. Outer and inner space change at the same time, as at the beginning of Brahms's F minor Piano Sonata (Ex. 3.2). 2. Both outer and inner space remain unchanged, as at the start of Scriabin's *Vers la flamme*, and the opening of the Adagio of Bruckner's Eighth Symphony (Ex. 3.3). 3. The outer space changes, but the inner does not; e.g., the Prelude to Wagner's *Rheingold* (Ex. 3.4). 4. The outer space remains unchanged while the inner changes, as in the preparation of the second theme in the first movement of Beethoven's Pastoral Sonata (Ex. 3.5), and in the enharmonic modulation from B major to E♭ major in the last section of the Finale of Beethoven's Op. 7 (Ex. 3.6).

Example 3.2. Brahms, Piano Sonata in F minor, Op. 5, mm. 1–5.

Example 3.3. Bruckner, Symphony No. 3, Adagio, mm. 1–6 (piano reduction).

Example 3.4. Wagner, Prelude to *Das Rheingold*, mm. 81–124.

Example 3.4. (con't.)

Example 3.5. Beethoven, Op. 28, mvt. I, mm. 71–91.

Example 3.6. Beethoven, Op. 7, Finale, mm. 169–72.

Toward a Kinetic Space

Evidently, musical space is always related to movement within it, that is, to a kinetic quality. To prove this, we shall make a preliminary classification of various kinds of musical space. This classification is "structuralist" in nature, since it starts from the smallest units and gradually combines them into larger ones. Basically, one may distinguish between three kinds of musical space:

1. In the first, we have only pointlike spaces, positions of separate sounds and pitches. All music is made of a given collection of pitches (this is the starting point of set-theoretical analysis of music). As Cogan and Escot have noted (1976), various styles in music emerge from a given store of tones, what German theorists call a *Tonvorrat*. "The Old Castle" from Musorgsky's *Pictures at an Exhibition* and Chopin's Mazurka, Op. 56 no. 1, are apparently quite different, but both pieces use tones of the B major scale. They emphasize them quite differently—the former toward minor harmony, the latter toward major (Cogan and Escot 1976: 88–90).

Musical language also consists of relations (intervals) between tones. To look merely at the notes of a tune would be a purely taxonomic approach which does not yet form a language. Even when we seem to have a musical space made of single points, as in Ligeti's *Aventures* and Webern's "pointillist" works, this space contains relations and tensions among its points. The first task of analysis is to make a topological map of these points, but we must also determine which points function as center(s) in relation to which any movement can be considered as either disengagement or engagement.

There exists a hierarchy of points in a musical space, such that they are provided with different values. These values represent what we have called modalities (Chap. 1.4), borrowing the term from formal logic and the semiotics of Greimas. Points in musical space receive modal values denoting how much they are wished for, expected, desired, obtainable, possible, necessary, facultative, fortuitous, etc. Even completely serial pieces, like those of Webern or Schoenberg, are modalized in the listener's mind and according to an implicit modal structure of the musical text itself. Thus, if the first task of a spatial analysis of music is to make a rough topological analysis of what "points" the piece employs, the next is to clarify how those points are modalized.

2. Here we examine how musical space consists of transitions from one point to another. The routes between points may be called musical vectors or lines. Composers of electronic music often use a computer when faced with the problem of moving from the sound of, say, a flute to that of a violin: one may calculate the classes of timbral transformation needed to realize this transition as an unbroken line. In tonal music, the transition from a point A (dominant) to a point B (tonic) can also be modalized in many ways, e.g., provided with an intense drive or 'will' for something, as in the outburst of the main theme in the slow movement of Tchaikovsky's Fifth Symphony.

3. Finally, in addition to points and transitions between them, musical spaces can consist of whole fields,[6] which are not felt as conglomerates of discrete tone points but as more or less articulated sonorous masses or timbres. This is true not only for modern "sound mass" works, such as those by Ligeti and Penderecki, but also for tonal pieces, such as Chopin's C♯ minor Scherzo, in which melody and accompaniment often constitute one and the same texture in transitional sections (see Szabolcsi 1965: 173). Cases like the Chopin show that even sound fields or sonorous surfaces are not neutral entities; they too become modalized when moving toward or away from some fixed point or center of a musical space.

Charles Morris (and G.H. Mead) spoke of three kinds of movement: toward, against, and away from something (Morris 1956). This classification suits musical kinetic spaces, and using the theory of modalities, we can give this classification a more precise content. The central idea of spatiality in music is that there are different "microspaces," "registers" in music which are modalized in various ways that cause tension and compel them to move toward, against, or away from each other.

Let p and q represent two musical microspaces (points or fields). Adopting the symbols of von Wright's logic of change (discussed in Chap. 1.2), we can formulate how these microspaces can be modalized in different ways: (m) p and (m) q. There may also be a transition from one space to another: pTq. The kinetic moment in this space would be the quality of movement represented by T. For example, let p be a motif on tonic, and q a motif on dominant. One may move from p to q either by accelerating or by slowing the movement. The movement can be felt as a 'will' of p toward q, but this 'will' might be obstructed, which would signify an obligation or compulsion to resist this movement. This situation involves two modalities: that of 'will' (*vouloir*) and its negation, 'not-will' (*non-vouloir*); and the *surmodalization* of 'will' with 'must' (*devoir*). This means that p must move to q although it does not want to. Using all the cases of modalities of 'will' and 'must' we get four articulations: 'must/will': the music must proceed and it also wants to proceed from p to q; 'must/not-will': the music must, but does not want to proceed from p to q; 'will/not-must': the music wants although it does not need to proceed from p to q; 'not-will/not-must': the music neither wants nor needs to proceed from p to q. We can also interpret our symbols p, q, and T in terms of modalities. All music consists of stasis (something which only 'is') and of dynamism (something which 'does' or makes something happen). This should be intuitively clear to any musical mind. Let p and q represent static moments of 'being' in music; then T would symbolize the 'doing' or action in a musical text.

Using these concepts we can formulate a tentative program for the analysis of any musical space. One should first search a piece for moments representing the 'being' (*être*) and 'doing' (*faire*) (Greimas 1983: 67), i.e., the static moments and the active transitions between them. For example, in the first movement of Beethoven's Pastoral Sonata, the first theme would serve as the 'being 1' and the secondary theme as the 'being 2'. How the transition from 'being 1' to 'being 2' takes place is a crucial moment which the theory of modalities can make explicit. The same situation can also be projected into larger syntagmatic units, as in the transition from the first to second movement in Beethoven's "Waldstein" Sonata (analyzed in Chap. 5 below). A more extensive paradigm of these transitions reveals particular spatial "figures" or common patterns of musical 'doing'. For example, the diminished seventh chord, in which any note may serve as leading tone, is a harmony that easily moves us from one musical space to another. On the other hand, modulating sequential passages can also operate in the T-function of our theory. Likewise, enharmonic reinterpretations move us to a new musical inner space. All the rules of modulation can thus be given a semiotic reading, as shown in Fig. 3.1.

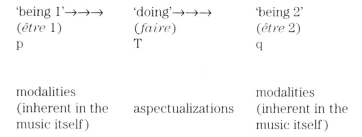

Figure 3.1. Semio-modal reading of modulation.

Modalities and Modalizations

We need a chart that allows deeper reflection on the modal nature of musical space, much like the serial matrix that shows all the transpositions and inversions of a twelve-tone row. If we combine the basic modalities of 'being' and 'doing' with the four additional modalities of 'will', 'must', 'can', and 'know', we get two charts (Fig. 3.2). The first, related to the 'being', articulates the musical space; the second, related to the 'doing', shows the organization of the musical time. (We shall soon see, however, that space and time in music are inseparable.)

Musical Space

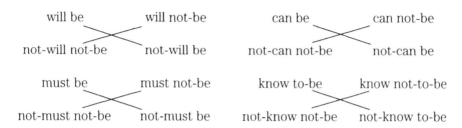

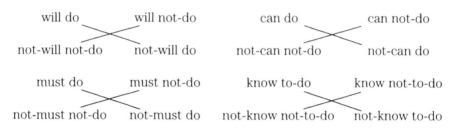

Figure 3.2. 'Being' and 'doing' combined with 'will', 'must', 'can', 'know'.

It is highly probable that the modalities as construed by Greimas (1983: 86–87, 99) cannot be directly applied to music. They have to be retitled following the basic significations of musical modalities we defined in connection with Ernst Kurth's theory (Chap. 1.4 and Chap. 4). Referring to Fig. 3.2, we shall now take a closer look at all of these cases and their counterparts in musical terms.

In a musical space, or 'being', the 'will' (kinetic energy and goal-directedness) appears in such a way that some point of the musical space is the object of a particular striving; for example, tonic in the inner space, a certain register in the outer. We have to ask by what means that object is made to sound or seem desirable. Here, other mechanisms of the musical semiosis come to our aid: actorialization, where the main actor occurs in the desired register; or temporalization, where the desired object is situated in the final phase of a long temporal process, i.e., at the point of terminativity or perfectivity. Such is the characterization of the point 'will be' in a musical space.

'Will not-be' means that one wants to avoid some register. For example, a certain instrumental register might not produce the needed sound, as when Berlioz forbids the use of certain low notes with wind instruments, while Richard Strauss allows them (Berlioz and Strauss 1904: 205, 215, 242–43); and Rimsky-Korsakov does not recommend trills on certain strings (1914:

10–11). One might want to avoid certain places, such as the low register of the piano; or, following the principle of *horror vacui* in its inverse form (*amor vacui*), a gap can be intentionally created in a musical space, a gap that is deliberately not filled and awaits completion till another, more effective moment.

The category of 'not-will be' means that some register or point in a musical space, though used, produces an unpleasant and unwanted effect. For instance, the grotesque transformation of the *idée fixe* in the last movement of Berlioz's *Symphonie fantastique* makes this actor and the space filled by it not-wanted. It is true that this case relates more to actoriality than to spatiality, but there are many works in which certain places are provided with the modality of 'not-will be', such as the register of bass clarinet and tubas in the depiction of Alberich's cave in Wagner, or when some register is occupied to the point of undesirability.

Such an effect also relates to sequential passages. When a sequence begins in a tonal piece it is usually experienced as a point of rest, a pleasant relaxation or 'will be' (*vouloir être*). The listener wants to stay ('be') there, but the music continues, and soon the problem arises of how to finish the sequence. If the composer does not know how to end a sequence early enough it becomes a place of 'not-will be' (*non-vouloir être*), where one no longer wants to dwell. How elegantly Chopin finds a solution for this situation in his F minor Ballade, when the homophonic texture returns after a polyphonic sequence; how skillfully Saint-Saëns, in his Piano Concerto in G minor, gets out of the cadence in the first movement when he proceeds almost unnoticeably to the thematic material of the introduction (Ex. 3.7); and Mozart has the ability to emerge unscathed from vicious circles of sequences, as in the dialogue between soloist and orchestra in the Finale of the C major Piano Concerto (Ex. 3.8).

There remains the category of 'not-will not-be'. This is the well-known principle of *horror vacui*, the "fear" of any gap or place of 'non-being' in the music. Leonard Meyer's implication model (1973: 110) is based precisely on this modal situation: the hypothesis that both composer and listener act in accordance with the idea that no gap can remain unfilled in any "good" composition, lest we feel that it represents an unbalanced use of the musical space.

Next we shall scrutinize spatial articulations according to 'must' (*devoir*). If the foregoing reflections belong to the sphere of volitive logic (Greimas 1979: 422), then this case illustrates deontic logic. It depends somewhat on the attitude of the analyst as to how important this normative dimension is for musical semiotics.

'Must be' means that a certain point in tonal space has been "ordered" and must occur there. In serial music a tone row constitutes the source of this type of 'obligation'. According to Schoenberg, even in tonal music the beginning tone and the first digression from it create the first obligation, which determines the future course of the piece (1975: 269). Which point of the musical space (both inner and outer) must be used is most often determined by the musical

Example 3.7. Saint-Saëns, Piano Concerto No. 2 in G minor, Op. 22, mvt. I, F.

Example 3.8. Mozart, Piano Concerto in C major, K. 467, mvt. III, mm. 266–80.

context; this context is either the work itself or the tradition of genre or form. Sometimes it can even be hard to distinguish between 'willing' and 'obligation', since the norms can manifest themselves as the internalized will of the composer.

'Must not-be' means that certain stylistic norms determine that a given portion of the musical space must not be used. Greimas lexicalizes this case with the term "impossibility." For example, in "classical" atonal music, there must be no repetitions or octave duplications. In a good orchestration, no instruments should go unheard. In turn, 'not-must not-be' refers to the fact that it is not necessary to leave a certain point unused; it is possible not to use a certain point, but not compulsory. Finally, 'not-must be' means that a certain point in the musical space is not forbidden, but is optional.

There are various degrees of 'must'. In some cases something is strongly obligatory, in other cases less so. In the same way, Greimas speaks of epistemic acts as having four aspects: to confirm, to refuse, to admit, to doubt, where admission and doubt are milder forms of affirmation and refusal. In the musical universe, too, something can be absolutely affirmed or refused but also admitted to be possibly true or untrue.

This brings us to 'can be', *pouvoir* in music, which relates to technical rendering, virtuosity, power, and efficiency. 'Can be' means that some point of a musical space has been provided with great power and effect. Thus, affirmation in music, as in the finales of "victory" symphonies, often involves orchestral tutti effects. Likewise, virtuosity in solo cadenzas also displays 'can'. 'Can not-be' signifies refraining from the use of an effect, say, in a place where an inferior composer might use it. Sibelius, for example, frequently ends a work without a powerful coda or definitive closure. The work simply ends when the 'know' and the 'will' of the musical material are exhausted. There occurs no glorification of the main theme or climax required by aesthetic-stylistic obligations or norms. In Anton Webern's music, as well as in modern pointillist orchestration, one also senses this power of abstinence.

'Not-can not-be' represents the case in which no (musical-technical) impressive effect occurs at a place that 'is not', i.e., does not exist musically. When a certain place is missing or an obvious gap occurs, this modal combination is quite evident; but even nonpertinent material, such as transitions, might not require exceptional technique or virtuosity. 'Not-can be' means that some point or event of a musical space exists but does not occupy a crucial position in the technical realization of the piece; for example, in an orchestration that would otherwise foreground the event.

We arrive at our last spatial modality, that of 'knowing', which refers to the information that the music contains, its cognitive moment. 'Know to-be' signifies that some point of the musical space exists and at the same time offers us new information about the piece. For example, to start a composition directly with the main theme, in its proper register, would mean "affirmation" of this "place."

'Know not-to-be', according to Greimas, makes us regard something as illusory or imagined. This situation involves the absence of a certain "place." At the same time, this absence, 'not-being', forms a cognitive element of informational value in the course of the composition. For example, a sonata may deliberately not have a slow movement, or the first movement of a sonata may lack a development section.

'Not-know not-to-be' means that the absence of a certain point in the musical space does not form any cognitive moment; this absence is not pertinent in the work in question. For example, Leopold Godowsky added octaves to Chopin's Etudes. The octave duplications are supplemental, nonpertinent elements, and when playing the original version we hardly miss them.

'Not-know to-be', on the other hand, is difficult to lexicalize as an "impossibility," since this case involves a musical space that exists but does not form a cognitive unit, i.e., does not provide new information. For example, two thousand singers and players in an open-air concert produce as great an effect as one hundred musicians in a good concert hall. The refrains in a rondo form are repeated and thus they "are," but they do not give us any new information.

Now we are ready to examine transitions from one musical space to another. The latter space, or 'being', can have entirely contradictory modalities in relation to the first, in which case a tension emerges between a musical space having the modality 'm' and another space with the modality 'not-m'. In its smallest form this tension, which can occur between two hierarchically contrasting tones, involves the modalization of 'doing' (*faire*) in music. We recall that 'doing' presupposes the existence of a tension and its increase, while 'notdoing' means a decrease in tension, a movement toward rhythmic or harmonic consonance. Here we move from mere 'being' into action, into the temporal processes of music (refer again to Fig. 3.2). Without a certain amount of temporality it is hard to imagine any musical event, or 'doing', though one might argue that in a musical simultaneity two musical spaces can be juxta- or superimposed without forming a musical event.

'Will do' means that a musical text strives for increase of tension by a strong tendency toward a goal. The musical processes have a clear direction. 'Will notdo' depicts the contrary situation, where the music aims to decrease tension and moves away from dissonance. If, say, point x of a musical space has been modalized with 'can do' (*pouvoir faire*) and we proceed from x to a point modalized with 'can' and 'will be' (*vouloir être*), one generally finds a gradual decrease in musical tension, thus avoiding a very abrupt transition. 'Not-will not-do' is the case where music does not strive for a tensionless space; i.e., the music allows the tension, the 'doing', to continue. 'Not-will do', on the other hand, means that the kinetic energy of the music tends toward dissonance and aims for a continuation of 'being', as in a *sotto voce*, detensional gliding between two differently modalized musical spaces.

'Must do' in music follows the logic of "if p then q," on the supposition that musical universes p and q are in mutual tension, thus forming contrasts with each other. It is then necessary to move from p to q, which only increases tension, dissonance, and feeling of action. 'Must not-do' refers to a transition that diminishes tension. It often occurs in sonatas, at the transition from development to recapitulation, especially if the development dramatized various theme-actors, say, with the figure of Battle. Correspondingly, 'must-do' in sonata form appears in the transition from exposition to development, or in rondo form, from a *lied*-type main section into a more active subordinate section.

'Not-must not-do' occurs when no norm determines whether the tension is permitted to resolve toward a consonant state of rest; for example, instead of a tensional, virtuoso cadence, the composer writes a thematic, polyphonic solo part. 'Must not-do' means that a composer is not obliged to choose a tensional, active transition from space p to space q, but is able and permitted to do so. Also, the listener realizes that the contrasts in transitions are not obliged to be so sharp, but somehow this happens nevertheless.

The modality of 'must' also influences that of 'believing' (*croire*) to the extent that the increase of musical tension is convincing and persuasive. Pieces might also contain a final climax that is not actually credible or necessary, in which case the music resorts to the modality of 'willing'. If a musical work only obeys external style norms and accordingly situates the climax at, say, the golden section (approximately .618 of the total length of the piece), without this point being made necessary by any inner energetic 'will', then such a climax is certainly not felt as an efficient, believable solution.

'Know to-do' contains the idea that a transition from p to q also includes certain information; the transition is made surprising in a way that increases tension. For example, a diatonic fifths progression does not project the modality of 'knowing to-do'; but a skillful, dramatic modulation through reinterpretation of a given key certainly exhibits this modality (as in Schubert's *Erlkönig*). 'Know not-to-do', in turn, means that the tension lessens; the composer attempts to move away from tension with some inventive way of offering us new information (as in a false or "wrong-key" recapitulation).

'Not-know not-to-do' represents a case where the decrease of tension takes place by some cliché, such as an unimaginative thematic liquidation. Examples include Schubert's Impromptu in F minor, Op. 142, No. 4 (middle section); any overlong return to a subordinate section in Brucknerian symmetrical formal construction; and the liquidation of the development section in the first movement of Beethoven's G major Sonata, Op. 14, No. 2. 'Not-know to-do' means that the tension increases, but how this is accomplished contains no further information. Iconic repetition of the same motif, with only an increase in dynamics, would serve as an extreme illustration of this category.

'Can do' means that the tension increases when we shift from one to another place, while at the same time the technical realization of this shift comes into the foreground; i.e., there is power and effectiveness in the music. We can illustrate this modal combination with the transition section in the second movement of Rimsky-Korsakov's *Scheherazade* (Ex. 3.9), where enharmonically reinterpreted chords alternate with the trumpet call.

Example 3.9. Rimsky-Korsakov, Scheherazade, mvt. II, mm. 12–19 after E.

'Can not-do' refers to the use of technical resources of music in order to diminish tension, as when orchestration moves from "heavy" to "light." For example, in Veljo Tormis's choral piece, *The Nights of Inkeri*, the pitch suddenly falls, following the natural respiration of the singers—a conscious use of choral technique as an artistic device. 'Not-can not-do' denotes a decrease of tension without any musical-technical resources contributing to that decrease. 'Not-can do' can be illustrated by cases where a composer tries to increase tension, without using any special technical skills or effects. Someone may thereby fail to write a good climax or development.

We have just explored musical 'being' and 'doing' in combination with various other modalities. Still, even the primary modalities of being and doing most often vary and alternate within a musical piece. To explore further these basic modalities, we now put them and their negations into the semiotic square shown in Fig. 3.3. The epistemic modalities can be similarly positioned (Greimas 1983: 120), as shown in Fig. 3.4. Quite often, a composition that follows the norms of Western art music is programmed in such a way that it starts with 'being', with affirmation; i.e., some place in a musical space is provided with euphoric and actorial cogency. Then we relinquish 'being', by doubting or gradual negation of this euphoria, and move to the category of 'not-being'. From here we soon proceed to a negation and refusal of 'being', that is, to true action and 'doing'. After the 'doing' has been realized, it starts to negate itself: we give up 'doing' and shift to the state of 'not-doing'. This shift means a move away from tension, toward a 'being' that differs from the 'being' from which we started. This movement, in very general terms and with all manner of variants, is well illustrated by the beginnings of Bruckner's Seventh and Ninth Symphonies (Exx. 3.10 and 3.11).

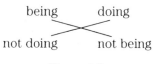

Figure 3.3.

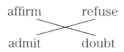

affirm   refuse

admit   doubt

Figure 3.4.

We have thus far produced a taxonomy of various musical spaces and their modalities. For a musical enunciator (composer) they form a subconscious paradigm of various possibilities to be fulfilled when writing a musical text. Often these categories unite to form spatial figures, as mentioned above. Figures, as specific and recurrent musical situations, enable the process which we call *narrativity* in music. Only the analysis of concrete musical texts, in all their richness and intricacy, can show us whether this paradigm would be of any real use or remain mere speculation.

Example 3.10. Bruckner, Symphony No. 7, mvt. I, mm. 1–27
(piano reduction).

For example, one might analyze the figure of ascending stepwise motion in musical space. On the level of the signified (content) this ascent brings about the aesthetic emotion of the sublime. Such a figure has a certain universality in the context of Western art music. One needs only mention cases like the second movement of Bruckner's Eighth Symphony, where we find a solemn stepwise upward motion with the change of chord on each scale degree, as an enactment of this sublimity. Likewise, we find the same figure in the slow movement of Sibelius's Violin Concerto (Ex. 3.12a), the slow movement of Beethoven's Fifth Piano Concerto (Ex. 3.12b), Wagner's *Parsifal* (Ex. 3.12c), and Bruckner's Eighth Symphony, in the rising strings before the trombone theme (Ex. 3.12d).

Example 3.11. Bruckner, Symphony No. 9, mvt. I, mm. 1–26 (piano reduction).

Example 3.12. a. Sibelius, Violin Concerto in D minor,
Op. 47, mvt. II, mm. 38–42; b. Beethoven, Piano Concerto in
E♭ major, Op. 73, mvt. II, mm. 7–10; c. Wagner, *Parsifal*, Grail motif;
d. Bruckner, Symphony No. 8 in C minor, mvt. III, mm. 40–43.

Other Musical Spaces

Looking at more metaphorical musical spaces, one finds that the distinctions
Greimas made for narratives hold true for musical texts as well. He posited a
zero-space, called *topical* space, from which the narration begins. Topical

space is surrounded by other spaces, situated before or after it, which he called *heterotopic* spaces.

It is often necessary to articulate the topical space further. There is a *utopic* space, where action transforms 'being'; this is a space for performances (in myths these places are often subterranean or celestial). In addition there is a *paratopic* space, where competencies are acquired. In music the paratopic space is the place where the musical substance reveals its own competency ('knowing') and performance ('being able to do'). For example, in sonata form the exposition is typically a utopic space, where themes are innovated and introduced (Mäkelä 1989: 36–39); the development section is the space where thematic performances occur. Most often this paratopic space is at the same time a heterotopic space: the performances take place "elsewhere," that is, in keys other than that of the utopic space.

Even in avant-garde music, paratopic spatiality plays a crucial role. In Magnus Lindberg's *Kraft*, the movement of the musicians around the performance space creates an interesting fusion of the subjects of enunciation with what is enunciated (*énoncé*), a fusion upon which many effects of the piece rely. In the same work, impressions of topical and heterotopic spaces are also created: the electronic intensification of the sound of blowing soap bubbles alludes to an aquatic, submarine space, which contrasts with the "celestial" space represented by the sound of gongs and bells.

Likewise, the narrative "arch" of such multimovement works as Musorgsky's *Pictures at an Exhibition* (analyzed in Chap. 8) exploits the distinction between topical and heterotopic space. After the introduction of the center of the narration (the *modo russico* of the first Promenade), the music moves through various heterotopic spaces, such as "The Tuileries," and "The Old Castle." The music returns "home" to the center with "Baba-Yaga" and "The Gate of Kiev."

IV

MUSICAL ACTORS

4.1 Ernst Kurth as a Precursor of Musical Semiotics:
Steps toward the Definition of Actoriality in Music

> Melody is movement. It is erroneous to investigate only acoustic sound phenomena and to consider sounding [material] and tones, with all their implicit harmonic relations, as the most essential and significant factors, without accounting for perceptions and sensations of energy between tones. In this context the melodic progress from one tone to another has to be considered a factor inseparably and even originally related to these [acoustic] aspects.

These words launch the *Grundlagen des linearen Kontrapunktes* (1922), a monograph by Swiss music psychologist Ernst Kurth. Why should a 1990s theory of musical semiotics return to ideas first presented in the 1920s, ideas evoking German speculative philosophy—perhaps the extreme antipode of the contemporary sciences of simulation and cognition? One reason is that a clear line of development leads from turn-of-the-century energeticism, first to Kurth and Schenker, then to French music philosophers Gisèle Brelet and Vladimir Jankélévitch, and finally via Kurth to the Russian Boris Asafiev, whose intonational theory one may consider an implicit musical semiotics (see Jiránek 1967). Yet of all these theoreticians, Kurth seems to be the most neglected, though some of his ideas have become crucial to present-day Schenkerian analysis (e.g., the idea of *Linienzug*).[1] Despite this neglect, I predict that Ernst Kurth's theoretical thinking will one day attain a status in musical semiotics equal to that of Heinrich Schenker in contemporary music theory.

The passage quoted above reveals Kurth's fundamentally semiotic starting point: in any complex of signs, such as a series of pitches forming a melody, the essential relation is always the reference of a physical stimulus (signifier) to what Kurth calls a "state of forces" (*Kräftevorgang*). Even if it is true that in the twentieth century the acoustic analysis of sound has reached unprecedented exactitude (Cogan and Escot 1976: 77), it in no way follows that we have attained equivalent depth and accuracy in the semiotic inferences we make from sound phenomena when we listen to a musical work. Crucial to such inferences is the relation between the musical signifier and the deeper forces it represents.

Another feature of Kurth's enterprise, one that forms the basis of our own theory of musical semiotics, lies in the thoroughly temporal nature of music: the essence of melody does not consist in the succession of tones, but in transitions between them. Transitions involve motion, and from this it follows that only the motion between tones and one's experience of this motion lead to the true nature of music. According to Kurth, the basic postulate of such a view is:

> The experience of movement felt in a melody is not only a kind of subsidiary psychological phenomenon; rather, it leads us to the very origin of the melodic element. This element, which is felt as a force streaming through the tones, and the sensual intensity of the sound itself both refer to the basic powers in the musical formation, namely to the *energies* which we experience as psychic tensions. [1922: 3]

Is this *fin-de-siècle* mysticism, which should be replaced by modern scientific theories? Hardly. In his epistemological foundations Kurth is simultaneously a semiotician, cognitivist, and generativist: semiotician in the sense that he sees or hears the sound stimulus of music always as a *sign*, as something which refers to something beyond itself; cognitivist, because he attends to what happens in the human mind in the act of perceiving music; generativist and structuralist in that he starts from the "inner" and moves toward the "outer," from deep structure to surface organization:

> The energy of movement is a tensional phenomenon which precedes sounding. . . . The tones of a melodic line are surface levels of these streams of psychic energies which break forth. Therefore one must not only speak of feelings of forces between tones, but also *over* them. The sounding shape represents to a melody what a drop of water represents to the tensions of a mass of water. [1922: 5]

Kurth considers all earlier music theory misguided insofar as it has investigated music primarily from acoustic-physical and physiological phenomena. To his mind, music and the audible material (tonal sensations) relate to each other as a 'will' relates to its manifestation, as power to its actualization, as an abstract idea to its concretization, or, as a Lévi-Straussian might add, as the intelligible to the sensible.

One could even speak of semiotic forces within ourselves, which Greimas's generative trajectory, among other models, has tried to explicate and formalize. Neither the semantic investment which at each moment can be inserted into this generative course nor the elaborated material is essential; rather, what is crucial is the energy of elaboration, "the compelling movements of psychic powers in us, which only grasp 'the musical substance' when they try to concretize and become a sense phenomenon" (Kurth 1922: 8). The semiotics of Greimas and Kurth therefore aim for the same goal. And it is no wonder that Greimas and Schenker, the twentieth century's other great "energeticist" of music theory, seem to fit well together, especially with regard to the notion of tri-leveled generation of texts (as demonstrated by Littlefield and Neumeyer 1992).

Adopting the Kurthian perspective as the point of departure for a musical semiotics immediately raises important issues as to analytic method. Let us begin with Kurth's view that "the energy which flows through melodic lines influences all single tones in a melody, which we experience as a closed whole, a linear unit" (1922: 11). Therefore music divides itself into phases of movement whose length is determined by their inherent kinetic energy. In other words, a segment in music lasts as long as there is enough power in its initial impulse to keep the motion going forward. Kurth's theory accordingly revolutionizes traditional criteria of segmentation; and using it one can also treat music that analysts have generally had trouble segmenting, such as electronic music, freely pulsatile music, "sound mass" compositions (for example, some works by Ligeti and Penderecki), minimalism, spectral music, and computer works.

Kurth warns that kinetic impressions in a melody must not be confused with rhythmic/metric impulses. The kinetic energy, the melodic course streaming through and binding together all the tones, represents a far more general and deeper phenomenon than rhythmics and metrics.[2] Kurth postulates as a basis some *Bewegungsphase*, with all its energies, which we expect to continue in a given way unless a composer interrupts it in order to withhold fulfillment of forward-driving energy for another, more narratively effective point. Even narrativity in music is realized precisely as a deliberate disengagement/engagement of the enunciator (composer), by which he or she diverts the primal energy of movement from its "normal" course, manipulates the phases of the melodic line and harmonic tension, and guides their resolution. Such a shifting or disengaging activity is possible only when realized against this innate kinetic quality of music.

Outer rhythmics and inner kinetics coincide in Viennese Classical and Romantic *lied* melodies, but not necessarily in other music styles. Kurth in fact reaches the same conclusion as Schenker, namely, that the spatial element dominates musical kinetic energy. In Greimasian terms, kinetic energy is not a temporal-rhythmic but a spatial category. Thus one may conclude that, as regards musical actoriality, the energy of some theme-actors can be determined by purely spatial factors. For instance, Cogan and Escot have analyzed the *Benedictus* from a Josquin mass and demonstrated how its kinetic energy arises from spatial activity (1976: 17–24).

This evidence strengthens my view that a semiotic analysis of music must first search out spatial fulcrums and only thereafter define their modal values; that is, whether certain tones serve as goals, and whether there are "desirable" or even "inevitable" passages. Often some tone is, on first occurrence, something only desired or "wished for" and in later occurrences proves to be the "inevitable" center of the whole melodic course (as with the tone A in the cadences of Josquin's mass). One must also determine which points, such as neighboring tones, are swiftly visited and thus "avoidable," and from which one quickly returns to the energetic sphere of the central, structural tones (e.g., C and G in the Josquin mass). Only after this modal mapping can one examine how movement to and away from tones has been temporalized. Then one can engage Kurth's thesis that rhythmic and kinetic energy do not always coincide.

In Kurth's view, however, this should not lead to reduction of the melodic movement to harmonies alone, as if melodic shaping were only passive shifting from one note, fixed by the harmony, to another. Whether one takes the scalar passage C–D–E as an extension of C major harmony, with D as a foreign tone, or whether one experiences these three tones as expressions of a tonic–dominant–tonic function—both these perceptions are *post facto* rationalizations. We might add that, even here, such interpretations of individual melodic tones represent semiotic reasoning, since the tones as signifier relate to an invisible meaning, a signified, a concept or abstract content, whether it be simply a "tone that belongs to a chord" or a "tonal function." Schenker's theory starts with such an assumption and claims to depict the genesis of music in the mind of the composer, an activity in which the composer improvises from a given *Ursatz*. By contrast, Kurth's method centers entirely on the music's destinatee, the receiver, and on the music as a heard and experienced reality. Still, from this difference in methodological orientation one cannot draw any conclusion as to which theorist is the more "semiotical."

Kurth considers the smallest unit of musical segmentation, the motif, as the offspring of a certain kinetic energy. The fundamental character of a motif is based on the play of its inherent forces. If we identify melody or theme with a musical actor, then the actorial analysis of music is the analysis of the motifs constituting a theme, and the reduction of those motifs to their energizing, kinetic tensions. Among other things, this explains why the signifier of a motif can be transformed so easily: a motif remains recognizable even when its intervals are expanded or contracted, its metric values distorted, or its melodic direction reversed. These operations do not necessarily disturb the identity or inner iconicity of a motif, for their signified motifs carry a certain kinetic energy.

We thus conclude that precisely this kinetic energy forms the purely semiotic signification of a musical text, as a whole or in part. Though I have earlier understood by pheme analysis of music the dissolution of a musical lexeme into smaller motifs and intonations, such as intervals, such analysis operates only on the level of a signifier and its taxonomy. In addition to such semes we must designate units of a properly semiotic content, units which we might call *kinemes*, the smallest units of kinetic energy. They refer to the binding force of a phase of melodic movement, which makes us experience both stepwise melodic motion and intervallic leaps as manifestations of a semio-kinetic content. What are these basic kinemes of music like? Are they numerous or few in number? Answering these questions is one of the primary goals of music analysis.

If we hold as a minimum requirement of musical semiotics that it distinguish at least the levels of expression and content, signifier and signified, then Kurth's theory meets this demand by identifying these levels in music: "A written or sounding melody, with all its intervals and leaps, constitutes only a reference to a real melody" (1922: 27). In other words, Kurth sees even musical notation as a sign system. This system refers to a "real melody," which is in turn the same as the *Bewegungsphase*, or kinetic energy, inherent in a sounding melody. Therefore a music semiotician is faced with the paradoxical task of developing, alongside traditional notation for music performance, another notational sign system that can portray this "real" melody. This real melody might be indescribable in principle, at least not with a prescriptive notation that would enable its production or performance. As with graphic descriptions of computer and tape music, these structural descriptions cannot serve as tools for reproducing the music. The real melody, the same linear progression, can have several audible melodies. In other words, two or more traditional notations can in this new kinetico-semiotic analysis be reduced to one and the same structure. Kurth's method in his examples (mostly fugue themes by Bach) is to search for musical lexemes that illustrate the same figure of kinetic energy.

The usefulness of Kurth's theory lies in the fact that it is not overly limited to the harmonic parameter. Therefore the validity of his theory reaches beyond Western tonal music (the absolute limit for Schenker's method). The Kurthian kinetic energies can also apply to atonal, *concrète*, and computer music, although the principles of application would have to be redefined in each case.

Kurth also illustrates his theory with an example of two phases of motion in the ascending C major scale, the movements C4 to F4 and G4 to C5, with all their inner tensions: "In relation to c [C4] the tone f [F4] is in the strongest energetic relation. G [4] again is a new initial tone toward c [C5], and g aims at c as c aims at f; thus g, b, and f carry the strongest tension in this scale" (1922: 43). But how to interpret and describe semiotically all the inherent tensions of these scale tones, since they undoubtedly form the semiotic moment in the proper sense?

First, each tone assumes its meaning only through its function in a continuum of signs, a semiosphere or tonosphere. In Kurth's system, as in phonemic systems of some languages, individual tones have no meaning except in relation to other tones. Notice that the tonic C, the starting point, already represents a latent kinetic energy, an intent to ascend to the upper tonic, so that it is not a completely stable element; thus all nongoal tones in the narration represent a situation in which a subject has been disjuncted from an object (S ∨ O). We must define how far it has been disjuncted and how much energy these tones contain, that is, how much energy and will they have to re-conjoin to the object. One might depict the value of a leading tone B as (C)→→→B, with G represented by (C)→→G and F by (C)→F, in which the number of arrows indicate greater and smaller degrees of tension.

Tension is not only a horizontal, syntagmatic concept, but also a vertical phenomenon. Both horizontal and vertical movement bring about dissonances and their resolution to consonances. This can be explained by Greimasian concepts of disengagement/engagement: all musical disengagement in the spatial, temporal, and actorial senses means a formation of dissonance, which in turn requires a resolution or engagement. By what formal notation can we describe kinemes in the sense of both horizontal and vertical flows of energy? In Cogan and Escot's system, a number within a single circle denotes intervals as horizontal units; numbers within double circles, vertical units. We too can describe the intensity of tension by using a numerical scale; for instance: a consonance = 0, a mild dissonance = 1, a moderate dissonance = 2, a fairly strong dissonance = 3, and a striking dissonance = 4. In the horizontal sense, this scale would depict how close/far one is from an "object." Correspondingly, in vertical formations the intervals might be classified according to their degree of dissonance.[3] If p is a given tone or passage, insofar as it is a horizontal (melodic) unit representing a Kurthian *Linienzug* or *Bewegungsphase*, a symbol above it and a number represent the amount of melodic tension. Thus $\overset{\text{③}\rightarrow}{\text{p}}$ means that a tone or passage p has the tensional value of 3, a disengagement of three points from the state of rest and consonance (engagement). In the same way, an arrow and number placed under the symbol can show the tensional value of a vertical unit, in terms of the mean value of the intervallic tensions that the unit contains. This method of analysis clarifies the amount of tension inherent in a motif (pheme) or musical actor. Slightly transformed, the method might prove useful for investigating serial music, rhythm, dynamics, and timbre.

It is particularly noteworthy that music has tensions in two directions: horizontal (kinetico-melodic) and vertical (harmonic). Although a tension might resolve vertically, this need not mean a complete resolution of tension, which would require at the same time a similar dissolution of energy in the horizontal movement; and vice versa. A good illustration is provided by the bitonal music of Darius Milhaud's *Saudades do Brasil*: the superimposed F minor and F♯ minor of the "Botafogo" form constantly unresolved dissonances, at the same time as the kinetico-melodic lines resolve "normally." In other words, harmonic tension can be 0, while melodic tension is great: $\overset{\text{③}\rightarrow}{\underset{\underset{\downarrow}{\text{⓪}}}{\text{p}}}$

It is easy to see, then, how crucial the definition of both horizontal and vertical energy is to a complete semiotic analysis of a musical composition.

For Kurth the influence of kinetic energy reaches deep into chords. Often a potential energy occurs in the harmonies, which appears as latent, especially in dissonant altered chords. For example, in the chord E–G♯–B♭ (as derived from the triad E–G♯–B) occurring without preparation, the kinetic energy of the B♭ is experienced as inclined toward A. B♭ has thus parted from the B, and its kinetic energy is now directed toward A. Such altered chords carry within themselves a tension that demands resolution and that can appear without any preceding linear development (Kurth 1922: 74).

Semiotic analysis should reveal this latent tension by showing the progress of a chord's kinetic energy through all its phases of generation. The description of musical tension starts from the realization that the 'being' of music is the same as consonance or state of rest, whereas the 'doing' of music is the dissonance or contradiction demanding resolution or continued elaboration. Consonance and dissonance should be conceived of not only as properties of vertical harmony but also as linear, temporal formations. The notion of dissonance can even be extended to cover whole sections and movements. For instance, as a whole the storm movement in Beethoven's Pastoral Symphony represents "dissonance," musical action, in relation to which the entire last movement confirms the pastoral euphoria of F major. The same holds true for the relation between the first and third movements of the "Waldstein" Sonata. Therefore the Greimasian categories of S ∧ O and S ∨ O (subject conjuncted to or disjuncted from its object) can be interpreted in music in a broader sense, as consonance (subject possesses its object) and dissonance (subject lacks its object).

How can one distinguish between subject and object in a piece of music? In the state of consonance or 'being', subject and object form a syncretic entity; that is, in 'being' we do not experience music as a stage on which a subject moves while attempting to reach an object. It is rather in dissonance, 'doing', that we feel music lacking something and that its energy leaves us unsatisfied. What is missing can be felt as a disjuncted, sought-for object. But where is the subject who searches for this object? Is the subject a given part of the musical text in which this "something" is missing, as, for example, a dominant seventh chord awaiting resolution to a tonic? Would it thus not be more appropriate to speak of the way a subject appears in the music's kinetic energy, which from dissonance strives for a state of rest? That is, would the subject be the hidden element in music, the energetic impulse on a deep level, which determines the sounding, manifest reality of music? In the framework of a kinetico-energetic theory it can be difficult to speak of a discrete subject, since the very concept of energy seems to be subjectless. Of course in some music a subject appears as musical actor(s); but there is also deactorialized music, in which the problem of an absent subject arises.

Thus we arrive at the problem of the musical subject, or, in semiotic terms, to actoriality. Kurth opposes polyphonic, linear art to homophonic, classic melodics. At the same time, in my view, he accurately describes the birth of the whole concept of actoriality in Western art music. In Classical *lied* melodics, the multipart texture and the melody mask each other. The lines of the texture maintain rhythmic symmetry of accentuation and therefore end up as two-bar groups. So a two-bar, symmetric melodic-harmonic section is created in which other parts are subordinated to the melody. Kurth illustrates two-bar groups with an example from the Allegretto movement of Mozart's Piano Sonata in C major, K. 330 (Ex. 4.1). Two-bar grouping is the fundamental trait of Classical melodics and the basic manifestation of the actoriality and "rationality" of Western art music. Kurth believes that, in our music history, polyphonic linear development, which is free of two-bar periodization and accentuation, forms the great counterforce to actoriality. Nevertheless, in the phases of development of European rationality it was the two-bar melodic-harmonic entity that was assigned the task of carrying and representing the subject in music. This assignment marked a crucial epistemic change in Western music. Kurth bursts forth in eloquence when describing this epistemic shift (1922: 184–85):

> Whereas the polyphonic line was based on a mystical progress towards the distance, Classical melodics conceals an inner quality [*Innigkeit*] of an emotion in its expression. The *lied*-likeness is in many respects connected to the melodic language of all Classic art. Melodic expression is always (and not only with regard to vocal music) a "singing," "speaking" emotion of subjectivity . . . even when the expression goes far beyond the simple *lied* character in the adagio themes by Mozart or in the melodic language of Beethovenian thematic processes. . . . Nevertheless, we are always dealing with a "pathos" which forms the basis for the artistic expression of melody and which takes shape deep in human nature. . . . In the Classical work of art, the subjective expression, passion, atmosphere, personality always come to the foreground in an impression; with a Classical artist the characteristic features of his personality always come through first in the work, and only later do the basic traits of the period and style emerge. The older polyphonic art considered the manifestation of personal expression as profanity. The artistic language of a Classical man is freer, he problematizes feeling and passion. . . . The language of a Classical artist is always "confession." . . . Therefore the Classical period laid the foundation from which an unlimited and growing subjectivism could develop. . . .

Example 4.1. Ernst Kurth's illustration of two-bar groups in Mozart, Piano Sonata in C major, K. 330, mm. 9–16.

One could not better describe the emergence and development of actoriality in music. Kurth thereby connects a theory of musical subjects with the musical text itself, which manifests actoriality by use of two-bar symmetric-periodic actors. The birth of such actoriality in music cleared the way for narrativity, and actoriality formed so strong a model that any deviation from it meant alienation from the epistemes of European culture itself. Consider, for example, the so-called synthetic style in Sibelius's music, in which melodic lines are freed from the constraints of conventional *lied* melodics and follow "continuous and alternating mutuality of rising and relaxing developments" (Normet 1989: 137), thus producing ornamentation typical of *l'art nouveau*. This synthetic style was promptly condemned in Germany, where it was regarded as a weed to be cut away from the field of Classical tradition. This explains the unpopularity of Sibelius's music in central Europe and also accounts for many other reception-historical phenomena.

From the semiotic viewpoint, the strong connection of actoriality with a specific style period of Western art music might be viewed as a restriction that threatens the general validity of the whole theory. Yet we should first try to establish the basic manifestation of actoriality in our own musical tradition before we extend our definitions to cover other musical cultures.[4]

4.2 From Musical Subjects to Theme-Actors

To speak of time and space in music seems legitimate, but the mere mention of musical "actors" might sound mystical or at least problematic. Nevertheless, I believe that actorial analysis is possible within musical texts, as Ernst Kurth so strongly hinted. The concept of actant or actor comes from Russian Formalist Vladimir Propp, whose ideas were used by Greimas in his famous model of mythical actants: subject, object, sender, receiver, helper, and opponent (Greimas 1967: 180). Even these early concepts can serve as tools for music analysis, as I will show in the analysis of Chopin's *Polonaise-Fantaisie* (Chap. 6.1).

Only the first two actants, subject and object, remain in Greimas's later narratological model (1979: 124–25). There the basic activity of any narration is defined as that between a subject and an object or, more precisely, between two subjects, S1 and S2, and their 'doing' (F). A subject can be either conjuncted to $(S \wedge O)$ or disjuncted $(S \vee O)$ from an object of value. Furthermore, subjects S1 and S2 can act in such a way that one subject does something that causes the other to possess or to be deprived of the object. Any narration starts, according to Greimas, with these simple actions, and these actions are also relevant to the narrative analysis of musical texts. On a larger scale, actoriality in music is represented by all those features that render abstract musical structures as anthropomorphic.[5] Let us now explain what we understand by actorial analysis of music. I distinguish the following phases:

1. We observe whether a given musical text is oriented toward subject or object. In a "normal" case this orientation may be defined as conjunction (the subject possesses an object) or disjunction (the subject lacks an object). Conjunction creates a euphoric meaning-effect, disjunction a dysphoric one. Sometimes music can be purely subjective in character—*innig*, as the Germans say—without any objectal thing-likeness (*Dinglichkeit*). But music may also be like an "object," for example, in iconic portrayals of some phenomenon. In any case, we have two "negative" cases of a fundamental structure constituted by two terms, subject and object: "subject without an object" or "object without a subject."

2. We examine subject and object as such, that is to say, music *as* subject or object. All three categories (temporal, spatial, and actorial) can be used in these two cases. When we experience in a musical text the development of a subject and its transformation over time, we perceive a temporal subject. When

we attend to the place (topos/heterotopos) in which a musical subject moves and acts, we get a spatial subject. When we examine a subject as part of musical communication, we encounter an actorial subject, either within a musical enunciate in a metaphoric sense or in the act of musical enunciation (by composer, performer, listener).

The expression "actorial subject" is not tautological, since its opposition, "de-actorial subject," is a meaningful term. For example, in Schoenberg's *Erwartung*, the subject is de-actorialized and made "athematic" on the level of enunciate (*énoncé*) but is quite actorial, in the form of a soprano, on the level of enunciation (*énonciation*). This contradiction yields the effect of a de-actorialized subject. Correspondingly, the expression "de-actorialized object" is not tautological, because even its negation conveys a new meaning. For instance, an actorialized object such as the Grail motif in Wagner's *Parsifal*—a musical manifestation of the searched-for value object on the level of the enunciate—can interact with several other motifs in the musical action and thus become part of the actorial network of a musical text. In another example, the movements "Bydlo," "Baba-Yaga," and "Great Gate of Kiev" in Musorgsky's *Pictures at an Exhibition* are not only de-actorialized descriptions of certain objects but clear anthropomorphizations of those objects, objects that have been musically actorialized.

As a consequence of whether a subject is disjuncted from or conjuncted to an object, we obtain two kinds of subject: the subject of 'being' and the subject of 'doing'. The subject of 'being' is euphoric when it has an object in its possession. If it lacks an object, it is a dysphoric subject that represents 'not-being' and perhaps implies movement toward the subject of 'doing', which by its action attempts to regain the object. A subject in the state of 'not-doing', about to reach the object, is already a euphoric subject. The subjects of 'being' and 'doing' might also be called patient-subject and agent-subject respectively. The patient-subject experiences or is submitted to various emotional states and passions but does not act or do anything. The agent-subject, in turn, actively does or causes something.

3. The subject is the element of discourse that opens the dimension of modalities. Even the fundamental modalities of 'being' and 'doing' lead to a typology of subjects. When one says that 'being' determines or modalizes 'doing', we have a competent subject; when 'doing' determines 'being' we get a performing subject. To scrutinize closely the content and quality of these performances and competencies, one needs other, supplementary modalities that allow us to designate a subject who 'will', 'must', 'can', 'know', and 'believe'. The intentions and acts of an agent-subject, as well as the emotional states and passions of a patient-subject, can be more subtly defined as various combinations of these modalities. After establishing, on temporal, spatial, and actorial criteria, the fundamental features of the music in question and its nature as a Firstness or immediate quality (in Peirce's sense), the next step is to analyze more accurately this quality in terms of the modalities of these musical subjects.

4. A crucial methodological question that must be answered during this phase is: Where are the musical subjects? Are they in the music, the musical enunciate itself? If so, where exactly? Is the musical subject revealed, say, when the actorial category is most prominent? When the composer employs the actorial category in order to make a melody or theme emerge? Or can spatial manipulation, such as placement of musical material in a certain register, produce a musical subject? Or can some passage emerge temporally as so cogent and significant that we experience the presence of a musical subject? Or does the musical subject manifest as the general character of the whole composition, as a "semantic gesture," as Russian Formalists and Prague Structuralists suggested? If so, we would not be able to locate the musical subject at any particular place in a musical text. In this case the musical subject does not "live" at any exact "address" but is omnipresent in a musical text, just as everyone feels the presence of Tartuffe in the first two acts of Molière's play, though the character has not yet made his entrance.

If the subject is in no way concretely present in a text, then subjectivity represents a derived concept whose existence must be inferred from features of the text itself. Is the subject consequently a mental construct or cognitive unit? Is it the same as the composer's intention? If so, on what grounds is the subject the intention of a composer who has been privileged? Isn't the intention of a performer or a listener equally valuable for the discovery of such a subject? The whole concept of intention can be easily reduced to the intention of skill, knowledge, norm, idea, or belief, that is, to a composer's techniques, cognitive competence, submission to normative and stylistic constraints, will to self-expression, and attempts to persuade others, to make listeners believe in what she or he says musically.

Viatcheslav Medushewsky's (forthcoming) typology of musical subjects concerns precisely this kind of non-actorialized theory. When Medushewsky distinguishes the "motoric I" in Schumann and Scriabin, the "meditative I" in slow movements by Bach and Shostakovitch, and the "narrative I" in Bizet, and further speaks of lyrical, dramatic, and epic "I's," he means this kind of general and intentional musical subjectivity.

How does an intentional subject differ from an actorialized subject in music? Is this difference a projection of the eternal philosophical problem of mind/body onto musical semiotics? That is, does the "mind" correspond in music to the more or less inarticulate, aura-like subject, while the "body" takes shape as concrete sound entities with measurable properties, entities we meet in music and consider as actorial subjects and objects? Here we enter a confused, philosophical-conceptual jungle, in which one is tempted to react like a commonsense British empiricist: What is mind? No matter. What is matter? Never mind.

The crucial issue for a semiotician is the level of analysis and description on which to operate. Since all meaning arises from dialogue between researcher and his or her object, and is therefore clearly something we produce, we have to regard both kinds of musical subject, of enunciate and enunciation, and our talk about them as our own semiotic constructs, whose usefulness depends on the kind of knowledge we seek. Because we are intentional subjects as we listen to or produce music, we can seek signs or traces in music that were encoded by other subjects more or less similar to ourselves. As biographers, for example, we might discover a composer's diaries and directly read about his or her intentions, or at least what a composer wanted us to believe they were. This modal configuration is complex:

$$S1 \text{ v } F \ (S2 \ \wedge \ mO+), \text{ where } m = fS1 \text{ c, s, v, non-p, non-d}$$

The logical symbols are abbreviations of French terms for the modalities: v = *vouloir*, or 'will'; f = *faire*, or 'doing'; c = *croire*, or 'believe'; s = *savoir*, or 'knowing'; p = *pouvoir*, or 'can'; d = *devoir*, or 'must'.

The formula reads: Subject S1 (composer) wanted (v) to create (F) a situation in which a subject S2 (contemporary reader) gets ($\wedge$) a value object O (diaries), already a modalized entity (m), which the composer meant to serve as a positive (+) intentional object in order to convey the following: The object O+ reveals subject S1 as an active subject (fS), i.e., as a person composing or producing sonorous sign objects who wants to make the receiver S2 'believe' (c) and who reveals to us information (s) about himself and his actions; the composer expressly wants (v) this, whereas the object in question (the diary) does not contain the 'ability' (non-p) of this subject in the proper sense—that is, his or her abilities as a composer—but instead uses verbal discourse. The diary does not include any normative 'must' (it is non-d), since this case most closely represents autocommunication, though a secondary intention might be the subsequent discovery of these diaries. In that case, the three aforementioned "positive" modalities would be revealed to a future addressee; for example, in a case like Richard Wagner's autobiography, in which the normative 'must' is strong, since it constitutes the official image of the composer (subject S1) and is intended to be read by other people.

Diaries and other autobiographical documents bring insight into the "soul" or "mind" of a composer-subject (verifying this insight is another matter). But in most cases we have before us music written or produced with intentions about which we know nothing. This is the normal situation of music listening. If the music we listen to has any subject in front of or behind it, we must be able to perceive, experience, and infer that subject from the sonic design and according to our own competence. In other words, we run the risk that the subject we have found in the music is none other than ourselves.[6]

Music always has subject and object somewhere, just as it always has "sound" and "sense" (Lévi-Strauss 1971: 578–79). Hence we can experience true spiritual adventures with a music alien to us, whose signification we attempt to grasp by constructing subjects for it. The "objectal" nature of such a music is always easier to explain. We feel that in this kind of music the subject is absent; for example, in the famous interpretations of Sibelius by Akeo Watanabe and the Tokyo NHK symphony orchestra, despite the musicians' high artistic qualities, the modalization of the music is strange to Finns, because in our way of performing we do not recognize those modalities of 'will' and 'can' which we believe the musical subjects carrying them should convey (however much this "difference" from supposed "authenticity" might fascinate us).

A musical subject in the intentional sense is perhaps nothing but the sum of modalities. A musical subject is perhaps the very factor that integrates these modalities. On the other hand, we know that not all the modalities are compatible.[7] For example, Watanabe's interpretations might contain all the modalities presupposed by the music itself, but they do not appear in the right proportions and quantities. In other words, one has to account for such aspectual semes as insufficient/excessive, beginning/enduring/terminating, accomplished/nonaccomplished, and so on. Thus when we ponder the problem of musical subjects we have to introduce more and more concepts which are meaningful and possible only if we suppose that there is a subject that supports and carries those concepts.

This brings us to the crux of our speculations on the musical subject. Is it only an intellectual excuse? Does an intentional musical subject exist only in order to justify our semiotical-conceptual network, and ultimately the whole generative course? We resort to the concept of musical subject as a high-level cognitive principle which we must postulate in order to get the whole mechanism of musical discourse to function. Yet this cannot be taken as proof of the existence of musical subjects any more than the reasoning of the medieval scholastic philosopher proved the existence of God: "The concept of God includes His perfection. Such a thing that does not exist is not perfect. Therefore God must exist." On such reasoning we would establish the existence of musical subjects by first assuming that there must be certain mechanisms functioning in music (such as spatial-temporal-actorial shifters, isotopies, modalities). We would infer that these mechanisms cannot operate without a musical subject that launches them. But despite the doubt cast by these philosophical reflections, we may content ourselves with the fact that the concept of musical subject is obviously useful to us, in both the intentional and the actorial sense.

What is the connection between the intentional and the actorial subject? The Russian Formalists taught that the subject of an enunciate (utterance) is not the same as the subject of the enunciation (uttering). Musorgsky as a living man, as a psychological subject, is quite different from the musical-actorial subject in his songs, operas, and instrumental works. Neither is Musorgsky the real man the same as Musorgsky the composer; this is a basic truth taught by the structuralists. Nevertheless, *tout se tient*: there must be some correlation between these two aspects of discourse.

In concrete semiotical analyses, some of which follow in Part Two, I have tried to show how the inner narrator of a composition creates the musical shape and moves the musical actors,[8] like an actor behind a puppet in the Japanese *Bunraku* theatre. Put another way, it is the intentional subject emerging from the cooperation between composer, performer, and listener, and living in the no-man's-land between them, who is the subject properly speaking and who programs musical actors on the textual level. This subject places musical theme-actors in different narrative situations: one as a sender, the other as a receiver, one as an subject, the other as object, some in the role of opponent, some in the figures of Battle, Return, Victory, Destruction, or Glorification.

Here end our preliminary speculations on musical actoriality. In the analyses in Part Two of this volume we shall have occasion for further speculation, not just on actoriality, but also on the other categories and processes of our generative model. Nevertheless, the analyses that follow aim primarily to illuminate the music in question, at the same time as they provide more material for elaboration and modification of the theory. To this end, and because the model developed out of a chronological approach to these musical texts, the analyses are arranged by style period and not in theoretical "steps."

II

Analyses

V

SEMIOSIS OF THE CLASSICAL STYLE
BEETHOVEN'S "WALDSTEIN"

Beethoven's "Waldstein" Sonata, Op. 53, is a central text of German culture. By means of the generative course, we shall investigate the first movement and see how modalities emerge from preceding phases of generation, that is, from isotopies and disengagements/engagements.

In Beethoven's case, it would seem possible to formulate a modal grammar expressly in connection with the analysis of musical actors.[1] As musical actors I regard certain motifs or themes which in Beethoven are clearly distinguished from the musical discourse surrounding them. In his time it was not at all uncommon to think of music in actorial terms. The eighteenth-century music theorist Heinrich Koch compared the antecedent and consequent of a musical phrase to the subject and predicate of a sentence. And Joseph Riepel, another theorist of the day, developed an actorial terminology for describing the hierarchical relations of chords in a key: tonic as "landowner," dominant as "overseer," subdominant as "day laborer"(in Ratner 1980: 36, 40).[2]

A basic hypothesis of the present analysis, one which made me select only the first movement of the "Waldstein," is that a musical actor does not disappear "from the stage" even though it is not "speaking," just as theatre performers in dialogue do not disappear when the speaker changes. On the contrary, the actors remain present throughout the discourse, but *in absentia*, as destinatees who immediately interpret and respond to the utterance of their interlocutor. What happens in music corresponds to theatrical communication: a musical theme-actant might disappear from the score at moments when its opposing theme occurs in another register, but it does not disappear from the listener's mind.

Although music is basically a linear art of time, it can create the effect of superimposed and simultaneous levels of musical action, much like Bakhtin's concept of "polyphonic consciousness" in the novel (1970). A quick search finds examples illustrating this effect: the beginning of the Allegro movement of Haydn's Piano Sonata in E♭ major, Hob. XVI: 49; the chorale versus the consequent phrase in the upper register of Chopin's Scherzo in C♯ minor; the theme and arpeggiated-triad figure in the third movement of Schumann's C major Fantasy, where the triad always seems to cut across the melodic course, creating the impression of two superimposed levels (see mm. 34–37); and the beginning of Beethoven's "Waldstein," where two motifs, each in a different register, "fight" each other. They alternately modalize each other and follow a certain narrative program, constituting a narrative function, in Propp's sense (1958).

One must also consider the music's spatial and temporal structures. Yet a musical analysis that stops with these would be like a review of a play that critiques the scenery and stage positions but ignores the dramatic course of events, the identity of the actors, what they said, what they did—in other words, what really happened. My objective is to depict *was es eigentlich gewesen ist* in music—the alternation between 'being' and 'doing', tension and rest, dissonance and consonance in the broadest sense of these terms—and to specify that activity in a proper metalanguage.

When the object of analysis is a musical text representing sonata form, we can distinguish among the following *topoi*: 1. Thematic areas, places in which theme-actors move. Thematic areas are to a great extent determined by spatial-temporal criteria and characterized by certain modalities. Within and "upon" these isotopies, theme-actors move with their particular modal contents. Sometimes there can be musical thematic areas without any actors, and sometimes the force that catalyzes the musical motion lies in the juxtaposition of a theme-actor with its modalities and the modalities of the surrounding area. 2. Transitions between thematic areas. Transitions maintain the processive aspect of music. The motion represented by transitions can be analyzed into semiotic aspectual categories such as inchoativity/terminativity, perfectiveness/imperfectiveness, punctuality/durativity. The fundamental modality of transitions is 'becoming'. 3. Developments constitute areas of musical action whose modality is 'doing'.

How does musical 'doing' differ from 'becoming'? 'Doing' suggests a stronger activity than mere 'becoming'. The 'doing' sections must contain ample musical substance, such as *savoir*, other modalities and their contrasts—in short, events which produce a feeling that something is happening. One may well ask, What are the criteria for a musical event? Doesn't an event or action always require someone to whom something happens (a patient-actor) and someone who produces the action (the agent-actor)? On this view, the concept of action would be linked specifically to the actorial category. Yet sometimes a musical event can arise simply through sharp contrasts in spatial-temporal dimensions, such as deceleration/acceleration of tempo or abrupt changes of register. In some works the mere alternation between 'being' and 'doing', along with their indexical connectives, creates the action, as occurs in the first movement of Bruckner's Ninth Symphony, Musorgsky's *Pictures at an Exhibition*, and Magnus Lindberg's *Kraft*. Sometimes the distinctions between 'being' and 'doing' have been deliberately obscured, as in the late symphonic style of Sibelius. We shall now segment the first movement of the "Waldstein" into the following isotopies (see Baur 1985):

Exposition (mm. 1–86)
First thematic area
(mm. 1–13): C
Second transition
(mm. 14–34): C → E
Third thematic area
(mm. 34–50): E

Second transition (mm. 50–73): E

Codetta or closing theme (mm. 74–86): E

Development (mm. 87–155)

Recapitulation (mm. 156–249): C → A → C
Coda (mm. 249–302): D♭ → G → C

Example 5.1. Beethoven, Op. 53, mvt. I, mm. 1–13: actors *a, b, c, d.*

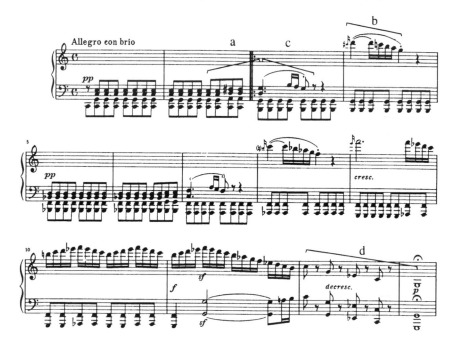

Exposition: First Thematic Area or Isotopy and First Transition (mm. 1–34)

SPATIAL DIMENSION

This section leans strongly toward the flatted key area, which in our terminology signifies a *débrayage* (disengagement) in the non-tensional direction. It is particularly surprising that the second phrase begins in B♭ major. The transition compensates for this non-tensional move by a complementary ascending modulation, C–D–A–B (V/E), to the key of the second theme.

These observations concern the inner spatiality. With regard to the outer spatiality, attention is drawn to the juxtaposition of two registers, two octaves apart, which unite at the end of this isotopy. The deliberate creation of a "gap" in the tonal space at the very beginning of the piece provides a strong implication for further developments. The second theme, among other things, fills this gap; similarly, the usage of the entire range of the keyboard, in the last movement, fills this gap with arpeggiated chords.

A further feature of the inner spatiality is the acceleration of harmonic rhythm over the dominant in mm. 9–11. This acceleration may be why August Halm, in his *Von zwei Kulturen der Musik*, chose the beginning of this sonata to illustrate the phenomenon of *Steigerung* (intensification), or semiotically, tension and its growth (Halm 1916: 107–17). Halm interprets this *Steigerung* using modal concepts and distinguishes between two kinds of intensification: 1. growth of tension through greater distance, *débrayage* (or disengagement) from the tonic, as exemplified by the harmonies C–G–B♭ in mm. 1–6 and by C–G–D minor in the transition, mm. 14–19; and, paradoxically, 2. growth of tension through *embrayage* (or engagement), harmonic motion toward the tonic. The latter can be illustrated by extended pedal tones on the dominant (typical of Beethoven as well as Bruckner), which Halm calls *vermehrte Ladung*, "multiplied storing" or "charge" in the sense of electrical energy (1916: 110): a great dominant construction that sounds more and more dissonant, through prolongation and withholding of resolution becoming more and more tensional, signifies the growth of a forward-driving, energetic force.

But when a tonic is prolonged as a triumphant homecoming and expression of definitive completion, emphasizing the category of perfectiveness, then attainment of an inner, spiritual consonance ('being') is involved, rather than a focus on the consonant aural quality of the tonic itself. These two cases produce intensification by means of an *embrayage*, particularly that of inner spatiality. As Halm puts it, the increase of a certain constant, whether it be dominant or tonic, effects a rise in tension. Precisely this type of growth in tension through *embrayage* occurs over the dominant pedal in mm. 9–11.

In contrast, the transition realizes growth of harmonic tension through *débrayage*. Halm suggests that the transition represents a "*crescendo*" and a "*decrescendo*" in the harmonic action, but not in the modalities of 'willing' and 'obligation'. If one compares the first isotopy with the subsequent transition, thus accounting for the temporal paradigm of musical memory, this increased tension comes clearly into the foreground. Halm's concepts of *Steigerung auf Distanz* (intensification by distancing) and *Nahsteigerung* (intensification by drawing closer) correspond to our *débrayage/embrayage* of inner spatiality. This is in fact the same idea suggested by Victor Zuckerkandl (1959: 34–35), who notices that, in the ascending D minor scale, the motion from D to A is felt as an increase of tension—Halm's *Steigerung auf Distanz*, our tension through *débrayage*. But as the motion continues upward from A to D, completing the octave, we sense a decrease in tension but at the same time an intensification. The latter motion exemplifies Halm's *Nahsteigerung*, our tension through *embrayage*, a tensing motion toward the tonic. Simply put, the entire process entails movement away from tonic toward the dominant, then back toward the tonic. In Zuckerkandl the arrows pointing in opposite directions, D4→ A4 ←D5, illustrate this process (1959: 35).

We can measure *débrayage/embrayage* by assigning numerical values based on the circle of fifths to various points in relation to their distance from a tonic.[3] In this way we can evaluate with some precision the degree of tension for the inner spatiality of each musical section. Motion toward the left side of the circle (flat keys) is indicated by minus signs, motion to the right (sharp keys) by plus signs. Numbers show distance from the tonic in terms of fifths in either direction, and asterisks signal parallel major or minor. The following gives *débrayage/embrayage* values for this movement's first isotopy and subsequent transition: m. 1: 0; m. 2: +2; mm. 3–4: +1; m. 5: -2; m. 6: V of -1; m. 7: -1; m. 8: *-1; mm. 9–11: +1; m. 12: *0; m. 13: +1; m. 14: 0; m. 15: +2; mm. 16–17: +1; m. 18: *+2; m. 19: V of +3; mm. 20–21: *+3; m. 22: V of +5; mm. 23, 28: +5; and +4; mm. 29–34: +5.

We next examine the outer spatiality. Fig. 5.1 shows the abrupt shifts between registers C4 and C6, especially in mm. 1–10. The piece begins with a disengagement of the external spatiality: the dislocation caused by centrifugal tendencies results in a detached and disjunctive placement of the musical material. The category centripetal/centrifugal aptly characterizes the outer spatiality, where centripetal motion equals engagement and centrifugal movement equals disengagement. In this case, the shifts in outer spatiality parallel the growth/decay of tension in the inner spatiality.

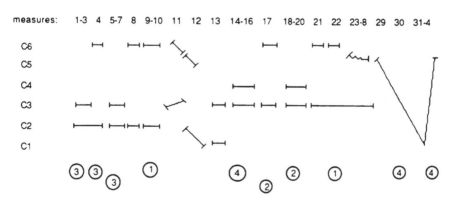

Figure 5.1. Beethoven, Op. 53, mvt. I, outer spatiality of mm. 1–34.

We can determine similar tension values for the external spatiality, in order to provide a basis for comparison with the inner spatiality. The outer spatiality can also be digitalized with discrete units. As a criterion for the degree of centrifugal tendency one might consider only the alternation of different registers, and not the fact that two extreme registers are in use. If, for example, a composition employs the same registers throughout—say, the melody remains near C6 and the accompaniment at C2—its centrifugal tendencies are weak. But if extreme registral shifts take place, a centrifugal effect strikes one immediately. Numerical values can be assigned to every change of register, depending on the degree of shift. Let us assign the value 3 to the leap from C3 to C6 in m. 4 of the "Waldstein," signifying a leap of three octaves. The value 0 represents mm. 1–3, a case in which the register does not fluctuate radically; other values are shown in circles at the bottom of Fig. 5.1, at points where registral changes occur.

One could measure the intensity of disengagement or centrifugal tendencies in a musical segment by simply adding up the values of registral shifts; the greater the number the greater the disengagement through centrifugal motion. This method of measurement might be refined by distinguishing between registral shifts occurring by leap or by step, since one experiences a scalewise shift as less abrupt than a direct leap. One must assume also that each musical text, and sometimes a particular section, has unique outer-spatial norms in relation to which even the slightest deviation represents a centrifugal tendency. Such a registral norm may remain completely independent of the fulcrum (tonic) of inner, tonal space. By simply measuring changes in the outer spatiality, it would be difficult to infer the norm of a particular musical universe. Would it be the register used most frequently? The register in which the section or isotopy in question ends? It is impossible to decide by only these facts, since temporal and actorial categories can also influence outer spatiality.

For instance, the unity created through actorial similarities (discussed at length below) between the two registral extremes mitigates the effect of abrupt spatial disengagement in the first four bars of the "Waldstein." The opening passage introduces a symmetrical, four-bar actor typical of the rationality of the Classic period, with simple scale motifs making up the musical substance of this actor. On the other hand, the centrifugal tendency of m. 9 increases through the subsequent implied acceleration effected by the use of smaller time units, signifying growth of tension in the temporal domain. Likewise, at the end of the transition the temporal disengagement combines with the extremely heightened tension (+5 value) of the inner spatiality. Thus even though the outer spatiality in mm. 23–28 remains constant, an area of great intensity arises through a centripetal movement of engagement. The interaction and engagement/disengagement of spatial, temporal, and actorial dimensions is also affected by the modalities, which we shall soon discuss in connection with actoriality.

TEMPORAL DIMENSION

The outer temporality presents few obstacles to semiotic analysis and can be described to a great extent by a rhythmic study of the piece. In music generally, meter and tempo instructions (*allegro, adagio, vivace,* and the like) require expression of a basic pulse. Meter and tempo combine to form temporal "cultural units" (see Eco 1976: 67). For example, both listener and performer understand intuitively what an indication such as *tempo di minuetto* requires, and they further relate this tempo to gestures typical of that dance. Meter and tempo together govern the basic pulse, in relation to which accelerations/decelerations are disengagements, shifts out of the normal rhythm of the piece.[4]

In his novel *Muuttumisia* (Changes), Finnish-Swedish author Oscar Parland (1966) provides the first movement of the "Waldstein" with an interesting verbal interpretant that emphasizes the "drumming" character of the persistent eighth-note motif. Also concerning the outer temporality or rhythm of the piece, Charles Rosen writes: "The pulsating energy in this work is perhaps its most remarkable innovation" (1976: 398). Yet he admits that "Description in purely rhythmic terms, however, will not do." In the following discussion we shall try to make more precise the features of outer temporality mentioned by these writers and consider the inner temporality as well.

The first isotopy and transition contain similar programs of disengagement through rhythmic acceleration. The sixteenth-note figuration increases in the right hand (mm. 8–11), and at the end of the transition it dominates the registers in both hands (mm. 23–30). This temporal acceleration no doubt generates much of the *Steigerung* which August Halm believed permeates this sonata. The outer temporality can be measured in terms of changes in rhythmic time units: a plus sign denotes acceleration through temporal diminutions, a minus sign deceleration, both in relation to the basic time unit (though the basic time unit of a piece or section may sometimes be as difficult to determine as it is to determine the norm of the outer spatiality). Degrees of change in the external temporality can be accounted for in terms of measure units. If we assign the value 0 to the drumming motif, with its eighth-note rhythm as the basic time unit of the first isotopy and transition, we get the following description: mm. 1–2: 0; m. 3: 0, +1/8, meaning that on one eighth-note of the bar there occurs an acceleration of the basic time unit; m. 4: 0, +1/4; mm. 5–6: 0; m. 77: 0, +1/8; mm. 8–9: 0, +1/4; mm. 10–11: +1; m. 12: -1; m. 13: -3 (plus fermata); mm. 14–30: +1; mm. 31–34: 0.[5]

As regards the inner temporality of this section, we should, as does Halm, account for the paradigms of musical memory and expectation as well as their influence on musical form, since the temporal strategy of a musical text emerges from the cofunctioning of these two factors. By temporal strategy we mean the order in which events are introduced, how they relate to each other on the time axis, and how sections form a temporal fulcrum, which is retained in the memory and to which all subsequent intonations are compared.[6]

Halm asserts that the opening major chords, C–G–B♭, provide the memory with a paradigm to which are compared the C–G–D minor of the transition's beginning. Heard against the background memory of the former series of chords, the latter series represents an intensification: It "wirkt als Steigerung, wir finden uns da nach vorwärts fahrend, getragen und schon gehoben" (Halm 1916: 109). Halm also points out that, in relation to C major, D minor belongs to the "lower" side of the circle of fifths, as relative minor of the subdominant. Yet we experience a slight friction between G major and D minor, produced by the tritone dissonance B/F. This is a livelier friction than that produced by the G major/B♭ major chords. Thus of the two chord pairs, the G major/D minor friction generates more catalyzing energy. Finally, Halm says: "Above all what is involved is the comparison and measuring against that which has been heard earlier, and the impression brought about by [the comparison's] allowing us to experience an intensification [of tension]" (ibid.).

Such comparison makes possible the analysis of music's inner temporality, or, as it is called in linguistics, aspectualization: aspectual semes of inchoativity/terminativity, punctuality/durativity, perfectiveness/ imperfectiveness, excessivity/insufficiency, all of which depend on inner temporality.[7] Furthermore, inner temporality yields and is yielded by the modalization process of music. In our discussion of modalities below, we shall return to matters of inner temporality.

ACTORIAL DIMENSION

Actorial relationships remain quite clear throughout the first movement of the "Waldstein." Kurth states that the masters of the Classic style created the foundation of musical actoriality and that symmetry of phrasing (two-, four-, eight-bar) and other formal units enacts an archetype of Western rationality (1922: 149–51). This symmetry also serves as a legisign in the thematic-actorial structure of sonata-form pieces.

Musical actoriality presupposes certain general traits related to the concept of theme, such as distinct features, relatively simple chordal accompaniment, and predictable length. These features characterize musical actors—musical subjects that influence and perform within the musical discourse. Halm says:

> Every logical beginning of a theme, that is, every germ capable of musical life, contains its own ideal continuation, and also a great amount of potential growth. A composer's intention, his anticipating will, his attempt to determine the nature, size, and quality of a composition are, moreover, influential here—but only to a certain extent; and [these intentions] do not have unlimited power: they influence like the climate and the country: they can favor or damage [1916: 243–44].

Halm implies with this statement that the subject (the composer) and the subject's intentions might differ entirely from the subject of the musical enunciation. The last might appear as an autonomous actor or perhaps as several actors.

As for the actors, we must examine not only the inner qualities that Halm emphasizes, such as symmetry and ability to grow. Relations among these actors are also of primary significance. "The Waldstein also establishes its themes in a genetic order; that is, they appear to be born one from another even more than in Haydn's technique of thematic derivation, although the method is not very different" (Rosen 1976: 397). We shall first categorize the principal actors of the "Waldstein" according to Greimas's actantial model (1979: 3–6), which designates opponent-/helper-actants, and patient-/agent-actants (refer to Ex. 5.1).

The first motif, a, is a virile catalyzing agent that possesses a strong inner will toward dissonance. This main theme-actor contains a doubly tensional moment. It begins on the third degree of the scale, which has a tensional, leading-tone urge toward upward melodic motion. The ascent goes beyond expectations, thus following a seme of excessivity: E3 proceeds not to F3 but to F♯3, which has a strong leading-tone quality that strives for and demands further resolution to G3.

In a rhythmic sense, actor a likewise contains a double tension followed by a resolution. At first prolonged as part of the drumming accompaniment, a remains on E3 for the duration of a whole note. The faster motion of two eighth notes on F♯3 leading to G3 then compensates for this prolongation. This G3 serves as both the end of the first motif and the beginning of the next. In a small-scale rhythmic sense, the shape of actor a is repeated by the next motif, actor c : prolonged tone, two sixteenth notes, final tone. With regard to pitch, motif c seeks a return to balance by twining around G3. Still, the listener does not experience motif c as a satisfactory resolution of the tension of E–F♯–G in actor a.

Next, another motif, b, sounds in the upper register, as a reminiscence of or an answer to actor c , though it is condensed into a relatively brief reply. At this stage of the piece motif b is clearly a patient-actor, subordinate to the main actor, with as yet no life of its own. But the combined narrative program of the first isotopy and the transition produces a *Steigerung* that transforms patient-actor b into a domineering agent-actor that pushes actor c from its throne. Actor b leads the narration back to G3 (opening register) in m. 13. After the preceding events this G is ambivalent: because it forms part of a descending arpeggiation of the parallel-minor tonic chord, the G3 of m. 13 does not necessarily project a dominant quality. The contractual relation between the agent and patient themes nevertheless proves very strong. For when motifs a and c repeat over the chords B♭–C₇–F (mm. 6–7), the patient/agent theme b shifts back to the opening spatial dimension (m. 8) as a reflection of its former self. Analogous to *Stimmtausch*, here we have *Rollentausch*, an exchange of actantial roles: the agent of the beginning turns into a patient, and the patient of the beginning becomes an agent. In the next isotopy (mm. 35–49) the descending-scale motif of actor b will play an even more important role by providing the main action of that section. There it enjoys the euphoria of E major and becomes a symmetric, self-reflexive, and narcissistic second theme, all in accord with the 'must' (*devoir*) of sonata form.

Notice that Beethoven breaks and destabilizes rhythmic-symmetric actoriality in order to create the atmosphere of an artificial *inachèvement* (unfulfillment) or *imperfectivité*. The opening four-bar phrase is already asymmetric in the actorial sense, because actors a and b occupy three bars and actor c only one. Yet with harmonies of I (mm. 1–2) and V (mm. 3–4) the inner spatiality emphasizes symmetry (2 + 2). The eight-bar period is incomplete, however, since the consequent phrase ends in m. 13 (where it introduces a new actor, d), creating asymmetrical phrasing having the global form of 4 + 4 + 5. This five-bar extension expands considerably in mm. 22–34 of the transition, and it is precisely with such expansions that Beethoven and other late Classicists radically enlarged sonata form: in the transition the relations are 4 + 4 + 13!

In sum, we distinguish among four different actors: a, the ascending-scale motif; b, the descending-scale motif; c, the returning-note motif; and d, the arpeggiated-triad motif (of importance later on). Roland Barthes's observations on the economic organization of the Classic literary text (1964: 206) apply to this musical text: the first movement of the "Waldstein" constitutes an economy in which all the actors are employed to fill different actantial roles, and no actorial substance is wasted by occurring only once. We shall in fact exempt the entire second theme from this actorial analysis. Because of its serenity of 'will' and balanced phrasing, the second theme instigates no further development and no further action. Nor does it divide into smaller musemes resulting from musical 'knowing' (*savoir*). Thus in the universe of the piece the second theme represents 'being'.

Schenkerians often neglect actoriality by overemphasizing the importance of tonal, inner-spatial dimensions. In fact, the entire problematics of thematicity vs. tonality can be reinterpreted semiotically as the privileging of spatiality to the exclusion of actoriality, and vice versa. Yet musical actors and their modalizations strongly determine the form of a musical work. How can we otherwise explain deviations from the ideal type; for example, the unexpected, additional development sections in the recapitulation and coda of the "Waldstein."

Our actorial analysis will proceed as follows: Select the main actors of the text; indicate the modal content of each actor; and search for actors that belong to other actors' spheres of influence; that is, discover the ways actors modalize each other through their placement in various spatial-temporal fields. One can presuppose that in a Classical text modal balance will prevail. For example, if a certain actor has a strong 'will to do', or striving for dissonance and for tension, then the following actor will probably submit to or be subdued by the former actor's 'will' and therefore represent 'will to be' or at least 'will not to do'.

The first isotopy introduces the four principal actors, bracketed in Ex. 5.1. With respect to 'willing', the actors produce a relatively balanced situation which can be mapped onto a semiotic square, shown in Fig. 5.2. Actor a, with the energy and tension emitted by scale degrees $\hat{3}$ and $\sharp\hat{4}$, projects dissonance and 'will to do'. Its 'knowing how to do' likewise arises from the ascending tendency of the third degree of the scale. Being familiar with Beethoven's technique of thematic elaboration, we expect the *savoir* of this motif to be powerful enough to cover the entire movement and to have the capacity to generate further modalities. This capacity is latent in the museme E–F♯–G, comprising the tensest scale degrees. Of the seven available tones of the scale of G major forming the background of actor a, this museme uses the tones that best project the modality of 'will to do'.

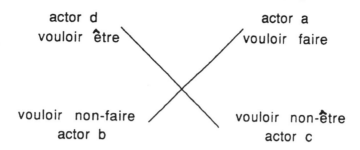

Figure 5.2. Beethoven, Op. 53, mvt. I, 'willing' of actors
a-d projected onto semiotic square.

In order to assess 'must', we first establish an actor's context and actantial role. The leading-tone action of actor *a* undeniably fulfills one requirement of that motif's *devoir*. If, however, one thinks of "normal" main themes of sonatas (as in Beethoven's Op. 2 no. 1 or Mozart's Sonata in B♭ major, K. 570), the museme of *a* runs counter to the expected 'must' of sonata form. And it is neither conventional nor necessary for a Classical sonata to begin with the kind of extraordinary intonation that opens the "Waldstein." Therefore we assign to actor *a* the values of 'not-must be' (*non-devoir faire*).

We must also scrutinize the modality of 'can'. This modality relates to the technical realization, dynamics, idiomatic nature, potential for fulfillment, and general musical effectiveness of a passage. The first four bars of the "Waldstein" exhibit a high degree of 'can'. This 'can' is not caused by the museme E–F♯–G, but by the rhythmic drumming motif and that motif's placement in an unusual bass register (compare the opening of Clementi's B♭ major Piano Sonata and the Allegro of the overture to the *Magic Flute*). In other words, actor *a* draws its modality of 'can' directly from its spatial-temporal isotopy.

Actor *c*, a rhythmic diminution of actor *a*, derives its 'knowing' from, and is therefore subordinate to, the latter. The modalities of 'must' and 'can' in actor *c* also remain under the influence of actor *a*, and according to the principle of contiguity must be considered the same as in the preceding actor of the musical syntagm. Intervallically, however, *c* produces its own unique modal content. By returning to its point of departure, G3, actor *c* seems to project the modality of 'will to being'. But since the point of departure/return is the fifth degree of the scale, *c* cannot represent the definitive 'being' of the piece. Actor *c* must instead represent 'willing not-being', as depicted on our semiotic square: *c* desires not to remain on G, the temporary resting place attained by the 'must' (signified by the leading-tone resolutions) of the preceding actor.

Actor *b* is obviously antithetic to actor *a* and seems to answer the "question" posed by the latter. Furthermore, *b* partially derives from actor *c*: *b* contains the last three notes of *c* (B–A–G), but in a different register. Altogether this descending motif works against tension but not to the complete dissolution of energy, since actor b (because of its placement two octaves higher) does not dispel the 'will to do' of actor a. Rather, b enacts the principle of 'willing not-doing', the contrary of all *Steigerung*. But even though this actor's kinetic energy at first impresses one as weak, b soon assumes the leading role and rules over the texture in mm. 9–11. As for its 'knowing', actor b, another scalar motif, derives from actor a (as did actor c), though the descending motion of b produces a detensional effect. Because it descends from $\hat{2}$ down to $\hat{5}$ (the goal of both a and c), b conveys no new information and thus remains subordinate to a with respect to *savoir*. One might also interpret the chromatic, chaconnelike, descent of the bass in mm. 1–11 as a transformation of b. This would not, however, change its derivative *savoir* content. By ending on the dominant, b obeys the *devoir* principle regarding symmetrical main themes, fulfills its necessary obligation, and thus receives a positive value for that modality. The high degree of 'can' in actor b comes directly from the sudden shift of register that produces a feeling of surprise.

Actor d, the arpeggiated-triad motif (mm. 12–13), completes the section and represents 'will to being', or the will-to-consonance. Actor d does not, however, provide a complete state of rest, or 'being' (C major tonic in root position). Instead the parallel minor chord appears, indicating that the process must continue and providing the passage with the aspectual seme of imperfectiveness. At the same time, actor d refers to the flatted key areas and thus to a tonal field with a 'not-doing' (*non-faire*) quality. Later in this universe (mm. 23–30, left hand especially), d moves center stage, again to provide terminativity/imperfectivity. At the very end of the movement, arpeggiated triads are rejected at the point (m. 300) where one expects an appearance of actor d. Instead a strong cadence occurs (mm. 300–302), reinforced with thick chords in contrary motion, to provide true closure through the aspectual seme of terminativity/perfectivity. Actor d is poor in 'know' (musical substance or informational value), though its 'can' is strengthened by triple octaves. Yet Beethoven does not place the *sforzando* indication at the beginning of this motif, but at the climax of the final repetition of actor b. Instead, d receives a *decrescendo* marking that produces a tendency to 'being'.

Modalization concerns not only musical actors but larger textual units as well. The first section introduces only the main actors, yet they provide abundant modal variety: none of the actors are redundant in the sense of repeating the same modalities. Therefore the first section does not in the least project pure 'being' or pure 'doing', though the small narrative program in mm. 1-3 is based largely on the performance of the tensest actors, a and b. (Recall that a was in the privileged position of opening the discourse and that its *faire* value at that point was very great, but b soon took the lead and by the end of the first isotopy had become the dominant actor.) We can now summarize the analytic results of the modal qualities of each actor: Actor a: 'will do', 'know to do', 'must not do', and 'can do' (*vouloir faire, savoir faire, devoir non-faire*, and *pouvoir faire*), owing to the background of this actor and its *pouvoir* caused by rhythm and register.[8] Actor *b*: 'will not-do', 'know to do' (the musical substance corresponds to the nature of its appointed task and will, in this case, 'will not-do'), 'must do', 'can do'. Actor *c*: 'will not be', 'know not-to-be', 'can be'. Actor *d*: 'will be', 'know not-to-be', 'must not-be'. In this last case the degree of information and of obedience to norm conflicts with the other modal values.

The beginning of the first transition (mm. 14–34) repeats the opening of the first isotopy, except here the bass line follows the modality of 'will to do' because of its higher registral placement, its ascending motion, and its move toward sharp key areas. We soon encounter a texture derived from actor *d*. Previously the actantial role of *d* was to close the first section, and the same holds true in this passage. The arpeggiations in the left hand, and finally in both hands, provide a sense of closure that lacks the seme of perfectiveness, since in terms of inner and outer spatiality we have progressed a good distance from the beginning. With its juxtaposition of homophonic melody against arpeggiated chordal accompaniment, m. 23 almost convinces us that the secondary theme area has begun, or at least that an area of thematic significance has arrived. But when the right-hand figurations continue into m. 24 and beyond, we find our initial impression of m. 23 to be illusory, 'appearing not-being' (*paraître non-être*). In the bars following m. 23 the degree of 'can' reaches high levels because of the virtuosic, chromatic right-hand figuration.

The first transition contains low 'knowing' levels, for it simply reintroduces the materials of actors *a*, *b*, and *d*, without further developing those materials in any particularly original or innovative way.[9] Measures 31–34 display an interesting modal combination: a strong 'will to do', since the musical substance originates from actor *a*; and on the other hand, 'can not-being' (*pouvoir non-être*) in which the degree of 'can' is high. The staccato arpeggiated octaves form an obstruction, a movement "against-something," in Charles Morris's terms (1956), as if the section were striving to prevent a 'being' which nevertheless must be. In other words a strong feeling of 'must' is involved, and this in turn leads to 'must be' in the next isotopy, or, in traditional terms, the second theme.

Exposition: Second Thematic Area or Isotopy (mm. 35–49)

SPATIAL DIMENSION

With regard to inner spatiality, this section moves within E major. Consequently this area contains a high degree of disengagement (+4) in relation to the main isotopy of C major. As to the outer spatiality, we remain in the middle register, hands close together, without gaps in the tonal space, all of which makes this a particularly engaged section.

TEMPORAL DIMENSION

The outer temporality divides this section in two. Dominating the texture is a dactyllic pattern that is answered in the consequent phrase by dactyls ornamented with triplets.

ACTORIAL DIMENSION

As we have said, the almost totally symmetric phrase structure of this section typifies the rhythmic-symmetric rationality characteristic of Western art music's Classic style, yet Beethoven imposes a slightly asymmetric de-actorialization. The last four-bar group does not repeat in full; only three bars of it are present. The entire second theme temporarily brings actors *a* and *b* into a peaceful confrontation between ascending and descending scale passages. Likewise, the ornamentation in the repetition of this theme makes use of these actors exclusively. Only in the last bar of the section (m. 49) does actor *a*, in the middle line, come to the fore. Actor *a* anticipates and thus becomes an index of the next isotopy (mm. 50–73).

In its modality the entire second theme represents *vouloir être*, a languishing of energetic 'will'. The inner-spatial fulcrum of E major has been so strongly prepared that the listener can temporarily relax into the euphoria of that tonality even though we have not yet reached the safe harbor of definitive 'being'. As for 'must', this exceptional choice of tonal center (not V) articulates the modality of 'must not-being'. And as for 'can', a complete sense of 'being' has been attained, with all its corresponding performance instructions (*dolce e molto legato, piano*) and harmonies set in a chorale texture.

We face a problem when measuring the inner-spatial disengagement of this isotopy. Should it be reckoned from the basic C tonic, or from E, which has been strongly tonicized in the preceding transition? In my view the original tonic remains in the mind of the listener and thus constitutes a secondary point of reference for all inner-spatial motion within this text. The outer spatiality follows the scheme shown in Fig. 5.3. We notice extremely small disengagement values of the outer spatiality (circle, bottom of Fig. 5.3), since changes in register occur gradually. Even in m. 39, where the register shifts abruptly, the passing of A4 of m. 38 provides a smooth transition into the next phrase. The change of pulse requires a new time value (quarter note) by which to measure dis-/engagement: mm. 35–41: 0; m. 42: +2.5 (this value is assigned to the triplet figure as lying between eighth and sixteenth notes), mm. 43–49: 0/+2.5 (this means that the primary unit is retained while alongside it occurs a secondary rhythmic figure in eighth note triplets).

This section emphasizes the modality of 'knowing'. With respect to the foregoing paradigms of musemes, two innovations occur: the change of basic rhythmic unit (representing the musical *être*) to the quarter note, and the change of rhythmic pattern to dactyllic. The restlessness of these changes effects, if not quite 'doing', at least a sense of 'not-being'.

Exposition: Second Transition (mm. 50–73)

This isotopy strengthens the view that the essence of this work—what it tries to "say"—lies in the transitions rather than in thematic areas which present musemes and musical actors. These 'becoming' (*devenir*) sections do not

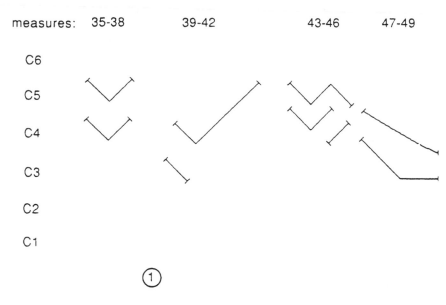

Figure 5.3. Beethoven, Op. 53, mvt. I, outer spatiality of mm. 35–49.

simply premodalize or attune the listener to the spatial, actorial, and temporal isotopies of an upcoming section. The preparation for the E major actor of the second theme, for example, was violent and labored and in no way prepared the listener for the symmetry and thematic synthesis of the ensuing section. The causal-indexical process of this music does not announce that an upcoming section will be dramatic, or, in semiotic terms, will contain abundant spatial-temporal disengagement and actorial juxtapositions. On the contrary, in the first movement of the "Waldstein" Beethoven presents the listener with a modal state antithetical to that of the next isotopy. As a Classic-Romantic composer, he could choose from among several narrative programs to articulate transition sections: a search for an isotopy, a gradual yielding of an isotopy, a surprisingly new or unprepared isotopy. Elsewhere in this sonata he follows a causal-indexical, generative principle of theme-actors. Think of the 'becoming' of the slow movement, which gradually evolves toward the theme-actor that begins the last movement; or of the transition to the Finale of the Fifth Symphony.

The outer spatiality of the second transition follows a clear-cut ascent from C4 to C6 and thus a very great disengagement, though it is softened by the gradual realization of this ascent (see Fig. 5.4). The climb to the upper register unfolds through an alternation of two mutually supportive lines, as in mm. 50–53, for example, where one line remains stationary as the other rises. Further, when the climactic goal has been attained momentarily at the beginning of m. 56, it is relinquished briefly in m. 61 so that a new and more dramatic climb may begin. The E6 of m. 74, which begins the next isotopy (closing theme), forms the musical object, a true point of conjunction; it was achieved in m. 56 and is painstakingly sought again until m. 74. A very simple narrative program of the outer spatiality here becomes as complex as possible through the aspectual seme of durativity and through appropriate modalities.

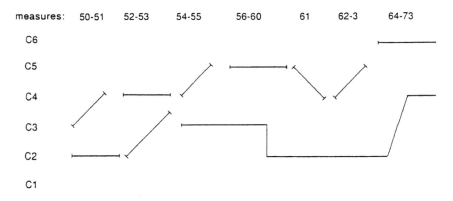

Figure 5.4. Beethoven, Op. 53, mvt. I, outer spatiality of mm. 50–73.

With regard to the inner spatiality, the music seems to embrace the tonic E. A subtle ear might make the following intonational analysis: when E major is so strongly emphasized in a work whose basic tonal isotopy is C major, compensation is necessary to reestablish tonal equilibrium. The slow movement's tonal focus of F will indeed provide this compensation by effectively dissolving the energy gathered in the chromatic-third related key. If we select E as a temporary but promisingly stable focus, we get the following degrees of disengagement for the inner spatiality: mm. 50–58: 0/+1; m. 59: 0; mm. 60–61: 0 (with lowered seventh); mm. 62–63: -1; mm. 64–65: V of +1; mm. 66–69: 0; mm. 70–73: +1. These values show that the inner spatiality becomes less tense as the harmonic rhythm slows toward the end of the section.

The temporal dimension of this transition is of greater interest than the outer and inner spatialities. Again let us recall that not all dimensions of a Classical text simultaneously embody a full 'knowing' (*savoir*). Some dimensions remain relatively stable, while others propel the narration forward. Here attention goes to the acceleration of disengagement of the outer temporality. The triplet ornamentation, introduced in the second theme, becomes a central musical substance of this section. The basic unit of the outer temporality remains the quarter note until m. 58, where the basic pulse of the first theme (the eighth note) returns, now delineated by the Alberti bass. With agitated left-hand syncopations mm. 62–65 continue to stress the eighth-note pulse, and mm. 66–71 retain the eighth-note pulse while referring to the staccatos that prepared the secondary theme. The section as a whole transforms the outer temporality through an acceleration from quarter to eighth note as the basic pulse.

The homogeneous rhythmic-metric texture of this transition needs little comment except to say that, in the paradigm of memory, the musemes therein originate from the actors introduced in the first isotopy. Does the extreme redundancy of this temporal strategy exhaust the material? Or does this section represent the *Nahsteigerung* discussed by Halm? The latter seems to bring a negative answer, since when the object of the search (E6) is attained it is almost immediately given up, and the reward seems incommensurate with the effort. Instead, this transition emphasizes durativity.

In the actorial dimension this section foregrounds the role of actor d (arpeggiated triad), which as the central actor subordinates everything else to itself. A close look finds actor a submerged in the right-hand then left-hand figurations of mm. 50–53, counting the pitches at half-bar units; and the upward gallop of mm. 62–65 also recalls actor a. This section does not, however, clearly present musical actors. It is a subjectless isotopy, a musical event, not an action.

Still, the allusions to actors d and a produce a certain modal content. The 'will to do' of a, its tensional growth, becomes quite obvious in the ascending motion of mm. 62–65. This tension is mollified by d, which represents the least tensional 'will to be' of all the actors introduced at the beginning. The 'must' content here is rather slight because of the persistence of E major. Yet the fact that the main theme is used in the lower register and the second theme is used in the middle creates a strong expectation, bordering on 'must', that the closing theme will occur in an upper register. With regard to 'knowing', this section represents *non-savoir/non-être*: 'not knowing' because almost no innovative material appears; 'not being' because the section pulls away from a state of 'being' while remaining within such a state, since the sought-for object of value is none other than the E6. Though 'not knowing' and 'non-must' (*non-devoir*) permeate this section, the 'can' content is quite high.[10] The use of the entire keyboard range signifies a strong value of 'can do', indicated also by the syncopated rhythms, difficult octave leaps (mm. 66–67), and the trill.

Exposition: Codetta or Closing Theme (mm. 74–86)

The outer spatiality of this section returns the action to its initial state, or *topos*. Thus the codetta represents an engagement, which occurs subtly and gradually, without conflict or violence. The obligatory return to the basic spatial isotopy is masked and sweetened by the overall euphoric nature of the passage, which signifies a desirable goal. Fig. 5.5 shows that no great disengagement, in the form of abrupt registral shifts, occurs in the outer spatiality.

The program of the codetta's inner spatiality must return us to the tonic C, in relation to which we get the following values: m. 74: +4; m. 75: *+3 and +4; m. 76: *+3 and +6; m. 77: *+4 and +5; mm. 78–81 = mm. 74–77; m. 82: *+4 and -1; m. 83: *+4 and +5; m. 84: 0 and -1; m. 85: 0 and +1.

A new basic time unit, the half note, governs the outer temporality in mm. 74–81. The retardation of pulse complements the closing function of this section and helps produce a durative ending, and an interesting combination results from the juxtaposition of half notes and sixteenth-note figuration, two extreme time units conjoined for the first time in this sonata. As to the inner temporality, a look backwards prevails.

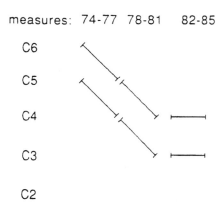

Figure 5.5. Beethoven, Op. 53, mvt. I, outer spatiality of mm. 74–85.

Engagement functions in the actorial dimension of this section. Actor *b*, expressing dissolution of tension, is finally given speech. The dactyllic rhythm of mm. 76–77 refers to the rhythm (in diminution) of the second theme, and the descending-triad arpeggiations allude to actor *d*.

The modal content of the section may be described as follows: 'willing not-being' (*vouloir non-faire*); 'not-knowing being' (*non-savoir être*), since no new material emerges; 'must be' (*devoir être*), because of the necessary return to the tonic key and engagement of the lower register; and 'not-can being' (*non-pouvoir être*), because of the relaxed dynamic-technical aspect of the texture, here polyphonic and noninstrumental, especially in mm. 81–84.

Development (mm. 86–155)

The development section forms the proper 'doing' of a sonata. It represents a heterotopos (Greimas 1979: 172) in the musical narration. In such a *topos*, actors of the exposition come to something like an incorrect isotopy in the spatial and temporal domains. They begin to struggle with each other and in the process modalize one another and reveal their inner potentialities.

Since the transition sections of this movement are themselves developmental, we might ask if there is enough 'knowing' (innovation, new information) and 'can' left in the musical material to allow building a proper development section. The modality of 'must' typically becomes less prominent in development sections, while 'willing' is realized without obstacles; and in the development section one often comes closest to the so-called structures of signification in music. On the other hand, the apparently fantasizing style of the development can be strictly determined with regard to the inner spatiality (tonality). Such is the case, for example, in Beethoven's Pastoral Symphony. The development section of the "Waldstein" might be taken as a syntagmatic whole, but we shall divide it into three narrative programs: mm. 86–111: struggle between actors c and b; mm. 112–41: heterotopos of "wandering" in the inner tonal space, development of actor d, and (as an implicit sub-isotopy) dialogue between actors a and b; and mm. 142–55: preparation for the recapitulation and sharpening of the relation between actors a and b during a *Nahsteigerung*, or engagement, over a dominant prolongation.

With regard to the inner spatiality, tonic ambiguity at the beginning of the development makes it difficult to estimate the degree of tension in the musical action. The development begins with a modulation to F major, perhaps as a temporary response to the E center of the previous sections, but does not remain in F long enough to disperse the tension and energeticism of E major. From C major we move quickly through its parallel minor to the dominant minor, G. Starting on F minor (m. 104), two-bar sequences develop over a stepwise descending bass and a circle-of-fifths progression (mm. 105–10) that passes solely through flatted, detensional key areas until arriving at C major in mm. 111–12.

Detensional harmonies also predominate in the second narrative program (mm. 112–41): F minor, B♭ minor, E♭ minor, F♯ (G♭) minor, B minor, C minor, D♭ major, and finally the dominant, G major (m. 136). Whereas the catalyzing force of the preceding narrative program was the seventh chords (every first half of the bar in mm. 105–109), in this section the dominant ninth prevails, always with lowered ninth. In these programs it seems futile to measure dis-/engagement values from a specific tonic, since the tonal motion fluctuates constantly. Directed motion is instead supplied by sequence, outer spatiality, and resolution of the seventh and ninth chords. For the first time in the universe of the piece, individual chords attain the status of a leading intonation, so values of centrifugal/centripetal tendencies have to be measured vertically, not horizontally as we have been doing.

Throughout the development section the outer spatiality forms the arena of an exciting fight centering on abrupt registral shifts. Fig. 5.6 depicts the outer spatiality of the development's first narrative program. One notices strong centrifugal motion of the upper line, in fact, the strongest of the entire movement. The uppermost line would thus receive a very high disengagement value. Its sharp profile stands out clearly against the relatively stable background of the lower part, though that part exhibits great variety with regard to inner spatiality.

The temporal dimension remains constant while the outer lines deactorialize, lose their individuality, and become parts of the musical narrative's figuration. Here we encounter another characteristic of the Classic musical text: one parameter dominates and draws attention to itself. In order to foreground a noteworthy event or action, other dimensions must remain unchanged or otherwise subdued. In the first narrative program, though the time values accelerate to sixteenths at m. 96, they are grouped in quarter-note pulses. In the second narrative program (mm. 112–41) rhythmic motion slows to triplets, recalling the transition to the second theme of the exposition. The third and final narrative program of the development (mm. 142–55) is based on sixteenth notes and galloping counterdactyls. With regard to inner temporality, only this last program is of interest, since it contains a built-in *accelerando*. The acceleration over the dominant, however, amounts to something like fraud and produces a disappointing result, because the dynamic growth of the inner temporality is out of proportion to the relatively static inner spatiality (the dominant prolongation).

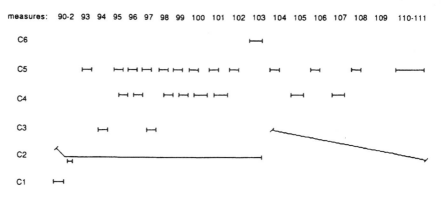

Figure 5.6. Beethoven, Op. 53, mvt. I, outer spatiality of mm. 90–111.

The outer spatiality of the second narrative program (mm. 112–41) follows an uneventful course. It contains no dramatic leaps, thus the disengagement values remain very low. The wandering of inner spatiality emerges even more clearly—a wandering rather than a search because in this section one senses no disjunction from any object. Rather, this narrative program claims no object; that is, the chords aim in no compelling direction. The outer spatiality of this narrative program sinks gradually to the opening register of the piece. Nevertheless, the return of the main motif does not occur immediately but only after a sudden increase of outer spatiality in the succeeding program (mm. 142–54), followed by a rapid decrease. The growing distance between the two outer lines emphasizes the latter program's centrifugal nature, which arises mainly from the convulsive quality of the upper line.

On the actorial level, development sections tend to be of interest. In the first narrative program, attention focuses on the struggle between actors *c* and *b*. Actor *c* transforms rhythmically into a more striking shape: the victory of *c* in mm. 104–11 is only temporary, though it is accompanied by the seme of perfectiveness, a feeling of achievement and completion. The second narrative program produces a highly deactorial effect, like riding in a train moving at high speed: one has little chance to notice the actors, only the constantly altering landscape. The third narrative program returns to focus on actorial functions, with the dialogue between actors *a* and *b* in their increasingly agitated dispute.

The modal values of the development's first narrative program come from its main actors, *c* and *b*, which articulate 'willing not-doing' (*vouloir non-faire*) and 'willing not-being' (*vouloir non-être*). Temporal acceleration emphasizes 'doing' and unrest, even though the section never reaches the level of a proper battle: a subdued passage such as mm. 104–11 always signifies a euphoric dissolution of tension, and the 'willing not-doing' of that passage arises only through the sinking bass line. The 'not-being' (*non-être*) of actor *c*, an actor that seeks to escape a state of rest, does not rule the section as a whole. Though the dominant ninths give the inner spatiality a slight feeling of 'will to do', a sense of stasis created by the arpeggiated triads prevails in the second narrative program. The third narrative program brings actor *a*, with its 'will to do', strongly into the foreground. With its agitation of both inner and outer temporalities, and explosive disengagement of outer spatiality, this program surpasses 'will to do' and attains the force of 'must do'.

'Knowing' values remain low in the first and second narrative programs, since the latter provides little new information. In contrast, the bridge (mm. 138–41) to the third narrative program (which delays the recapitulation even though the "correct" register has been regained) produces considerable 'knowing to do' (*savoir faire*). In relation to this bridge, the preceding narrative programs come nearest to 'not knowing to do' (*non-savoir faire*), since they do not manifest conspicuous musical action. Again, this is because the exposition contained so much innovative development that little remains for the development proper to do.

'Can' dominates this development section, which exploits virtuosic scale passages, disjunct motion, arpeggiation, and sustained chord tones serving as tension-creating finger pedals. The 'must' value is mildly positive since the development fulfills its traditional obligations, especially with regard to modulations and dominant preparation of the recapitulation—a *Steigerung* that strongly projects the *devoir* principle.

Recapitulation (mm. 156–302)

The last and most extensive syntagmatic whole of the movement restores balance to the modal field by repeating events from the exposition. It is important to remember which modalizations have taken place in the development, in order to perceive how the repetition of opening intonations influences our memory of those modalizations. Yet the recapitulation of this movement is incomplete, for Beethoven breaks the inner iconicity of the music in strategic places. These ruptures in the musical organization naturally capture a listener's attention.

The first break comes between the first thematic area and transition, where an extra development (mm. 169–73) emerges from the deceptive cadence in m. 168. In the spatial sense, this is an astonishing deviation into flatted key areas in relation to the C major *topos*. As to outer temporality, motion halts at the long, *fermate* whole notes. In the actorial dimension, *d* comes to the fore and receives development in this brief passage, which is perhaps meant to compensate for the relative neglect of that actor to this point. Modally, by its surprising deviation from the exposition, this brief section displays great innovation and offers new information, endowing it with much 'knowing'. A logical consequence of this *savoir être* value is that, running against the "normal" course of events in the recapitulation and thus against *devoir*, mm. 167–73 represent 'not-must being' (*non-devoir être*). Contradictory 'willing' values obtain in mm. 167–70 because the notes that begin mm. 167, 169, and 171 form a clearly perceptible step progression that calls to mind actor *a*, which was fundamentally a manifestation of 'will to do'. Still, the predominant modality of the ascending triads in this section is 'willing to be'. In spite of the octaves, the 'can' value is small, due to the *decrescendo* and *pianissimo* dynamics.

Another deviation, which however does follow the 'must' of a sonata recapitulation, occurs by the second theme's placement in A major. With disengagement value of +3 as opposed to the E major value of +4 in the exposition, the second theme now creates somewhat less tension, and the A major might even be interpreted as a mode change of the relative minor. The second transition (mm. 211–35), which in the exposition produced a tensional development that tonicized E major, is here presented completely in C major, our 0 point for the inner spatiality. After the closing theme, a new and fairly extensive developmental coda begins (m. 249). The coda displays extreme variation of the outer spatiality. As a parallel to the start of the development, the coda begins with abrupt leaps and registral shifts featuring actors *c* and *b*. There follows in mm. 259–60 a brief development of the drumming motif (the only museme from the opening not yet exploited), which accompanied *a* in the exposition.

In mm. 261–66 actor *b* broadens into syncopated quarter notes and sounds simultaneously with actor *a*, not after it, as before. As this secondary development continues, again the goal is to attain the register of C6, where a climax occurs that reverses the positions of actors *a* and *b*: the ascending passages, representing *a*, go into the upper part; the descending motifs, representing *b*, go into the lower part. A long sequence in mm. 267–71 accomplishes this *Stimmtausch*, which subsides to a stretto in mm. 272–74. Tension continues to build in mm. 275–76, with a rising chromatic line (G–G♯–A) finishing on the F major subdominant. The subdominant has functioned as a musical sought-for object since the very beginning of the piece, where the E3 above tonic C strove toward F but instead went through F♯ and on to G. Here we get the true answer, and the E at last secures its object of value. The diagonal melodic motion in mm. 276–82 (of high 'can' value) intervenes to delay the IV–V₇ progression accomplished via two sudden register shifts (mm. 282–83).

The second theme follows, now in the main key, the spatial isotopy of a true 'being'. We may consider this variant of the second theme to be innovative, because the antecedent phrase takes place in the "false" register of C3 and because the theme undergoes a slight rhythmic transformation when repeated. Temporal forward motion ceases in mm. 290–94, and the consequent phrase of the second theme becomes rhythmically static. A repeated striving gesture marks this section: from G through A/A♭ to the leading tone, B. This rising gesture refers to the earlier dramatic culmination in which the chromatic ascent of m. 275 only got as far as A (m. 276): the G♯/A♭ gesture reaches further and attains the leading tone. Contributing to the seme of perfectiveness that closes the movement, mm. 295–302 present all four leading actors in their original order of appearance.

VI

NARRATIVITY IN CHOPIN

6.1 *Polonaise-Fantaisie* and the Idea of Narrative Program

As much by his life as by his music, Chopin is considered a symbol of Romanticism. As a composer, he falls in the category of Schiller's "sentimental" artists, who attempted to reestablish a lost relationship with Nature. Early studies of Chopin rarely went beyond this typecasting, according more significance to the liberty of his formal structures than to their expressive, sentimental content. Later research on Chopin tried to retrace the passionate, dreamlike traits behind the composer's persona, and musicologists found that his compositions are grounded on rigorous principles of construction.

Chopin lived at the center of the literary-musical culture of Romanticism in an age that perceived the narrative content of musical works as the essential level of significance, and his music has prompted a considerable number of "programs" and literary commentaries. Indeed, there is an entire literary tradition of commentary on Chopin—going from Liszt to Prszybyszewski and Gide—though his music was rarely, if ever, directly inspired by a literary oeuvre. Liszt's point of departure was often literary, particularly in his symphonic poems, and the mission of literature was accomplished primarily in his music. In comparison to Chopin, there exist few commentaries about Liszt's works.

The following study of a work from Chopin's late period, the *Polonaise-Fantaisie*, Op. 61, pays special attention to its narrative content. It is not another literary commentary—the "story" this composition might tell—but reflects upon the semio-musical structures that make possible its concrete psychological contents, the intrigue associated with the piece. These semiotic structures need not correspond to those of conventional form analysis, whose error lies in slighting the energy and dynamism of the work, its internal tension or 'will' (*vouloir*). Segmentation of the work according to stereotypical form models leads to little, since in Chopin's late works we do not find the simple prototypes of Classical-Romantic music but a hybrid of several musical forms of his time, as shown by Zofia Lissa (1963), Gerald Abraham, and Hugo Leichtentritt. According to Abraham, this work has at least five different themes, three of which are never repeated. He views the global image of the work as follows (1960: 110):

Introduction: 23 mm., based mainly on section A, different keys

A: 42 mm.: A♭ major

B: 26 mm.: A♭ major but modulatory

A: 24 mm.: A♭ major

C: 32 mm.: B♭ major but modulatory

D: 33 mm.: B♭ major, etc.

E: 34 mm.: G♯ minor and B major; two bars as in introduction; ten final bars evoke E

Transition: 16 mm.

A: 12 mm.: A♭ major

D: 35 mm.: A♭ major

The form of the *Polonaise-Fantaisie* is somewhat problematic as compared, for example, to another major work from Chopin's late period, the Ballade in F minor: "The Polonaise-Fantaisie is admittedly a harder nut to crack," and yet, "the sequence and contrast of musical events are perfectly satisfying, and the whole piece rests solidly on its tonal pillars of A♭" (Abraham 1960: 110).

Abraham gives no reason why the contradictions and series of musical events are "perfectly satisfying," that is to say, why the work coheres. The predominance of A♭ major does not help, for psychologically there is a difference between the A♭ major of section A at the beginning and the final reprise of section A. This "difference" goes unnoticed in Abraham's analysis. Leichtentritt's (1921) is scarcely more enlightening:

I. mm: 1–24 Introduction, freely modulatory

      24–66 Development of theme a (A♭ major with numerous exceptions)

      66–71 Presentation of theme b (A♭ major)

II. 72–93 *Durchführung* of theme b (F minor, E major, F♯ minor, G♯ minor, A major)

      93–115 *Durchführung* of theme a (E♭ major, D♭ major)

      116–153 Theme c in free *Durchführung* (B♭ major, B minor, B major)

      153–181 Theme d (B major, D♯ major)

      182–213 Theme c (G♯ minor, B major

III. 214–216 Abridged introduction

      216–226 Theme c abridged

      226–242 Transition to the dominant of A♭ major

      242–254 Reprise of theme a as climax (A♭ major)

      254–268 Reprise of theme d (A♭ major)

Coda 268–288 Based on accompaniment figure of theme d

Leichtentritt sees the work as a three-part design that smacks of sonata form, and he considers the harmonic, pianistic, and timbral isotopies to be the most important. He confronts the work with criteria of his own (German) tradition. His analysis ignores other isotopies, such as motivic workings, and offers no reasons for the composer's choice of harmonic functions and tonal areas or for the order in which they occur.

expect a positive articulation, do we sense this arpeggio as affirming the plunge of the opening tonic? Probably not. Rather, the arpeggio represents a climb not only in register but also from the tension of a clear metric pulse. One might even take it as a musical echo of the overtone series, somewhat like the famous passage in F major at the end of Prelude no. 23, where we catch a glimpse of the overtone series with the appearance of E♭.

From the perspective of the semiotic square (Fig. 6.1), the arpeggio might represent the appearance of a contrary term. Put another way, the listener still awaits the appearance of the positive term S1 and the negative term S2, which in a sense is the negation of the negation. Thus, the arpeggio cannot be taken for S1 and can only be non-S1, the negation of a term not yet manifested in the piece.

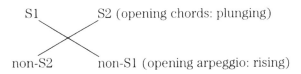

Figure 6.1. Chopin, *Polonaise-Fantaisie*, opening chords
and arpeggio projected onto semiotic square.

Measure 2 repeats material of m. 1 a whole step lower. The impression of plunging or collapse is reinforced when the downward motion continues in mm. 3–6. There, the semes of the arpeggiated and block chords of the beginning are gathered, and some are changed into their opposites: the opening dotted rhythm is changed into its contrary at the beginning and end of mm. 4–5. A variant motif from the small-note arpeggio of m. 1 makes a brief appearance in the bass. This passage is by nature redundant, a reinforcement. The balancing between the E♭ major and minor of m. 6 recalls Liszt's comment: "We might also say that these expressions make the corresponding sound of a third vibrate in the mind, which immediately changes our thought into a major or minor chord" (1963: 115). Then mm. 1 and 2 are repeated, but their dynamic isotopy changes into its antithesis, from *forte* to *pianissimo*, and here PN1 ends. Its essential content can be described by a complex isotopy in which plunging is the dominant isotopy and rising a simple allusion to the (as yet unrealized) contradictory category of affirmation:

plunging
———————
rising

PN 2: Birth of the Principal Theme (mm. 9–21)

The beginning of this program might be linked with the preceding section; but the semes here belong to a different energetic field whose central effect is a strong sense of expectation, tension, and beginning. The program begins in A♭ major, as does PN 1, but it modulates in mm. 11–12 to E major (A♭ = G♯ minor,

III/E). Here is another chromatic third relation that tonally represents the struggle between Hope and Despair. The passage is tonally symmetrical: mm. 9–11, A♭ (G♯) minor; mm. 12–17, E major; mm. 18–21, G♯ (A♭) minor. From the thymic perspective, the E major in the middle is only a brief taste of euphoria.

The primary function of this passage is to announce the coming principal theme, for here semes are introduced that will appear at the end of that theme (see Ex. 6.3). Semes from the beginning of the principal theme do not occur in this passage. The dotted-rhythm motif from the end of the principal theme (upper voice: G♯–A–F♯, beginning of m. 12) relates to the dotted-rhythm motif B♭–C–A♭ at the juncture of the third and fourth bars of the principal theme (mm. 26 and 27). Then the entire last part of the principal theme sounds; that is, all of m. 26 is anticipated in mm. 13–14. This is immediately taken up by the tenor voice, mm. 15–17 being basically a polyphonic-harmonic texture in four voices that duplicates the main-actant theme in the upper register. This situation recalls tragedies and novels in which besides the hero there is often an auxiliary character who reflects on the acts and feelings of the protagonists. This passage suggests that the narrative categories of subject/object, addresser/addressed, and adjuvant/opponent apply to music as well.

Example 6.3. Chopin, *Polonaise-Fantaisie*, mm. 13–15.

A similar relation between the subject and adjuvant themes was already operating in mm. 3–5 of PN 1, where the bass reinforced the upper voice by repeating the latter's motif. If in the present passage we consider the tonal isotopy of the lower register in mm. 17–21, we find a similar relationship of repetition and confirmation, now falling into the thymic category of frustration.

The theme-subject, relinquished by the upper voice at the start of PN 2, and the theme-adjuvant bass are locked in conflict. If the first theme represents the principle of plunging, the second theme encourages the former to revolt; it tends to rise menacingly, highlighted by the *crescendo* in mm. 10–11. The semes of the bass adjuvant-theme in m. 10–11 (Exx. 6.4b and c) come from the motif of the secondary notes of the arpeggiated chord in m. 2 (Ex. 6.4a). This motif passes through three different roles in a very short time. First, it is presented completely outside of the energetic field of the work; next, as an intensifier of the dysphoric principle of negation and resignation, that is to say, as submissive to the theme-subject of the upper voice in mm. 3–4. Finally, in mm. 10–11, it appears self-willed and achieves partial victory through its agitated motion, a temporary passage set alongside the coming euphoria of E major. But the final struggle between the theme-subject of the upper voice and the adjuvant-opposing, subversive bass theme will take place only in mm. 38–40, where the bass wins out but is then subjugated.

Example 6.4. Chopin, *Polonaise-Fantaisie*: a. mm. 2–4; b. mm. 10–11.

The conflict of two parallel themes is typical of actantial structures of Western music. The sonata-form dialectic between principal and secondary theme and that of subject and countersubject in certain Bach fugues are founded on this principle (for example, *Well-Tempered Clavier* I, Fugue in F♯ major). We can apply here the actantial categories of actant-antactant-negactant-negantactant to study how the same motif passes through several actantial roles in the course of a work. The question of whether any musical motif can occupy any actantial role forms its own theoretical problem, otherwise known as the classic problem between substance and function in music.

PN 3: Polonaise (mm. 22–65)

This PN is made up of two sections that follow the classical movement of x, x', z (theme, its repetition, something else). Its beginning is announced by a fanfare based on polonaise rhythm (Ex. 6.5). This fanfare belongs, on the principle of contiguity, to the succeeding musical phenomenon. Indeed, the theme we hear for the first time in mm. 24–27, and whose final part has been iconically prepared, is the first true theme of the work (Ex. 6.6). The same sentiments arise in the listener as when reading a novel or watching a play: "at last the protagonist enters!"

Example 6.5. Chopin, *Polonaise-Fantaisie*, mm. 22–23, announcement of principal theme (main actor).

Example 6.6. Chopin, *Polonaise-Fantaisie*, mm. 24–27, principal theme (main actor).

Let us study this theme's kinetic energy. B♭, the second degree of A♭ major, is emphatically repeated, twice on strong beats of the bar, twice on weak beats. The pull toward A♭ is made particularly strong by the accompaniment figure's dominant seventh chord. This principal theme qualifies as centripetal, for spatially it winds around scale degree $\hat{2}$ of A♭ major. In contrast, after the theme repeats, a spatial disengagement occurs in m. 31: the melodic line begins to ripple along and the frozen centripetal motion indicative of a dominating force becomes an oscillating, centrifugal motion that ranges from one part of the tonal field to another. This trait of the last part of the Polonaise theme is amplified upon repetition of the entire theme. Moreover, the principal theme blossoms out into the tonic from the previously cited B♭. The third bar of the principal theme (m. 26) shows the same activity in two of its voices: in the bass voice by a break in eighth-note motion and, a little later in the upper voice, by a contraction of temporal values and by a sixteenth-note pause—a catching of breath before the tonic A♭ in m. 27. This pause is particularly noticeable, inasmuch as the momentum in the preceding bar was pressing forward. The melody swerves suddenly into smaller temporal values, and in the accompaniment we glimpse the dactyllic, polonaise rhythm, which in this piece always signals forward motion. Because of the sixteenth-note pause, the B♭ seems to last even longer.

The continuation of the principal theme is cantabile in nature, not dancelike. In m. 31 Chopin is already imitating the motion of singing, creating the illusion of a *crescendo* between two notes by means of a pedaling effect and ascending harmonies in the left hand (see Ex. 6.7). He thus transcends the material, sonorous possibilities of the piano and creates an intertext of piano music that alludes to vocal music. The freely rippling melody that follows the principal theme soon becomes halting and discontinuous, as if under pressure from a signified of supplementary passion (mm. 34–35), finally crystallizing into the previous struggle between subject and adjuvant in mm. 38–39, which now has turned into the subject's opponent (Ex. 6.8). The melody ends in a second dotted-rhythm descent, which in Romantic music carries the nuance of plaint and supplication.

Example 6.7. Chopin, *Polonaise-Fantaisie*, mm. 28–31, continuation of principal theme.

Example 6.8. Chopin, *Polonaise-Fantaisie*, mm. 39–41.

Let us return for a moment to the study of the principal theme itself, the fundamental lexeme of the work. We have described it in terms of spatial and temporal connections but not actantial. Actantially, we can study the theme as we do any expression describing a state and an action; and the transition between the two can be described as follows, with the arrow indicating a transformation: F [S1 → (S2 ∧ O)], where F = 'doing' (*faire*). In music also, we can in principle distinguish between two types of expression, *open* and *closed*. Closed expressions describe or correspond to conjunctions; they are self-contained, with no desire to emerge from themselves. Open expressions require continuation; they aspire toward something else, and thus are disjunctions.

Which type of expression does the principal theme of the *Polonaise-Fantaisie* represent? There, a tension reigns between the tonic and scale degree $\hat{2}$; but these notes are not yet in a modal relationship of 'will' with each other. Rather, the tensional field separating them creates a harmonic isotopy in the immobile accompaniment part. We can consider the B♭ as a subject separated from the A♭, its object of value, which finishes by bringing the object into subjection. It is a matter of the situation F [S1 → (S2 ∧ O)], in which S1 is the B♭ trying to reach A♭, trying to merge, but is still separated. S2 signifies the same B♭, which finds its solution (object of value), the A♭. This simple plot is made complicated and more interesting by the obstacles and detours, the unexpected events that accelerate or slow down attainment of the final objective. Because the principal theme repeats in mm. 44–56, this disjunction is considerably magnified, and the expected B♭ in m. 50 will be heard only in m. 62, after the great climb and the passage which develops (by downward chromatic motion) the descending-fifth motif of the principal theme (mm. 56–59). In m. 56 the role of the B♭ is transformed; it is no longer the dominant of the dominant as it appeared in mm. 24–26 and mm. 45–46, but the dominant of the minor dominant (E♭ minor) of A♭ major. The true cadence for the bass's tonal isotopy in A♭ major is heard only in mm. 64–66 (Ex. 6.9), where another oscillation between parallel minor and major occurs, recalling m. 6 of PN 1.

Example 6.9. Chopin, *Polonaise-Fantaisie*, mm. 64–66.

PN 4: Modulations or Topological Disengagement (mm. 66–91)

Abraham and Leichtentritt have differing views about the segmentation of this passage. Abraham marks it with a B, without characterizing the content of this letter. We might consider Leichtentritt's interpretation arbitrary: in his scheme, a new theme (b) occurs in mm. 66–72 and is led through numerous tonalities in mm. 73–93, until the return of the principal theme in E♭ major in m. 94. According to Abraham, the *Durchführung* of theme B commences in section II.

Such a distinction does not seem founded on a study of the musical semes of this "new theme." To call it the second theme of a sonata form, new semes (at least) would have to appear and the tonal isotopy would be the dominant of A♭ major. Neither of these things happens; instead, this theme's initial part is derived from the accompaniment of the Polonaise theme (see the rising bass line in the left hand of m. 27). Its final part is derived from intervals from the central part of the principal theme. The motif, therefore, ought not to be designated a new, independent theme; although it is justifiable to wonder, from here on, what the modal value of the musical semes is. When the composer uses musical semes from the principal theme in the construction of an essential lexeme occurring elsewhere in the work, those semes are no longer neutral substances; in the listener's memory there remains an image or sensation that comes from the preceding modal content. (No motif or any other element is truly neutral in a musical work, except perhaps the free material found outside the temporal structure and tensional modal field of the work, that is, in the paradigmatic repertory of the composer's imagination.)

The modal content of the two preceding motifs of the present work served a transitional function in the micro-universe of the Polonaise theme, and they maintain the same function in the macro-universe. That is, they are enlarged in order to form the 26-bar transition section, where it is a matter of a level that is truly topological, not psychological or actantial. This transition takes us through several tonalities toward the return of the principal theme, which we find in new settings: A♭ major (m. 66), F minor (m. 72), E major (m. 80), F♯ minor (m. 84), G♯ minor (m. 86), and eventually in the dominant of E♭ major (m. 92), which, however, does not resolve to that key.

PN 5: Extreme Thymic States (mm. 94–115)

The transition to the repetition of the short Polonaise theme, now in a different setting, occurs in mm. 92–93 as a scalar passage that relates to the ascending arpeggiation that began the work. At its peak, in m. 93, there is a brief appearance of the motif G♭–A♭–C–B♭ (Ex. 6.10), which recalls the final motif of the arpeggiation, G♭–A♭–C♭–B♭, in m. 7 of PN 1. The Polonaise theme is transformed into triplet figuration in m. 95, whose impression of sweetness is reinforced by the fact that the dotted rhythmic motifs, according to the old tradition, should also be executed as triplets.

The principal theme in m. 95 occurs over B♭7, a fifth lower than its initial statement in m. 24. Here the continuation of the neighbor motif (mm. 99–100) is a step lower, differing from its continuation in PN 3, where it is always a step higher (mm. 28–29). From this euphoric state we will soon pass to its direct opposite, a period of dysphoric agitation in mm. 108–15. Perhaps Liszt had such brusque changes in mind when, in his essay on Chopin, he spoke of the extreme states one encounters in this piece (1963: 36–37).

PN 6: Mazurka I (mm. 116–47)

The transition to this PN is also brusque and surprising. The thymic quality, as well as the motivic material, again becomes graceful. Suddenly we intrude into the macrocosm of mazurkas, which Liszt analyzes in the following way:

> where one by one all the phases of passion are retraced: charming illusions of coquetry; strings of imperceptible inclinations; capricious façades suggesting fantasy; mortal depressions of weak joys which were born dying; flowers of grief

Example 6.10. Chopin, *Polonaise-Fantaisie*, mm. 92–97.

like black roses which sadden us by the perfume of their petals, petals which the least breeze causes to fall from their stems . . . pleasures without past or future, overcome by fate; illusions, inexplicable tastes, tempting us to adventure. . . . [1963: 54–55]

The Mazurka theme repeats several times consecutively, though it lasts only a bar and a half; but it always reappears embellished in different ways (see Ex. 6.11). Chopin has integrated into the texture a principle of expression typical of him: he never played a work the same way twice. Here also, nothing is repeated the same way. Moreover, the ornamentation is not without content. To paraphrase John Ruskin, Chopin does not try to give words more significance than they really have (1843/1987: 10). Certain musical semes in this theme also refer to the principal lexeme of the whole work; for example, the motif of the medial section (mm. 124–25), which is derived from the continuation of the Polonaise theme (see mm. 25, 29–30).

Example 6.11. Chopin, *Polonaise-Fantaisie*, mm. 116–19,
Mazurka I theme.

Mazurka I ends with a chromatic declamation that calls to mind the passionate violin figures of *Tristan*. The structure of this PN recalls that of PN 3, to the extent that here also the finale forms an oscillating passage of tonal space as the antithesis of the centripetal motif of the principal statement. The notes Bb–B–D–C of the Mazurka's main theme are a transposition of a motif that already appeared in PN 2 in the announcement of the principal theme (left hand, m. 10, A–Bb–Db–Cb). On the other hand, the beginning of the Polonaise theme is not used here at all, but is withheld as the central motif of the following PN. In mm. 148–52 we pass to the next PN, and this transition itself is of a paradigmatic nature, similar to the transition in mm. 64–65 which led to PN 4. This bridge does not lead to an intermediary passage based on motifs from the end of the principal theme, but to an oasis of calm—a Nocturne that brings a variant of the beginning of the Polonaise theme.

PN 7: Nocturne (mm. 153–80)

A change of inner-spatial isotopy puts the entire Nocturne section in B major, the enharmonic equivalent of the opening Cb major. Thus, a tension is born between the tonic of Ab major and its third-related scale degree. Again we find two superposed themes, one the actant, the other the negactant; but this time it is not a matter of musical expression describing the action, other than a phrase describing F (S1 ∧ O). The motif of the actant (upper part) and the motif of the negactant (bass) are introverted themes that search for no object, since an object has already been reached. Still, this does not precipitate a plunge into tonalities rich in flats, but on the contrary, a rising into the chromatic tonal field of A♯ major and C♯ major. Unlike the passionate last part of the preceding Mazurka section, the chromaticism here is introverted.

In Example 6.12, actant and negactant are not in conflict with each other, but sing a conciliatory duet. Notice that the former, derived from the Polonaise theme, rests on scale degree $\hat{5}$ of B major, not on $\hat{2}$, which would produce too much tension. This dreamlike section trails off in mm. 178–80, when three independent parts begin to move toward the G♯ minor of the next PN. In this section, the Polonaise theme's semes appear but distantly related to the original signified, as though to a distant memory. Here Chopin creates an aesthetic of the doubly signified in music.

Example 6.12. Chopin, *Polonaise-Fantaisie*, mm. 153–57, Nocturne theme.

PN 8: Mazurka II (mm. 182–225)

This program is a nostalgic version of PN 6, Mazurka I. There is an interesting subconscious connection between the first chords of the work (A♭ minor and C♭ major) and the basic harmonies of the passage, G♯ minor and B major (see Exx. 6.13a and b). Although it is a matter of harmonic interpretation, the tonal isotopy refers to the problem posed by PN 1, in its negation of the generalized notion of "polonaise."

Example 6.13. Chopin, *Polonaise-Fantaisie*, Mazurka II
theme: a. mm. 182–83; b. mm. 186–87.

Melodically, mm. 182–85 remind us of Mazurka I. Soon afterwards, in mm. 189–98, the semes of PN 3 (Polonaise) come into play. In fact, the bass is in a paradigmatic relation: it evokes the descending chords of the last of the Polonaise theme (see mm. 32–37, 55–69). At the same time, the melody of the upper part in mm. 190–98 is a variant of the sentimental, singing melody of the final part of the Polonaise theme's first appearance (mm. 32–36). In mm. 194–95, the dotted anacruses which have appeared throughout the work are rhythmically condensed as antitheses to the ornamentation of the actant-theme's second appearance in the preceding Nocturne section (end of m. 169 onward); and whereas the earlier theme descended with a sigh, here the dotted rhythms ascend. It is as if a reservoir of ambivalent reminiscences were crystallizing in Mazurka II, a storehouse of memory in which preceding intonations of the piece are fondly recalled. In this memory of happiness there is a direct relationship to, among other works, Albéniz's *Iberia*.

PN 9: Departure and Return (mm. 199–241)

This PN can be seen as a continuation of the preceding one, for here also there are numerous, previously heard intonations; but their modal value is reversed, as in Mazurka II. Here the modality of *vouloir* is completely disengaged. The trills of mm. 201, 203, and 205 are analogous to the relaxing solution of the Nocturne. Chopin does not end the trill directly on the tonic; instead, the long trill of m. 205 goes first to a Vb♮ chord. Only after a pause do we reach the object (tonic) in m. 206. So this miniature PN in mm. 199–205 slows down events, though it is at the same time dominated by the seme of tension.

A tension-free area occurs in the following passage, mm. 206–13. The bass theme-negactant of the Nocturne section takes center stage and directs the motion, seconded by the theme actant. Here the energetic wills of the themes are modalized contrarily to the Nocturne. The theme-actant undergoes diminution, while the theme-negactant expands. This leads to a short echo of PN 1 in mm. 214–15 (third-related chords and small-note arpeggiation). Whereas in PN 1 the first dotted-rhythm chord was accented and the second unaccented, now for the first time this relationship is reversed (m. 215).

In mm. 216–25 the departure is completed with a triple recollection of Mazurkas I and II. It leaves everything unresolved, as if forgotten in the midst of being announced. As the transition motif between this departure and return (which fills the final part of this PN), an intervallic expansion of the negactant theme intervenes. Measures 226–41, a "call to attention," form a brusque contrast to the preceding section. The Polonaise's dactyllic rhythm reappears. Earlier we noticed that in this work it accelerates the action. The function of the climbing chromatic figure in sixteenth notes in mm. 238–41 is the antithesis of the descending chromatic sixteenth notes in mm. 140–43, which preceded the Nocturne. There, the chromaticism expressed the anguish and helplessness of inaction. Here, it expresses the anguish that precedes the culmination of action. Thus Chopin creates modal contrast. The motif that formerly expressed quietude of will now expresses the positive category of 'will do' (*vouloir faire*).

PN 10: Fulfillment (mm. 242–88)

In mm. 242–48 we hear, in its entirety, the Polonaise theme borrowed from PN 3, the theme that all through PN 9 appeared as either moving away or as an object of 'will'. The transformation here leads to its goal, the Polonaise theme now reaching a higher register, as if victorious (Ex. 6.14).

Then comes a surprise. Soon after the Polonaise reprise, a résumé of the Nocturne section begins in m. 249. The allusion to the Nocturne first appears in tonal relationships: we are now in B major, and this ascent in key level, coming just after A♭ major, brings the effect of heroic elevation. Ornamented variants of the Nocturne motif sound, lengthened by dotted anacruses. The theme-negactant, heard beneath the theme-actant (Nocturne theme), is the same as the bass line that accompanied this theme on first appearance (starting in mm. 152–53), though in dotted rhythms here. From m. 254 onward, the

Example 6.14. Chopin, *Polonaise-Fantaisie*, mm. 242–44.

principal theme of the Nocturne section reappears, here modalized into its exact opposite: now the negactant rules over the theme-actant. Finally we hear the resolution of the last of the Polonaise theme, developed into an impressive cadence in m. 268—a true affirmation of the tonic A♭ major (Ex. 6.15).

Example 6.15. Chopin, *Polonaise-Fantaisie*, mm. 266–68.

Before affirming or denying something, it is necessary to want to affirm or deny. This process of 'willing' was described by the preceding chain of PNs whose different sections put obstacles in the way of this 'will' or pushed it to the fore. It all ends, however, in the sovereignty of the theme-negactant. In mm. 268–82 the latter escapes from its subordinate role in the bass, to become a true actant, a principal subject as opposed to its opening, adjuvant role (see Ex. 6.16). Now a surprising relationship is unveiled: the true identity of this theme, which has functioned as a negactant, is revealed. It is a modalized variation of the arpeggio motif that signified rising in PN 1. Which is to say that term S1 of the semiotic square manifests itself as a response to the problem of the fundamental narrative program of the entire work, namely, that of the deep structure.

The E♭ on the *sforzando* strong beat in m. 272 corresponds to the dotted-rhythm chord of the opening. In m. 1 the accent was, contrary to all expectation, on the sixteenth note and not the dotted eighth note. Here, the relationship is reversed. The rising melodic minor third, C–E♭ (end of m. 271–m. 272), responds melodically to the harmonic relationship of the opening A♭ major to C♭ major. The positions of the semiotic square are filled, and the musical narration is completed, led by its contrary relationships, both contradictory and implicative, to its final fulfillment.

Example 6.16. Chopin, *Polonaise-Fantaisie*, mm. 272–74.

We could have produced several, parallel semiotic squares for this piece; for example, those concerning the tonal isotopies of A♭ major and B major. And the analysis of a single work is a far cry from bringing to light all of Chopin's narratology; it only opens the way for such an enterprise. It would be necessary to analyze in addition, the Ballade in F minor and the Fantasy in F minor, whose narrative programs differ enough from those of the *Polonaise-Fantaisie* to give proof of the individualism in the creations of Chopin's late compositional period. Nonetheless, this analysis of musical-narrative tensions in this one piece has revealed the principles on which Chopin bases his musical narration.

6.2 Writing a Modal Grammar: Chopin's Ballade in G Minor

The following analysis of the Ballade in G minor goes still deeper into details of semiotic investigation of music and leads to the most formalized grammar of a musical work in this volume. The main isotopies of the piece and their modalities are:

I   Mm. 1–7. Introduction: arpeggio that in m. 5 turns into a recitative; change from spatial to actorial articulation in mm. 6–7; subdued temporal articulation, almost disengaged; 'not-doing'.

II   Mm. 8–35. Waltz: a somewhat "estranged" waltz, a *valse oubliée*; clear and somewhat syncopated rhythmic-temporal waltz pattern; 'being'.

III   Mm. 36–65. Indexical development of Waltz; 'doing'; waltz+.

IV   Mm. 65/66–81. Quasiparlando motif dominates; 'not-doing'.

V   Mm. 82–93. Transition: sequel to the previous section, codetta, postmodalization, "après"; 'not-being'; trans-.

VI   Mm. 94–105. Transition: anticipation of the next section, premodalization; subordination of the main actor to a helper actor in relation to the quasiparlando motif; transfer of the main actor to the role of a sender; 'not-being'; trans+ (waltz).

VII   Mm. 106–23. Glorification of the quasiparlando, secondary actor: quasi-'doing' or 'appear to-do'; epistemic value of 'lie'.

VIII   Mm. 124–37. Transition: premodalization of the next section, "avant"; 'becoming' (*devenir*); 'not-being'; trans+.

IX   Mm. 138–65. *Scherzando* combination of the quasiparlando and waltz motifs: 'appear-to-be'; also a 'lie'.

X   Mm. 166–93. Return of the quasiparlando motif: now not incognito, with the correct epistemic value; 'being', which is nonetheless full of inner modalizations.

XI   Mm. 194–205. Waltz actor: functions again as a sender, but this time resulting in a dysphoric transformation of the quasiparlando motif at the same time as there occurs an engagement to G minor, which is no longer destabilized; an indexical, forward-directed, but repressed 'not-being'; movement away from 'being'; waltz, trans+.

XII   Mm. 206–50. Tragic ballade prevails: 'doing'; temporal shift to *presto con fuoco*.

XIII   Mm. 250/251–64. Coda: 'being' postmodalized by all preceding elements; definite negation of the secondary actor; synthesis of the introduction and the waltz actor; 'doing' = 'being'.

In this list, waltz+ means an indexical development of the waltz motif; trans- means a transition that both closes and is postmodalized by the preceding section; and trans+ designates a transition that serves as the introduction to, and is premodalized by, the following section.

As early as this phase one may draw some general conclusions about the narrative content of the piece. It involves a struggle between two theme actors, the waltz motif and the quasiparlando motif, in which the latter threatens to become overwhelming (see Exx. 6.17a and b). Between them there prevails a relation of sender/subject, in the sense that the waltz actor serves as a sender both for the glorification of the parlando motif (Ex. 6.18) and for its destruction in the coda (isotopy XII), where dominance of the parlando motif is definitely overcome (Ex. 6.19). This is not a Hegelian composition that proceeds from the antithesis of these two actors to a synthesis on a higher, third level. It is significant that once the waltz motif (in III) functions as if it were its own sender, it leads to dissolution and chaos. In this story, there is no *deus ex machina* solution, as in the *Dante* Sonata by Liszt, but at the end there is a return to the dysphoric isotopy of the waltz, which has grown from mere nostalgia into tragedy.

Example 6.17. Chopin, Ballade in G minor, Op. 23: a. Waltz-actor,
mm. 8–10; b. quasiparlando actor, mm. 67–69.

a.

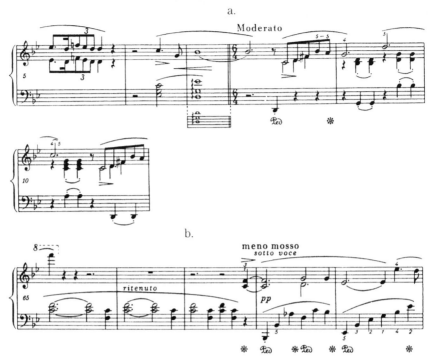

b.

Example 6.18. Chopin, Ballade in G minor, mm. 105–108,
glorification of quasiparlando actor.

TEMPORAL ARTICULATION

    I   *Largo*: A section apparently intended as an almost atemporal, freely preludizing moment; mm. 4–7 with more varied time units, reminiscent of a recitative.

    II   *Moderato*: The waltz rhythm prevails, but with continuous syncopation and absence of a strong pulse in the bass; upbeat to m. 9 starting on the weak part of the measure; at the end of the section (m. 33) surface ornamentation with smaller time units. All these factors create a hesitant, lingering effect.

Example 6.19. Chopin, Ballade in G minor, mm. 206–10,
quasiparlando motif overcome.

III *A tempo, agitato*: Faster version of the waltz rhythm; strong down-beat, but again a syncopation covering the second beat of the bar; the figuration turns wholly to eighth notes and, at the same time, the formerly syncopated bass shifts to provide an anacrusis to the first beat of each bar; distinct accentuation finally disappears altogether in mm. 58–65.

IV *Meno mosso*: Quarter-note arpeggio figuration in the bass, without the accentuation and syncopation of the waltz; freely developed ternary rhythm in the melodic line; a lingering quality.

V *Meno mosso*: Rhythmic diminution to eighth-note triplets, which now dominate; hence a disengagement in relation to the preceding quarter-note figuration; anacruses to strong beats, otherwise equal figuration.

VI *A tempo*: Return of the original lingering rhythms of isotopy II, now more consistent.

VII Rhythmic articulation the same as in IV; waltz pattern reinforced with triads and dyads in the bass; in the right hand, rushing anacruses to first beats (especially mm. 119, 121, 123) over consistent wavelike figurations in the left hand.

VIII *Più animato*: The +disengagement (acceleration from the "normal" pulse) changes into -disengagement (slowing down from the normal pulse); i.e., a shift from the overly slow tempo (in relation to the main waltz tempo) of the previous section to an overly fast tempo; figuration of eighth-note triplet *accelerando*, which gradually becomes lighter.

IX *Scherzando*: Combination of the intensified waltz rhythm (see III) of the accompaniment to waltz+ and the fluttering, consistent triplet figuration of the upper part. At the end of the section, variants of the basic waltz rhythm return in the bass.

   X   In the bass, a quotation from the triplet figuration of V, combined with time units of the melody borrowed from the melodic line of IV; if in the previous section (IX) the following situation prevailed:

upper part = +disengagement

---

lower part = -disengagement

then here we have the situation:

upper part = -disengagement

---

lower part = +disengagement

In other words, there occurs a rhythmic-temporal *Stimmtausch*; in the transition at the end of the section, the upper part follows the lower, complementing it with triplet figures.

   XI   Return of the original version of the waltz rhythm, thus a rhythmic engagement.

   XII   At first the rhythmic figures of the upper part are freely declamatory, in mm. 206–207, recalling the free rhythmic units of the recitative in I. Then they become denser and faster, and here for the first time there is a dotted rhythm and a hemiola, 2/8 against 3/8. In the continuation, there is a strong rhythmic +disengagement to *alla breve* and an abrupt rejection of ternary rhythm, a shift to a totally new rhythmic field in which the time units of the previous section no longer hold.[1] Here we move outside the "normal" ternary waltz *topos* of the narration; in the bass there is a complete inversion of the waltz rhythm, from the pattern of bass note followed by chord alone, to that of chord followed by bass note alone. The only reminiscence of the waltz is the syncopation to the weak second beat, appearing from m. 216 on. Dominance of the eighth-note figuration gives way to virtuosic scale passages which are *en dehors du temps*, notated in smaller time units.

   XIII   Detached rhythmic motifs in mm. 253 and 257 recall the waltz *topos*. In mm. 258–61, in the context of the new quadruple rhythm, a -disengagement occurs; it signals the return of the waltz pattern, but now in a metric context that distorts its original rhythmic essence.

SPATIAL ARTICULATION (O = OUTER SPATIALITY; I = INNER SPATIALITY)

   I   O: The work is launched with a three-bar disengagement via an arpeggiated ♭II of G minor that covers a range of three octaves, followed by a gradual descent to the "proper" register. This is followed by an engagement of three consecutive bars. I: g: ♭II–IV–I6/4 (to V in m. 8, next isotopy).

   II   O: The whole section dwells on the main topical space of the work, the middle register, from which it deviates only in the ornamentation of m. 33. The value of disengagement/engagement is 0. I: The section centers on tonic G minor. The essential forward-driving tension is produced by the dominant seventh and its resolutions, emphasized by placement of the seventh (C) on a syncopation where it is sustained as a finger pedal. The main motif is based on a typically Chopinesque, arpeggiated dominant seventh chord, in contrast to that of mm. 27 and 29.

III   O: gradually descending, partially chromatic motion in the upper line and bass; wide leaps in the accompaniment. From m. 44 onward the spatial sequence is resolved first by contraction into a sinking, four-note group of eighth notes (mm. 44 and 46) and then by development of the descending minor second, which is projected into different octaves. In mm. 44–47 there is a strong +disengagement and intensification in both hands; mm. 48–50 keep to the upper register; in mm. 51–55, another descent; mm. 56–65 contain a ++disengagement that covers the entire keyboard with arpeggiated triads. I: First a sequential, chaconnelike bass, mm. 36–44, with more variety in seventh chords than earlier. The main G minor harmony continues, with some subdominant emphasis via secondary diminished seventh chords. At the end of the section a disengagement occurs that briefly tonicizes B♭ (m. 63 onward), the dominant of the main key (E♭) of the next section.

IV   O: The spatial implication of the melody is clear: first it climbs upward by leaps, from F4 to B♭5 in mm. 68–71, then this gap is filled stepwise. The accompaniment figure expands, disengaged into quarter-note arpeggios in wide leaps. I: The dominant B♭ major, preceded by its dominant (F) in mm. 65–67, begins the section in m. 68. The local tonic of E♭ is weakly established in mm. 69, 72, and 77. Notice the prevalence of the interval of the fourth, harmonically in mm. 66–68, 70, and elsewhere, and melodically in the bass, mm. 69, 71, 72, and elsewhere.

V   O: An engagement to the same register as the waltz *topos* of section II. The section ends with a dissolution to figuration. Typical of this Ballade is a spatial rupture at the end of each section, which in this phase of analysis does not yet have a structural meaning. I: The whole section is in E♭ major, tinged with modal mixture (iv). The end of the section moves toward the A minor tonic of the section to follow; in D minor: m. 91, iv; m. 92, VI; m. 93, i = iv of A minor; m. 94, arrival at dominant of the new key.

VI   O: Concentration in the register of the waltz *topos*, from which the music, pushed by a great tension, gradually rises toward the upper register. I: The dominant pedal point (E) produces tension for the entire section; a tendency to dissonance, produced especially by the diminished seventh chords of mm. 102–105.

VII   O: Disengagement over a wide expanse. A *tutti* effect arises through the "orchestral" usage of the piano. Otherwise this section refers to the space of section IV, except that here we have a spatial extension, with octave duplications of melodic lines. The wide leaps at the end of the section (mm. 117–23) "crystallize" and extend the spatial-melodic program begun in section IV. I: Strong affirmation of A major.

VIII   O: First a sharp engagement to the low register, as a reductive effect, then a gradual rise or slight disengagement to the new (high) register, forming a temporary spatial fulcrum in mm. 133–37. I: An abrupt shift of tonal-harmonic color so that the tonic chord of G♯ minor with raised sixth is interpreted enharmonically as A♭ minor (m. 125), followed by prolongation of B♭ harmony (mm. 126–37), dominant to the E♭ major of the next section.

IX   O: First the upper register provides a new spatial fulcrum in which a fluttering and somewhat disengaged motif is placed. There follows a descent into the middle register (mm. 146–52); but the upper register soon returns (its space may be characterized as transparent and light), until a descending scale passage from F7 to B♭1 shifts the action to a new *topos*. I: The main tonal areas are E♭ major (mm. 138–50), a modulatory passage (mm. 151–53), F♯ minor (mm. 154–55), a modulation (via an enharmonic diminished seventh chord and an augmented sixth, mm. 156–57) back to E♭ major (mm. 158–65).

X   O: The entire section is based on the undulating, arpeggiated accompaniment chords in a low register, and on a spatial strengthening of the upper part as compared to its original form in section IV. The original quarter-note motion has now been filled in with eighth notes to provide broader and richer chords (see, for example, m. 174 onward). Some disengagements occur, into the brilliant upper register of the previous section, which thus modalizes the present isotopy. At the end, again, the rich texture dissolves into chordal arpeggiation. In Chopin all the usual means of filling tonal space, such as simple arpeggiated chords, get a quite different epistemic content than they generally do in the music of the time. In his works such means usually portray transitions or illusory *topoi*, that is, heterotopic tonal spaces, which are not expressly topical, narratively pertinent functions that stress moments of "here." I: The section is firmly in E♭ major until mm. 190–93, which move to the main key, G minor.

XI   O: Return of the register of the waltz *topos* and from there a gradual disengagement toward the upper register. I: The dominant (D) pedal point injects the whole section with a tensional element; dissonant diminished seventh chords over the dominant pedal.

XII   O: Use of registral extremes; a strongly centrifugal tonal space caused by the chordal leaps in the bass, in reverse order from the beginning. Measures 216–27 fix on one register, especially in the bass. Except for the bass register, which remains relatively engaged, a general scheme of the tonal space follows: a sinking from on high (mm. 206–15), staying at one level (mm. 216–27), rising (mm. 228–37), rushing down (mm. 238–41), gradual rise (mm. 242–45), gradual sinking (mm. 246–50). In other words, the tonal space is filled by a chordal zigzag movement, by ascending and descending scales, or alternately broken and continuous lines. I: The whole section is already in its definitive tonal isotopy of G minor. A noteworthy deviation, also reflected in the stagnation of the outer tonal space, is the use of the Neapolitan (mm. 216–26), a reference to the arpeggiated chordal passage that began the piece. Chromatic neighboring and passing tones enter the texture beginning in mm. 208–209. Notice also that the sonority in m. 246 (D–A–C–G–E♭) is almost like a combination of the chords accompanying the recitative of the introduction (mm. 6–7) and that the right-hand figuration in m. 246 begins with the same notes as in m. 5: E♭–D–F–E♭–D.

XIII O: Two quick elements of disengagement, in the form of ascending scales, immediately followed by an engagement to the basic register; at the end, still an extreme disengagement in broken octaves and contrary motion, leading to an engagement with the descent to the tonic. I: Affirmation of G minor; in m. 258 an extreme tritonal tension at the beginning of the parallel octaves, where the motion converges from a tritone to unison octaves.

This spatial analysis also reveals interesting deficiencies in the method. Namely, the terms *disengagement* and *engagement* alone are insufficient to depict with enough subtlety the filling of tonal space with music. One needs further terms of description and formalization in order to describe the manner of shift in tonal space (stepwise or by leap) and the extent and density of shift: does the motion occur on a broad or restricted field? It is clear, for example, that a disengagement occurring over a broader scale is less tensional than one happening on a smaller scale.

ACTORIAL ARTICULATION

Actoriality forms one of the most pertinent and most clearly foregrounded levels of the work. The most obvious—emotional and phenomenal—Firstness impression is that this level is based on a few clear-cut actors and that it does not rely on Beethovenian, "developing variation" techniques of generating motifs. Still actorial analysis shows that Chopin has generated all his most important actors, and indeed the whole actorial content of this piece, from the short preludelike introduction (see Fig. 6.2). He nevertheless masks this technique of generation with many other musical devices, in a way that the listener does not readily notice. In other words, he exploits an epistemic category of 'not-to-appear/to be' or 'secret'. He does not permit the generative nucleus to manifest itself conspicuously, but presents the "row" in the form of a free preludization. The listener believes that what takes place is only the opening of the spatial field of the composition, the display of its palette of colors, when in fact what is offered are the keys to the whole production of actoriality in the composition—something like a code for the growth of forthcoming theme-organisms.

I The introduction contains no clearly profiled theme-actors. Taken as a whole, it serves as a sender for subsequent actors and functions as a hidden source for the inner 'must' (*devoir*) of the work. None of the elements in this preludizing introduction contain any outer iconic or indexical sign relations. The musical substance is purely and innerly musical. At the highest point of the melody a cambiata motif occurs (Ex. 6.20). The antecedent phrase perhaps refers to the recitative style of vocal music; a striking feature is that the cambiata motif, now an octave lower, begins the cadence, in mm. 6–7. A spatial-actorial implication is created in that the second half of m. 2 opens gaps from C5 to C6 which the subsequent part of the introduction fills with a gradual and partly chromatic passage.

Figure 6.2. Thematic-actorial chart of Chopin, Ballade in G minor,
Ballade, Op. 23.

Example 6.20. Chopin, Ballade in G minor, m. 3, cambiata motif.

II   Introduction of the main actor, which follows a Kurthian, rhythmic-symmetric principle of *lied* melodies. It borrows from the *topos* of salon waltzes of the time, so that the actor includes an iconic sign relationship to the external reality of the composition. What is involved is a *Satz*-type theme: a motif, its repetition, and development (8 + 10 + 10 measures). There is something lingering and non-dancelike in the character of the main actor, which is caused by the arpeggiated chord used as an anacrusis and by that chord's constant recurrence. At the end of the section, after a de-actorial ornamentation, the cadence in mm. 34–35 is realized through a quotation of the cambiata motif of the introduction, now transposed down an octave.

III   This section consists of frequent repetition of a variant of the cambiata motif. The repetition is so abundant and gradually becomes so agitated indexically, that the whole section becomes deactorialized through its fifteen repetitions. The listener starts to pay more attention to the harmonic events, the chromatic movement of the extreme parts, and the stepwise temporal acceleration. All this illustrates how a theme changes from a specific to a general character (as Carl Dahlhaus 1988: 159–82 outlines the difference between these concepts). Also, from m. 48 onward the cambiata motif occurs, now transformed into a harmonic fourth followed by a melodic second. This expands the actoriality of the cambiata motif throughout this whole section and takes one out of the intonations of the waltz actor. At the end of the section the deactorialization culminates with the protagonists entirely disappearing from the stage. As the only reminiscence of the protagonists, there remain the open fourths, sounding quite empty, and forming a bridge to the beginning of the next actor.

IV   This section is dominated by an actor that we have called quasiparlando. It too originates from the motivic paradigm of the introduction; here it is reactorialized as an independent musical actant. It does not attempt to negate the main actor, though it happens to occupy the same spatial register. It enters modestly, *sotto voce*, as silently as the *valse oubliée* of the main actor. It is subordinate to the first actor, perhaps in the role of helper, which can be inferred from the continuation in the next section.

V   This aftermath of the quasiparlando actor refers to the main waltz actor of section II, but in no energetic sense. Instead, between the actor of this section and the waltz actor there exists a contractual relation. At the end of this section there is again a deactorialization through dissolution of the characteristic motifs into arpeggiations.

VI   The waltz actor returns, not as a main subject, but as a sender, since it occurs over the tension-creating E pedal point. Its descending seconds turn suddenly into the stubborn gesture of a rising second that demands resolution (mm. 101–105). The result of this indexical "signal" is not at all the apotheosis of the main actor, the waltz theme, but surprisingly the glorification of the secondary actor, which completely occupies the next section, where it emerges as the product of the efforts of the present theme.

VII   The quasiparlando actor here should rather be called a "quasiclamando" actor. Especially in its descending course (which is an icon of an icon), it contains an immediate genetic connection to the corresponding point in section IV, and it also alludes indirectly to the recitative of the introduction. The nobility of the theme gradually becomes more and more imposing and declarative as a rising gesture in octave passages (m. 188 onward), while at the same time it becomes deactorialized.

VIII   In the figuration of this transitional section there is some preactorial material borrowed from, among others, the cambiata motif. Otherwise this section is almost deactorialized, with emphasis instead going to the spatial-temporal dimension.

IX   As a contrast to section VII, there is a *scherzando* development of the cambiata motif, and thus a rejection and lightening of the preceding heroism. At the end of the section, virtuoso elements contain only minimal actoriality.

X   This section presents the quasiparlando motif as a main actor that has pushed the waltz actor aside, as proven by this, its second affirmation. Nevertheless, what is involved in the epistemic sense is 'to-appear/not-to-be'; that is, the actor seems to be something other than what it really is. Yet for someone who knows the end of the story, the quintuplet figure of m. 170, iconically derived from the recitative of the introduction, is enough to mark the beginning of the loss of this actor. Thus it fulfills a Romantic doctrine according to which the kernel of a hero's defeat lies dormant within his greatest brilliance and heroism.

XI   The waltz actor returns again, as if secretly, *sotto voce*. The quasiparlando actor whom it had sent for the action in section VII has occurred in the role of the main subject in all the preceding sections. The waltz actor again adopts the role of sender, but we cannot know in advance the subject or object that the present actor sets in motion as a manifestation of its 'will'.

XII   As a peripety, or unexpected turn, of the narration, one hears as extremely stressed something other than the quasiparlando actor. Consequently the latter actor is strongly denied and revealed as a false hero by this declamatory motif, which comes from the recitative of the introduction. This recitative has undergone a gradual transformation—from a speech to a shout. It is a musical sign that has shifted from the Jakobsonian *emotive* function, where it served mostly the phatic function of maintaining communication, to a *conative*, 'to-make-believe' function. The music continues, with actorial references to, among others, the chromatically sinking, four-note group of the waltz actor (compare mm. 39 and 210–11). This gives us a hint: mm. 208–15 are a more strongly indexical, passionate, further development of the waltz section (III). The Neapolitan chord in turn alludes to the beginning of the introduction. It signals the end of the work and therefore contains a seme of terminativity and perfectivity. Even the virtuosic scale passage in mm. 246–48 is not totally devoid of actoriality; it derives from the last part of the recitative motif of the introduction, which has not been used until now.

XIII   At the end, the waltz actor is heard twice, as a threatening gesture.

Its initial, languishing and lingering character of a *valse oubliée* has turned into a call to battle. The chromatically sinking passage of mm. 258–61 is not actorialized by any previous element, unless one views the passage's intervallic expansion as an answer to the spatial panorama of the beginning.

In our actorial analysis we have proceeded on two different levels. One is a surface narrative level that places the theme actors in the roles of a mythical actant model, as sender, adversary, helper, receiver, subject, and object. The other is the level of deep narration, which shows how actors have been generated from a code or paradigm created by the composer-enunciator—a code which in the case of this Ballade is meant to be heard quite clearly by the perceptive listener, but which the composer might choose to hide.

There remains the task of elucidating the modal level of the piece; that is, how its modalities emerge from articulations of the basic modalities of 'being', 'doing', and 'appearing', and also from the temporal, spatial, and actorial disengagements and engagements that we have just described.

'WILL'

I   In the introduction the value of will+ prevails, in the sense that the tones of the arpeggiation have a clear-cut direction and intention to fill the spatial field of the piece. Moving by the pitch C on metrically stressed beats, the first three measures open up a three-octave registral space. This section begins quite disengaged, with Neapolitan harmony, so that even the inner spatiality manifests will+. In the temporal respect, the introduction, with its free pulsation, has no goal-directedness, and thus gets a zero value of 'will'. This section as a whole, however, is characterized by the value will+. By which criteria we estimate the 'wills' distributed to different parameters (for example, can a strong rhythmic 'will' compensate for a spatial 'not-will'?) is a question that remains without formalization. Consequently, such estimation will be based on the judgment and competence of the analyst.

II   This section is dominated by repetition of the waltz actor. Since it is based on a seventh chord and its numerous resolutions and on mere recurrence, it has a negative value of 'will', or will-. The rhythmic value would perhaps be will 0, since this section dwells on the basic rhythmic unit of the whole composition, the piece's temporal engagement.

III   This section represents an indexical development of the waltz, here provided with a strong feeling of forward-directedness (which in the interoceptive sense is always a sign of indexicality in music). This directedness represents will++; so much 'will' occurs that one expects it to diminish in the continuation.

IV   This section neutralizes the preceding one. As stated earlier, it manifests a tendency away from action or 'doing'.

V   A tendency toward 'being' is obvious, particularly at the end of this section, where actoriality dissolves into non-tensional, arpeggiated triads. The section thus receives the value will-.

VI The waltz actor comes back, but now in the role of a sender; that is, it functions to produce a musical object from which one is disjuncted. This disjunction is experienced as the narrative figure of the "emergence of a lack." Consequently it represents the search for a future object—we do not yet know which one—and there is will+, which at the end of the section grows to will++.

VII The quasiparlando actor appears, in all its deceptive brilliance. The moment of 'will' remains high (will++) although this section represents dissolution of the previous tension through the seme of terminativity and perfectivity. Notice also the spatial disengagement to the key of A major, strong emphasis on the outer spatiality by a filling of the tonal space with an orchestral *tutti* effect, and the actorial disengagement+ constituting a strong affirmation of the secondary actor of the piece. Such factors cause the degree of 'will' to remain ++.

VIII In this section the degree of 'will', or kinetic quality, sinks abruptly, but it remains basically similar in regard to the 'not-being' character of the whole section. That is, the section functions as an inner index that prepares and premodalizes the next section: will+.

IX At the beginning the degree of 'will' is negative, in keeping with this light *scherzando* section. Toward the end of the section the 'will' rises to 0, as the 'being' of the subsequent section is prepared.

X The second affirmation of quasiparlando, with a deceptive spatial engagement to a nearly related key (E♭ major) of the main actor. Nevertheless, some amount of 'will' remains, because in the temporal-spatial-actorial sense we are still not yet completely engaged to the starting point of the narration. Therefore will 0 → +.

XI The waltz actor returns, but in an incorrect spatial isotopy. Again a great increase of 'will' occurs throughout the section because the actor functions as a sender whose object we do not yet know (the first time it was the quasiglorification of the secondary actor). Consequently the degree of 'will' increases from + to ++.

XII The degree of 'will' in this section remains at ++ because although we are engaged spatially to the starting point (G minor) of the narration, temporally we remain amidst an extremely agitated *presto con fuoco*, and actorially, amidst a completely actorless or disengaged state. Thus will++, since the piece has not yet ended and the 'will' been dropped.

XIII In this section extreme values of 'will' alternate. The ascending rush of octaves gets the value of ++; on the other hand, the calming triads and return of the main actor receive values of 0 or +. The desperate and dysphoric octave passage at the end represents ++, whereas the final tonic chord represents 0. This section has its own, miniature narrative program with respect to its 'will': ++, 0, ++, +, ++, 0.

In this description of the 'will', one notices the 'becoming' of music, the effect of music's basic temporality, since it is not enough merely to describe any section in terms of either ++ or 0 or -. One should also be able to depict the movement from ++ to 0, or from + to ++, if such is the precise content and order of the element of 'will'. A compound symbol is suitable for such a description; for example, + → ++.

'KNOW'

It was noted above, in connection with actorialization, that the seven-bar introduction contains the most essential musical-thematic substance or cognitive moment of the piece. Yet this is not the only issue relevant to 'know', since we are also interested in precisely how the composer creates cognition and information over the temporal course of the piece. It is therefore crucial to discern how the musical substance serves this informative function, in which repetition always means a negation of 'know' and difference means its affirmation.

The 'knowing' in music also pertains to particular informational structures in the sense that a complex fugue seems to contain more knowledge invested in music than does a melodically simple, theme/accompaniment situation. Even here the outer/inner distinction holds: a complicated polyphonic texture contains more outer 'knowing' than does a homophonic structure. As to the inner 'knowing', the degree of organization of the musical substance does not mean anything as such, since what matters are the relative values that appear during the temporal unfolding of a piece. It is obviously necessary to determine both these values when speaking about 'knowing'.

I   In the introduction, the degree of outer 'knowing' is small. Naturally anything heard first in a composition strongly determines all of what follows— the opening moment is decisive to the development of the informational network throughout the piece. There are two kinds of texture in this section: unison lines and melody/accompaniment. Thus although the cambiata motif of mm. 6–7 already appeared at the beginning of m. 3, at the peak of the melodic curve, it is heard in mm. 6–7 as part of a new texture. This situation militates against basing a motif's value of 'knowing' merely on recurrence. Hence the only repeated or redundant element is the repetition of the arpeggiated triad of A♭ major in different registers, though even there a slight *différance* comes about because the repetition occurs in different registers. Consequently section I projects a fairly rich and expectant 'knowing': knowing+.

II   This section consists of simple spatial relations, waltz rhythm, and repetitions of a simple melody. The overall redundancy caused by the repetition does not change, despite the fact that a development takes place toward the end of the section. As a whole, the section represents a simple melody accompanied by chords, with virtuosic figuration in m. 33, which never strengthens the 'knowing'. (Here again one notices the incompatibility of modalities: the plus value of 'knowing' does not measure up to the plus values of 'can' in the sense of virtuosity.) On the other hand, when the cambiata motif of mm. 34–35 is provided with a surprising moment, this ornamentation erases from memory the thematicity of the section's beginning. Altogether, the degree of 'knowing' is positive, know+, due to the phenomenal, Firstness quality of all the musical material.

III   This indexical waltz development does not contain mere repetition: the waltz rhythm becomes stereotyped, and the recurrent cambiata figure deactorializes the section by adopting the function of an indexical 'can'. The degree of 'knowing' is negative: know-.

IV   The quasiparlando motif, in turn, is something "new" which emerges as the result of the preceding indexical process. Also, the accompaniment texture is varied, and is not a schematic repetition of the same figure. The 'knowing' of the melody is diminished, however, by the sequential passage in the consequent phrase (mm. 71–75), which follows a circle of fifths with respect to inner spatiality (sequences always mean a fall in the values of 'knowing'): know+.

V   This section, postmodalized by the previous section, introduces no new musical substance; rather, it tries to finish the isotopy created by the preceding section. This section also refers (m. 84) to the waltz actor heard earlier. This reference lowers the degree of 'knowing', despite the astonishing context in which it takes place: know 0.

VI   This section is based on the return of the waltz actor, but difference arises by that actor's placement over a tension-building pedal point. Yet this is not enough to prevent one from experiencing the section as a very abundant repetition of the same motif; accordingly, know-.

VII   The quasiparlando motif unexpectedly appears as the object of the 'will' of the preceding section, and is transformed into a quasiclamando. In the cognitive sense, this transformation creates new information. Also, the spatial disengagement to A major has a surprising effect. The accompaniment figure stabilizes from a changing line into repeated figuration, and this in turn diminishes the 'knowing'. The repetition of the quasiparlando in m. 114 produces a small ABA form that changes the positive values of the first half of the section to negative in the latter half. All this constitutes a move from know+ to know-.

VIII   With its surprising spatial disengagements from the upper register downward, and with its enharmonic modulations (G♯/A♭, E♯/F), the beginning of the transition is rich in information. As the section continues, 'can' comes to the fore, and mere figuration steps in to prepare the *scherzando* texture of the next section. Thus this transition, like the preceding section, moves from know+ to know-.

IX   The *scherzando* section lightens the atmosphere, but at the same time keeps the 'knowing' at 0.

X   The return of the quasiparlando motif is heard as a logical consequence of the preceding section. The result of such a teleological-causal process can only be very uninformative. Such a process strengthens the symmetry, or 'must', of the global form, but for 'knowing' represents the most redundant possibility, as well as the fundamental modality of 'being': know--.

XI   Similarly, the next transition, with its return of the waltz actor, is, as to its kinetic energy, a tension-producing and positive event, but not as to its informational content. Toward the end of a piece, possibilities of choice automatically decrease. Uncertainty diminishes and is replaced by surety, especially insofar as the material of the first half repeats. 'Must', 'can', and 'will' grow, but 'knowing' stays at its lowest degree: know--.

XII   This is the peripety of the narrative process, though actorially an engagement prevails. The return of motifs from the piece's introductory recitative is experienced as surprising, since the waltz actor last functioned as the sender for the object constituted by the quasiparlando actor in a euphoric A major. Now the result is a tragic G minor, with all its dysphoria, which will be underscored by the entire succeeding section. The peripety is also emphasized by the fact that an entirely new temporality, quadruple meter, begins. It differs strikingly from that of the waltz and thus forms the beginning of a new cognition. This difference is so abrupt and unexpected that at first the degree of 'knowing' leaps to know+, but it soon decreases gradually, because of the repetitiveness of the figures. Although the virtuosic, descending scale passage at the end is such an innovation, it is nevertheless an expansion of the recitative motif of the introduction, and thus a kind of repetition.[2] If the composer had not presented the paradigm of the most relevant musical substance at the beginning of the work, this moment of 'knowing' might be heard as positive. It therefore changes from + at the beginning of this section to 0 at the end (a hidden repetition can be considered as zero information; an apparent and recognized repetition, as a minus).

XIII   The last section brings about new information by the simple means of choosing from the intonational store formed by the piece itself, the piece's inner (paradigm of) memory, elements that one would not expect to hear in combination. It creates new 'knowing' precisely from these unexpected combinations. This is the means by which, for example, a music based on a technique of citation tries to destroy its own redundancy, and by which postmodern music operates (for one example, see the sudden changes of texture in Poulenc's *Concerto for Two Pianos*). Also, musical humor is often based on this usage of the modality of 'knowing'.

The scale passages form an entropic element, whereas the G minor tonic chords and the declamatory-heroic variants of the waltz actor which follow serve as a redundant factor; however, when they occur successively, to form a strong contrast following the principle of anti-indexicality, the redundancy— the inner iconicity formed by the waltz actors—disappears, replaced by a new value of 'knowing': know+. The value rises for a while into know++, caused by the parallel-octave passage proceeding out of a tritone; such a passage is a new element in the work.

'CAN'

This modality focuses our attention on the instrumental, in this case pianistic, aspect of the piece. Anything that causes the technical aspect of a performance to flourish, even at the expense of other modalities, is noteworthy in this phase of the analysis. Accordingly, at those moments when the texture of the piece begins to approach the ideal of nonidiomatic writing—as in the Baroque era, in pieces which could be performed equally well regardless of the instrument or ensemble—the degree of 'can' is 0. Chopin's writing is very idiomatic, however, as evidenced by the fact that few composers have succeeded in orchestrating his piano pieces.

I   The arpeggio of the beginning is perhaps an imitation of the overtone series, although it is considerably more distant and weaker than the passage that begins the *Polonaise-Fantaisie*. Instead, this recitative, with its unison passages, contains no particularly instrumental innovation: can 0.

II   The arpeggiated chord of the upbeat of the waltz actor has been placed in an advantageous position. Chopin's own fingerings require gliding the fifth finger from a black to a white key. Otherwise the first half of the section is completely neutral in instrumental value. A surprising figuration in m. 33 suddenly pushes the 'can' of the piano into the foreground, from 0 to +.

III   Only the development of the waltz actor, which was for the 'knowing' a purely negative phenomenon, makes the instrumental aspect thrive. The degree of 'can' grows gradually toward the end of the section, from + to ++, reaching its peak in the difficult but instrumentally imaginative figures of mm. 48–53. Nevertheless it diminishes at the end to can+, with shifts to "normal" chordal arpeggiations.

IV   In the quasiparlando section there is no particular instrumental innovation, but since it does not directly repeat any previous figuration, its degree of 'can' remains 0.

V   Neither does this section, which closes out the previous one, offer anything instrumentally new, although it has been written very aptly for the instrument when the waltz actor bursts forth in a middle part.

VI   The premodalization of this section by the foregoing one does not increase 'can' to the same extent that it strengthens 'will', forward-directedness, and indexicality. 'Can' is 0 because this texture has occurred before in the piece.

VII   In the return of the secondary, quasiparlando motif, what is essential is the instrumental *tutti* effect. The octave passages in sequences have been skillfully written so that the middle parts give support to the right hand. Toward the end of the section, virtuosity flashes out in the ascending octave passages, so that here 'can' moves from + to ++.

VIII   The transition is instrumentally very innovative. With regard to several other modalities, it is an insignificant passage, but for 'can' it is a noteworthy section: can++.

IX   'Can' remains high throughout this *scherzando*. In fact, various virtuoso piano textures alternate so frequently that this section represents a particular 'knowing' of what one 'can'. The same techniques are not repeated but are creatively varied throughout: fluttering, *détaché* texture in the upper part, a chromatic scale against a waltz rhythm in the bass, an octave sequence, scale/broken chord, and again a scale.

X   Perhaps in order to emphasize the character of a stable 'being', the instrumental inventiveness suddenly stops completely, and the actors are allowed to return as such, while borrowing elements of accompaniment from the old technical store: can-.

XI This transition forms part of a continuous sinking, eventually into can--, since instrumentally it is a texture quite similar to that heard as early as section VI.

XII As surprising as this section is regarding 'knowing', it is equally so in its 'can'. There is an extremely abrupt shift from can-- to can++. From beginning to end this section is an extremely virtuosic instrumental passage, and in this respect also innovative. For example, mm. 208–209 exhibit not only the tonic chords of G minor; Chopin inserts nonchord tones that make the technical performance much more difficult, while also providing a refreshingly new sound. At the same time, the 'can' unites with the 'knowing', or cognitive moment; as almost always happens in Chopin, the figuration is thematically-actorially motivated (see the scale in mm. 246–49, which derives from the motivic paradigm of the introduction).

XIII To the very end the effectiveness of the piece stays at can++. In the last measures this value arises through the alternation of different instrumental figures and technical devices.

'MUST'

At first, one might be tempted to think that the analysis of the modality of 'must' would come closest to traditional style and formal analysis of music, since stylistic *topoi*, as well as formal schemes (sonata, chaconne, menuetto, and so on) and genre traditions, constitute the normative ground against which the 'must' of a musical text is investigated (see Ratner 1980). Yet 'must' extends to still broader areas; for instance, orchestration has its own rules, or 'musts'. The maxims in Rimsky-Korsakov's instrumentation treatise—"Every composition has to be written in a way which renders its performance easy" and "The work has to be written taking into account its orchestral effect"—represent a combination of 'must' and 'can'.

In contrast to 'knowing', 'must' grows toward the end of a composition because its formal type is often not revealed until the scheme is completed. We do not know, for example, whether a work is in sonata form until we have heard its development or its recapitulation. Some methods pay attention to this aspect, but they remain mere score analysis and probably practice the stiff "geometric" segmentation belittled by Kurth, since a listener cannot hear this 'must' of a form, which therefore does not influence the experienced form.

Also, when we evaluate the degree of 'must' in its various manifestations, we are faced with the difficult task of imagining ourselves in the position of a listener at the time of Chopin or Mozart, and we have to approach the work from the stylistic and formal norms of its period. In this sense the analysis of 'must' in our semiotic methodology perhaps comes close to historical musicology. On the other hand, we suggest that a music text also has its own, inner and structural 'must', which is established by the text itself and is open and universally definable for listeners having sufficient competence. An analyst of new music has no 'must' other than that offered by the piece itself: part of the inner 'must' of an avant-garde musical work is that it denies all outer 'must'. Therefore regarding 'must', we also have to distinguish two aspects: the outer, which refers to style-historical and traditional generic norms; and the inner, which for the listener takes shape in the unfolding of the musical work itself.

Quite often the title of a composition includes a normative reference to what the piece will convey. If the title is "sonata" then the composer makes a commitment to the outer 'must' of a certain formal type. Contrarily, if it is a "fantasy," he or she is bound to a certain 'not-must', which permits formal liberties. The designation "ballade" is common to Romantic pieces and does not necessarily say anything normative about the form of a piece (for example, compare the ballades by Liszt and Brahms to those by Chopin). Instead, "ballade" undeniably refers to a certain narrativity, a certain semanticity, although Chopin has left it completely open as to what kind. Therefore, in a semiotic analysis it is better to investigate the structural level and to look for those significations one can find by using the generative trajectory of a piece.

I   The introduction displays no consistent temporal program; spatially, normal chord functions guide the course of the music; the actoriality remains quite open (we do not know that here we in fact have the kernel of the actoriality of the whole piece, its thematic 'must'); must 0.

II   The waltz section takes shape according to the rhythmic-symmetric *lied* form so-designated by Kurth: 4 + 4 + 4 + 4 + 2 + 3 + 3 + 4: The accompaniment figure of the waltz is kept on as a "norm"; it is temporarily abandoned in mm. 26–33 but returns at the close of the section, a return which means a spatial engagement according to the norms of tonal music. This section contains elements that break waltz norms, for instance, the pianistic figuration in m. 33, thus: must+.

III   In this development of the waltz a shift occurs, from an oft-repeated texture containing much 'must' to a seemingly free development in which the instrumental 'can' is rather overwhelming. Even this early in the composition one notices that the 'must' of the form and the 'can' of the technical realization are incompatible—instrumental virtuosity has never helped fulfill strict formal schemes. So we have here a shift from a must+ to must 0.

IV   The quasiparlando section follows sonata norms, inasmuch as the subordinate theme occurs in a third-related key (a commonplace in sonatas of the time). In character it differs enough from the main theme that it forms the secondary theme of the composition. As a rule, in compositions of this style period one might expect something new to be introduced at this moment in the piece, regardless of whether it is in sonata form. Even this theme follows a symmetric *lied* form: must+.

V   This transition freely fantasizes, though hints of the waltz theme produce a certain amount of 'must'; not, however, as anything particularly obligatory, but rather as a fortuitous remembrance: must 0.

VI   The return of the waltz actor, here with the function of a sender, would be for the 'must' a significant strengthening, if it were to appear in the same thematic role as at the beginning or as the main subject. But that is not the case: the pedal point causes the listener to give up the idea of a formal scheme based on repetition (such as a rondo). Rather, the value of 'must' is negative: must-.

VII   The triumphant return of the quasiparlando motif, or secondary theme, would perhaps be a repetition making the 'must' grow, but the unexpected spatial isotopy (A major) and virtuosic 'can' reduce the probability of 'must'. However, repetition is always a factor that increases 'must', so the modal value of the section is must 0.

VIII   Again, instrumental 'can' is so prevalent in this transition that the 'must' stays at 0.

IX   This *scherzando* section follows the temporal scheme of a waltz, the fundamental isotopy of the piece, though in a remarkably accelerated rhythm as compared to the beginning. Nevertheless it is experienced as a lightening, a capricious episode which could just as well have been left out of the piece, considering the formal outline and progress of narrative plot. On the actorial level, this section in no way attempts to sharpen the competition and opposition of the two actors of the piece: Must-.

X   The return of the quasiparlando motif, even in its original spatial isotopy of E♭ major, necessarily serves as a form-building element.[3] The degree of 'must' grows constantly in relation to the preceding section. The listener anticipates completion of the formal scheme of A (Introduction)–B (waltz)–C, C′, C″. Now, after an episode inserted into the waltz isotopy, one expects B′: must++.

XI   The return of the waltz actor, however, is not a "correct" return of section B, but again the waltz actor plays the role of sender and not of main subject. The listener's thwarted expectation is diminished by the fact that this same situation occurred earlier, in section VI. The value of 'must' accordingly decreases to must+.

XII   This section, the result of the preceding indexical process, is heard as a psychological surprise and, regarding the global form, as a sort of return of the Introduction; B is left out entirely. This is not a conventional resolution, though in the narrative sense it is completely justified. Also, the section contains normative spatiality and actoriality, so much so that the decisive point in mm. 206–207 has in a way already been heard, in mm. 3–5 of the introduction. The following texture has a codalike character, caused by the abandonment of triple meter. The high value of 'can' means a low 'must' for the formal design, so that we have must-.

XIII   At the end of the piece the expected waltz actor finally arrives, but in truncated form, like the "last words of the hero before death," so that it no longer realizes any formal scheme, properly speaking. The somewhat artificial increase of 'knowing' automatically means a very low degree of 'must'. This is in no way an anticipated ending for the work: one does not think that the higher-level semantic narrative program, to which the balladic nature of the title refers, would presuppose the occurrence of such astonishingly sharpened, tragic-dysphoric situations. Considering the form as heard, the closure is therefore not normative.[1] Actorially (return of the main subject) and spatially (return of the tonic) the closure follows the modality of 'must', but neither the temporal nor any other modal constellation would favor a fairly high value of 'must' (the 'can' and 'knowing' naturally decrease its value). The closure is thus must 0.

'BELIEVE'

As the last modality, we shall consider the epistemic structure of the piece, its truthfulness or persuasiveness. For Umberto Eco, it is characteristic of any sign that it can not only speak truths but can also lie or betray. Without arguing that the narrative figure of Betrayal or Deception would be central for a listener to Chopin, the piece undoubtedly provides material for an epistemic interpretation. With regard to the categories of truth/untruth/lie/secret of the veridictory square, we have discussed the secret code, or resolution, hidden in the introduction of the piece but uncovered in the surprising and tragic-dramatic turn of mm. 206–207 (beginning of section XII). Thus we have already found at least the categories of secret and truth. Where can we find other terms, and how does the work unfold via operations of affirmation, denial, doubt, and other epistemic entities?

First of all, the waltz isotopy with its actors proves to be a false subject, since it does not return in correct form at decisive moments in the global design of the work, that is, in the narrative trajectory. Still, the category of a musical lie in the correct sense would instead be occupied by the misleading program of the secondary theme, with its apparent glorifications. Therefore the waltz actor falls into the category of untruth. Departing from this fundamental epistemic articulation, we now examine how epistemic operations of affirmation/denial, admittance/doubt, and the aspectual semes of excessive/insufficient, sufficient/inexcessive appear in each section.

I   For a listener, the atmosphere at the beginning of the piece recalls the start of a story. Like a writer, Chopin first outlines the topical space of the ensuing action. However, the Neapolitan arpeggio of the beginning functions to mislead the listener as to what the tonic is. Therefore what is involved is m̄ab (not 'make-appear-to be'), or preventing something from appearing as what it is, here preventing the emergence of G minor.[']

At the beginning, we are unsure, and we doubt whether we are in the correct isotopy. The actorial cambiata motif appears in m. 3. There we learn that Ab major is not the tonic, though it would appear to be; that is, we have the uncovering of a deceit or a betrayal (m̄ab). In m. 3, C minor is offered as the tonic, since that is the most obvious harmonic implication of the melodic perfect fourth, C—G on beat 1. Yet the continuation in mm. 4–5 denies C minor, and so we have the modal constellation of m̄ba. Finally, in mm. 6–7/8 the "ears" of the listener are opened as to the correct key, when the G minor is established and affirmed (mba). Consequently, as early as the brief introduction the listener is led through four epistemic modalizations in the order shown in Fig. 6.3. On the level of the musical enunciation and utterance itself, this corresponds to the operations shown in Fig. 6.4.

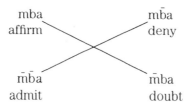

Figure 6.3. Epistemic modalizations by listener, Isotopy I.

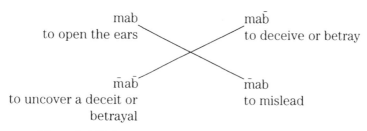

Figure 6.4. Epistemic modalizations on the level of musical
enunciate and enunciation, Isotopy I.

In Fig. 6.3, 'being' modalizes 'appearing', whereas in Fig. 6.4, 'appearing' modalizes 'being'; thus the square in the former approaches modalizations from a listener's standpoint, while the latter describes them as acts of a composer. However, the effects of meaning are similar in both cases.

II   Even on first hearing, this isotopy, the waltz, contains a far from affirmative, distant, and illusory *valse oubliée*. It thus appears to be something quite different from what it is. Chopin borrows characteristic waltz features from the intonational store of his time; but since the listener knows that the composition in which they are placed is a ballade and not a waltz, he or she has a presentiment that the waltz actor is no true waltz. This situation falls in the category mab. Notice also that mm. 34–35 of this section bring back the cambiata motif of the introduction, which at first was provided with the epistemic value of the "uncovering of a betrayal" and then of "affirmation." These values have clung to this motif, but they now assume a different content in the new epistemic isotopy. In this case, they only affirm the epistemic value of the entire section, its illusory character or mab.

III   In this section the development of the waltz proves to be a "true" one (mab), but toward the end of the section the waltzlike character is transformed from the category of sufficient to that of excessive, through extreme repetition of the cambiata motif and the waltz rhythm. This brings us to the category of mab: the waltz is shown to be something other than it first seemed. So we have a shift from mab to mab.

IV   The quasiparlando motif, like the waltz actor, is not particularly affirmative in nature, even though the tonality and sequential passages provide it with a certain safe and convincing character. It is a detensional, consonant 'being', but only temporarily. It is an 'inexcessive being' which one might soon have to give up. What is involved is not a strong tonic but tonicization by secondary dominants and hints of minor VI (mm. 74–75). This section should thus be interpreted as in the category m̄ab; its 'being' is somewhat unsure and doubtful.

V   The transition section aims to emphasize and strengthen the epistemic situation of the preceding section, that is, the temporary tonic of E♭ major. Also, the waltz actor, which hitherto has served as the main subject, touches on an incorrect isotopy. As already stated, this section is premodalized by and contains the same epistemic value as the foregoing one; but its 'being' is somehow stronger, m̄ab+, because of I–V alternations over the E♭ pedal (temporary tonic).

VI   This section first strives to show that the 'being' of the preceding section was only provisional and deceptive, that it represented m̄ab̄. There, however, the waltz actor was experienced as a true affirmation and occurred in an incorrect spatial isotopy, which made it a sender-actant for someone whom we would now presume to be mab, or true, and experienced as a veritable affirmation. So here we have a movement from m̄ab̄ toward mab. One might add that this action is very indexical by nature; the 'doing' is very underscored, even excessive. In other words: m̄ab̄ → m+ab.

VII   Here we are surprised by the apparent glorification of the second theme, or the category mab̄. Even here one could say that the aspect of 'doing', or the way this "betrayal" is realized in music, is strongly tensional, provided with a *tutti* and with *fortissimo* dynamics: m+ab̄.

VIII   In this transition the epistemic situation changes abruptly. The listener is kept in a state of uncertainty as to what will follow. It represents a premodalizing section whose value can be determined only when one knows in which direction one is headed. The premodalization is already evidenced by the texture's gradually thinning; this involves a movement toward the transient and euphoric illusion of the *scherzando*, a fictional state in which the virtuoso 'appearing' (in the form of technical 'can') dominates, and the modal value is m+āb̄ → mab̄.

IX   The temporary illusion of a *scherzando*: mab̄.

X   This is the return of the quasiparlando motif, now showing its true character. The prolonged E♭ major key area prevents this subordinate actor from appearing to be the main actor, which it strives by all means to be. Nevertheless, the 'appearing' and 'being' of this section remain doubtful, in spite of this passionate striving: m̄+ab.

XI   The waltz actor comes back, now in its correct spatial field, as we start to approach that actor's definitive affirmation. The starting point of this section serves as the denial of the lie of the preceding section, then as a movement toward the truth, or m̄+ab̄ → mab.

XII   Strongly premodalized in the preceding section, this is the climax of the whole piece, the height of its 'making to believe', or persuasion. The ears are ready for the moment of the truth, or mab, but only via a disappointment on another level, namely, for anyone who has followed the development of the waltz actor. Because at the beginning this actor appeared as a denied and uncertain subject, then twice as a sender, one would now expect it to send itself to definite glorification. This does not happen; instead, what really corresponds to the category of truth is the unveiling of the recitative motif of the beginning as the most important element of the work. The dysphoric G minor this motif reintroduces is reinforced as the section continues: m+ab.

XIII   The waltz actor reenters, but now too late to be convincing. It has become merely a defiant but powerless gesture. The tragic dysphoria of the Ballade, which was hidden at the beginning of the work, has now been revealed, to end the piece with a modalization of mab.

The whole field of modalities in the Ballade in G minor is shown in Fig. 6.5, which might be useful in comparing all of Chopin's Ballades with each other. This chart might also be written in syntagmatic form (as a linear series of signs) according to the rules of Greimasian narrative grammar. As we have mentioned (Chap. 1.2), in Greimas's theory the starting point of the description of narrativity is the scheme F S1 → (S2 v Ov), which means that a subject S1 acts—and the nature of this activity can be specified with a modality—so that a subject S2 becomes disjuncted from a value-object Ov. For example, in the *Ring des Nibelungen*, Alberich (S1) acts so that the Rhinemaidens (S2) lose their value object (Ov), the Rhinegold.

	'Be/Do'	'Will'	'Know'	'Can'	'Must'	'Believe'
I	not to-do	+	+	0	0	māb
II	to be	0	+	0 → +	+	mab̄
III	to do	++	-	+ → ++	+ → 0	mab → m̄ab̄
IV	not-to-do	0	+	0	+	m̄ab
V	not-to-be, trans-	-	0	0	0	m̄ab+
VI	not to-be, trans+	+ → ++	-	0	-	m̄ab̄ → m+ab
VII	to appear to do	++	+ → -	+ → ++	0	m+ab̄
VIII	not-to-be	+	+ → -	++	0	m+āb̄ → mab̄
IX	to appear to be	- → 0	0	++	-	mab̄
X	to be	0 → +	--	-	++	m̄+ab
XI	not-to-be, trans+	+ → ++	--	--	+	m̄+ab̄ → mab
XII	to do	++	+ → 0	- → ++	-	m+ab
XIII	to do= to be	++ → 0	+ → ++	++	0	mab

Figure 6.5. Modal activity in Chopin, Ballade in G minor, Op. 23.

The scheme can also be written in a more general form, as Fm S → (S ∨ Ov). Yet if we start to elaborate a modal grammar on this basis, we are faced with the problem of distinguishing between subject and object in a musical discourse. Doubtless, in some cases music is so anthropomorphic at the surface level that one can distinguish formations there which may be called subjects, and others the objects they seek. Such a case undeniably forms an exception. Rather, it usually holds true that, if Lévi-Strauss says music is *le langage moins le sens*, then for us it is perhaps more *langage moins l'objet* or *récit moins le sens*. The greatest obstacle to formalization of musical narration seems to lie in distinguishing between subject and object. As long as we understand this distinction as a relation between the subject (composer, performer, listener) of the act of enunciation and the enunciate itself, everything seems logical. But what would correspond to a subject and object within a musical piece?

One might think that both subject and object are purely intentional entities which cannot be identified with any physical place or point. The subject of musical narration would then be an inner narrator of music, the "I" who experiences various phases and changes between 'being' and 'doing', but who cannot be identified with any real subject. This problem has been much discussed in musicological literature. For Adorno, Mahler as a person was not the same as the fictional hero of his symphonies. According to Dahlhaus, Beethoven himself is not the same as the victorious or tragic hero-subject of his symphonies. The goal of the musical process, the searched-for object, need not always be visible or, rather, audible. Perhaps in all temporal processes this object is a euphoric final-state in which all tensions have been resolved and in which something is experienced as being achieved, fulfilled, as in the finale themes of Beethoven's Ninth Symphony, Brahms's First, and Sibelius's Second. In these cases it is quite clear what forms the object in music. Yet on the other hand, the musical object may vary throughout the same piece, making it impossible to determine with certainty. Hence in writing a modal grammar, I leave open the subject/object problem, but reserve a place for it in the logical-formal scheme.

According to Greimas the basic situations of any narration are S ∨ O and S ∧ O, that is, a subject is disjuncted from or conjuncted with an object, which states, roughly speaking, appear on the thymic level as either dysphoric or euphoric. In music, disjunction would equal the musical 'doing', since the lack of some object is experienced as tensional and catalyzes the action. Correspondingly, conjunction produces a resolution of tension and thus musical 'being'. When these terms are placed onto a semiotic square, two other cases arise: S ∨̄ O, in which a subject is going to be re-conjuncted with an object; and S ∧̄ O, in which a subject still is or has conjuncted with an object but is about to lose or become disjuncted from it (see Fig. 6.6). The latter two cases fall under the categories of 'not-doing' and 'not-being'.

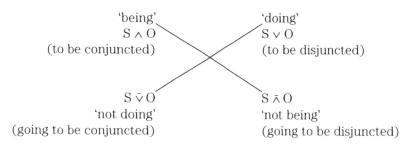

Figure 6.6. Conjunctions and disjunctions in Chopin, Ballade
in G minor, Op. 23.

Now we return to Chopin's Ballade in G minor and segment the work into categories of being/doing, not-being/not-doing, considering all thirteen isotopies as narrative programs (PNs):

PN I: F (w+, k+, c0, m0, māb) [S v̄ O] T

PN II: F (w0, k+, c0 → +, m+, mab̄) [S ∧ O] T

PN III: F (w++, k-, c+ → ++ → +, m+ → 0, mab → m̄ab̄) [S ∨ O] T

PN IV: F (w0, k+, c0, m+, m̄ab̄) [S v̄ O] T

PN V: F (w-, k0, c0, m0, m̄ab+) [S ∧̄ O] T-

PN VI: F (w++, k+ → -, c+ → ++, m0, m̄ab̄ → m+ab) [S ∧̄ O] T+

PN VII: F (w++, k+ → -, c+ → ++, m0, m+ab̄) [S v̄ O] T

PN VIII: F (w+, k+ → -, c++, m0, m+āb̄ → mab̄) [S ∧̄ O] T+

PN IX: F (w- → 0, k0, c++, m-, mab̄) [S ∧̄ O] T

PN X: F (w0 → +, k--, c-, m++, m̄+ab) [S ∧ O] T

PN XI: F (w + → ++, k--, c--, m+, m̄+ab̄ → mab) [S ∧̄ O] T+

PN XII: F (w++, k+ → 0, c-- → ++, m-, m+ab) [S ∨ O] T

PN XIII: F (w++ → 0, k+ → ++, c++, m0, mab) [S ∨ O → S ∧ O][6]

Most analyses using formal symbolism stop at this phase. Once the living musical figures, the inner dynamics, and other audible aspects have been captured by schemes which at first sight may frighten some readers, the analyst considers the task finished. Yet to all this the reader can with full justification ask: so what? I respond by saying that analysis also requires common sense. When the formalization is completed and the narrative grammar is written, one has to find a use for it. The grammar can elucidate diverse and problematic situations on different musical levels, situations which might present difficulty in listening to or performing the piece.

The next phase of analysis would be to find the typical figures of a composer and to scrutinize them in the light of a previously revealed semiotic structure. On the other hand, if we consider as a figure some musical situation typical of a composer, that figure can be examined only after analysis of the whole corpus, when one can see precisely which figures recur. In the G minor Ballade, for example, one may consider several features as figures: In isotopies VI and XI, "damming the tension"; in IX, the texturalization of actoriality, that is, transformation of the thematic material into mere texture, produces a virtuosic variant of the modality of 'can'. The balladic and fateful twist, which occurs between XI and XII, is a figure also realized in the F minor Ballade. The dissolution of a previous texture at the beginning of a succeeding section is a figure (which Chopin perhaps uses to greatest effect in the finale to his B♭ minor Sonata) that is realized in XII. The introduction, the onset of narrative time, forms its own figure in isotopy I. In the G minor Ballade the introduction figure performs an important structural task, whereas in some other ballades we have a different type of introduction, in the manner of a true improvisation, such as the famous search for the "blue" note (see the Fourth Ballade); in still other cases this figure is deliberately omitted (the Second Ballade). Very often in the middle of a composition there is a polyphonic development section (as sometimes happens in Beethoven) which realizes the aspectual seme of durativity. No such figure occurs here; cf. the Second (mm. 96–133) and Fourth (mm. 135–45) Ballades.

From these observations one may conclude that "figure" is an intertextual concept related not only to genre but also to a more extensive paradigm of intonations. Whether the figures in music always follow a certain order, in the manner of Proppian functions, is impossible to say before one has thoroughly analyzed a sufficient number of works of the composer or the music-historical period in question.

VII

MUSIC AND LITERATURE

7.1 The Case of *Obermann*: Franz Liszt and Marie d'Agoult in Switzerland

In 1836 Franz Liszt and Countess Marie d'Agoult decided to leave Paris and journey to Lake Geneva. For travel reading they took along Etienne de Sénancour's *Obermann*, a novel which, along with *Réné* by Chateaubriand, George Sand viewed as French counterparts to Goethe's *Werther*. During the trip Liszt wrote a collection of piano pieces that he later compiled as an album of Switzerland in his *Années de pélérinage*. Among the pieces in this album is *Vallée d'Obermann*, which alludes to its literary starting point with quotations from the novel placed at the beginning of the piece.

These are the simple facts of an event that belongs to the cultural and biographical history of Romanticism and to its literary and musical tradition. My objective is to provide a semiotic interpretation of this entire phenomenon. This interpretation proceeds from the fact that the behavior of Liszt and Marie d'Agoult can be characterized as semiotic or at least strongly symbolic. As true Romantics, they were inclined to identify themselves with the protagonists of novels they read and to fashion their own lives and acts by imitating their literary models. This inclination has been well demonstrated by Juri Lotman in "Theater and Theatricality": as their last words, heroes of the French Revolution might utter citations from some ancient Roman hero. Or one need only think of Goethe's notion of life itself as an artwork.

When Liszt and d'Agoult left Paris to begin their aimless travels, they enacted one of the central epistemes of Romantic culture: the idea of wandering. It is not by accident that Schubert's piano work the *Wanderer Fantasy* found a permanent place in Liszt's repertoire. His admiration of this piece is also mirrored in later works from his middle period, for example, in the structure of the B minor Sonata. The *Wanderer Fantasy* provided an example of sonata form united with the idea of monothematicism—the "wandering" of a single theme, in various guises, throughout an entire work.

The allegorical, semiotic meaning of the journey of Liszt and d'Agoult has been explored by many scholars. Entire monographs have been published about this journey, including Robert Bory's *Franz Liszt und Marie d'Agoult in der Schweitz* and the detailed study by Jacques Vier, *La comtesse d'Agoult et son temps*. The latter study gives a detailed, day-by-day account of the couple's travels. Other details about the trip can be found in their correspondence, as well as in the memoirs later published by d'Agoult. George Sand and two young students of Liszt later joined their company, and everywhere they went this strange group aroused great attention, creating a spectacle for local people. The following entry was found in the guest book of Hôtel l'Union, in the small town of Chamonix: "Name of passenger: *Family Piffoël*; permanent address: *Nature*; coming from: *God*; destination: *Heaven*; place of birth: *Europe*; profession: *Loiterer*; date of departure: *sometime*; authorized by: *General Opinion*." For a semiotician, this reads almost like a variant of Greimas's mythical-actantial model!

The first half of the trip, when Liszt and d'Agoult were alone, is the most interesting for my purposes, since it constitutes the actual Obermann phase of the journey. D'Agoult's account of this part of the trip is perhaps the most intriguing document of the episode. Her memoirs show that d'Agoult was not a particularly gifted writer, borrowing her style from the authors she admired, from Sénancour among others. This emphasizes the central role Sénancour played in the creation of Liszt's piano work. If the narration of Sénancour's *Obermann* turns around its solitary hero, the focus of d'Agoult's memoirs is naturally Liszt himself, the object of her adoration. Her literary style was not faultless, and there are often some comically pathetic expressions. The fifth chapter depicts, in a Sénancourian way, the couple's loneliness in the middle of Nature:

> Like granite battlements, unscalable mountains jutted tall between us and the world, as if to shield us from the world's gaze. Jet-black fir trees shrouded us in shadows. The muted murmur of lakes, the enchanting, ominous rumblings of deep chasms, alpine vistas that gave to our day of rapture a presentiment of things eternal—bittersweet specters of my youth, I conjure you here in my pitiful memoir, for the last time. . . . Only for a day—then you will return with me, into the mute shadows out of which God called us. Shall we remain forever as ghostly shadows—dispersed and unconscious, in the silent void? Or shall we plunge into the inexhaustible richness that ever comes from death—life—and give form and thought to those empty shades?

This outburst, which addresses Nature in the second-person plural, contrasts with the next section, which switches to a more reporting style. It shows quite clearly how the protagonists of this spectacle became aware of the semiotic-allegoric nature of their behavior:

> Franz and I had no itinerary, no travel plan. Happenstance led us toward Switzerland; where we went mattered little to us. To live alone, together, to put a vast gulf between us and our past; a change of view to accompany our change of daily routine—we sought nothing else. We wanted solitude, contemplation, work. Abandoned, a little humiliated by brief moments of fame that led to nothing else, and tormented by higher ambitions, Franz wanted to withdraw from notoriety and the duties that brings, in order to study in peace the great Masters, and to compose a great work of art.

Of the pieces written during this period only *Au lac du Wallenstadt* is mentioned by d'Agoult: "We stayed on the shores of Lake Wallenstadt for a long time. There, Franz composed for me a quite melancholy piece that sounded like the lapping of the waves and the cadence of oars—a piece I could never listen to without crying." She says, in passing, that they also read *Obermann* and *Jocelyn*, but does not mention Liszt's *Vallée d'Obermann*.

One need not study all of Liszt's music to realize that this work is very different from the other pieces in the collection. In her study on the morphology of Liszt's piano works, Marta Grabócz (1986) has even argued that this piece already includes all the central Lisztian isotopies: the isotopy of a Faustian question, or "why," a quest for something; the isotopy of pastoral expression; the pantheist feeling of nature and exaltation; religious expression; sorrow; storm and macabre fight; and heroism. Using the theories of A. B. Marx, Grabócz points out that all these isotopies are to some degree present in *Vallée d'Obermann*, along with techniques of character variation. Moreover, most of these isotopies can also be found in the novel by Sénancour and in d'Agoult's memoirs, which faithfully reflect the book's content.

D'Agoult was completely aware of the unreality of their whole trip. No letters came to the place where they lived. And when Liszt finally gave a recital in Geneva, d'Agoult suddenly saw him in a new light: he was no longer the protagonist, the main actor of their common story, but had been unexpectedly transferred, as it were, to the level of a secondary representation. When she saw Liszt on stage she noticed this difference:

> It was Franz whom I saw, and yet it was not Franz. It was as if a person represented him on the stage, much like him, but nevertheless having nothing in common with him except the apparently similar outward appearance. Also his playing confused me: it was his wonderful virtuosity, splendid and unequalled, but still I felt it as strange to him. Where was I? Where were we? Did I dream? Was I about to become insane? Who had brought me to this? In what sense? . . . It was incredible anguish.

This fragment from d'Agoult's memoirs is very illustrative, for it could almost be a direct quotation from the passages of *Obermann* that Liszt chose as the mottos of his musical work:

> What do I wish? Who am I? What shall I ask from nature? . . . Every cause is invisible, every end is deceitful; all forms change, all durations finally come to an end. . . . I feel, I exist only in order to waste myself in untameable desires, to drink of the seduction of a fantastic world, to remain a subject of its sensuous illusion. [Sénancour, *Obermann*, Letter 63].

These literary fragments could easily be read as interpretants, or as verbal legisigns for the music in question and that music's implicit isotopies. They would thus exhibit the isotopy of a Faustian "why?" in the first *Più lento* section of *Vallée d'Obermann* (see Ex. 7.1).

Example 7.1. Liszt, *Vallée d'Obermann*, mm. 26–31.

Also characteristic of Liszt's musical narration are complex isotopies, that is, passages with two or more superimposed isotopies. Therefore Ex. 7.1 could also be read or heard as the manifestation of a religious isotopy, because of its chorale texture. This isotopy, too, is found in the memoirs of d'Agoult, who tells that Franz's secret wish was to restore sacred music to the temples from which worldly taste had expelled it. She reports how much biblical stories and Christian legends fascinated him even this early in his life.

In any case, there exist several studies of Sénancour and his novel. Particularly noteworthy is Irene Schärer's *Obermann: Versuch einer Analyse* (1955), which analyzes the structures of landscapes where Obermann wanders. Even in this somewhat naive sense there is a parallelism between Liszt and Sénancour, if one merely observes the main theme and its particular shape, as well as its tonal and spatial organization in Liszt's piece. The theme of Obermann can be considered an iconic image of the valley itself, and the use of various registers throughout the piece illustrates the peaks and valleys of those landscapes (see Ex. 7.2). This main actor also conveys metaphysical disquietude, longing for the infinite, and the theme of "boredom" (*ennui*) so crucial to the Sénancourian universe.

The Basic Isotopies of Vallée d'Obermann

Vallée d'Obermann represents a typical monothematic work. All the musical events center around its main theme, which appears transformed in many ways. It is not only the character variations, which we might call interoceptive iconicity, that are essential but also the text strategy: the technique of dramatic narration. The stabler it is the more the narration becomes evident to a listener; that is, the more the narrative events are based on inner iconicity, similarity, and repetition of the musical substance, the more readily the listener perceives the text strategy. The iconicity of the piece also forms the foundations for what we call its basic isotopies. The piece divides into five main sections, all characterized by a unique aesthetic expression and a textual strategy manifesting that expression. In the attempt to invent verbal titles for these isotopies we may employ terms offered by Sénancour's novel itself and by critiques dealing with that novel.

Example 7.2. Liszt, *Vallée d'Obermann*, mm. 1–25, main actor.

Isotopy I (mm. 1–74) *Ennui*: This introduces the main thematic material but is quite fragmentary in nature, though tensional, and contains several *fermate* which interrupt the musical continuity. There is something hesitant and re-strained about the whole section. Its main moods are melancholic—*espressivo,*

sotto voce, smorzando, dolcissimo, dolente. All this justifies our title for this isotopy: boredom. Jankélévitch (1974) has aptly defined boredom as "time in disorder." The extremely slow progress of this section seems to bear out this definition (as does the modalization of the piece in the interpretation by Vladimir Horowitz).

The choice of the appropriate isotopy and basic mood ultimately determines subsequent choices of sign processes. Accordingly, one consequence of the isotopy of boredom is that all indexical signs turn out to be anti-indexes; that is, the music tends to stagnate, and motion stops altogether several times in the section. This section does not convey the sense of something narrated in the past tense, the "then." To a great extent it represents music of the present, the "now." Its tensions do not culminate in deeper conflicts or catastrophes, but remain somewhat hidden and suspended.

Isotopy II (mm. 75–118) Wandering: In contrast to the first isotopy, this section progresses continuously and fluidly. The tensions now relax, and the theme-actor does not appear as detached from its background accompaniment, but merges with the latter's sonorous environment. The dramatic conflicts recede into the background, and the music seems to contain no inner contradictions. Rather, it appears to narrate something in the distant, epic past. The choice of register and the quietly descending motion, as if sinking down from the top of a mountain, also display these qualities (see Ex. 7.3). The section begins in the upper register with a tranquil movement, like the prelude to *Lohengrin*, which Liszt greatly admired and for which he even wrote a literary program. The novel *Obermann* contains several possible literary interpretants for this kind of wandering: "But there, on those solitary mountains, where the sky is bigger; where the air stirs less and time moves more slowly, where life is more permanent: there all of nature eloquently expresses a grander order, a more visible harmony, an everlasting ensemble. . . ."

Example 7.3. Liszt, *Vallée d'Obermann*, mm. 75–76,
beginning of Isotopy II.

Isotopy III (mm. 119–69) Fight or Storm: The tension becomes extremely acute (see Ex. 7.4), leading at the end of the section to a violent outburst and conflict of thematic elements introduced in the first isotopy. What remained latent in the first isotopy now becomes overtly chaotic, passionate, and stormy. Temporally and spatially the section is extremely varied, active, and disengaged. The contrast between the theme and its background is at its sharpest here. Liszt might have had in mind the storm movement from Beethoven's Pastoral Symphony, which he had also arranged for piano; it might have served as a legisign for the construction of this entire isotopy.

Example 7.4. Liszt, *Vallée d'Obermann*, mm. 119–22, beginning of Isotopy III.

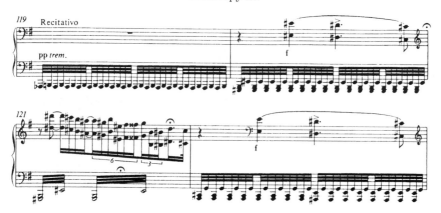

Isotopy IV (mm. 170–203) Pastoral: This is one of the most typical Lisztian isotopies (see Grabócz 1986). It is an objective, distanced commentary, a view of the battlefield from afar, like "the sun casting its last rays upon a field full of corpses after the struggle." This naive-sounding metaphor evokes the subjects that Liszt's great contemporary Delacroix chose for his paintings. The narration moves again as if in the past tense, "then," but "now" in relation to the preceding fight section (Ex. 7.5).

Example 7.5. Liszt, *Vallée d'Obermann*, m. 170, beginning of Isotopy IV.

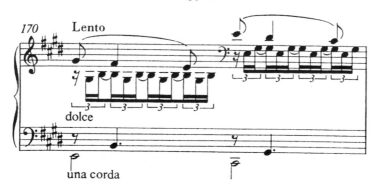

Isotopy V (mm. 204–16) Pantheist Apotheosis of a Sense of Nature (see Ex. 7.6): This isotopy could as well be characterized as an exaltation, which also reflects certain passages in Sénancour's aesthetic model, when he has the hero say: "the two hours of my life when I was most alive, the least unhappy with myself . . . [now,] for this moment only, I want to do what I must, and do what I want to do." This forms an epic-dramatic culmination of the preceding lyrical isotopy, a movement from "then" to "now."

Example 7.6. Liszt, *Vallée d'Obermann*, m. 204, beginning of Isotopy V.

Moving to the next level of the generative trajectory, we now consider various disengagements in the piece. Particularly important in the Lisztian universe are the gestural shifters. Among the idiomatic or instrumental shifters are those passages that take the hands away from their basic position at the keyboard. Various scales, arpeggios, trills, tremolandos, and octaves are typical devices in Liszt; but there are also subtler techniques, such as rinforzandos, various ways of playing scales (either with a deep *espressivo*, cello-like legato touch, or by letting the fingers lightly glide over the keys, *dolcissimo*), with woodwind-like timbres and, in general, all the imitations of various orchestral instruments by the piano, accomplished by hand-crossings and the like.

The common shifters—temporal, spatial, and actorial—are also relevant to *Vallée*. For example, for the spatial category in this piece, as for all shifters, one can distinguish inner and outer articulations. In the first isotopy the outer spatiality reaches its extreme at the same moment in which the inner spatiality reaches the dominant function, that is, at the same time that the maximum of internal disengagement occurs. Thus the inner and outer spatial disengagements culminate at the same time. This does not always happen in music. In order to clarify to what extent these two networks are independent or support each other, one could prepare a chart of the outer tonal space of the piece, in which we could indicate which tonal fields or registers the music occupies in each isotopy. The register in which the piece starts is a factor that also determines the spatial point of "here"; all movement away from this "here" represents the act of disengagement.

In *Vallée d'Obermann* the point of "here" is the registral field one octave below middle C. It occurs often in the first section of the work, and it returns in the somewhat distanced, fourth isotopy, where the temporal now-moment also evokes the beginning of the piece. The "here" engagement occurs at the very end of the piece, in the brief summary phrase which reminds the listener of the basic problem, still unresolved, of the narration. Furthermore, the first and second isotopies end in a low register, unlike the third and fourth. The purpose is to increase tension: two endings in the low register make the listener consider them "normal," and a deviation from them creates a moment of tension. Only at the end of the fifth isotopy does the low register return, its dark sonority strongly emphasized. Isotypy II keeps to the same register longest, and it is also the least tensional section of the piece. From this we may draw the conclusion that tension can arise through any change of register, contrary to the assumption held by some, that tension automatically increases only with an ascent in tonal space. Remaining in the same registral space, or on the same pitch, can also create tension. For example, the *sotto voce* theme of the first isotopy, the "oboe" motif (Ex. 7.7), contains extreme inner tension, although it seems to be stuck on one level; whereas the same motif forms a mobile and relaxed motion at the end of the second isotopy.

In contrast, through the entire third isotopy there passes a chromatically rising bass line which builds tension. Notice that the outer space is at the same time extremely disengaged; that is, the register changes are very abrupt (This is also a characteristic of the fifth isotopy, in which one hears parallel ascending and descending motions which are otherwise rare in the piece). Thus the interesting point in the third isotopy is that in the inner spatiality a chromatically ascending line takes place at the same time as the outer space projects abrupt register changes. These two aspects convey, each in its own way, the same modal principle: growth of tension.

Example 7.7. Liszt, *Vallée d'Obermann*, mm. 5–10, Isotopy I.

The changes of register are made by both leap and step. The leaps are naturally the more dramatic, except when the register shifts are separated by a *fermata* pause and a detensional moment in the inner space. This happens, for example, when the tonic has just been reached at the end of a section and the narration continues in another register, as if in a different isotopy. This separating device is also exemplified by the smooth change that takes place between the first and second isotopies. Therefore, one can by a change in register also emphasize a change of isotopy. On the other hand, abrupt register changes can also belong, especially in rapid passages, to the same isotopy, as in the third isotopy of the piece, which portrays syntactically the idea of a macabre fight (see Ex. 7.8). There the changes serve as a question/answer textual strategy in which the direction of motion may change; that is, the "question" can be situated in either of two registers, as also holds true for their "answers." It is precisely the changes in this question/answer, attack/defend constellation in the middle of this section that so aptly illustrate the nature of a "fight" isotopy. In the case of Sénancour's narration, it appears as a struggle between the hero and natural forces, the storm, or within the hero himself. (These extreme disengagements of the outer spatiality are also closely related with gestural shifters, and further with the temporality as regards the basic time unit, which changes from eighth-note to thirty-second-note figuration.)

Actoriality is a category that is particularly central to Liszt's music, and especially to *Vallée d'Obermann*. The outer actoriality is represented by an intonational figure, usually called a theme. The listener can identify with this theme, which forms a clearly distinguishable, musical-psychological unit. One important factor is the way a theme is distinct from the other musical material. It can clearly differ from its accompaniment, as at the beginning of the first isotopy (Ex. 7.2), or it can merge with its background, as in the second (Ex. 7.3). According to this merger (or not), one may describe, for instance, the relation of a theme-actor to its environment, a relation which can be either harmonious or contradictory.[1]

Example 7.8. Liszt, *Vallée d'Obermann*, m. 133, "Struggle" in
Isotopy III.

What then is the basic nature of the main musical actor of *Vallée d'Obermann*? The opening theme consists of two half phrases, which are strangely asymmetrical (see Ex. 7.2, mm. 1–4). In a spatial sense, the theme comprises descending scale segments of E minor and G minor in mm. 1–4, shown in Ex. 7.9. These scales do not coincide in their rhythmic-metric articulation, which seems to divide the theme into two equal parts, the second of which (mm. 3–4) is obviously a rhythmic augmentation of the first. The rhythmic division thus supports the grouping relation of 1:2, while the pitch articulation would divide it as 2:1. In this thematic intonational figure the most outstanding event is the beginning of the G minor scale segment, starting on E♭, heard on a strong beat in m. 3. The listener would expect D♯, the leading tone to the tonic E, to be established in the first two bars. In a sense this happens, but it produces frustration when the D♯ turns out to be the enharmonically transformed E♭ and does not "properly" resolve to the tonic E minor, but modulates to a flatted tonal field.

Example 7.9. Liszt, *Vallée d'Obermann*, mm. 1–4, atemporal reduction of main actor.

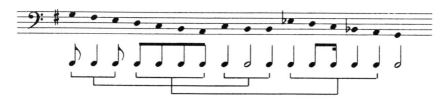

Because the E♭ occurs at a point of metric and tonal stability, it has great intonational power. When the E♭ is intoned so strongly at the beginning of the work, the listener's ear remains receptive to it, even as the music continues, and awaits the "correct" resolution of D♯. This resolution is also implied by the E minor six-four chord in m. 2, which, however, does not proceed to V, as one would expect. In fact, as a leading tone the D♯ is systematically avoided in the whole first isotopy, among other ways, by transforming it into part of a descending "gypsy" scale on G (m. 13). Notice especially that the whole section ends in a highly stressed way, following the dominant function (marked *rinforzando*) on the D♯ in m. 25, which occurs immediately afterwards as E♭ (m. 26). If we compare the opening to the end of the piece (Ex. 7.10), we notice that the last musical motto, intoned very heavily in *fortissimo*, is a truncated version of the opening theme-actor, now simply ending with the first half phrase. It thus avoids the contradictory intonational element, the leap to E♭/D♯ of mm. 2–3. This gives the closure of the piece an unfinished quality, which is quite appropriate to its narrative program and serves well as a musical portrayal of Sénancour's frustrated hero.[2]

Example 7.10. Liszt, *Vallée d'Obermann*, mm. 214–16.

On the other hand, the whole first isotopy (*ennui*) ends with a six-four chord of the E minor tonic (mm. 73–74), that is, on the chord that should have followed this stressed intonation. The six-four chord sounds alone and waits for its resolution during the *lunga pausa* of m. 74, which underscores the disappearance of the theme-actor from the stage. This resolution never comes, since the whole narrative isotopy changes in m. 75. Likewise, such deliberately created incompleteness keeps up the tension in longer and shorter sections. Thereafter, the plot proceeds so that the theme-actor always comes back, but transformed, often in such diminutions that only a part of it is recognizable, as if according to the principle of *pars pro toto*. It would be unnecessary to repeat the whole theme, in the same way that when one is performing a fugue it is enough to emphasize only the beginnings of the fugue subject as a sign for the whole. The fragments of the present theme also function as signs for the complete theme.

There are also thematic occurrences that are not experienced as new actors or subject-actants, but perhaps as opponents or adjuvants. For example, in the first isotopy the chorale topic is twice repeated, a glimpse of the religious isotopy so characteristic of Liszt. But only twice: the choralelike texture does not occur later in the piece, which does not seem to require it any more, unless one considers as its distant reminiscences the chromatic half-note chords in the same register at the end of the stormy second isotopy. There they should be interpreted as a decisive, almost furious negation of the religious isotopy.

Another *topos*, typical of Romantic music, appears in the middle of the storm section, namely, the outburst of the theme-actor into *bel canto*, parallel thirds (Ex. 7.11), as were written by Mendelssohn in his Venetian gondola songs and by Beethoven in his piano sonatas. In Chopin, parallel thirds (with sixths as an alternative) form the particular paradigm of imitating a vocal duet. In Liszt, they have an *amoroso* connotation. In addition, in *Vallée d'Obermann* one notices a special *Spielfigur* used as a gestural disengager: the *appassionato* parallel thirds are picked up by the left hand above the operatic *tremolando* of the right hand, as shown in Example 7.11.

Example 7.11. Liszt, *Vallée d'Obermann*, mm. 129–30.

In the end, a theoretical problem remains, namely, that of the musical-psychological mechanisms by which the actorialization of certain musical units is created. Mere general thematic features, such as sufficiently characteristic traits, simple chordal background, repetitions, and so on, do not seem to be satisfactory as explanations. Moreover, one has to account for all those transformations and consciously juxtaposed theme-actants whose conflicts emphasize the nature of music as drama, with all its attendant roles and figures.

7.2 "Après un rêve": A Semiotic Approach to the Study of Musical Performance

Musical performance is one of the most fascinating and at the same time most neglected areas of research. As a basic truth concerning musical interpretation, one might say that performance can only be analyzed in relation to the musical enunciate itself. Perhaps this explains why the analysis of musical performance has not become an autonomous discipline with methods of its own, but has been considered a mere extension of ordinary means of music analysis.

True, in 1932, Carl Seashore developed several methods for accurately measuring and analyzing the physical products of musical interpretation, such as recordings. Yet both musical pieces and their interpretations are created in order to produce certain musical significations. In this regard, one has to ask if there exists a method that would approach the interpretation and the musical work itself expressly as meaning-producing processes. In what follows, I shall compare and analyze various interpretations of the well-known song "Après un rêve," by Gabriel Fauré to a poem by Romain Bussine, as well as examine the musical-poetic text (see Ex. 7.12).

> Dans un sommeil que charmait ton image
> Je rêvais le bonheur, ardent mirage;
> Tes yeux étaient plus doux, ta voix pure et sonore.
> Tu rayonnais comme un ciel éclairé par l'aurore;
> Tu m'appelais, et je quittais la terre
> Pour m'enfuir avec toi vers la lumière;
> Les cieux pour nous entr'ouvraient leurs nues,
> Splendeurs inconnues, lueurs divines entrevues . . .

Hélas! Hélas, triste réveil des songes!
Je t'appelle, ô nuit, rends-moi fes mensonges;
Reviens, reviens radieuse,
Reviens, ô nuit mystérieuse!

In a slumber charmed by your image
I dreamed of happiness, ardent mirage;
Your eyes were more tender, your voice pure and clear.
You were radiant like a sky brightened by sunrise;
You were calling me, and I left the earth
To flee with you towards the light;
The skies opened their clouds for us,
Splendors unknown, glimpses of divine light. . .
Alas! Alas, sad awakening from dreams!
I call to you, oh night, give me back your illusions;
Return, return with your radiance,
Return, oh mysterious night!

Example 7.12. Gabriel Fauré, "Après un rêve," mm. 1–11,
poem by Bussine.

Greimas's generative course constitutes a many-phased and complicated chain, from which one can select those phases relevant to the text under investigation. In music, which lacks lexicographic meanings, we may thus restrict ourselves to some levels of the generative course. The present analysis of the text (*énoncé*) draws mainly on the second level, with its temporal and actorial shifters; the level of modalities is used in the analysis of different interpretations (*énonciations*). (See Appendix.)

It will be helpful to review what these categories mean in general and, more particularly, in music. The classic example, given by Greimas (1979) to illustrate the functioning of disengagement/engagement, are the various forms of military roll call. In the German army soldiers respond with the word "hier" (here), that is, by using the spatial engagement. In the French army they respond by saying "présent" (present or now), referring to the temporal category. In the Lithuanian army (in which Greimas served) one answers by shouting "I," thus applying the actorial engagement.

As discussed in Chap. 1.6, these three categories, or "shifters," also operate in music (see Fig. 7.1). First, there exists the so-called tonal space, a structure consisting of pitches and revealed in the broader sense by the use of different registers.[3] Music is made up not only of vertical relations but also of horizontal, linear elements, since it is of course a temporal art. Thus rhythm and meter, as the articulation of time in music, form another essential level of analysis. Finally, music contains figures and shapes with which the listener can identify, because they contain anthropomorphic units that encourage such identification. Such units, with regard to the Classical-Romantic style period of Western music, are typically "themes," in that a theme serves in music as a narrative subject— "the faded hero of a novel," as was said of themes in Mahler's symphonies. Applying these three levels to the Fauré song, we shall articulate our analysis and show how signification is produced on each level.

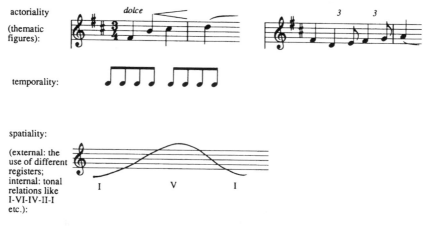

Figure 7.1. Actorial, temporal, and spatial categories in Fauré, "Après un rêve."

Spatial analysis has been applied in many ways to the study of music performance. In Chap. 5 we utilized a model developed by Johan Sundberg, Lars
Fryden, and Anders Askenfelt (1983), which is based on a definition of tension
in terms of the distance from the tonic, around the circle of fifths (Fig. 7.2).
The tonic receives the value 0, dominant and subdominant the value 1, dominant of the dominant and subdominant of the subdominant the value 2, and so
on.[4] To some extent, Sundberg's model answers well the needs of our analysis.
Ex. 7.13 shows the melody of the Fauré song reduced to a series of simple,
chorale-texture chords, along with the harmonic distances of the chords from
the tonic. Their numeric values depict the degree of tension they contain (following Sundberg's method, the values of the subdominants in Ex. 7.13 are
increased by additional half of their values).

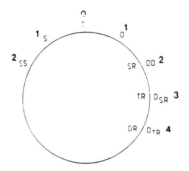

Definition of *harmonic distance* by means of the circle of fifths. For a given
chord this distance equals the number of chord changes which is required in
traditional harmony in order to reach the tonic chord again.

Figure 7.2. A means of measuring inner spatiality
(after Sundberg et al. 1983).

Example 7.13. Fauré, "Après un rêve," mm. 1–11, harmonic tension in
numerical values (after Sundberg et al. 1983).

It is tempting to imagine that these tensional values might also serve as a
norm for interpreting the level of musical enunciation (performance). Yet such
calculation involves problems even at the textual level (enunciate). For ex-

ample, which value goes to parallel-mode (major or minor) chords of the same degree? It is essential to the coloristic effects of the chords in this song that, instead of an expected minor or major chord, one hears its parallel, as in the culmination point on "hélas" (m. 31) and "radieuse" (mm. 40–42). Furthermore, how should we interpret altered chords? For example, should the Neapolitan in m. 27 be construed as a maximally distant and therefore tense chord, or as a lowered second degree, whose numeric tension value would be much smaller? Besides these and other problems,[5] such an analysis only defines the tensions of the tonal space, tensions that can be supported or weakened by other musical parameters and by matters of performance.

The Musical-Poetic Text (énoncé musical)

As to the tonal-spatial structure of the melody of Fauré's song, the first two stanzas (mm. 1–8) are harmonized with a descending movement in the circle of fifths toward the dominant and tonic of the main key. Only in the third section do the chordal processes become more varied. In Classical-Romantic melodies in general, the first eight-bar period uses the common chord progression I–IV–II–V–I—the "words" of harmony (Salzer 1960). Only after that does the melody move beyond circle-of-fifth sequences. Another typical example is the beginning of the *Canzone* from Tchaikovsky's "Pathétique" Symphony, shown in Ex. 7.14 (circle of fifths motion bracketed). As a rule, such a sequential passage in fifths functions as a transition and thus represents the impression of movement, a feeling of going toward something, in contrast to more static passages, where no sense of motion occurs.

In the semiotic sense, let us recall that there are two kinds of movement: either disengagement (*débrayage*), moving a distance from the center of the narration, or engagement (*embrayage*), a return toward that center. Such a sequence, both at the beginning of the Fauré song and in the consequent phrase of Tchaikovsky's *Canzone*, of course functions as an *embrayage*, and more particularly as a return, a shifting in, which lets us know that we are safely proceeding toward the repose of the tonic. The tension is thus not dysphoric but euphoric. In sum, the first phrase of the Fauré song is ruled by the spatial semes of mobility, euphoria, and tension.

In the poem as well as in the song, a decisive peripety, or turning point, occurs at the juncture of lines 8 and 9 (mm. 30–31). There degree $\hat{4}$ is tonicized by means of a secondary dominant. The poem dramatizes this change of atmosphere—the awakening from a dream. The three dots eliding into the exclamations of the following lines (9–12) lead one to expect a corresponding dramatic musical gesture, such as a sudden pause, transition, or unexpected modulation (as occurs, for example, with the awakening in the song "Ich hab' im Traum geweint" in Schumann's *Dichterliebe*). Fauré, however, goes quickly to the exclamation "Hélas!" in mm. 30–31. He has prepared the (spatially) high E5 in m. 31: where we might have expected the use of the upper register for "splendeurs inconnues" in line 8 (mm. 26–28), there was instead a downward octave transfer, with the effect of saving the brilliance and dramatic power for the climax in m. 31. In the last two lines (m. 38 to the end), which recall the main actor, the harmonic rhythm is especially dense: chord changes occur in quarter-note values and turn around the subdominant, not escaping the influence of that harmony until the return to the tonic in mm. 46–47.

Example 7.14. Tchaikovsky, Symphony No. 4, *Canzone*, mm. 1–23, harmonic sequence in vertical brackets.

The analysis of the temporal level of the song is not so rewarding, since its basic unit is the eighth-note figuration which recurs throughout the piece. This figuration is the basic rhythm, in relation to which temporal variations of the melody always mean a disengagement. The fact that the temporal category, on the level of musical utterance (*énoncé*), proves to be rather unequivocal does not exclude possibilities of variation on the level of uttering (*énonciation*) or intoning. Nevertheless, if we are aiming for an original interpretation, we should remember French baritone Pierre Bernac's observation that in French music *rubato* is rarely used. In his view, in French art song (*mélodie*), accuracy, punctuality, and lyricism have to be interlinked (1978: 108).

Of more interest than the temporal category is the analysis of the actorial level: a close investigation of the melody, its figures, and its thematic elements. In this music, an actorial analysis is often possible only after the spatial and temporal analyses have been completed. The main actor first contains an intense rising movement in quarter notes. Immediately after the highest point has been attained, it is negated or given up, so that it fades away like a dream (which is also referred to by the poem itself). In the consequent phrase (mm. 5–8), the deviation from the basic temporal and rhythmic pulsation of the antecedent is balanced: the antecedent's rising sixth, F♯4 to D5, is intoned in reverse, as a quick downward leap of a sixth in m. 5, while balance between actorial, temporal, and spatial categories (a *harmonia praestabilita* prevalent in all tonal music) is gained by the use of eighth notes, the "normal" time values of the temporal articulation.

At this point it should be clear that, if we pay attention to the performance directions of the piece, we cannot simply apply the numerical values of Sundberg's system. For example, in the movement toward the dominant in mm. 7–8, there is a *crescendo* on the words "ardent mirage" (mm. 6–7). Yet according to Sundberg's system, the chord in m. 7 would receive a value of 1, since it lies but a short distance from the tonic (see Ex. 7.13). Another contradictory situation is on the word "rayonnais" at the start of line 4 (mm. 12–13), where the VI chord occurs, provided with the value 4.5, which is at first sight supported by the *crescendo*. But the chord is interrupted with a breath mark, after which the word "comme" (on III) clearly expresses an understatement, as a subordinate clause, and sounds much quieter and weaker (see Ex. 7.15).

At the end of the consequent phrase, the musical repetition becomes more pertinent than the poetic text. In order to make the consequent finish with the same triplet figure as the antecedent, the last syllable of the word "mirage" is stretched out melismatically in mm. 7–8. Elsewhere in the song, this triplet figure is always associated with a melisma. This stylistic device, not so common in Fauré, can perhaps be explained as a melodic interpretation of the last word, "mysterieuse." This allusion to the melismatic style of plain chant brings about a mystic, spiritual, unearthly connotation. On "Tu rayonnais" (Ex. 7.15) there occurs a Wagnerian intertext, or *topos*. The descending chromatic passage refers to Wolfram's song to the evening star, Elsa's prayer in *Lohengrin*, and to many similar Wagnerian melodics.

The end of the second phrase on major III (m. 15) forms a tone painting for "l'aurore" by brightening the harmony that accompanies the ascent from minor I to major III. After this follows one bar of accompaniment alone (m. 16), which modulates chromatically back to the tonic through the augmented triad (V+).

This chord frequently has the connotation of openness, emptiness, and a *funèbre*-flavored transcendence. In the four final lines (starting in m. 30), attention is drawn to the frequently recurring intervals of a fourth, on "Hélas . . . Je t'appelle." These intervals are internal indexes in the music, "call" *topoi*, as are almost all such motifs with rising fourths from upbeat to downbeat.

Example 7.15. Fauré, "Après un rêve," mm. 12–14.

The last phrases synchronize in an interesting way the actant and anti-actant, the two main motifs, introduced in the first section: the ascending dream motif which represents the "I" (je) of the poem (mm. 2–3) and the triplet motif that winds around scale degree 3̂ (mm. 9–10) and represents the "you" (tu). At the beginning, the "you" of the poem calls to the subject of the poem. Toward the end, when the "I" calls to the "you," this actant is not the previously mentioned anti-actant, but the negactant, or "the night" ("Je t'appelle, ô nuit!"). This can be felt as a surprise that has been deliberately saved till the end. At the same time, it is revealed that the hidden neganti-actant of the beginning of the poem is the nameless subject, who was provided with attributes of light ("lumière") and heaven ("ciel"). Thus we can fill all the corners of Greimas's semiotic square and articulate the song's proper actants (see Fig. 7.3).

As the title indicates, the most important *topos* of the poem is the state that comes after the dream: the awakening, the "après un rêve." It is the place of the subject, the "I," at the moment of enunciating the poem. But the poem (or at least its first eight lines) mostly takes place in the *heterotopos* of the dream. In turn, this *heterotopos*, the category of "elsewhere" as seen from the *hic et nunc* point of the poem, has a mystical property: it is temporally situated in the category "night." Yet, when it is stated at the end of the poem, this night has features of its opposite, the day. It is a "nuit radieuse"—a radiant night. This is a real unification of opposite poles on the imaginary level, which is revealed by

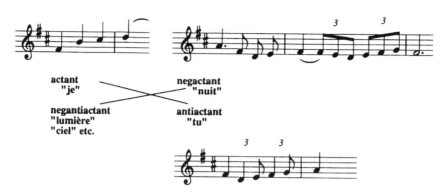

Figure 7.3. Actants in Fauré, "Après un rêve."

the fact that in mm. 36–38 the singer asks the night to return its lies to him. Analyzed together with the veridictory category (Greimas 1979: 419), the semantic universe of the poem appears as in Fig. 7.4. The dream state of the beginning has remained hidden, as a secret. What happens in the awakening is really the uncovering of the truth, after which the night represented by the dream seems to be a mere lie, albeit a pleasant one, which is asked to return.

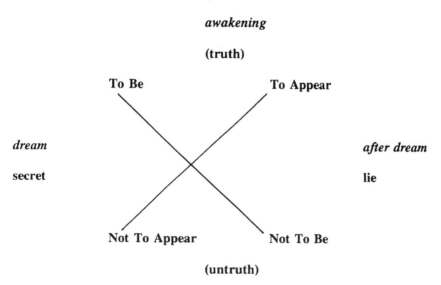

Figure 7.4. Veridictory square for "Après un rêve."

The ego of the poem again directly addresses himself to the negactant night, not the anti-actant (tu). For he knows that the "you" of the poem can only return through the arrival of the negactant "night"; i.e., the negactant "night" serves as the subject's helper (Greimas 1967: 174–81). On the musical level, the actant motif expands into three parts separated by breath marks, while the musical motif of the anti-actant fuses on the textual level with the negactant "night." This fusion depicts the blending together of "you" and "night." By calling to the night, the "I" of the poem at the same time calls "you."

Melodically, the actant motif contains an obvious implication. As a reply to the ascent in mm. 2–3, from $\hat{5}$ to $\hat{3}$ in an upper octave, the listener awaits the final resolution of $\hat{5}$ via the (Schenkerian) linear passage $\hat{5}$–$\hat{4}$–$\hat{3}$–$\hat{2}$–$\hat{1}$ as the music resumes. The listener will accept only this as the definitive solution, with the final $\hat{1}$ (in the original register) accompanied by the tonic chord in root position. In other words, the ear expects the descending fifth cadence of F♯ major to B minor at the same time as the melody comes to rest on the tonic. The fact that the first four lines of the song end with a descending fifth in the voice (m. 15) provides a strong cadential feeling; but the song cannot end with this, since the cadence is on III, not on the tonic. In lines 7–8 (mm. 24–30) one hears the intonation of a descending fifth twice more, but both times other parameters suggest that this is not the final cadence. The melodic fifth on the words "leurs nues, splendeurs" (m. 26) is provided with an entirely different harmony: the tonal movement is toward the subdominant, and the notes of the interval are even separated by breath marks. True, tonic harmony occurs on "inconnues" (mm. 27–28), but in the parallel major—a modal shift which forms one of the typical devices of this song. Therefore the "true" and "correct" descending fifth is saved for the very end of the song, where it occurs in the right (opening) register and with the proper harmony (minor I).

In sum, we have combined Meyer's melodic implication model (1973) with the Greimasian semiotic square: The first phrase of the "Après un rêve" forms an implication that is not fulfilled until the final verses. The action of the musical actant of the song takes place between the tensions constituted by the beginning and end—the narrative arch proper.

Now the musical character of the various *topoi* of the song and poem can be explained: the *heterotopos*, the "elsewhere" of the dream, is depicted as a euphoric sequential passage along a circle of fifths, while the topos of "après un rêve"—the "here," or "being awake" of the poem—is tonally portrayed as a state in which one desperately searches again for the tonic of the dream (Fig. 7.5). The relatively quick changes of harmony toward the end of the song (mm. 36ff.) illustrate the unquietness that relates both to the musical and to

dream	→→→	*awakening*	→→→	*after the dream*
heterotopos:		moving from heterotopos to topos		topos: "Here"
"elsewhere"				
Secret		Truth		Lie
(euphoric)		(dysphoric)		(nostalgic)
circle of fifths inward tonic		subdominant area		search for tonic, errant tonal plan

Figure 7.5. Motion from heterotopical to topical space in "Après un rêve."

the inner world of the poem. As for tonality, all the transitions take place with abrupt and simple chromaticism, without enharmonic reinterpretations, diminished sevenths, or other modulatory means.

To discuss the tensions in the song, such as the way the transition from *heterotopos* to *topos* is realized by aspectualization, it is essential that we first uncover the engagements and disengagements on all three levels. The transition is depicted by the aspectual seme of accelerating, as is the state after the dream. In the former case, the acceleration occurs within the temporal-actorial category; in the latter case, within the spatial category. It is also clear in this connection that, as regards the spatial level, it is almost impossible to provide each chord with a tension value according to some external category or preconstructed, albeit correct, taxonomy. Nevertheless, in analyzing the degree of tension of a text, one must consider the isotopy in which the tension occurs. In other words, if a chord is part of a sequential passage, its value has to be given the coefficient determined by its isotopy. This coefficient is in turn decided by the position of the isotopy in the narrative course of the entire piece. In the case of Fauré's melody, the highest tension values occur in the latter half of the song, starting with the "hélas" exclamations. It is interesting to observe how the main musical actant of the song relates—in its *Bewegungsphase*, its shape of motion, to use Kurth's term–to some other Fauré themes; see, for example, the main theme at the beginning of his Ballade in F♯ major (Ex. 7.16).

Example 7.16. Fauré, Ballade in F♯major, mm. 1–3, opening theme.

Both there and in "Après un rêve" Fauré attempts to avoid the angularity of German melody, so that the stressed, long values are immediately followed, as if in impatient compensation for slowness, by a movement in smaller time units. The energy of the movement first accumulates and then dissipates. On the other hand, in the last section of "Après un rêve," when the "je" and the "tu" motifs return, they have been transformed, masked into unidentifiable units, so that from a veridictory point of view, one has moved into the category of lie, to complete the use of the former categories of secret and truth.

It is also rewarding to analyze the phonetic-musical features of the song, i.e., the musical points where the marked phonetic values or long vowels are placed. A map of the places where a vowel with a duration of at least a quarter note occurs on a strong, stressed part of a bar shows the location of the most important vowels. The first half of the poem has more /e/, /a/, and /o/, while towardthe end /ö/, /y/, /ä/, and /e/ predominate. The vowels /a/, /o/, and /u/ are dark and are thus more suitable for illustrating the desolate night; however, the distribution of these phonetic units over different registers does not occur systematically (see Ex.

7.17). Another phonetically pertinent figure is a longer triplet motif, frequently sung over the length of one bar. This figure is placed on the vowels of /a/, /e/, /ö/ and /ä/, /o/, and /ö/, alternating the vowels to avoid monotony.

Example 7.17. Fauré, "Après un rêve," vowel sounds.

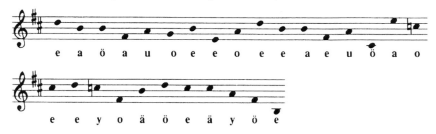

Musical Enunciation (énonciation musicale)

After clarifying the inner kinetic-semiotic structure of the tune, we can now move from the study of the musical enunciate, or intonation, to the structure of enunciating, or intoning, of the music. There are two main types of interpretation of "Après un rêve," one by singers, the other by string players. Comparing these interpretations provides interesting material concerning the extent to which instrumental intoning differs from vocal. Guido Adler, the founder of style analysis in musicology, considered instrumentality/vocality as an essential criterion of stylistic research (1911: 170–82). In the case of the Fauré song, the melody itself is equally suitable for singing or playing. The respiration slurs in the score (see Bernac 1978: 110), or "junctures of respiration" (see Pierce 1987: 1–12), give the melodic line its own articulation, which may differ completely from a purely instrumental articulation.

One level of analysis, which in fact belongs to temporality, is the segmentation of larger units of form. It may be that segmentation through intoning differs greatly from the musical articulation of the intonation itself. A traditional formal segmentation is shown Fig. 7.6, with brackets marking where the singer takes a breath. Note the difference between the segmentation of the intonation (text) itself and of its intoning. From this we can infer how the segmentation of the intoning is based on the semiotic structure of the musical enunciate (composition), whether it increases or diminishes, supports or rejects the interpretation made on the basis of the enunciate itself in the first half of the song, the breaths and the analysis of the form by and large coincide, while toward the end the breath slurs exceed the limits of the traditional segmentation. In other words, at the beginning, the form units of intonation and intoning are the same; at the end they differ, almost completely systematically. Because the second half of the song also has a more dramatic content, one may suppose that it is the need to express, the modality of 'demanding' ("Reviens, reviens"), that breaks the conventional limits.

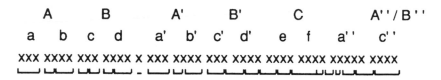

Figure 7.6. "Après un rêve," formal segmentation of song with segmentation by respiration of singer.

My study of the interpretations of this song by Fauré, of the way the previously analyzed musical enunciate (*énoncé*) becomes manifest in the performance and the way it changes and becomes modalized therein, is based on empirical material from sound recordings,[6] twelve vocal and ten instrumental (nine cello and one violin) performances. The renditions consist of the recordings in the archives of the Finnish Broadcasting Company in Helsinki. They represent an adequate sample on which to base a study, and they differ enough that it is possible to discern how the same musical enunciate changes character in the act of enunciation and to what extent a semiotic analysis of the musical enunciate itself (in this case, the poetic-musical text) might explain those differences. The assumption is that musical performances cannot be studied without a prior examination of the inner kinetic energy of the work itself.

In the empirical phase the plan was to note the differences, in all their subtleties, among the various interpretations. Yet a semiotic analysis cannot stop here, but must attempt to reveal each interpreter's way of modalizing, and to explain this modalization as but one variant of the internal, energetic-semiotic paradigm of a composition. The first empirical observation was that each interpreter has one or a few characteristic features, a "semantic gesture," which dominates his or her interpretation and distinguishes it from other performances. After the first listening it was possible to define eight pertinent parameters of analysis of the musical enunciation.

TEMPO

This includes alternations of the general tempo among various performers and also more limited temporal strategies, such as retardations and accelerations, within the basic tempo. In some interpretations one could even distinguish a gliding from tempo *a* to tempo *b* throughout the performance.

INSTRUMENTALITY/SPEECH-LIKENESS OF THE VOICE

The term "instrumentality" is less appropriate here, since the question is whether a singer takes into account the comprehensibility of the words and to what extent he or she focuses on the recitation of the poem. Kiri Te Kanawa, whose interpretation is such that one completely forgets the words, has an extremely "insrumental" voice. On the other hand, reciting style covers several variants, from a pathetic Italian operatic sigh, where the aspirant quality is very strong and almost a stylistic device (Katia Ricciarelli), to a light *chanson*-type reciting, as in spoken theatre (Claire Croiza), or exaggerated stress on the semantic content of certain words, as in the "low" style of entertainment music (Barbra Streisand).

VIBRATO

This concerns both singers and instrumentalists. As Ernst Kurth says, in his *Grundlagen des linearen Kontrapunkts* (1922: 30):

> A characteristic symptom of a psychic energetic experience occurs in tones with a longer extension (for example, in string instruments or the human voice), namely, in their tendency toward vibration. The ordinary explanation, according to which an intensified sound impulse forms the kernel of the artistic use of vibrato, the coloring of a tone with a vibration bursting out from it is not satisfactory. From the point of view of the sound, the aim of sound formation would on the contrary be only an absolute pitch. Vibrato rather manifests a need to provide a tone with a movement, as it were, with something to be understood in terms of the body. Vibrato means clinging to a tone and shaking it. A tone kept in a state of complete rest is only an aural sensation, not a musical tone. Through vibrato a tone assumes more intensity; it is an awakening from a state without any energy. With it musical life starts to pulsate in a pure sound impression. . . . The whole phenomenon of vibrato is only the manifestation of kinetic energy within a stable tone, it is a swaying forward to one or the other side. For tones held for a longer time the vibrato emerges—particularly with string instruments, where the sound is produced with a fingertip—most often unconsciously, at least in musical performance displaying some sensitivity. It is the excitation of the player, whereby he expresses himself; and this musical arousal is, with respect to its instinctive, unconscious part, a compelling kinetic energy.

When we clarify or at least make ourselves conscious of the somewhat mystifying way in which Kurth talks about "an instinctive musical excitation," his ideas are fully acceptable in the semiotic analysis of the interpretation. Yet the twenty-two interpretations studied here suggest that the use of vibrato is not at all arbitrary and unconscious, but a device that is economically distributed to different sections of the piece according to what is needed. Only one performer (Nikolai Gedda) seems to use it in a wasteful way throughout the entire work. Vibrato is a musical sign for the modality of 'will' in music, its *vouloir* and *pouvoir*.

The negation of vibrato, leaving it unused, becomes a device which is especially important in this song, particularly in the passages where a lack of vibrato aims to emphasize the dreaminess and "archaism" in the melismas. As a counterpart to vibrato, there can be a light, sustaining way of singing or playing, which might create, after a more stressed antecedent, an echo effect, a distanced understatement in the consequent.

BREATHING

Breathing, or phrasing, is an important style feature. It creates the impression of continuity/discontinuity. In Kurth's view, what is essential in a melody is the *Linienzug*, or *Bewegungsphase*, passing through individual notes, not these tones taken separately, as *Einzeltöne*. However, in proper places, individual tones of a melody can be emphasized as an efficient stylistic device. For example, some performers emphasize the first three ascending quarter notes, accentuating them separately. On the other hand, Pierre Bernac faithfully follows the breathing marked in the text itself, while other interpreters freely connect phrases and thus create their own "slurs" according to their own aesthetics.

DYNAMIC CHANGE

Dynamic levels are distinguished either abruptly following so-called terraced dynamics or by gliding between different degrees, yielding *crescendos* and *diminuendos*. Deviations from instructions written in the score can be very great. In almost all the interpretations the dynamic culmination of the piece did not come where *forte* is marked in the text, but one bar before or after it. In the cello arrangement by Casals, there is an instruction to play the repetition of the main period in the upper register and more intensively. Some but not all the interpreters did so. In most cases there was a direct correlation between the intensity and the loudness of the sound. However, in Streisand's interpretation recording techniques are used to expand the voice as well as to make it thinner and disappear into space at the culmination a little before the end. There is a growth of intensity but not of volume.

A particularly interesting technique is that of understatement, a sudden change from *forte* to *piano*, that is, a sudden change of level which produces the impression of a parenthetical statement before the narration resumes its course. This stylistic device is very useful for changing a one-part, linear text into a polyphonic, many-layered texture. A typical opportunity arises in m. 27, with the sudden move to the Neapolitan chord (which functions as something distanced and "strange"): the energy is accumulated and dammed up before the next rise and culmination. The vowels in the poem also enable some singers to broaden, lower, or change the voice into an open, dull intonation (which is employed very skillfully by Regine Crespin). Such an understatement technique is often used by singers aiming for expressiveness but very rarely by instrumentalists. Among the violoncellists only Antonio Janigro clearly displays this feature. Fauré wrote *crescendo poco a poco* in m. 27, and unfortunately many interpreters start their *crescendo* as early as that bar itself, though a basic rule of interpretation states that the sound must only begin to strengthen at the place where a *crescendo* is marked.

GLISSANDI

The *glissando* constitute a means of expression and a semiotic process of its own. The conscious destabilizing of the intervals between two notes plays an essential role, particularly in vocal and string performances. This does not necessarily mean a broader intervallic leap (Casals, for example, expressly avoids the use of an octave *glissando* at the climax; see m. 31); a *glissando* can also occur between intervals of a second. The use of *glissando* can be considered another energetic means, just as Kurth regarded vibrato as a sign for a need to increase the energy ("A tone at rest is a will to movement and this will swell during its suspension").

The kinetic-modal value of a *glissando* is more varied and more difficult to determine. One may emphasize the tone after the glissando, if the intention is to foreground it (Kiri Te Kanawa, m. 3, on "charmait"); or one can stress the *diminuendo* phase, when it functions as a "sigh" (Croiza, m. 19). It can convey a passionate submission, particularly in descending passages (Merrimam, mm. 6–7, or Crespin in the same place and elsewhere); a *glissando* can likewise express sensual languor or pining away.

PHENOMENAL QUALITIES

The softness/hardness, lightness/gravity of the voice itself can also function as signs that catalyze a semiotic process, but this largely depends on the recording. Particularly in older recordings these qualities run the risk of disappearing into the background. Together with other means, this device can also express the distance of a subject from an object in the process of musical signification. For example, the lightening of the voice or the sound can serve as a temporary strategy, conveying a relinquishing of the object, pushing it aside for a while, in order to grasp it even more passionately the next time. Furthermore, these qualities can precisely express matters that are difficult to describe or make explicit, namely, the place where the singer or player situates himself/herself most cogently as a musical subject, so as to participate most strongly and decisively in the transmission of the kinetic energy of the music. Each interpreter has personal spiritual techniques with which to regulate the streaming of his or her energy into the work: here one gives more, there less; here one spares energy, there one gives up that nuance in order to sustain overall coherence; here one decides not to be moved by that chord, that turn, in order to save more expression for the culmination point. This spiritual, inner strategy forms the kernel of the modalization of the musical enunciate. It is the semiotic moment of the interpretation in the true sense of the word; it is built on the 'will' expressed by the composer in the score as a surmodalization. Therefore the quality of the voice may convey the last important dimension in the analysis of an interpretation.

GLOBAL FORM

This dimension has to do with the construction of a musical piece as a semiotic object proper. The whole of a composition is dominated by a certain textual strategy of enunciation. At this level the interpreters manifest their own views of the fundamental isotopies of a musical work, in this case the topical narrative space, which is articulated through the musical-poetic text. It would be naive to search for direct counterparts to actants and to suppose that each artist would exploit a given quality to enact a given actant in the musical narration. Still, performers may emphasize some actantial role or isotopy in their interpretation, like the dream, awakening, mysticism, night, and possibly the transitions from one state to another.

After determining the basic categories of the analysis, we can proceed to a second listening of all the interpretations, this time paying attention to only one musical parameter (and its performance) at a time. In this way we can form a profile of each interpretation with respect to these eight dimensions. We may be able to complete the global view of each interpreter and his/her interpretation by drawing on extra-semiotic knowledge of the artist's life, style influences, or school and even sometimes about his or her aesthetic, verbally conveyed thoughts.

VIII

MUSIC AND VISUAL ARTS
PICTURES AND PROMENADES—A PEIRCEAN EXCURSION INTO THE SEMIOSIS OF MUSORGSKY

The choice of a piece such as Musorgsky's *Pictures at an Exhibition* for a semiotic analysis needs no extended explanation or justification. If one considers musical signs as obvious iconic cases where a musical motif or passage represents an object in the external world, Musorgsky provides a gold mine for a semiotician. Even one who has heard Musorgsky's *Pictures* innumerable times will experience surprise on seeing the original paintings, aquarelles by the Russian architect Viktor Hartmann, the source of inspiration for the composer (Figs. 8.1–8.4). Music can create its own, inner and purely virtual pictures so powerfully that concrete visual shapes can cause disappointment. The fantastic universe produced by music alone is so intense that when we really see the Great Gate of Kiev, through which we have entered many times, we feel a frustration and a fading of our fictive world.

One may therefore understand why this analysis goes a little further: to ponder how so-called musical realism in general is possible, and to examine how, almost unnoticeably, one is shifted from musical realism into "absolutism," even in such an evidently programmatic piece as Musorgsky's *Pictures*. By this I mean the way a composer transforms external icons, indexes, and symbols into internal ones. To my mind, inner iconicity and indexicality are not only manifest in the movements, known as Promenades, that hold the piece together; these sections naturally seek to serve as inner indexical passages leading the narration from one scene to another and to provide the piece with substantial coherence by forming series of iconic transformations of the same motif. Within each "picture," realistic and representational elements borrowed from the natural, external world are internalized into the musical discourse, into the kinetic-energetic network of the musical text. As soon as the Musorgskyan icons and indexes in each movement have been introduced and their representational nature is revealed, they become signs for totally different things. It is the task of semiotic analysis to clarify the aesthetics of this deeper level, which lies beneath the more superficial programmatic contents of the piece.

Figure 8.1. Viktor Hartmann, Design for unhatched chicken
costume from the ballet *Trilby* (aquarelle).

Thus certain aspects, even in the Firstness reception, may have an immediate impact on the listener, at least on a competent listener. Only on the later
level of Thirdness can we explain the factors on which these "first" impressions
are based. One such passage is the unexpected shift in "The Great Gate of
Kiev" to the gloomy atmosphere characterized by the bell-like timbre. In the
inner spatiality this means the use of the key of A♭ minor, while externally the
music moves to a lower, darker register. Yet this passage is actually a self-
quotation from the Coronation Scene of *Boris Godunov* and at the same time
a reference to Boris's end. Since all this takes place amid a triumph—a function of glorification in the musical narration—it reminds the listener of the
dysphoria of death and casts a shadow over the festive mood. The aesthetic
effect, *effet de sens*, is one of the most impressive moments of the whole piece
(see Ex. 8.1), even for those who do not know its symbolic value.

Figure 8.2. Viktor Hartmann, *Samuel Goldenberg*
and *Schmuyle*.

Musorgsky also guarantees this effectiveness by purely musical means. At
the very beginning, the pentatonic theme of the Promenade captures our attention by its avoidance of the leading tone, A (see Ex. 8.3). When A finally
arrives, in mm. 8–11, it appears as A♭. This point (A♭) of the tonal space is
thus marked and given a special value, precisely by its being unused here and

Example 8.1. Musorgsky, "The Great Gate of Kiev," mm. 77–84.

Figure 8.3. Viktor Hartmann, *Hut of Baba-Yaga* (aquarelle).

exploited only where needed for a stronger expression. Similarly, in the first 29 measures of "The Great Gate of Kiev," the A♭ is intentionally understated, saved for the tonality of A♭ minor. In addition, A♭ minor is also an enharmonic reference to the key of G♯ minor of the "Old Castle." These brief examples represent the inner musical semiosis in terms of shorter musical units. Joined together, those units form a musical narration in the proper sense.

Figure 8.4. Viktor Hartmann, *The Great Gate of Kiev* (aquarelle).

The narrative arch of such multipart works as *Pictures at an Exhibition* also exploits the Greimasian distinctions between topic and heterotopic spaces. After introducing the center of the narration in the *modo russico* of the first Promenade, the music shifts to various heterotopic spaces and to the periphery (such as the garden of the Tuileries, the Italian castle, etc.) and then back home to the center of the narration with "Baba-Yaga" and "The Great Gate of Kiev." Thus the different pictures appear in an order that reflects their distance from the topic place (the Promenades) in which the narrating subject is present. Moreover, these spaces are always pre- and postmodalized by the previous and succeeding sections.

We can now present a schematic actorial, spatial, and temporal articulation of the whole piece:

1. Promenade: temporally, attention is caught by the steady quarter-note rhythm and its aperiodic disengagement; the actorial dimension is realized through the actor "I."

2. "The Gnome": asymmetric, rhythmic disengagement; the actors are distorted and strongly opposed to the "normal" actor of the first Promenade, a negation of the previous section in every sense; the modality of 'doing' dominates; much harmonic disengagement in relation to the beginning; notice the tritones in the bass.

3. Promenade: premodalization of the next picture, a rising spatial movement as a symbol of the gothic Middle Ages.

4. "The Old Castle": Musorgsky's Italian pastiche (compare Busoni or Glinka writing in the "Finnish" style); Siciliano rhythm prevails; an enharmonic modulation from the A♭ major of the previous Promenade to G♯ minor; temporal disengagement: "old castle" alludes to the past, a heterotopic place, "elsewhere" with respect to the musical narration.

5. Promenade: an alienating effect produced by the postmodalization, i.e., the abrupt return to the present time and place.

6. "The Tuileries": Children quarreling at play; Musorgsky's French pastiche; notice the actorial disengagement.

7. "Bydlo": again an actorial disengagement, in such a way that the heaviness and slowness of the Polish wagon is anthropomorphized.

8. Promenade: an indexical pre- and postmodalization, i.e., the limits of the piece are made to disappear.

9. "Ballet of the Unhatched Chickens": actorial articulation in the foreground.

10. "Samuel Goldenberg and Schmuyle" (two Polish Jews): again actorial articulation as a Bakhtinian "polyphony of consciousnesses" appearing amid Musorgsky's musical discourse. A unison style similar to that in the "Gnome."

11. Promenade: repetition of the first Promenade; engagement (*embrayage*) by recall of the starting point of the narration; a reference to the act of utterance (enunciation) and to the subject interpreting the pictures.

12. "The Market Place at Limoges": on the level of plot, an actorial and spatial articulation at the same time.

13. "Catacombae": a spatial disengagement; "Con mortuis in lingua mortua": actorial interpretation of the preceding section.

14. "The Hut on Fowl's Legs (Baba-Yaga)": an actorial and spatial articulation; a return from the heterotopos to the topos.

15. "The Great Gate of Kiev": a merely spatial articulation and at the same time a symmetric culmination of the Promenade of the beginning; the glorification of the topical space.[1]

Pictures at an Exhibition basically consists of two kinds of movement: promenades and pictures. As regards their cognitive function, these movements are situated on quite different levels. In the Promenades the emphasis is always on the *énonciation énoncée*, the uttered utterance or enunciated enunciation, that is, on the fictive spectator (here, the listener), who modalizes and is modalized by different pictures. The "pictures" themselves are like objectively depictive musical "language," which is commented on by the Promenades. If this technique is compared with some works by Robert Schumann which form a "gallery" of portraits (for example, *Kreisleriana* or *Carnaval*), the difference is that Schumann does not present the subject of the enunciation as a text apart, i.e., as an individual voice of the narrator. In the Musorgsky, the narrator always emerges in the Promenades, where almost the only factor creating continuity is produced by actorial iconicity; that is, the actors of all the Promenades are based on the same thematic-actorial material. The music also depicts various approaches of the narrator-spectator to the pictures he views: when he is putting his whole soul into the picture, when he maintains an ironic distance, when he is flatly stating something objectively, when he becomes overwhelmed by what he sees, and so on.

This psychological-semiotic binarity, the distinction between two levels, makes *Pictures* a truly fascinating work. It also explains the work's musical form, which does not grow from the possibilities of the thematic substance of the material or end according to the latter's inner laws. Rather, it is finished when the observer of these first-order signs, on the level of secondary modeling, tires of them, wants to get rid of them, forgets himself, or sinks into them for indefinitely long periods. Consequently, the form of these pictures is sketched on the psycho-semiotic level, not through the formation of any strictly inner kinetic musical energy. Thus the "pictures" are most often based on certain external iconic signs that constitute their Firstness. But as soon as the composer starts to repeat them or confront them with other musical signs, their quality of Firstness disappears, replaced by the Secondness of the purely musical formation.

The level of Thirdness is realized through the idea that, for the inner narrator-spectator of the work, the pictures finally become symbols of certain properties, to which the inner listener-spectator of the music reacts on the level of Thirdness. This way of reacting or modalizing is reflected by the musical form of each movement. To note the fulfillment of this Thirdness, particular attention must be paid to formal closure, when aspectual semes such as insufficiency/excessiveness characterize the way the movements end and how those endings are reflected on the level of Thirdness. The individual movements hardly ever end according to "normal" musical logic, but always last either too long (the first Promenade, "The Old Castle") or too short a time (the Promenade after "The Old Castle"). Musorgsky's aesthetic is one of extremes, offering either too much or too little.[2] Hence all the signs in *Pictures at an Exhibition* should be interpreted first, signs as such; second, as part of the chain they form with other musical signs; and, finally, in relation to something third, which is the narrator of the work, whose voice is heard both in the Promenades and in the creation of the global form of each "picture."

The way this interpretation is realized more precisely depends largely on the use of modalities. For example, one may speak about 'will' on these three levels, as opposed to our earlier analyses (Chaps. 5–7) of Beethoven, Liszt, and Chopin, where it sufficed to distinguish between only two levels: the outer and inner modalities. To illustrate, let us take the main motif of the "Gnome." First, it has the kinetic 'will' and goal-directedness formed by the complex of its tones. Second, it has 'will' that grows from its relation to the preceding and succeeding signs of the musical syntagm. In addition, the motif's 'will' can originate from something third, that is, from a subject of musical narration (enunciation) which through the operation of disengagement has moved to the level of the musical discourse itself. We can clarify these three levels of 'will' by analogy to a linguistic utterance: the phrase "The Gnome is a limping troll" depicts the 'will' of the first degree; "The Gnome is a limping troll who is searching for a princess" consists of several signs between subject and object and thus contains a certain 'will' emerging from the interrelations of these signs and objects; "The Gnome is a limping troll who is searching for a princess and who frightens me" forms 'will' of the third degree, wherein the narrator-subject reacts to the Gnome and expresses his reaction with a certain modality, that is, with a special part of the text on the level of the discourse itself.

Translating this situation into the musical language of the "Gnome," we may take the quick opening eighth notes as a sign of the first degree, with its particular 'will'. Alongside it, another motif of heavy half notes emerges in mm. 38–41. A kinetic tension arises between these two musical signs, since they are so different in their respective kinetic energy, or 'will'. The 'will' that arises between the two motifs represents 'will' on the level of Secondness. In the musical process these motifs develop in sharp contradiction to each other: the half-note motif tends upward and expresses striving toward consonance, a state of rest, for example, by resolution of the tritone; while the eighth-note motif strives toward dissonance and tension. The eighth-note motif always interrupts the more stable development promisingly begun by the half-note motif, as if the viewer of the picture were mentally comparing the two contradictory motifs that he sees, unable to decide on which one he will set his euphorizing modalization, or empathy. This juxtaposition on the level of the musical discourse therefore manifests the 'will' of the musical narrator toward the actors of the narrative itself and their respective 'wills'.

Orchestration as a modalization can strengthen or weaken any segment of this three-phase process. For example, by choosing some instrument to portray the primary sign of the "Gnome," the orchestrator can either emphasize or weaken its qualisigns. If he uses the same instruments for both the lively, jumping motif of the Gnome and the subsequent *pesante* motif, and then takes the same instrumental "actor" to function as an actor in the background of each musical object, he can greatly mitigate the tension between the two motifs. Such orchestration might follow the rules or 'must' of Rimsky-Korsakov/Berlioz/Strauss orchestration, but it might also go totally against the modalities of the Musorgskyan tonosphere. Correspondingly, by choosing apt instrumental actors to support actors of the musical utterance itself, the orchestrator can also reveal entirely new modalities in the latter actors, perhaps completely remodalizing them, and thus adding a fourth dimension to the semiosis of the piece.

Of further interest is the concept of "border" in the Tartu School of semiotics. Many of the movements in Musorgsky's piece are not articulated according to traditional musical criteria; rather, the composer has attempted to eliminate clear-cut border lines between movements. This is nothing new—one need only think of Schumann's piano suites. This disappearance of borders seeks to describe the reaction of the musical narrator on the level of Thirdness.[3] For example, the fact that "The Great Gate of Kiev" bursts upon the listener without any mediating Promenade also reflects the idea that the consciousness of the narrator is, as it were, merging with its object. A syncretism takes place between the subject of musical narrative and the subject of narration, limits disappear altogether, and the levels become fused. From this point until the end of the work, the subjects of narrative and of narration are the same.

Promenade I (Allegro giusto, nel modo russico, senza allegrezza, ma poco sostenuto)

The inner spatial articulation is the key of B♭ major, with projections of pentatonic content. Another way of viewing the inner spatiality is with the modal element of a raised (Lydian) scale degree $\hat{4}$ (E♮). The modal pitches are avoided in the two opening bars, but are introduced as the texture becomes chordal. From B♭ Lydian we take a short excursion into D♭ major in mm. 8–11, after which we return to B♭ major, now without any modal features.

In the outer-spatial sense a striking antiphonal feature in the first two phrases is the contrast between thin and dense filling of tonal space, the alternation of unison and chordal textures. The chords change with every quarter note, although this is neither a chorale nor a march.[4] The tempo of chord changes becomes faster, but it returns to the quarter-note rhythm to close the movement. In the harmonic sense the texture is simple, naive, arousing no particular attention. The spatial is not the most pertinent level of articulation in this movement.

The temporal articulation proves to be much more interesting and pertinent by virtue of its complexity and degree of disengagement. Segmentation of the movement is problematic, to the extent that this problem can be regarded as the central compositional idea. This evokes the so-called versification problem, particularly if one thinks of the allusion to the antiphonal peasant choirs on the spatial level. In this respect the movement might be taken as a *chant sans paroles*. Can any valid metric theory be applied there?

An appeal to rhythmic theory based on beats (e.g., Cooper and Meyer 1959 or Krohn 1945/46) does not suffice, for here it is hard to define beats unambiguously. Barlines offer little guidance, since the rhythmic articulation moves by alternation of quarter and eighth notes; the movement contains no other time units. The meter varies between 5/4 and 6/4 without any apparent scheme. Accordingly, it is better to establish first the rhythmic scheme of the whole movement, to find any repetition on the basis of which we might set up a paradigmatic chart. If the changes of meter are omitted, the organizing criteria become the alternation of quarter and eighth notes and the slurs toward the end of the section (not shown in some scores). The oft-repeated rhythmic figure of two eighths plus a quarter may also be considered a structuring principle: it forms an anapestic motif and should be conceived as such according to Musorgsky's slurs. One might thus take this unit as the basis of segmentation at the beginning. Why does Musorgsky write this slur so carefully at the beginning, but not at the end? Probably to prevent this figure from becoming a dactyl, which would turn the accentuation of the beginning into the monotonous scheme shown in Ex. 8.2.

Example 8.2. Musorgsky, Promenade I, opening, rebarred as dactylic rhythm.

An analysis of the rhythmic values shows three paradigmatic rhythmic criteria in the first two measures: three quarter notes, the anapestic motif, anapest + four quarter notes (see Fig. 8.5). A simple tally of the frequency of various rhythmic cells shows that the piece includes a tendency of engagement toward two rhythmic figures: a group of three quarter notes, and a group of two eighth notes followed by a quarter note. Further, the piece uses all possible articulations of these rhythms. One cannot show any rhythmic-temporal fixed point other than the recurrence of certain rhythmic figures. This recurrence is in no way periodic, so that part of the movement remains without a rhythmic center, and the overall impression is one of disengagement. On the other hand, in relation to the next Promenades, whose paradigm this section constitutes, mere disengagement can serve as engagement. In other words, the establishing of irregularity as a starting point entails that any overly periodic metric transformation of that starting point will weaken the original rhythmic iconicity. This is the process of deiconicization, disengagement in the inner sense. Hence on this level, similar to the inner and outer spatiality, the rhythmic motion does not function as a source for establishing the iconicity. This task is left to the actorial dimension.

Figure 8.5. Paradigmatic rhythms in Musorgsky, *Pictures at an Exhibition*, Promenade.

The actorial articulation takes place as follows: The first two measures introduce the main actor of the movement, first as a single melodic line, allowing the listener to focus on its pitch content (see Ex. 8.3). All that follows in the continuation is generated from this motif. It consists of a series of successive groups of six notes which are organized to form a symmetrical, closed, reflexive whole. The actorial symmetry forms a counterpole to the fragmentation, asymmetry, and threatening monotony on the spatial level. How then does this main actor, which also has the task of portraying the spectator of the pictures, expand over the whole movement? First, with regard to larger periods, it exceeds the Kurthian rational principle of rhythmic symmetry (1922: 149–51) by always adopting new arrangements of formal units:

1. According to the scheme: theme-repetition or solo-tutti (mm. 1–4); A, A´.

2. From the inversion of the theme a formal unit abab´ is built (mm. 5–8); B, B´.

3. A developmental section follows, representing durativity and mostly elaborating intervals of a second (from previous motifs) with neighboring and passing notes as central components. The formal principle is a motif and its extension: C (mm. 9–10), C´ (mm. 11–13).

4. Gradual development/transformation of a motif: D (m. 14), D´ (m. 15), D´´ (m. 16).

5. Reorganization of the cells of motif C according to the formal principle of motif-repetition-condensation: C + C + c (mm. 17–21).

6. In mm. 21–24 the first sequence of the beginning is repeated, now harmonized each time, albeit somewhat differently from the first occurrence.

Although similar actorial substance is used throughout, and although it is fully recognizable, each of the movement's six sections displays a slightly varied principle of formation. This creates *différance* in the text on the actorial level, yet not with so much variety as to inhibit the aspectual seme of excessiveness.

Example 8.3. Musorgsky, Promenade I, mm. 1–2.

Examination of the qualisigns of the motifs reveals that, just as in the rhythmic-temporal paradigm, certain intervals become pertinent through mere repetition, clearly dominant intonations which the listener's ear can grasp. One such element is a falling-fifth motif, which becomes pertinent not only through recurrence but also through its consistent placement at the ends of phrases (see Ex. 8.4). The neighboring-tone motif likewise belongs to this group of dominant intonations.

Example 8.4. Musorgsky, Promenade I, mm. 4–8, falling-fifth motif.

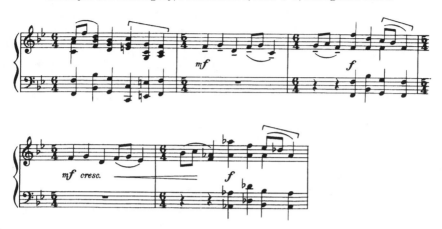

To make the repetition of intervallic motifs perfectly explicit would require a list of 24 paradigmatic units. Even on the level of two- and three-note units the actoriality dissolves into a great many proto-actors. Naturally in such a paradigmatic chart the essential question would be from which notes to count the intervals. The last note of a frequently repeated motif can also be considered the first note of the subsequent motif. Such a paradigmatic method has not been followed in the present analysis. Instead, choice of actors has been made on spatio-temporal criteria, in favor of one or the other motif. On the microlevel this movement exhibits the generation of actoriality from minimal units of signification. A motif (musical pheme) has to be repeated a certain number of times in relation to surrounding motifs in order to win in this competition of intonations, or in order to exceed the limit after which it becomes a content-bearing unit (seme) with the characteristic trait of a musical actor. Musical cells or phemes are not yet actors, but serve as their constituent units on a subactorial level.

From the actorial point of view, what is surprising in this movement is that the phenomenal impression is that of identity; i.e., the whole movement is dominated by one and the same actor. This "superactor" consists of 24 different elements, four of which are particularly pertinent. Why have these four elements been selected? The investigation of modalities below will provide an answer to this question, and also to the question of how these proto-actors are used later in the piece. Similarly, further comparison will reveal which phemes of this paradigm the semiotic process later brings to the fore. In any case, the paradigmatic store for later transformations and selections for the syntagm of the whole work is very rich. In this sense Musorgsky's *Pictures* fulfills Roman Jakobson's requirement for the poetic quality of a work of art, namely, the condition of richness of the paradigmatic store.

Finally we have to look briefly at the modal content of the first Promenade. Regarding the 'will' (*vouloir*), the first two bars of the main actor manifest two implications: an ascending and a descending motion, which is at the same time fragmentary, due to two missing notes, E♭ and A. In its inner spatiality, this actor is a plagal melody, in which the tonal range extends to the dominant on both sides of the tonic. It is significant that actors with a length of two or three bars almost always begin and end on the same note. The actors are thus by their nature closed within themselves: they manifest a 'will to something' and then a negation of this striving, a principle of *de-vouloir*. Therefore the basic function of the whole section is 'becoming', transitivity, not the creation of tension or an initial lack for the musical narration or a completely stable state of rest (the passage is marked *Allegro giusto*). The degree of 'will' is balanced, a neutral value of 0.

Regarding the 'knowing' (*savoir*), we have already seen that much new spatial-temporal information is given, especially on the microlevel, for the "phonemes." On the "word" or "morpheme" level, the overall impression is much more redundant. Yet in spite of the repetition at certain levels, this movement contains much information, which is stressed by its placement as the first Promenade: the first Promenade is the legisign of all the ensuing Promenades, all of which are iconically related to the first; thus, know+.

In the sense of technical efficiency the whole movement is very unrewarding, almost unimaginative. The solo/tutti effect and the choralelike harmonization are used abundantly and hence cause monotony. All other parameters vary, yet the technical-instrumental level remains the same. The movement therefore receives a negative value of 'can' (*pouvoir*): can--. If one thinks of norms, style obedience, and so on, then on the level of formation this Promenade follows a series of traditional formal principles, though it is richly varied within those limits. Nevertheless, in principle the piece ends with a symmetrical repetition. On a stylistic level the piece represents folklike art music, *modo russico*, but it adds no new interpretation to this paradigm. The determinant role this movement has for what follows, and its functioning as the substance (legisign) for future Promenades, cannot yet be seen. Thus the degree of 'must' (*devoir*) remains neutral: must 0.

As to the epistemic position of the movement, if we assume the role of an omniscient enunciator, we know that the first Promenade will undergo complete affirmation only at the end of the work. Nevertheless, nothing is denied or hidden here. The 'appearing' of the movement corresponds exactly to its 'being'. If this 'being' is understood to be the fact that this movement's intonations are based on the store of popular intonations of Musorgsky's time, its motifs undeniably fall into the Asafievian category of "true musical speech." Indeed, for the Promenade as a whole, for its parts, actors, and even the characteristic traits of these actors, one can find interpretants in the Russian folk music of the time, that is, corresponding folkish *arguments, dicents,* and *rhemes.*

When pondering the epistemic value of the whole movement we have first to think of the subject according to whom we make this evaluation. As already stated, the Promenades represent an imaginary spectator-listener with whom the receiver of the message is intended to identify. Thus the Promenades represent modalizations (evaluations, interpretations) of the "pictures." The pictures aim to convince us with their truth, untruth, lie, and secret; whereas the Promenades alone cannot convey these epistemic values, since they are not in front of us on the same level as the musical objects of the pictures themselves. Therefore during the Promenades only the epistemic values of the pictures are reflected, or rather created. So the first Promenade, coming before any pictorial scene, cannot represent by its epistemic interpretation anything other than an innocent, inexperienced *tabula rasa*. We naturally assume that the intonations contained in the Promenade form the inner store of intonations to which all future intonations will be compared. Only by this relationship can one later define the 'being' or 'appearing' of future intonations derived from this store. Notice that here the term 'being' does not denote a state of rest or consonance, but the existence of some musical intonation in an immanent store of intonations, in contrast to the concrete 'appearing', or sounding, of this intonation.

Before examining the first "picture" we must comment on the transitions, the border lines between the movements. Musorgsky paid particular attention to the variety of these transitions. Their quality reveals the way in which the inner narrator of the work, the receiver of the enunciation, has experienced the aspectual content of the preceding section, as excessive, sufficient, not-excessive, or insufficient. From the viewpoint of excessiveness, one might think it desirable to get as quickly or indexically as possible to the following section; and indeed, this has been musically realized with various *attacca* beginnings. A section experienced as sufficient needs no postmodalization by a separate Promenade; in such a case the transition can set up some quite new modalization and orient itself toward the particular atmosphere of the next picture. On the other hand, a section that remains insufficient might require a long postmodalization, as does the Promenade following "Catacombae" (which is not entitled "promenade" but given a Latin name). A not-excessive but still abundant modalization would cause the next movement to be premodalized by its preceding Promenade.

When the first Promenade ends we do not sense closure; the movement lacks achievement, the seme of perfectivity. It ends abruptly, without warning, and one moves quickly to the first picture, "The Gnome." Although this transition is not marked *accelerando*, it happens quickly and without preparation. By so many alternative motifs, rhythmical-temporal repetitions, and spatial monotony, the Promenade has given the "spectator" such an impression of excessiveness that an *attacca* transition is necessary.

"The Gnome"

The strongest Firstness impression of this movement, coming after the first Promenade, is of striking contrasts on many levels at the same time. If the preceding movement was characterized by actorial-temporal excess, then here we meet an insufficiency, since even slightly lengthy developments are immediately interrupted. The movement is based on three musical actors which have unambiguously iconic and representational tasks as musical signs in relation to their objects in the real world.

The first motif, Gnome I, strikes a sharp contrast to the Promenade-actor, although it has undoubtedly been derived from the latter's descending-fifth motif by slight intervallic alteration: the fifth has become a sixth and the major second a minor second (see Ex. 8.5). Moreover, since this motif is symmetrical, like the Promenade-actor, it appears as a strange and grotesque distortion of the latter, and the walker recognizes in the Gnome something of himself.

Example 8.5. Musorgsky, "Gnome" I, mm. 1–3.

Spatially, we have moved to E♭ minor, the minor subdominant of B♭ major, the opening key. In the outer tonal space the middle register, used extensively before, is now avoided, and the music remains mostly in the bass range, apart from an abrupt leap to the upper register at the very end. The tonal space is thus deliberately disengaged, unbalanced. In the temporal respect the movement alternates between an extremely fast eighth-note figure and a half note lengthened by a *fermata*, like the damming of kinetic energy followed by a violent outburst. Only in mm. 8–9 do the meter and tempo become clear, but even there they are partially masked by hemiolas. There is an alternation of temporal + and -disengagement. Actorially, this takes the form of a motif, its repetition, and its development.

The changes of the modality of 'will' alternate abruptly, which we can indicate by the symbol +/-. The degree of 'can' is high in relation to the uninstrumental nature of the previous movement: can+. The degree of 'knowing' is also great, since the transition was quite unexpected, and the temporal imbalance and disengagement gives this movement much information and entropy: know+. The degree of 'must' is again minus, since we have here a relatively free formal design.

The motif of Gnome II is based on elaboration of the seconds in the initial melody line and on a new, ascending-tritone motif in the bass (Ex. 8.6). Spatially, these factors represent a diagonal move from the extreme register toward the center. We remain in E♭ minor, but in the temporal sense we again hear an oddly syncopated rhythmic figure that can serve as an external icon of many a dwarf. Nevertheless, in the actorial-temporal sense this iconic sign embodies the scheme of a motif and its repetition. In m. 29 this is interrupted by Gnome I.

Example 8.6. Musorgsky, "Gnome" II, mm. 19–22.

Gnome II contains two, mutually contradicting kinetic tendencies: the value of will+ in the ascending motion and dissonant, tension-increasing intervals in the bass; and will- in the upper part and its figure, consisting of resolutions of appoggiatura chords and accented passing tones. Accordingly this represents a counterpoint of modalities, a simultaneity that produces a peculiar meaning-effect of strangeness. The modality of 'knowing' also forms a complex isotopy. The upper part is based on a falling melodic second derived from earlier material; consequently this constitutes a moment of know-. At the same time, the lower part introduces new intervals, thereby representing the value of know+. As to the modality of 'can', this section is innovative in its joining of different registers to produce its unique timbre (can+). Regarding 'must', this otherwise strange section is symmetrical (motif plus repetition) and accordingly must+, even though its interruption (m. 29), which results in a truncated period, or *Satzform*, leads to a break of norm, with the value of must-.

Gnome III (Ex. 8.7) is steadier than the temporally capricious texture of the previous sections. In the actorial sense it is derived from the bass line of Gnome II, but it also refers vaguely to the fifth motifs of the Promenade actor. Moreover, the two consecutive descending seconds originate from Gnome I. Its iconic impression is that of heaviness and persistence, as if it were pushing or dragging a burden. It occurs in the form of a motif, its repetition, then its development; but its quiet unfolding is interrupted by Gnome I (mm. 45, 54, 58). The degree of 'will' in the two first repetitions of the phrase expresses a growth by striving or laborious ascent. In the last repetition, which develops the motif, a resolution of the tension and a descent are accomplished by means of sequence (mm. 60–71). 'Can' is still high, owing to the parallel-octave motion. The degree of 'knowing' is small since the most essential motivic substance derives from what was heard earlier (know 0). The degree of 'must' is almost positive in its regularity, save when Gnome I interrupts the normal progress of the form. This interruption results in something like a conversation between two actors (as Musorgsky would later describe it) in the Bakhtinian polyphonic sense.

Example 8.7. Musorgsky, "Gnome" III, mm. 38–41.

There follows a development of Gnome II, now with trills and chromaticism evocative of melodramatic horror effects (mm. 72–93). The kinetic energy of the section increases toward the end, culminating in two chords that simultaneously crystallize the intervallic content of Gnome I. The coda releases the accumulated energy in a *velocissimo* figuration and engages the section to the tonic (mm. 94–99). The degree of 'knowing' remains positive in spite of repetitions, and the 'can' is likewise positive because of the new instrumental devices. The 'must' also remains on the plus side, and the 'will' grows until the end.

On the thematic-actorial level, the global form gives the impression of three subactors whose iconic qualities awaken extramusical associations, but who also follow purely musical logic so that they function as inner icons. At the beginning, the anti-indexes of the *fermata* pauses prevail; they are balanced by the *poco a poco accelerando*, which increases indexicality at the end. Yet normal musical processes are interrupted often and abruptly, and this interruption doubtlessly conveys the modalization of the spectator with respect to the representational icons of the picture itself. The spectator-walker is surprised and upset by the actors he sees (hears). Their images pursue him incessantly (notice the disturbing penetration of Gnome I into Gnome III, breaking down the latter's form), so much so that he decides to get rid of the world of the picture quickly, to flee from it with the *velocissimo* of the coda. As a whole the movement has been so disengaged from the "normal" situation of the beginning that with respect to its epistemic value it falls into the category of the untrue, grotesque, or unreal. The coda of this movement constitutes its postmodalization with the epistemic value of denial, in the sense of denying this "picture" as untrue or unbelievable.

Promenade II

This promenade, with its gothic linear motions, serves as a transition and premodalizes the next picture. The character is euphoric and striving upward, but without any violent 'can', as though seeking an object far "above." In the spatial sense the section is in A♭ major, which is first hinted at in m. 8 of the first Promenade. This choice of key suggests that the whole next movement, in G♯ minor, should be understood as an excursion to the heterotopos, to "elsewhere" in the course of the narration. Temporally, the basic pulse of the Promenade remains the same, slowing with longer time units (half notes) toward the end. Actorially, we hear fragmentary reminiscences of the subactorial motifs of the first Promenade. The descending fifth and fourth of the bass in mm. 9–10 and the ascending fourth in the right hand of mm. 11 are strongly foregrounded, referring to the characteristic intonations of the next picture.

In terms of the subject/object distinction, this section represents a subject that has sunk or will sink into a euphoric 'being': euph. mod. (S ∧ O). The other modalities are as follows: 'Knowing': 0 or scanty, since there is no new musical substance in the section. 'Can': slight, although the contrapuntal arrangement of the parts is new. 'Must': moderate, since this is a relatively regular *Satzform*. 'Will': minus articulation or negative value, since the only real striving is the sinking motion of the bass in mm. 9–10 and the rising movement in mm. 11–12. 'Believe': the movement attempts to affirm something denied above, but it contains no strong persuasive or conative epistemic value.

"The Old Castle"

It is amazing that Calvocoressi, among others, considered this movement less than successful: "The only complete failure is *Il vecchio castello*" (1946: 174). And yet it is among the most charming and impressive in the whole series of pictures. The basic atmosphere is nostalgia (see Ex. 8.8). A subject has lost the euphoric object, now far away, either in the past (the musical archaism of open fifths in the accompaniment, and the constant G♯ pedal point) or in some distant place (the "orientalisms" of the melodic line). This picture also takes us to a "strange" and distant isotopy in the sense of inner spatiality: G♯ minor (enharmonically transformed A♭ minor). All this represents S ∨ O, a subject who has lost the valued object that he once owned.

Example 8.8. Musorgsky, "The Old Castle," mm. 1–12.

The compound duple meter suggests balladic narration, as does the fact that nearly every phrase ends with the same melodic figure, B to G♯. In the middle sections, however, the subject of this narration disengages himself from the melancholy present and returns to the past tense, referred to by the Neapolitan and subdominant tonal areas of the transitions (mm. 29–37, 38–46), whose rich chordal textures contrast with the barren and empty timbre of the open fifths and linear activity. In the middle sections the subject remembers, as it were, how in some golden past he still possessed a valued object, the identity of which is never revealed to us (was it the tonic B♭ major?). If, therefore, the first transition section portrays the modal state of a subject remembering his euphoria due to the possession of a value object O, then in the second transition this same subject expresses a small effort of will to retrieve this object. Yet the refrain always returns that attempt back to the basic nostalgic mood. The movement therefore contains this modal definition: a subject m (S ∧ O), a subject wants to be conjoined anew with the object.

In front of an old castle, the inner narrator of the movement—whether a balladeer, a bard, or a bayan playing archaic instruments—passes through three modal states: m (S ∨ O), where m= 'not-willing, being'; m (S ∧ O), where m = the aspectual seme of "past," euphoria; and m (S ∨̌ O), where m = 'willing', or the subject S wants to deny his disjunction from an object or be reunited with it. In linguistic terms, transition I may be compared to a subordinate clause beginning with "although," and transition II to a sentence beginning with "however" or "on the other hand."

The frequent repetition in "The Old Castle" emphasizes the "timelessness" of the whole movement and the way all actoriality finally disappears with the thematic liquidation at the end. This represents a musical "forgetting," an immersion in the way the picture is presented, not so much in the objects presented. Orchestrations that try to change the timeless and monotonous contemplation of the movement into an excessively narrative plot, by constantly alternating instruments that carry theme-actors, lead listeners astray as to the character of the piece. This is meditative music of a contemplative, nonmotoric "I." The epistemic modality of the movement is 'secret' ('not-to-appear/to be') or 'doubt', an ambiguity arising from the three modal states mentioned above.

Promenade III

This transition in B, the relative major of the previous G♯ minor, brings the narrator-ego back "to earth," to decisiveness and affirmation. It represents the epistemic category of 'truth'. In the spatial sense the movement repeats the rising line of the preceding picture, but heavy octave duplications and full triads add heaviness to the linear rising motion. Of all the modalities, only 'can' is provided with a positive articulation, because of a new piano-technical device, but the other modalities remain at zero. Above all, this movement represents the uncovering and breaking of the illusion, the 'secret' of the previous section. In this sense, the 'will' at the beginning of Promenade III attains a strong value as it tries to negate the preceding narrative program. This Promenade is also remarkably condensed and entirely post- and premodalized by the pictures that frame it.

"The Tuileries"

Musorgsky's musical map of Europe starts to take shape. Children playing and quarreling in the garden of the Tuileries are still placed in a "strange" isotopy (B major) in the inner spatial sense. The basic modality is $S \vee O$, a subject disjuncted from an object. Yet the 'doing' caused by this lack is not very serious but playful. The impression of a light scherzo is brought about by the parallel fifths in the outer parts of the main motif, and by the capriciousness of the temporal program that combines quarter and eighth notes (see Ex. 8.9). In the actorial respect the movement consists of a repetition of an "infantile" descending minor third, reminiscent of children's playground taunts. In the subordinate section, the motif of mm. 14–19 quotes from the third section of "The Old Castle" (e.g., mm. 55–58).

Example 8.9. Musorgsky, "The Tuileries," mm. 1–2.

The way that Musorgsky uses musical analogy becomes manifest in this movement. What do we understand by "musical analogies"? Nothing other than the musical imitation of external reality, or, to put it in semiotic terms, musical iconicity. Marianne Kielian-Gilbert (1990) takes her definition of musical analogy from Douglas Hofstadter, who calls this phenomenon a case of "me, too." For example, two listeners to Musorgsky's *Pictures at an Exhibition* sit side by side at the concert. One whispers to the other, "I forgot to put coins in the parking meter." The other person replies, "Me, too." Everyone understands that the second speaker is not referring to his friend's car but to his own car. The scheme of such inferences through analogy is A:B :: C:D (read: A is to B as C is to D). In other words, both sentences are analogous to each other, having certain features in common, while other factors vary.

This scheme suits Musorgsky very well, since translated into our own semiotic terminology it signifies the inner iconicity and indexicality as well as their joint effect. For example, m. 1: m. 2 :: m. 14: m. 15 in "The Tuileries." The situation of mm. 1–2 is repeated so often in the inner iconic texture of the movement that against this background even the slightest common element suffices later to catalyze the mechanism of analogy. In this case it is the staccato sixteenth-note figure of the latter half of m. 15. Such inner iconicity functions within various movements, as in mm. 8–14, 29–37, and 61–68 of "The Old Castle," which form a corresponding chain of analogous relationships. And inner iconicity also functions between movements; for example: "The Old Castle" : "Bydlo" :: "The Tuileries" : "Limoges"; or "Limoges" : "Catacombae" :: "Baba Yaga" : "The Great Gate of Kiev" (especially with respect to the transition between A and B, and C and D). Accordingly, *Pictures at an Exhibition* exhibits a more sophisticated network of inner iconicity than would be brought about by mere unvaried repetition of similar elements. In fact, Musorgsky has his own particular manner of repetition, which might be called gradual condensation or exaggerated repetition—further evidence for our thesis that Musorgsky's aesthetic manifests the principle of excessiveness.

In the spatial sense the movement is based on an axis formed by a minor third, an imploring or even deriding motif, around which other material entwines. As to the inner spatiality, we have alternating I and VI chords (the latter with added sixth) in B major. In the temporal respect the movement is based on a contrast between quarter and sixteenth notes, so that the impression of *accelerando* is created by actorial condensation: denser motifs consisting of both these elements. In a broader sense the movement has the form ABA´, in which A sections are provided with Tchaikovskyan cadences of fleeting scale passages and diagonal lines. The B section provides a brief development. In the actorial sense the movement shows a confrontation between human types, which are typical of Musorgsky. The "speaking subjects" include an imploring or deriding subject (mm. 1–2) and a "self-satisfied" one (mm. 14–21). So, if the beginning of the movement portrays a subject who has been disjuncted from an object, the B section describes a subject conjuncted to an object. Of all the modalities 'can' is perhaps the most striking here as a pianistic innovation; this appears in particularly varied types of texture, which would justify different colorful orchestrations.

"Bydlo"

The Polish wagon, with rough wheels and drawn by a pair of oxen, returns to the spatial *topos* (G♯ minor) of "The Old Castle." The main actor is also based on the same scale as the bayan's song in "The Old Castle," but otherwise the narrative plot of the movement differs. The piece can be segmented into ABA´, as in the previous movement, but here the middle section forms an indexical culmination leading to the glorification of the main actor in the A´ section.

If "The Tuileries" described a modal situation in which the subject had lost an object but played with or experienced the disjunction euphorically, this movement in turn depicts the conjunction of subject and object as dysphoric. The subject possesses an object, and the music is full of the might and power of this ownership, 'can' (*pouvoir*), but this fundamental modal state is dissonant in character. In this way, Musorgsky shows that conventional articulations do not necessarily hold in his universe. Just as Wagner teaches us that a dissonance can also be sweet (according to Adorno), in these movements the normal thymic values of 'being' and 'doing' (euphoric/dysphoric) are inverted: in "Bydlo" 'being' is dysphoric and 'doing' is euphoric.

In the spatial sense the movement starts and ends in a low register. The A and B sections have dissimilar textures, the former octaves, the latter triads. As to the temporality, eighth-note figuration is engaged from the beginning. From the actorial viewpoint, we have already stated that the musical substance of the main actor recalls the principal motif of "The Old Castle." The subordinate actor (beginning in m. 21) is reminiscent of the descending octave passages of "The Gnome" and also alludes to the descending thirds of "The Tuileries." The heavy, arduous progress of the wagon, iconically portrayed by an ascending fifth in quarter notes (mm. 5–6 and elsewhere), is a device that appeared in "The Gnome." The thematic liquidation of the ending evokes the close of "The Old Castle" as it iconically depicts the disappearance of the wagon over the horizon.

Promenade IV

This Promenade exhibits an abrupt inner-spatial change: a shift from G♯ minor to D minor (Aeolian). In its outer spatiality there is a strong disengagement from the low bass of the end of the preceding movement to the high and expressive legato line here. In the middle section, a canon in octaves occurs, as in the earlier Promenades. As a premodalization, the figuration of the succeeding movement appears at the end of this Promenade. Diatonic D minor prevails in the middle section, and mm. 6–8 return to D-Aeolian.

In terms of inner spatiality and actoriality, the opening of this movement projects nostalgia and a sharp contrast reflecting the disjunction of subject from object," contrasts in which only the temporal dimension and the dynamics remain the same. The end of this Promenade, especially the last two measures, is indexically engaged, however, as preparation for the next picture.

"Ballet of the Unhatched Chickens"

This movement is related to the ballet *Trilby*, for which Hartmann drew sketches for the costumes. It was choreographed by Petipa and performed in St. Petersburg. The outer iconicity involves the imitation of birds, which has a long paradigm, from Rameau's *La poule* to Tchaikovsky's "Dance of the Swans." Musorgsky represents an intermediate position between these two works.

The outer spatiality favors the upper register. The inner spatiality makes use of the lowered submediant (augmented sixth chord on D♭) to embellish the tonic, F major (Ex. 8.10); this chord combination occurs in other parts of *Pictures*. In the temporal sense the whole movement, apart from the coda, remains in equal eighth-note figuration. Actorially the movement is uninteresting insofar as no clearly individualized theme-actor emerges; this is quite apt since the movement portrays a collective actor: chickens. The A section culminates with the exaggerated repetition of a right-hand figure that later appears in mm. 25–30 of "Baba Yaga" (another musical analogy). In the trio section, which is still in F major but somewhat Lydian-tinged, the listener's attention is caught by certain orientalisms (such as the melodic minor and augmented seconds in mm. 31–33), perhaps as an index to the augmented scale passages in the musical actor of Samuel Goldenberg. The whole movement has the flavor of a playful 'doing'. In the sense of inner spatiality it functions as dominant of the B♭ minor tonic of the next picture, but temporally and actorially there is a strong contrast. The instrumental innovation, or the modality of 'can', is again very high, and the dancelike character provides the scene with its 'must'. The musical substance of the movement is in no way outstanding, and the 'will' is likewise quite neutral here. The distinction of subject/object would be irrelevant to the text itself, which represents the depiction of a euphoric, hilarious object, striking in its outer iconicity.

Example 8.10. Musorgsky, "Ballet of the Unhatched Chickens," mm. 1–2.

"Samuel Goldenberg and Schmuyle"

It is not known who named these two Polish Jews, one rich and one poor, but Musorgsky's imagination is similar to Bakhtin's when juxtaposing two sharply contrasting consciousnesses and describing with outer iconic means the struggle between the two.[7] The narrative program of the movement is clear: A, introduction of the first actor (mm. 1–8); B, introduction of the second actor (mm. 9–14); A/B, juxtaposition of the two actors (mm. 15–21); C, coda, final comment (mm. 22–25). Both actors have been made iconically speechlike. In section A/B each loses some of his individuality and becomes texturalized, so to speak. Ex. 8.11 shows actor A in the left hand, actor B in the right. The movement has a strong outer iconic content, particularly since actors A and B engage in a struggle that ends with the defeat of B and the dominance of A. At the same time, this struggle is without object in the musical discourse.

Example 8.11. Musorgsky, "Samuel Goldenberg and Schmuyle," m. 15, motifs A and B.

Both actors are furnished with a humorous, if grotesque nuance, in that both have a legisign in previous pictures. Samuel Goldenberg is identified with the Gnome by unisons, rhythmic fragmentation, and an interrupted, nondurative nature, which in this case may also be taken as speech-likeness. Schmuyle, in turn, recalls the chickens in the Trio of the previous movement. The transition in mm. 13–14 is very typical: the roots of the chords of A minor (spelled Bbb), C augmented (with Fb for E), Db minor, and Bb minor derive from the melodic material already actorialized in Samuel Goldenberg (second half of m. 1). This epistemic gesture is in the category of "misleading": making something appear to be something it is not.

The modalities occur as follows. Section A: willing+; can+; knowing + to-; must+ (normal periodic form); 'doing'. Section B: willing-; can+; knowing- (because of frequent repetition); must+; 'being'. Transition: 'to appear/not to be'. Section A/B: willing++; can++; knowing-- (mere repetition); must++ (normal development in regular periodic form); epistemic modality of 'making something appear what it is' or to 'open the eyes (or ears)'. Coda (diminution of B):

all the modalities on the minus side; Coda (diminution of A in the last two bars): all the modalities again on the plus side, even 'knowing', since the closing comment is unexpected in the narrative sense.

Promenade V

This transition repeats the opening Promenade exactly, except for small changes in mm. 14–15, 19, 21, and at the very end. These changes have no particular meaning, since the overall impression remains the same. Therefore this represents a complete return, an engagement to the inner narrator of the whole work, the subject of enunciation. It is revealed only at the close of the work that these Promenades really serve as an upbeat, a dominant to the E♭ major tonic of the end.

"The Marketplace at Limoges"

After the highly individuated actoriality of the preceding movement, we have a collective event, in which spatial articulation and temporality are central. What is involved is a "motoric I" or "we." The literary program of the movement, which was deleted by Musorgsky, depicted the quarreling of French women at the marketplace:

"Great news: Mr. Pimpant de Panta-Pantaleon has found his cow, The Runaway."

"Yes, madame, it was yesterday."

"No madame, it was the day before yesterday."

"But listen, madame, the animal was wandering in the neighborhood."

"No it wasn't, it wasn't wandering anywhere."

And so on. Musorgsky portrays this parody musically with continuous sixteenth-note movement set in the spatial *topos* of E♭ major, and with a phenomenon referred to above as "a penetrating repetition."

The movement represents the modality of 'doing' because of the disjunction of subject and object. Both spatial and temporal dimensions are extremely disengaged and scattered, consisting of brief fragments, especially in the developmental section starting in m. 12. There chord changes first have a clear direction, which then becomes vague (mm. 20–22) and turns into a texture of altered chords with neighboring tones. The rate of chord changes accelerates to an extreme, and at the same time the rhythms become irregular and additive (mm. 16–24).

In the actorial sense the connection of this movement to the "Ballet of the Unhatched Chickens" is quite obvious, in that "The Marketplace at Limoges" is an almost grotesquely intensified, exaggerated transformation of the former. As to the modality of 'believing', the rhythmic and inner spatial disengagement here are "too much." The iconic unity with the "Chickens" appears on the actorial level as follows:

"Ballet of Unhatched Chickens"	"The Marketplace at Limoges"
main motif, mm. 1–2	upper voice, m. 3
left-hand scale, mm. 5–8	upper voice, ascending scale, m. 2
main motif of the Trio	upper voice, m. 5

The iconicity of the movement thus has a triple character: The interprenetrating motifs and the additive rhythms serve as outer icons for the "dispute" at the marketplace; the actorial elements of the movement are in an internal iconic relation with the "Chickens;" and there are frequent recurrences of the same motifs. Correspondingly, the indexicality is also very strong, and the forward-rushing character of the music reaches its climax in the coda (*Meno mosso sempre capriccioso*), which is like a condensation from both the "Chickens" and the "Limoges" movements. One might say that the "semantic gesture" of the whole movement is a temporal and indexical *crescendo*.

"*Catacombae*" *(Sepulcrum Romanum)*

As a contrast to the modalizing transitions of the Promenades between previous pictures, here one goes *attacca*, without warning, into the extremely different next movement. Thus Musorgsky seeks to create a sharp opposition of structure and content between the profane and the sacred.

Whereas temporality was the most pertinent level of the preceding movement, here we are dealing almost exclusively with the spatial dimension (see Ex. 8.12). The basic nature of the movement is a dysphoria that depicts not only a subject that has given up the search for objects (where the situation S ∨ O would prevail) but also the way the subject itself has also "died" or disappeared. The subject is no longer actorially represented in the musical discourse. Only in mm. 18–22 does a reminiscence of the subject burst forth, a pale ghost rising up from the past. An iconic allusion to the main motif of "Chickens," it too originates in the Promenade actor.

In the temporal respect, the movement is an extreme contrast to the preceding one. "Catacombae" is totally anti-indexical; the rhythm and even time itself seem to have lost all meaning. This music is doubtless experienced on the level of Firstness as a series of chords far from each other, a series of sound events provided with *fermatas*, which no longer seem to have a logical-discursive, syntagmatic unity. The only logic left might be the contrast between dissonant *fortissimo* chords and their *pianissimo* echoes functioning as "resolutions." These hushed echoes are again intended to serve as external icons for the empty corridors of the catacombs and as external indexes for the horror aroused by those deserted hallways. This would thus represent a Berliozian aesthetic of the unexpected, *l'imprévu*. Yet the listener may also anticipate that this is not the whole truth, or that the epistemic value of the movement may still be such that not everything sounds or seems as it really is.

Example 8.12. Musorgsky, "Catacombae."

Let us scrutinize the inner spatial structure more closely, particularly its relation to the outer spatiality. Analysis reveals that the outer spatiality does everything it can to hide the inner spatial, or functional, harmonic movement from the listener. Since the texture of this movement can be considered a kind of chorale, the abrupt changes of register in the outer spatiality cause this texture to become a deactorialized or alienated chorale. Because the preceding movement ended in the tonic, Eb major, the contrast to the beginning of "Catacombae" is sharp in both outer and inner spatiality, for the first eleven bars of the movement can be interpreted in B minor. Hence a mediant tonal relationship, Eb–B, such as that favored by the Romantics. At the same time there also occurs an extreme outer spatial disengagement between the two movements, a leap from the highest to the lowest register.

In the continuation, the first three bars, in octaves, contain three notes: B–G–G. The first two bars are decisively important, set as an oppositional pair on the timbral level: B must sound *fortissimo*, G *piano*. These enigmatic tones are in fact the secret code of the whole movement: a descending major third in the bass is the central and all-pervading inner-spatial structure of the piece. When the same pattern of three *fermate* notes repeats in mm. 12–14, the pitch center changes from B minor to G minor, a major third down. The chords in mm. 12–24 can all be interpreted in the context of G minor. The modulation takes place enharmonically in m. 13, whose G minor tonic chord (missing the fifth) may be reinterpreted enharmonically as three notes of the VII diminished seventh chord in B minor. This particular harmonic isotopy is given the task of carrying the only glimpses of actoriality in the movement, in which the rising octave motif is filled and thus made melodic.

In mm. 22–23, the octave leap of the main motif, which has been heard twice, expands into an outer spatial disengagement of more than two octaves, obviously emphasizing the significance of E♭ major as the climax of the whole section. This has a certain meaning for the whole tonality of the composition, since the end of the work, in which the narration attains its culmination in the achievement of the action, is in E♭ major. Iconically anticipated in m. 23, the modal value of this triad remains hidden, however affirmative it might look in this catacomb of shadowy, somber chords. The E♭ major triad in m. 23 and the C-major echo in the following bar have also been provided with a *fermata*, an indication of stopping time. Both can of course be interpreted in the context of G minor, as VI and a major-mode variant of IV. But the latter chord also serves to connect the return to the basic tonal isotopy of B minor: in the inner spatial sense it is also ♭II (Neapolitan) of B minor, confirmed by the harmonic motion of mm. 25–30, which leads to a half cadence in that key.

Harmonic analysis thus shows that, from the end of the preceding movement, the inner tonal space is organized as a series of descending thirds: E♭–B–G–E♭–C plus the return to B minor. Falling thirds, as "madrigalisms," have been used as signs meaning "departure" and "death" since the unsettled tonality of the beginning of the seventeenth century and even earlier, for example, in some motets of Orlando di Lasso. Musorgsky uses this old principle as a hidden structure in "Catacombae," which also contains just such a "secret" iconic content.

"Con mortuis in lingua mortua" [Promenade VI]

The musical material of this movement recalls the dysphoric atmosphere of the previous one. It continues on the macrolevel the effects of *fortissimo/ pianissimo*, near/far, which typified "Catacombae." It is thus strongly post-modalized by the preceding music. At the same time, the actoriality repressed in "Catacombae" again comes to the foreground in the form of the Promenade motif. Thus in spite of its title this is also a "promenade" movement in which we return to the subject of the narration (see Ex. 8.13).

The pathemic, or inner-emotional, state is now revealed by the performance indication of *con lamento*. The subject is disjuncted from the object, particularly from a dysphoric object. For example, "The Old Castle" described the pathemic state of nostalgia, in which the longed-for object was presumably euphoric. Consequently, in nostalgia we are dealing with the positive value of 'will' combined with 'knowing': the subject of "The Old Castle" knows that the object is euphoric, but is forced (must-) to keep away from it and is not able (can-) to unite with it. But here we have a dysphoric object that belongs to the past ("death"), with which the subject will be inevitably united in the future, a fact which the subject very well knows but neither wants nor can prevent. The modal state of the subject in the present *meditatio mortis* differs completely from its earlier state of nostalgia. However small, this Promenade tells a miniature story, in that something becomes something different.

Measures 1–10 are formally articulated as *aba´b´* (2 + 2 and 3 + 3 meas-

ures). As an actorial dialogue between two subjects, the first half of this movement is, in the outer sense, a directly iconic and realistic description of
Hartmann's aquarelle *The Catacombs of Paris*. In this painting, two gentlemen
wearing silk hats, stand with their backs to the spectator, and look at the catacombs.[8] A third person, carrying a lamp, is in the foreground, also with his
back to the spectator. The light from the lamp is bluish in color and reflection,
like the coat of the person carrying the lamp. Musorgsky depicts this blue light
by an upper pedal point on F♯, which at the end of the movement proves to be
the fifth of B major. It is perhaps no coincidence that, in both Rimsky-
Korsakov's and Scriabin's charts of colors, B major is expressly related to blue,
dark blue, or steel blue.

Example 8.13. Musorgsky, "Con mortuis in lingua mortua," mm. 1–3.

The pedal point descends twice at the motifs *b* and *b´*, chromatically fluttering downward, perhaps expressing the modal state of fear of the third person
in the painting. Neither in the aquarelles nor in the first half of the movement
do we know what the real spectators of the Catacombs are thinking. Their
modal state is not revealed in the painting or in the music. From the perspective of the enunciator-composer, the epistemic modality of the first half of the
movement is 'not-to-do/to appear/to be', that is, to prevent something from appearing as it is.

The latter half of the movement (mm. 11–20) shifts to the epistemic state of
'not-to-do/to appear/not-to-be'; we find that something is not as it looks. First of
all, we move from the dysphoria of B minor into the luminous euphoria of B
major. At the same, a change occurs in the outer tonal space. The actors, instead
of floating back and forth, stabilize in a certain register. The Promenade actors
disappear altogether, replaced by the actor of death, borrowed from "Catacombae" (mm. 18–22). The latter actor has now assumed a positive thymic value,
with its neighboring-tone motion preparing for B major. In other words, the
object from which the subjects are disjuncted, but with which they are necessarily conjuncted in the future, unexpectedly receives a euphoric value.

The events of this movement can also be seen in relation to the fundamental
value model of any subject, which according to the semiotic square includes
cases such as life, death, not-life, not-death. Then we are dealing with trans-
fers of musical subjects and actors between these states of being. The motif

that originally depicted the unhatched chickens now changes into its negation, 'not-life', like the actor of "Catacombae," and this motif in turn becomes a representative of 'not-death' at the end of "Con mortuis."

"Baba Yaga (The Hut on Fowl's Legs)"

Toward the end of the composition the narrating subject and the Promenades that represent him give place to direct narration. That is, the subjects of the enunciation and the act of enunciation begin to fuse and to operate syncretically. At the same time, the actors of previous movements start to integrate. Regarding the modality of 'knowing', this means an increase of redundancy with respect to the musical substance; the material of the narration is generated from the inner-memory paradigm of the piece itself. In this sense, the outer iconicity on the actorial level becomes more and more internal. At the same time, other modalities, particularly 'can', are foregrounded in an increasingly significant way.

The subject of "Baba Yaga" is motoric-ecstatic and dancelike. The motifs of the main subject are taken from the Promenade theme, but the rising fifths of the main motif (e.g., mm. 29–30, 33–34) refer to the secondary theme of "Bydlo" in that they manifest the seme of heaviness and clumsiness. Similarly, the rising syncopated fourths of the beginning (mm. 17–24) derive from the opening of the Promenade theme (second interval), but they have already been used as upbeats in "The Old Castle" and "Bydlo." The chords with appoggiaturas that descend on an augmented scale (e.g., mm. 21–26) allude to the "Chickens," the octave leaps in the left hand to "Catacombs." On the other hand "Baba Yaga" is also related to "The Gnome" in the inverted sense that the unfinished, interrupted, and imperfect movement of the former is now realized in the latter with a rude power that combines 'will' and 'can'.

The normative modality of 'must' and the innovative attitude of 'knowing' step aside. If the subject of the previous movements has represented either an unsuccessful or clumsy 'doing' (or, rather, 'not-doing')—an agent without power or 'can' ("The Gnome," "Bydlo," "The Marketplace at Limoges")—or with an actoriality that has sunk into a pathemic 'being' ("The Old Castle," "Catacombae")—then we are faced with a subject that borrows all its cognitive content from other subjects. This borrowing of 'knowing' represents the epistemic figure of a 'fraud' (to make something appear what it is not), which, however, leads directly to the uncovering of the truth of the next movement ('to make appear-to be').

The temporal dimension is foregrounded with an indexical rush forward. The inner time structure of the movement represents an ABA form, in which the B section (mm. 91–121) controls the indexicality. It also contains internal iconic references to the angular tritone motifs of "The Gnome" (with intervals inverted) and to the descending chromaticism of "Con mortuis." Likewise, the rising octave-fifth motifs of mm. 100–102 in the B section recall the subordinate section of "Bydlo." Altogether we have a look backwards, an obstruction of motion by inner iconicity.

In the spatial respect, sections A and B are contrary. In the outer tonal space the actors of the A section move in all registers centrifugally, whereas the B section represents an engagement by its return to the middle register. In the sense of inner spatiality, the A section is mostly in C minor/major, while the tonal space of the B section is articulated chromatically, not functionally, projecting the whole-tone scale in the left hand. The indexical *martellato* motif, which closes the movement and builds a bridge to "The Great Gate of Kiev," has already occurred in the *attacca* transition between "The Marketplace at Limoges" and "Catacombae." There it signified a descent to the dysphoric principles of death and nature; here it portrays an ascent to the apotheosis of culture.

"The Great Gate of Kiev"

When comparing Hartmann's paintings and Musorgsky's *Pictures*, one is greatly surprised by the visual modesty of *The Great Gate of Kiev* in relation to its musical brilliance. Naturally one may see externally iconic semes in the movement: heavy, full triads, broad sonority, clocklike effects, and impressionistic blending of the chords, which would all refer to the church bells, as does the chorale hymn of the second theme. Actually, what we have is the exaltation of the musical subject, an exaltation further emphasized by the fact that actorially the main theme is obviously a condensation of the Promenade actor, its kernel purified into essentials.

Since the movement mostly consists of a euphoric E♭ major, how does the composer-subject bring shadows to this light in order to prevent the listener from getting bored with this celebratory procession? The disengagements take place in many ways and in many dimensions. In the sense of inner spatiality there are deviations to the minor-mode subdominant (G♯ minor) in the section that imitates church song and refers to the Coronation Scene in *Boris Godunov*. In the sense of outer spatiality, different registers fuse, with pedal points in common. The pianistic modality of 'can', which is central to the whole movement, operates through different means of filling the outer spatiality: by octave passages (in the third section, starting at m. 47), sometimes by broken chords shared by the two hands (the fifth section, m. 81, and elsewhere). In the temporal respect, the sixth section (mm. 114–38) is the most inventive, with its different uses of hemiola. The half-note triplets are first divided irregularly over strong and weak beats, and in the same manner the triple meter is transformed into binary by the end of the section. The seventh and last section (mm. 139 to end), with its *fermate* whole notes, steps entirely outside the temporality.

In this movement, the epistemic category of 'making something appear what it is', or revelation of the 'truth', may always be somewhat boring musically, precisely because the modality of 'knowing' does not flourish. The substance of the whole movement is based on the recurrence of similar material, but the modalities of 'will' and 'can' reach their peak. All this of course represents the conjunction of subject and object. Yet what may be even more essential is that the aforementioned *différence* between the subjects of narration and narratee, enunciation and enunciatee, disappears. The level of Thirdness—intellectual reasoning and reflection—vanishes almost completely from the music, because on that level such ecstasy would certainly not even be possible.

IX

THE SEMIOTICS OF SYMPHONISM

A DECONSTRUCTION OF NATIONAL MEANINGS IN SIBELIUS'S FOURTH SYMPHONY

Remarks on the Choice of Method and Subject

This chapter presents a narrative analysis of Sibelius's Fourth Symphony. To take a semiotical-narrative approach to a work representing "absolute" music is certainly exceptional, for we are used to relating narrativity with program music, which conveys a poetical idea or a visual image; in Sibelius's case, perhaps with works such as *The Swan of Tuonela, Kyllikki,* and *Historical Suite*. Yet in what follows I shall apply my theory to the analysis of an abstract piece. For semiotics to answer the challenges of music analysis, it must be able to deal with "absolute" music.

In such a task I find particularly pertinent Busoni's remarks in *Entwurf* about this kind of music, namely, his statement about Beethoven in the *Hammerklavier* and Schumann (see Chap. 1.3), who at their best moments anticipated an absolute music freed from normal dominant-tonic resolutions. Busoni's comment may also hold true for Sibelius's Fourth Symphony, which does not easily reduce to ordinary formal principles. In semiotic terms, the structures of *signification*, representing a composer's original, individual ideas and thoughts, break the chains formed by structures of *communication*, which are necessary to transmit these ideas to the audience.

There are other, purely musical codes that to my mind unite the Fourth Symphony with some central musical trends of the nineteenth century. Following the composer's own views, the Finnish tradition of Sibelius research has tried to minimize the influence of Wagner and emphasize the originality of the Sibelius. Yet to speak about the Fourth Symphony without mentioning *Parsifal* would be misleading. By this I mean not only direct allusions to the *Parsifal leitmotifs* (Ex. 9.1) but also certain harmonic procedures, the general spiritual atmosphere, the "semantic gesture" of the symphony, the impressions of a wide musical space, and then a negation of time—the anti-indexical nature of the symphony's temporal processes, which is manifested in the extreme slowness of all the events.[1]

Example 9.1. Sibelius, Symphony No. 4 in A minor, mvt. I, 2/5.

A principal objective of the present semiotic analysis is to join Sibelius and his Fourth Symphony to the general intellectual, philosophic, and aesthetic categories of European culture, and to show that his music has a particular message within and beyond the limits of European rationality. Semiotics is not understood here in the sense of the paradigmatic method; I am more interested in musical form as a kinetic process. As Pierre Boulez remarked, the essential point of analysis is not the mere existence of a twelve-tone matrix (paradigmatic chart) but rather how a composer uses it, that is, how he combines units and in this way effects transformations and changes in his work.

Nor do I feel that semiotic analysis is merely collecting and comparing what other scholars have said about the piece, although a semiotic analysis of a piece like Sibelius's Fourth has to take into account the tradition of analysis regarding the work. In this case semiotics can be used as a transmethod by which to reorganize previous knowledge. For example, a motivic analysis, such as that made by the Finnish composer Kari Rydman (1963), can be "semiotized" by using the Peircean notions of legisign/sinsign/qualisign and icon/index/symbol. In the Sibelian discourse certain motifs often become signs of other motifs within the same piece. This so-called domino-technique—a musical variant of Wittgenstein's *Familienähnlichkeit* principle—is also to be seen as a combination of indexicality and de-iconicity: it is a method for creating continuity (indexicality) and at the same time destroying similarity (iconicity).

The reader may now ask, Can a semiotic analysis obtain anything new regarding Sibelius? The main weakness of previous analyses relates to the unity-in-diversity of this piece, and in connection with this problem, to the way this music makes sense. The answer to these questions has been sought in three directions, which we can frame in terms of our own semiotic reading: 1. the temporal dimension, in the sense of a rhythmic-metric analysis; [2] 2. in the spatial or harmonic dimension by utilizing a Schenker-based method, which, however, at the same time tends to neglect other musical dimensions (Howell 1985, Murtomäki 1990); 3. in the actorial dimension, as motivic analysis, where the unity of the piece has been seen in the coherence of its motifs. We must pay attention to all these dimensions simultaneously; more particularly, how together, in the course of the piece, they constitute *narrative* structures. By narrative structures in music I mean those that function on the basis of spatial, temporal, and actorial categories and that through their collaboration continuously generate signification in the process of a musical piece.

If there are any narrative structures in Sibelius's Fourth Symphony, they obviously differ sharply from that era's conventional types of narratives and store of intonations. My hypothesis is that the Fourth Symphony possesses a narrative code that can be revealed by semiotic analysis, and that it so transformed commonly accepted narrative codes that it was felt as an almost anti-narrative musical event. For evidence, one need only look at documents describing contemporary reception of the piece.

Another, immediately striking feature of this symphony is that there are several narrative programs, moving in parallel, and realized phase by phase throughout the four movements of the symphony. A program might remain unfinished, to be completed only in a subsequent movement, as occurs in modern fiction. For example, in the novels of Marcel Proust, some personage may be introduced in the first volume and not return until the last, revealing there his true character after aging twenty years. Similarly, in this symphony there are several plot threads, which, while subordinated to the general flow of events, also live their own musical lives. We can distinguish two parallel narrative processes in the Fourth Symphony: The first should be called From Order to Chaos, which program is realized three times, each time with more cogency; namely, in the development of the first movement, in the counterstatement (Howell 1985) of the second movement, and in the latter half of the fourth movement. With each occurrence the degree of chaos becomes greater.

The second program—From Chaos to Order—runs conversely to the first, and is realized only twice: in the counterstatement, or recapitulation, of the first movement and in the third movement, where it forms the main idea. In addition, this latter program occurs in less extensive segments in the microcosm of the whole third movement's actorial and inner spatial levels (in the latter, affirmation of C♯ minor). In modal terms, this means that the program From Order to Chaos proceeds from the category of 'affirmation' to that of 'denial', after growing degrees of 'doubt'. From Chaos to Order reflects movement from 'denial' and 'doubt' to 'admittance' and ultimately to 'affirmation', that is, to the epistemic state of 'truth'. Thus the whole symphony can be seen as a fight between the categories of truth and untruth, lie and secret, in veridictory terms.

The Analysis

The first phase of a semiotic analysis of any piece is to find the fundamental isotopies and describe them. In Sibelius's Fourth they have been made clear by immanent, poietic studies, genre analysis, and historical-stylistic studies of the piece. The four movements of this symphony can be only partially reduced to the conventional formal schemes that we call structures of communication: Movement I (*Tempo molto moderato, quasi adagio*), Movement II (*Allegro molto vivace*), Movement III (*Il tempo largo*), Movement IV (*Allegro*). The tempo indications provide an idea of the basic character of each movement as regards the fundamental modalities of 'being' (*être*) and 'doing' (*faire*). Movements I and III represent slow tempos and accordingly stress 'being'. Movements II and IV are faster, with more action, thus constituting the principle of 'doing' (*faire*). This distinction is quite rough, since the static quality of the 'being' of the slow movements is very apparent, and they too contain great tension. The first movement contains abundant, tension-creating (especially spatial) disengagements that waver between 'being' and 'not-being'; and the *Il tempo largo* movement displays a clear shift from an unstable 'not-being' toward 'being' in the proper sense. On the other hand, the "active" Scherzo and Finale contain, through culmination of the action, a movement toward the principle of 'not-doing'. Movement II acts to "parody" a scherzo, as an interrupted process, or *inachèvement*; Movement IV projects a resignation that leads similarly to a state of unfulfillment.

In addition, as basic emotional distinctions we introduce the following rough articulations between the euphoric and the dysphoric: I: dysphoric 'not-being'; II: from a euphoric 'doing' to a dysphoric 'not-doing'; III: from a dysphoric 'not-being' to a dysphoric 'being'; IV: from a euphoric 'doing' to a dysphoric 'doing' and to a dysphoric 'being'. It is important to establish these isotopies, since they also determine the starting points for temporal, spatial, and actorial categories of the next level of generation. These categories enable us to determine what in each movement constitutes disengagement and engagement. (These determinations are thus completely relative and have to be made separately for each style, composition, and movement.)

In the temporal sense, and in spite of some highly energetic and mobile sections, the dominant feature of the entire piece is a *Parsifal*-like slowness of the musical process, a temporal looseness and ambiguity. The outer temporality (metrics) encompasses much syncopation and rhythmically ambiguous figurations. This rhythmic "dissonance" (Pike 1978) correlates with equivalent spatial inarticulation and the overall chaotic nature of the music. As regards the inner temporality, the philosophy of time in this work differs completely from that in Sibelius's three earlier symphonies; because of its particular treatment of time, it belongs to modernism in music and art in general. If a traditional symphony based on tonality relies on the intentional, or "protentional," conception of time, where time is constantly directed forward and where an indexical continuity prevails among all the musical events, then the basic temporal isotopy in Sibelius's Fourth Symphony represents a "detentional" conception of time. This means that its temporality functions in a way similar to the *mémoire involontaire* of Bergson or Proust, that is, not metonymically (contiguously) but metaphorically (associatively). This associative functioning allows one, within this time, to move from one event to another in the most unexpected and seemingly illogical ways. When the fundamental temporal isotopy functions in such a manner, then it follows necessarily that conventional temporal schemes are broken and a new vision of time emerges.

The basic distinction of inner musical space is the tritone, the tension between the diminished and the pure fifth. Even the tonal key relations between various movements of the symphony are largely determined by this primal intonation, its inherent tensions, or tensions related to it.[1] Furthermore, the outer spatiality unites with the inner in such a way that certain registers become "marked," and with their markedness produce coherence that spans the whole symphony. For example, the large intervallic leap in the modulation to F♯ major in the first movement furnishes the upper register of the violins with a markedness related to the temporary euphoric quality (in the context of A minor, the stabilization of F♯ major represents only a transient euphoria). This euphoria is fully realized only in the descending curve of the great theme of the third movement.[4] On the other hand, the outer space of the music has a characteristic linearity, in which different parts move without harmonic support.

There remain the fundamental actorial isotopies, which include the problem of the subject of musical enunciate and enunciation (utterance and act of uttering). The issue of the presence of the composer-subject in his discourse becomes particularly acute in connection with the Fourth Symphony. The subject of the musical enunciation, in this case the composer himself, can disengage from his discourse, disguise his presence, or render himself absent. Such actorial disengagement—withdrawal of the subject—is typical of this symphony and of other works by Sibelius that conjure up the image of a bleak "landscape devoid of actors" (as Raymond Monelle has commented).

Sibelius himself admitted that his Fourth Symphony portrays certain states of mind, thus affirming the psychological nature of the work. Do the "themes" then also represent the subject of enunciation in this discourse? Of course, not all proto-actorial intoning (motivics and thematics) reaches the level of musical actors in a proper sense. Still, in his diaries Sibelius often emphasized the importance of his themes, so that this isotopy should in no case be excluded. One trait of modernity in this symphony is that, for the most part, it contains no clearly distinguishable actors that carry the plot, as in his symphonic poems, the finales of his Second and Fifth symphonies, or in the way of the well-known trombone theme of his Seventh Symphony. The subject of the Fourth Symphony is *ex-centré*, driven from the center of his being, a modern alienated subject whose mere 'being' has a dysphoric character, as the outburst of the theme-actor of the *Il tempo largo* declares.

According to Tawaststjerna (1972: 251), the composer himself is speaking through the structures of this work: "In the tensions between the tritone motifs and major formations he gives us the key to the contradictions of his own ego, which is also the basic contrast of the symbolism: the conflict between the subconscious and the conscious." Sometimes Tawaststjerna even distinguishes between two subjects: the conscious subject, whom we might say prevails in the structures of communication during the first half of the second movement; and the subconscious subject, who speaks in the latter half of the same movement: "If the Scherzo in the proper sense represents the world of consciousness, then the *Doppio più lento* section seems to reflect the subconscious" (ibid.). Tawaststjerna thinks that these distinctions also have consequences for techniques of analysis: "It is precisely this psychoanalytical-musical viewpoint which makes it difficult to analyze the second movement with conventional concepts." It is therefore essential also to take into account the actorial isotopies, even in the sense of forming a typology of "subjects" who express themselves in the music.[5]

As important as the kinetic and continuous nature of music is, for practical reasons we must segment the piece. But it is difficult to segment it, because there already exist several competing formal-analytical segmentations of the work, and because the principles of segmentation may vary when one shifts from the spatial category to the temporal and then to the actorial. The segmentation should also anticipate, especially for this piece, the next phase of generation, that of a modal grammar. It would be reasonable, for merely technical reasons, to derive a segmentation that can be realized similarly on all these levels. Indeed, in the following I shall try to scrutinize spatial, temporal, and actorial articulations side by side. Each section is called a "narrative program" or PN (*programme narratif*); each is numbered, and together they form the whole narration of the piece.

FIRST MOVEMENT

PN 1: p. 1, mm. 1-6*

The inner spatiality involves ambiguous tritone motion which is open to many directions and to various tonal interpretations. Tawaststjerna speaks of "a space without gravitation," an apt description since at this point we do not yet have a tonal fulcrum for spatial engagement/disengagement, i.e., a center for the inner spatiality. As to the outer spatiality, note the low register and instruments of the orchestra: bassoon, cellos, and double basses. Since this is the opening of the piece, the place where its "code" is introduced to the listener, it is remarkable that in this outer sense the center of space is mostly situated in the octave C3–C4.

In the temporal respect, the musical material is syncopated, obscuring a sense of regular metrical pulse, save for the slow, mostly quarter-note motion. As Ex. 9.2 shows, the indefinite character of temporality correlates with indefiniteness in the inner spatiality.

The opening of the symphony offers a proto-actorial unit, a "nuclear motif" or "nuclear pheme," corresponding to the ambiguity of the tritone on the content level (the nuclear seme of Suffering), but not yet an entity rising to the level of a theme-actor properly speaking. Therefore, the beginning of the symphony is also disengaged actorially. We do not recognize here any personage on the musical stage or voice of the composer as narrator—yet.

* Page numbers refer to the Breitkopf & Hartel edition of Sibelius's Fourth Symphony.

Example 9.2. Sibelius, Symphony No. 4, mvt. I, 1/1–6.

PN 2: p.2, m. 1–p. 3, m.10

In the dimension of inner spatiality this section establishes A minor with modal features. According to Howell (1985), the A minor tonic in this movement is not established unequivocally by cadential motion here or elsewhere; rather, it is *implied*. Thus the movement has no inner-spatial fulcrum from which to compute the degree of disengagement. This PN represents an inner-spatial or tonal disengagement in depth. In this narrative program there is a shift from the implied A minor to C-Lydian and through it toward F♯ major. At the end of the section there occurs a struggle between C major and F♯(G♭) major. The thirds in the cellos, in G♭, suggest this possible interpretation of the tritone, creating a passing impression of bitonality. There is a complex isotopy of two superimposed keys, for example, p. 3, m. 6, where the drastic C# in bassoon, clarinet, and violas emphasizes the friction between these two keys. At the end of the section the harmonic rhythm accelerates, leading to a general effect of action.

The outer spatiality exhibits a stepwise shift from the low to the highest register, at first realized smoothly (p. 2, mm. 1–9), and finally by an abrupt leap at p. 3, m. 10 (see Ex. 9.3). In this way a great gap arises in the outer tonal space, which, according to the principle of "gap-fill" (Meyer 1973), forms an important implication as to the continuation of the piece. The listener expects this gap to be filled at some point.

Example 9.3. Sibelius, Symphony No. 4, mvt. I, 3/8–13.

In the temporal respect, the basic rhythmic unit (pulse) is the eighth note; however, this pulse is freely undulating, "organic," gradually unfolding. The inner temporality here involves an indexicalization of musical process: after an indefinite, errant, and disengaged beginning, the process takes a clear direction and goal, accompanied by a dynamic increase from *pianissimo* to *fortissimo*.

A theme-actor is introduced as one of the main motifs of the movement and the whole symphony (Ex. 9.4). Its actorial character is further emphasized by its placement in the solo cello. In all its monotony and modality, this actor functions as an epic, narrative voice. This narrator-actor soon disappears, however, so that the strings can "grasp" the rising-thirds motifs and let the actor fuse with the musical motion. The atmosphere changes from the primeval "sleep" of the beginning to a brooding, gloomy ambience, when we shift to the field of the struggling tonalities. The dissonant C# in the bassoon serves as an index sign of the impending brass fanfare. The brass symbolize on an actorial level some Finnish Hagen in this Fennougric *Götterdämmerung* and produce a certain actorialization in the universe of this symphony.

Example 9.4. Sibelius, Symphony No. 4, mvt. I, 2/1–5.

PN 3: p. 3, m. 11–p.4, m. 6

The inner spatial content of this section is a temporary affirmation of B major by its dominant, F♯. In the outer sense, the section starts with a great leap, as noted above, but there occurs another, even bigger leap to the upper register of the strings, followed by a stepwise downward sinking. The section also contains an expansion, an in-depth disengagement created by a horn signal, which is heard somewhat removed from the following brass motif. This motif returns the listener to the middle register and then to the dreary sonority of the foreground. Therefore the section is, in both inner and outer senses, very centrifugal.

Temporally, only individual motifs have clear metric articulation, but even they seem to float in a temporal "liquid," detached and seemingly without interrelationships. The temporal indexicality is therefore fairly small. On the other hand, actorial events are plentiful in this section: it contains an inverted, major-mode transformation of the epic narrating actor (p. 3, m. 11), a reference to the "Hagen" actor (p. 3, mm. 12–14), and an entirely new, euphoric descending-scale passage from the "heaven" of the strings. Thereafter, actoriality is conspicuous in the horn calls at p. 4, mm. 3–4 (which do not reach the status of an independent actor) and finally in the brasses' motif at p. 4, m. 5, which is reminiscent of the recurrent descending-fifth Wound motif in *Parsifal*. These actors are only introduced and do not (yet) interact, and are fairly contrasting in their mutual relations.

PN 4: p. 5, m. 1–p. 6, m. 4

This section, which in terms of sonata form presents a "development," can be interpreted on the whole as a movement from minor V of A minor to tonic in the parallel mode (A major). Howell (1985) has made a highly complex harmonic, inner spatial analysis of this section. Yet the section might prove even more interesting outer spatially, since it starts with an illustration of Sibelian "paralinear counterpoint" (Kurth 1922). The strings, without harmonic support, seem to draw lines in space; thereafter, in the tremolando section (p. 7 onward), they surround the woodwind signals. At first, this surrounded/surrounding constellation remains stable; then it starts to rise toward a resolution to A major in the upper register. The tonal space is at first filled by scale passages, as a contrast to the more open, arpeggiated chords of the preceding section.

In the temporal respect, this section as a whole contrasts with all the previous, fragmentary events. It is based on continuous lines and, toward the end of the development, on a still more clearly indexicalized, forward-rushing texture, as shown in Ex. 9.5. This activity is antagonistic to the detentional, errant time of the beginning. One notices here a clearly teleological process, a +disengagement, because the tempo gradually becomes more and more agitated, as the musical process assumes an obvious direction.

Whereas the Classical development section generally aims at destroying the iconicity of the exposition, here the degree of iconicity is very high, since all the musical substance originates from either the tritone motto or the fifth motif,

Example 9.5. Sibelius, Symphony No. 4, mvt. I, 6/1–2.

the proto-intonation already heard in connection with the main actor. Nevertheless, in the actorial sense this represents a -disengagement: actors are not foregrounded too strikingly, but instead disappear into the background as iconic material, or else return to the proto-actorial level of the opening tritone motif. PN 5: p. 6, m. 5–p. 10, m. 4

The apparent paradox of this section lies in its dwelling for a long time in a euphoricized F♯ major, which nevertheless 'appears' different from what it 'is'. In other words, this section misleads the listener, since the F♯ harmonies are in a tritone relationship of tension and dissonance to the C♮ of the beginning, and quite distant from the A tonic of the whole movement. In the sense of outer spatiality, this constitutes a stable 'being', a calm section that offsets the abrupt disengagements of the previous PN. The contrast between the brass ensemble of the preceding section and the triads of the strings in this one furnishes more proof for the *Parsifal* associations of this symphony.

In the temporal sense this forms a rhythmically-metrically clearly articulated section without any disengagement in either direction, neither positive (agitation) nor negative (retardation), but an engagement to the eighth-note figures of the beginning of the movement. The temporal interlacement of the woodwind motifs is also a softening element that lessens the dissonance.

As to actoriality, this is an innerly iconic section, which as a rule leads to stability and relaxation. Consequently, this section functions as an anti-indexical force by increasing the impression of 'being'. (Iconicity in general is a sign category related with the modality of 'being', while indexicality naturally evokes 'doing'.) There are two euphoricized motifs in the section, the narrator motif and the tritone motif, the latter now contracted to a perfect fourth. Here, at last, the tritone motif, transformed through new modalization into a figure representing 'not-willing', seems to have achieved the status of a true actor. Only at the very end of the section is the 'will'-principle of the tritone recalled, at the same time as we return to the register of low strings.

PN 6: p. 11, m. 1–p. 13, m. 6

In sonata form, the recapitulation serves, in semiotic terms, as the culmination of the principle of stabilizing iconicity, on the supposition that the development has been dramatically de-iconic and indexical. Many scholars have wondered why the recapitulation of Sibelius's Fourth Symphony is incomplete and does not include the main motif of the exposition or material related with that narrator-actor. But since in PN 5 (the development) the subject of the elaboration was the substance given at the beginning of the exposition (now omitted), even though in an iconically invariant form, one does not miss its repetition here. This explanation is also offered, in slightly different terms, by Gerald Abraham: "One feels that the development, being in the same grey, brooding mood, has taken the place of a reprise of the first subject" (1975: 25). Instead, what is crucial here is the strikingly dramatic transition to the recapitulation, that is, the border line between PN 5 and PN 6.[6] Whereas earlier the threatening brass harmonies were prepared by a spatial context that was very contradictory and dissonant, one now feels the outburst of these chords as a surprise, especially since the tonic of A major has been gained as a result of the preceding development. We must leave to the modal analysis the question of whether this moment belongs to the paradigm of Frustration in the Fourth Symphony, as evidence that there are no definitive achievements in this psychological "story."

On the other hand, the return of the brass ensemble can be seen only as a faded sign of inner iconicity, as a postmodalization of the threatening situation of its first occurrence, since in the continuation A major becomes convincingly established for the whole recapitulation. Even in a temporal sense, this recapitulation engages the music to 'being', now because of its temporal category. This is a return of organization, after the disorganization brought on by spatial-actorial-temporal dissonances. Also the recurrence of some actors strengthens their profile in the context of this movement and of the entire symphony.

PN 7: p. 13, mm. 7–11

A very brief coda alludes to the introduction, which is however not fully re-peated iconically. The tritone gesture is interrupted when it starts to rise from C. And it is shifted a third higher, to premodalize the following movement in the sense of both inner (F major) and outer (A tone) spatiality.

SECOND MOVEMENT

PN 1: pp. 14–15

Inner spatially, the movement begins in F major and should as a whole be in-terpreted in that key. Its most pertinent level is not inner spatiality, however. Rather, the action centers on temporal and actorial elements. In the sense of outer spatiality the movement is based mainly on a line descending from the upper to the middle register, where the string tremolando often serves as a ful-crum, or where these lines are left without reference to a spatial center, which accords with the overall "indeterminacy" of this symphony.

The temporal level involves a clearly articulated triple meter, whose basic pulse is determined by the eighth-note figuration. The texture is transparent and thin, far removed from the heavy brass sounds of the previous movement. Neither does it form a contrast, as does the episode of the flower girls (*Blumen-mädchen*) in *Parsifal*, to the sacral contemplation of the beginning. Actorially, the main motif contains the Sibelian elements of a long-held beginning tone and a triplet figure at the end, so that it represents a typical intertext in the work of the composer. The dancelike character and key (an inner-spatial relationship) refer also to another, more extensive musical text, namely, the second movement of *Kullervo*. As one of its phemes and intonations, the actor also contains allu-sions to the tritone. The two ascending fourths (violins, p. 15, mm. 2–5) have the exclusively temporal task of increasing the speed, but at the same time they serve as an anticipatory index to the main theme of the following *Il tempo largo*, with its two superimposed fifths separated by a major second.

PN 2: p. 16–p. 18, m. 34

According to some interpretations, this section constitutes the trio of a scherzo. Its most interesting moment is the sudden temporal disengagement from binary to ternary meter. Ballantine, in his study on the renovation of sym-phonic form in twentieth-century music (1983), lists cases in which the conventional three-part rhythm in a scherzo is replaced by a two-part rhythm (as in Shostakovitch's Seventh Symphony and Martinů's Fourth). Here it pro-duces an effect of true surprise, an apparently illogical and antidiscursive device.[7] The unchanging dactyl figure emphasizes a wavelike melodic contour (down–up and up–down), when suddenly, at p. 17, m. 7, a temporal engage-ment to the three-part basic pulse takes place. This engagement does not last, because the long notes of the brass ensemble again destroy the basic pulsation. The basic pulse is reestablished only tentatively, toward the end of the section, when the basic mode of the scherzo is gradually engaged.

Regarding the actoriality, note that the dactyl motifs are iconic transformations of the first movement's motif of a fifth filled by a triad (p. 16, mm. 5–6) and then of the main motif of the scherzo (p. 16, mm. 15–22). Also the use of the brass as a threatening gesture (p. 17, mm. 11–16, 21–28) is an iconic reference to the corresponding actors of the previous movement, namely, to those which represented its somber dysphoria. At the same time, the brass function as premodalizations of the unexpected ending of this movement. That ending consists of tritone intonations emerging from a fairly redundant field, intonations that, because of their recurrence, lose their tension and serve merely as a bridge in the shift in outer spatiality, from a low register to that of the main motif of the scherzo.

PN 3: p. 19–p. 22, m. 27

After an excursion into the flatted tonal field (D♭ major: ♭VI of F), this section constitutes the repetition of the scherzo, in which the F is reestablished as the tonic. A new actorial element occurs: a descending passage borrowed from the previous trio section has been transformed into an almost unrecognizable motif, but it still (at least subconsciously) preserves the iconic connection to its origin (p. 16) when it appears with graceful parallel-thirds passages (p. 19, mm. 14–19, p. 20, mm. 4–9). This new actorial element is not mere decoration; it has the narrative function of contrast and implication with other actors elaborated from the same material. By coincidence, there are precisely four actors in this movement, which tempts one to form a semiotic square consisting of actant, anti-actant, negactant, and neganti-actant (see Fig. 9.1). The

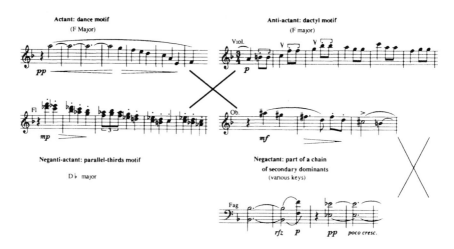

Figure 9.1. Sibelius, Symphony No. 4 in A minor, actors in PN 3 projected onto a semiotic square.

chain of actants can continue from any corner of the square, which allows formation of ever-new "squares." In other words, in the course of their development, musical actors get ever-new anti- and negactants. In fact, this is a typical *Durchführung* on the actorial level. Though some consider it strange, only in this coda (or counterstatement) of the scherzo has Sibelius provided the traditional actorial development which the first movement lacked. It is one of his techniques of iconic transformation of actors (the so-called domino technique) that produces actorial squares in which the last corner of the square is no longer in direct contact with the actor that was the starting point.

PN 4: p. 22, m. 28–p.28

This somewhat enigmatic section was anticipated. It is based on a Sibelian figure of narration in which tension increases through rising tremolando strings. Against this figure sound dramatic, "expressionistic" wind motifs. The actors formed in this way are surrounded by a gradually intensifying indexical texture which gives the impression that they are moving toward a definite goal—chaos or order, euphoria or dysphoria. In a sense, in this music one is seeking the object whose absence always forms the initial situation of narration. Naturally this represents a tensional phenomenon on the surface level, which we could easily reduce on the inner spatial level to contrapuntal and pitch structures that are strong as iron; overall, this PN has a compelling tonal progression. Nevertheless, such a figure is in this case experienced as stepwise, unfolding chaos, as fulfillment of those threatening tendencies already evoked by the previous musical signs (tritones, brass signals).

In the inner-spatial sense, we move through secondary dominants toward the F tonic. In the outer sense, the texture becomes denser, producing a *tutti* effect through the simultaneous use of different registers. In the actorial regard, the tritone is now used expressly as a gesture, whereas earlier it was utilized to create inner tension; now it appears dramatically as a theatrical and impressive gesture at the end of each actor. The main actor of the section (the negactant in the actorial square shown in Fig. 9.1) and its inversion are repeated ten times. These repetitions, plus the recurrence of phemes not related to this actor, act as confirming indexes.

The closure of the section and the whole movement is also surprising, since the tonic F major returns only at the very end, so unnoticed that the impression is one of inachievement—an interruption that seems to halt the action before its time. This interruption recalls the gesture at the end of the first movement, where the tritone motif started from C. But this is a more fatal interruption regarding the inner spatial structure of the symphony, in the sense that it serves as an obvious narrative device: the creation of a lack. The object (stable tonic) remains unattained, and the listener wonders in which phase the true achievement, *perfectivité*, and the completion of the narration will appear; to use literary analogies: the finding of the lost ring, the revelation of a murderer. The answer is provided by the third movement of the symphony.

THIRD MOVEMENT

This movement has been generally regarded in the Sibelius literature as rhapsodic, loosely organized (Abraham 1975), or improvisatory (Tawaststjerna 1972).[8] Perhaps the movement has been considered an improvisation because

of the difficulty of finding in it any structure of communication, that is, a previously coded principle of form to which the movement could be reduced and
against which its formal solution could be matched. As to finding structures of
signification, perhaps those scholars who have paid attention to the inner spatiality have been most successful (Jordan 1984, Murtomaki 1990, Howell 1985).
But even they speak about the enigmatic character of the movement.

In Abraham's view, there are two actorial elements, motif A (opening wind
lines) and motif B (rising fifths culminating in C♯ minor), and their alternation
is the core of the movement (see Ex. 9.6). Lionel Pike (1978) accounts for
both the spatial and the temporal dimensions when he states that the movement "works in the opposite direction . . . from atonality and unequal rhythm
towards tonality and regular rhythm"; in semiotic terms, from spatial-temporal
disengagement toward spatial-temporal engagement. Also, the Estonian
scholar Leo Normet (1970) emphasizes actoriality as he stresses the growth of
the C♯ minor theme and mentions as its particular property the modality of
'will' (*vouloir*), whose counterforce, an anti-actorial element, appears in the
tritonality and whole-tone scales. Robert Layton (1978) likewise focuses on
what we might call the modal signification of the piece, when he states that it
is "One of Sibelius' most deeply felt utterances . . . the emotional peak of the
work." The movement can easily be divided into narrative programs, mostly on
the actorial basis of motifs A and B. We shall see that these motifs sustain two
superimposed narrative programs that interact throughout the movement.

Example 9.6. Sibelius, Symphony No. 4, mvt. III: a. 29/1–3, motif A;
b. 30/1–5, motif B.

PN A: p. 29–p. 30, m. 2

This section starts rather far from the C♯ minor tonic, with arpeggiations of
the A minor, G♯ minor, and C minor triads, in the form of a dialogue between

two flutes. In the continuation the clarinet joins in. In fact, as early as these three "statements," divided between three instruments, one finds the code of the whole movement, just as the tritone intonation formed the code for the first movement.

The arpeggiated triads of the first flute represent minor harmonies, "hidden tritonality," and chromaticism, while the "answer" by the second flute contains a strong reference to whole-tone scales. Thus the diatony/chromaticism versus whole-tone pitch material forms one important opposition in the inner spatiality. It is symptomatic that since the beginning these opposing harmonic elements have been divided into two different levels, as a dialogue between two instruments, since the whole movement can be seen (Abraham 1960) as a simultaneous process of two opposed materials.

The musical narration involves two narrative programs that proceed in tandem. Since they occur in the same temporal syntagm, they doubtless interact with each other. What is the nature of this interaction or communication? And does that communication explain the structure of this music and its most important event (as some have argued), namely, the gradual growth of the C♯ minor theme? The whole movement would thus be better depicted by two parallel narrative programs that intertwine in the following way:

$$A \quad A1 \quad A2 \quad A3 \quad A4 \quad A5 \quad A6$$
$$B \quad B1 \quad B2 \quad B3 \quad B4$$

In the inner spatial respect, we have already noted how this section disengages from the tonic of C♯ minor. In principle the section forms a symmetrical structure such that the beginning and the end are based on triadic harmony—on the motif of a fifth and its filling, which is central to the whole symphony. Interlaced are scale passages that contain tritones, filled by whole-tone or chromatic scales. The outer tonal space again involves the combination of a high and low register (flute/clarinet vs. cello/double bass) without any mediating levels, such that both lines have clear profiles in the external space. These profiles are also in inner dialogue with each other, as 29/5 shows. When one falls silent, the other enters. In the temporal sense, the basic time unit is the sixteenth note. The rhythmic pulse is never emphasized, but is syncopated and undulating.

The instrumentation is so important that the theme-actor and the instrument-actor coincide. The actorial character of the whole movement becomes clear as early as in the dialogic structure of this first narrative program, first between flutes and clarinet, then in the opposition of woodwinds and low strings. The whole PN can be characterized as a dialogue between two subjects of utterance, which materialize in the music as the figures of the tritone motif (A) and the fifth motif (B). Subject A represents a meditative, passive element. It is therefore not an active subject like the motoric, dancing subject of the previous movement, but, as a modal analysis would show, a subject of 'knowing' (*sujet selon savoir*). Instead, subject B proves to be the 'willing' subject (*sujet selon vouloir*).

PN B: p. 30, mm. 3–4

The first occurrence of this parallel narrative program is only two bars long and is based on A major harmony (VI of C♯ minor) in the horns. The outer spatiality thus differs greatly from the space occupied by PN A, which underlines the dissimilarity of these two elements. Even temporally this PN represents quite another universe, a more rigid metrical-rhythmic articulation, in which the motif starts immediately on a stressed part of the bar. The four-part harmony evokes choralelike associations and, together with the horn timbre, a German chorale (more Brucknerian than Wagnerian). This clear-cut theme-actor emerges with a totally different character from the unsure and somewhat ambiguous motifs of the A section. The certainty of this actor is strengthened by the aforementioned clarity of inner spatiality (A major).

PN A1: p. 30, m. 5–p. 31, m. 4

As a reply to the multipart texture of the previous B section, we now hear chromatic and syncopated elaborations of the A motif, imitated by the strings and twice repeating the chromaticism of the *Tristan* chord. As a contrast to section A, A1 uses the low register of the outer space, ending with arpeggiated triads of C♯ minor and F/E♯ minor in the bassoon and clarinet.

PN B1: p. 31, mm. 5–10

The fifth motif returns, temporally augmented from its first occurrence. As a consequence of the events of the preceding A section, this section also appears in the strings; and the rising fifths culminate in a scale passage that remains on an A (violas and cellos), which now interpreted as part of a D minor chord (p. 31, m. 10), thus adding a Phrygian quality to the C♯ minor. The harmonies C♯/D are "after-effects" of the A/G♯ harmony (likewise a half step from each other) that appeared at the beginning. The temporal articulation here is quite similar to the first occurrence (PN B); this dimension has not yet come under the influence of the narrative program of A. In the actorial regard, this theme-actor projects a higher degree of individuality, because it emerges in the unisons of one instrument (cello) against the choralelike polyphony of the previous section. This emergence of individuality can be read as a transformation of a collective actor ("we") into a singular actor ("I").

PN A2: p. 31, m. 11–p. 32, m.8

This section also starts with three arpeggiated-triad figures (D minor, F♯ minor, and A major) and continues as a rising scale passage; the instrumentation is also new: viola, flute, and clarinet. This constant change of instruments emphasizes the diffuse nature of actor A, or rather that group of actors whose members have not yet attained sufficient individuality. The dialogue between bassoon, clarinet, and flute leads to the same conclusion: all three fill the tritone with a whole-tone scale. The section does not end here, but when the flute switches to the oboe, the three instruments adopt as their material the passionate B actor, which perhaps threatens them. In any case, they at the same time try to negate actor B, by turning the fifth motifs of B around, and by furnishing them with dysphoric chromatic passages. This inverted form and the violin tremolandos, which at the same time unite the A program spatially to the same C♯ minor as the B section, allow actor B to penetrate the domain of actor A.

PN B2: p. 32, m. 9–p. 33, m. 7

The tremolando figure of the strings with the same material as the fifth motif rising from the cellos–a classic example of the way melody and accompaniment are derived from the same material–constitutes an indexical sign for the change to goal-directed temporality. It is a sign for the move from *temps d'espace* to *temps de durée*, from a detentional to a protentional time. The whole-tone quality and chromaticism, with the tritone as their common denominator, represent a detentional, associative time at its most typical, while the diatonicism and functional harmony, with their root relations by fifths, are manifestations of a protentional time *par excellence.*

The inner spatiality is now entirely in C♯ minor. In the outer tonal space, within a string orchestra, a high line and a low line rising from the bass are united. The ascent of the lower actorial melodic line is interrupted on the cellos' B with the unexpected fall of a major seventh (p. 33, mm. 3–4), reminiscent of the great dramatic leaps in the vocal writing of Richard Strauss or the mature Wagner. Such leaps are appropriate for this emotional-indexical section, in which the desire of the C♯ minor theme increases.

PN A3 and **PN B3**: p. 33, mm. 8–17

This is one of the few sections in which narrative programs A and B intermingle; therefore they should not be dealt with separately but together. The low register of the strings prevails, supported by brief comments from the clarinet and the oboe. Here we approach C♯ minor, while also in a dysphoric field of errant tonalities. The contours of the outer musical space move diagonally, in contrary motion; and narrative programs A and B are now set upon each other. In the actorial regard, the A program twice offers a negation of the C♯ minor theme or its inversion. In the low strings, the theme itself occurs in a somewhat transformed manner, then bursts out all the more complete, though without the passionate intervallic leap in the climax. It is provided with a prolongation of the A program, and it ends with Wagnerian harmonies (p. 33, m. 16). Even in other respects, the inversion of the C♯ minor theme changes into a *Parsifal*-like figure, with its sinking fifths (e.g., at p. 33, mm. 10–11).

PN A4: p. 33, m. 18–p. 34, m. 8

We again return to program A, in which the fifth motifs of three woodwinds are filled by C♯ minor scales with a Phrygian tinge. Together they form a collective actor similar to that of earlier instances of this program, but also as an allusion to the corresponding woodwind combinations that closed the first movement. As the background, we hear a pedal point on G♯, the dominant of C♯ minor. In the external temporal sense, the woodwind solos occur first in alternation, then superimposed, and finally as the background ostinato for the next B section. At this moment, the oboe ostinato starts to serve as a clear index sign for a transition to protentional, forward-directed time, a moment underlined by the sudden *crescendo* indication at the beginning of p. 34, m. 8.

PN B4: p. 34, m. 9–p. 35, m. 6

This section helps to bolster Howell's thesis (1985) that the basic character of the movement is "compression" or condensation. In the framework of C♯ minor, the outer tonal space is shaped again as diagonal motion. The tempo (pulse) accelerates from quarter notes to eighth notes in this indexical section. The ascending motion of the theme is interrupted by a leap of three octaves (p. 35, m. 5), which produces a striking gap in the outer tonal space. The gradually descending motion, implied by the ascent and the gap, remains so short that a listener cannot consider this (so far the most extensive) occurrence of the theme-actor as its definitive portrayal. The section is left unfinished, just like the whole preceding scherzo movement.

PN A5: p. 35, m. 7–p. 36, m.5

Whereas the B program develops into ever-growing and more extensive forms, the A program exhibits an entirely contrary development. As if always looking backward, it represents a return to the past by repeating the dialogue-like, arpeggiated, and unrelated triads of the beginning (G♯ minor and C minor in the clarinets, then D♯ major in the strings). Returning also are the whole-tone scales and the sign representing the C♯ minor theme, played twice by the cellos in the opening bars, and now heard as a distant reminiscence of that which the A program had already definitely given up. Hence the A program represents frustration, abandonment, disjunction from an object.

PN B5: p. 36, mm. 6–11

This section signifies the final achievement of the B program, in narratological terms: the functions of fulfillment and completion of the action, perfectivity, and terminativity. A functional cadence in C♯ minor, realized with full harmonies, makes the minor key sound euphoric as compared to the brasses' *fortissimo* dysphoric allusion to the symbol of the A program: the tritone and its expansion to a perfect fifth. This gesture is pathetic in Tchaikovsky fashion, perhaps an instrumental remembrance of the finale of the *Pathétique* Symphony. Accordingly, amid the unfolding of the B program one is reminded of the existence of the A program and its loss (see Ex. 9.7). In a temporal regard, this also constitutes an engagement to the basic tempo of the B program.

PN A6: p. 36, mm. 12–37

The movement closes with program A, with cadential triplet figures already encountered in PN A5. Its normal rhythmic-metric pulse continues, now slowed down. In the inner spatial sense, the motifs outline the Neapolitan chord of C♯ minor (see p. 37, m. 2). The outer tonal space sinks toward the low register of the strings and returns to the pitch of C♯. In the actorial sense, these triplet motifs appear as disengaged transformations of the figures of the A program, now somewhat vague and unprofiled, and are repeated in various instruments, as if seeking support from one another. As a premodalization, at the beginning of the section we hear a parallel-motion passage in the clarinets and bassoons, on C♯–E–A–C♯, the pitches that will open the next movement. Therefore this passage serves as an index sign for the continuity of the work.

Example 9.7. Sibelius, Symphony No. 4, mvt. III, 36/1–7.

FOURTH MOVEMENT

PN 1: p. 38, mm. 1–15

Inner spatially, this introductory section is postmodalized by the previous program in the sense that it wavers between A major (with Lydian D♯) and C♯ minor. In the outer space, all the material is presented by the strings, without harmonic support of the bass except in the crucial beginning and closing bars. This emphasizes the plasticity of the violin lines. In the actorial respect, this can be held as a complete theme, though it is not much used later on. One of the intonations of this theme-actor is used subsequently as important material: the *sforzato* ascending third in p. 38, m. 7.

PN 2: p. 38, m. 16–p. 47, m. 11

As regards inner spatiality, after the confirmation of A major, E♭ major enters, thus causing complex isotopies of bitonal passages (e.g., p. 42, mm. 18–20). This tritone relation creates tension in the tonal space, underlined by instrumental actoriality: the contrast between strings and woodwinds, as in the preceding movement. A striking feature is likewise formed by the redefinition of the actorial role of certain instruments in relation to their earlier roles. For example, the cello, which in the *Il tempo largo* movement appeared as a lyrical introducer of the great theme, now occurs with a capricious, cadencelike *affettuoso* (p. 40, mm. 1–5).

In the outer spatiality, this narrative program uses an alternation of orchestral *tutti* effects and strings, and very active shifts of register. One of the basic problems of the whole symphony is the filling of the tritone and the fifth, and here it is accomplished by torrents of scales that extend anywhere from a third to an octave in range. After the actors heard in the introduction and at the beginning of this section, there occur brief (indexical) signs that refer to these actors. Besides the proto-intonation of the tritone, we hear a new motif of an ascending second/descending fourth, which becomes a central actor in what follows (e.g., see basses, p. 40, mm. 4–5, 12–13).

As those in Sibelius's earlier symphonies, the present actorial elements have a characteristic tendency to rapid growth and expansion; for example, the cello obbligato (p. 40, mm. 1–5) turns into an agitated, forward-moving texture that soon engages all the strings. Certain instruments represent actorial values; for example, the four-note motif in A major, which is constantly repeated by the Glockenspiel. In the temporal sense, the speed continuously accelerates and thus represents a +disengagement.

PN 3: p. 47, m. 12–p. 50, m. 14

In this section the E♭/A tritone dissolves to G♯ minor via C minor. Accordingly, this constitutes an inner spatial engagement, or diminishment of tension. An abrupt change occurs in the outer space, from the dramatic registral shifts of the preceding program to complete stasis and stabilization. Also, in the temporal sense we do not get the "normal" pulse of the beginning, but a motion that is half as fast dominated by half notes. This combination of registral and temporal stasis represents a negative disengagement, which is further stressed by the events of p. 48, m. 19 onward. There the music is stuck on the strings' ostinato and the violins' descending syncopated chromatic line. At p. 48, mm. 8–16 the horns present a completely new actor, which is based on the aforementioned intonation of second/fourth. It is hard to determine the character of this actor, who is rather like a "guest" from beyond the isotopy of this work. PN 4: p. 50, m. 15–p. 56, m. 11

The inner spatiality of this section centers on the tonality of C, both major and minor. In the outer sense, the strings' ascending and descending scale passages fill the space of one and a half octaves, thus forming an iconical-indexical elaboration of the rising-triplet motif and its extensions, heard at the beginning of the movement. Other instruments hold a pedal point for the ascending-fifth motif played triple *forte* in the trumpet (p. 52, m. 4–p. 54, m. 2) and the delayed sign of the glockenspiel in the "correct" key (p. 53, m. 1–p. 54, m. 4). Spatially, this is a relatively static section, although this moment is called a development in many analyses.

In the temporal regard, the first half of the section (through p. 54, m. 3) is likewise outside the "normal" metric pulse of the movement. The glockenspiel motif and the trumpet signal are slower than normal and thus represent a negative disengagement, while the scales of the strings are so fast that they are heard not individually but as a cluster, evoking an extreme +disengagement. In the actorial sense, from this spatial-temporal field spring references (index signs) to actors that were earlier heard in complete form.

The latter half of this "development" starts unexpectedly (p. 54, m. 4), without preparation, and in all respects it forms a contrast to the beginning of this section. The inner spatiality is C minor; in the outer sense, it is based on a new, angular, arpeggiated-fifth motif, played pizzicato in the strings. This figure becomes the ostinato "bridge" that guarantees indexical continuity from this narrative program to the next. It also functions as a background for completely contrasting motifs, the faded "ghosts" of the true actors, which are now heard in the winds. (For example, the syncopated, chromatically descending half-note motif of the strings occurs in inversion.) In actorial terms, disengagement prevails. In the temporal sense this half of the section is rhythmically-metrically engaged to the same time values as at the beginning of the movement.

In the first movement of the symphony the sense of key was vague (the spatiality was indeterminate), and in this section and elsewhere in this movement, the spatiality is articulated distinctly. But now the actorial level is again indefinite, as contemporary critics have remarked: among others, Heikki Klemetti noted that, in the Fourth Symphony, "Strange, transparent beings are floating here and there, telling us something which we do not understand" (quoted from Tawaststjerna 1972: 230). To a contemporary listener, still living in the codes of the Romanticism, the actorial level was very important for the conceiving of music. Actoriality, then, should be understood in the broader sense of concerning the subject of the utterance, which is hard to establish. We do not know who or what kind of subject-actor is expressing himself here.

PN 5: p. 56, m. 12–p. 58, m. 13

The material of PN 3 returns, now transformed into a dialogue between woodwinds and violins. At the same time, that material has been indexicalized by moving to a temporally accelerated process. Since it has been heard once before, the process gives the impression of forward motion and rushing toward the continuation.

PN 6: p. 58, m. 14–p. 62

Motifs of PN 2 come back, but developed into even more brilliant forms. In this section we return to E♭ major (pp. 60ff.), so that the movement starts to look more and more symmetrical. All this affirms the iconic global structure of the movement—a distinct contrast to the asymmetrical formation of the previous movement. At the same time, the indexicality is fortified throughout with eighth-note string tremolandos that keep getting stronger. There is a feeling of speed and progress in the music, making it impossible to say precisely where we are transferred to the additional "development"—or chaos—that emerges next.

PN 7: p. 63–p. 66, m. 6

In the spatial sense a return to A major takes place, but in a tonally extremely complicated and poly-isotopic texture, which fills the whole range of the orchestra as a gigantic stretto. In terms of outer spatiality, the sound effect is "simultaneistic," as in a Charles Ives symphonic movement. In the temporal respect, a retardation or -disengagement occurs in relation to the Allegro that started the movement and prevailed until now. In the actorial sense, the tonal field is so densely packed with recurrent actor-signals that they can no longer be distinguished one from another. The tritone and fifth intonation, so central to the whole symphony, constitutes the nuclear pheme of the "calls for help" by the winds. At the same moment, the strings start to glide toward the following narrative program and its strikingly contrasting isotopy.

PN 8: p. 66, m. 7–p. 68

This time chaos does not lead to imperfectivity, as in the Scherzo of the second movement, but rather to a Tchaikovsky-like resignation. The inner space glides gradually from a chromatic tonal field to that of A minor, the tonal fundamental isotopy of the Symphony. In the outer spatiality, this takes place as a dialogue between the registers of the strings and of the woodwinds. The chromatically descending string passage occurs seven times; the rising minor-third motif of the woodwinds, nine times. All the motifs undergo so complete a diminution that their actorial features totally disappear. For example, the oboe's descending, major-seventh motif, marked *forte* at 68/16–17 and repeated three times, could allude to innumerable events heard earlier in the work. Yet amid this extremely redundant anti-indexicality representing -disengagement, a single motif arises that is not recurrent: the ascending, melodic-minor scale (cellos and double basses, p. 68, mm. 7–10) of A minor, or if one wants, remnants of a whole-tone scale (C–D–E–F♯–G♯), with two notes interpolated and ending on C, the note that launched the Symphony.

Conclusion

This basic mapping of the spatial-actorial-temporal structure should in our semiotic analysis be followed by a phase in which the modal contents of these articulations would be observed with the ultimate goal of writing a modal grammar for the Fourth Symphony. This would constitute a decisive step in the whole analysis, since on the basis of several sources, not least the comments of the composer himself, this symphony should not be interpreted as the narration of a "plot" but as a description of certain modal states. All narrative grammars with overly "concrete semantic investments" (such as that by Ilmari Krohn 1945/46) have to be rejected straightaway and the "signified" of the symphony must be sought elsewhere.

Scholars have emphasized different modalities when speaking about this symphony. Cecil Gray, for example, considers the general thymic nature of the work to be dysphoric (deeply tragic and melancholy) and its most pertinent modality to be 'knowing': "The thought is so concentrated that it demands from a listener as high a degree of concentration" (Gray 1935: 50). Normet (1970) stresses 'will' when dealing with the main theme of the third movement, and in other regards, when he speaks of the energetic nature of the symphony.

It thus remains the task for a modal analysis to investigate the following: 1. starting from a thematic analysis, the way the modality of 'knowing' prevails or is distributed among the different movements of the work; 2. the way the modality of 'will' appears in the kinetic-expressive solutions of the symphony, say, in the orchestration, yet also with regard to its negative aspect, the power of abstinence and limitation; 3. the way the 'must' manifests itself in the exploitation of old Viennese-Classical forms and their filtering into the work as external sources of formal norms (one should also study the operation of inner obligation created by the material itself, which would represent a 'willing' crystallized as inner obligation); 4. the way the source of kinetic energy in the proper sense is nevertheless the modality of 'will' (so far, few have scrutinized the kinetic quality of Sibelius's music; e.g., what is the 'will' inherent in musical actors, and how does it relate to the tonosphere surrounding a particular actor?); 5. the way epistemic value, 'believing', is expressed throughout the work, that is, which passages are experienced as 'true' or 'untrue', which constitute an affirmation, which a doubt, denial, or admittance; for example, the 'parody' of a scherzo, at the end of the second movement represents a denial, or 'lie', in the Greimasian veridictory square, but is balanced by a strong epistemic meaning-effect of 'truth' in the emergence of the theme-actor at the end of the third movement. It is possible that only the level of modalities holds the key to the semiotics of Jean Sibelius's music, and more particularly, to his Fourth Symphony.

X

TOWARD THE MODERN SCENE

10.1 Debussy's Impressionism in the Prelude "... La terrasse des audiences du clair de lune"

General Remarks

What is Impressionism in music in semiotic terms? It is at least not musical realism in the common sense of an iconic correlation between music and exterior reality. Nor is it musical expression of emotions in the sense of an index. Impressionism in music as well as in painting must be a Thirdness, to borrow a Peircean term.

As for their relationship with their object, musical signs in Debussy are in the phase of Thirdness; that is to say, they are interpretants of secondary signs. In this respect we would be wrong to say that Debussy is a narrative composer in the vein of Berlioz or Musorgsky. Rather, he represents a post-narrative composer who tells no particular story, a composer for whom individual signs (*sinsigns* in Peirce's terms) or sign-complexes are *rhemes, dicents,* or *arguments* for a story already told. Listening to Debussy's "... La terrace des audiences du clair de lune," *Préludes*, Bk. 2, no. 7, we sense that the audience has left the salon or theatre. Something has happened there, music has been played, and an impression has remained in the mind of a spectator—an impression which he interprets through the intermediary of secondary musical signs (musical interpretants). We do not know if the work played was *Pelléas et Mélisande* or perhaps *L'après-midi d'un faune*, even when those two works are alluded to in the composition in question. What is important is that, through the musical signs of this prelude, Debussy is thinking about a story already narrated.

The symmetries and mirroring motions of this music imply that Debussy's musical signs seem to realize the principle of self-reflection (*autoriflessività*, to use Umberto Eco's term). They are signs locked within themselves, signs that do not necessarily have a referent. It is paradoxical that, even though nearly every Debussy prelude seems to have its own extramusical program, on the musical level we find no emotional indexes of the Romantic era and few iconic imitations of external reality. The referent has disappeared entirely from the musical discourse. If we were searching for musics that illustrate various philosophical doctrines, we could take Debussy's music as an example of nominalism, a music aimed toward a theory of truth based on the internal coherence of musical signs. Thus we find there are many iconic and indexical relations in the internal sense. How might we define Debussy's music from the epistemic point of view, since it seems to operate mainly through the categories of 'being' and 'appearing'.

A static feeling of 'being' permeates the piece, caused by the pedal point C♯. This note is constantly repeated, first in a low register, then higher. At the same time, the C♯ represents a secret 'doing' in its function as a dominant that does not resolve in the course of the piece. So even though it seems to represent 'being', the more profound nature of C♯ reveals a tension and a 'doing' that for the most part remain implicit, in the category of 'not-appearing/doing'.

Can we find any section of the piece that overtly represents the modality of pure 'doing'? Certainly we do not meet with any developmental section in the traditional sense, even if we conceive of the piece as a usual ABA form. It is typical of Debussy to create superimposed levels, complex isotopies, and their deliberate nonconcomitance; he does this by having the different levels or lines proceed nonsimultaneously. For example, in m. 5, which lacks repetition of the principal motif, the descending, thirty-second-note figure occurs a little sooner than on its first appearance, in mm. 1–2. Instead of a development section proper, all the motifs are elaborated and developed immediately after being repeated at least once, as in mm. 3–4.

Repetition is therefore an extremely interesting category in Debussy's works.[1] Repetition may occur immediately or at a remove. It seems that Debussy tries to subordinate all the principles of composition to variation. He not only varies and transforms the musical substance but even varies the manner in which the music is varied and transformed. He develops the principle of development, transforms the transformation. Even in this respect he is on a meta-level with regard to composers preceding him and with regard to formal principles and conceptions of preceding stylistic epochs. An example of such a "variation of variation" are the changes of perspective, by expansion or by diminution. Expansion can be illustrated by variants of what I shall call the neume motif in various proportions. As Ex. 10.1 shows, that motif is not only inverted, which also happens rather often in the piece, but also gets larger and larger at the very beginning of the work.

Example 10.1. Debussy, *Préludes*, Bk. 2, no. 7; transformations of neume motif in actor A.

Further, there are several types of repetition: either directly indexical (repetitions placed one after the other, in a contiguous relationship) or where repeated units are located at some distance from each other, in the same section, or among different sections. The paradigmatic diagram in Fig. 10.1 makes this usage of repetition more explicit and also demonstrates how the listener is invited to follow several superimposed "stories."[²] More particularly, it is necessary to note that the main actor or principal theme (element A in Fig. 10.1), contrary to what usually happens in Debussy's works, is not repeated right away. It is characterized by the fact that it always emerges without direct repetition, as if all alone. Such a nonrecurrent element is of interest precisely because it breaks the continuity and serves as a discrete unit in a discourse that is otherwise very continuous and coherent.

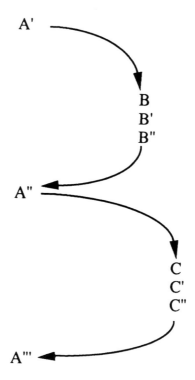

Figure 10.1. Superimposed "story" lines in Debussy,
Préludes, Bk. 2, no. 7.

The Global Form

It is first necessary to examine in minute detail what occurs in the piece. We designate A (m. 1) as the principal actor of the piece. Its modality of 'knowing' (*savoir*) is very great. In fact, the way in which Debussy spins out the entire form from this single element reminds one a little of Liszt: the content of a composition, the material from which the whole work derives, is presented at the outset (see Ex. 10.2). This principal actor contains at least the following musical phemes or units on the level of the signifier: the repeated-note idea; the appoggiatura figure; the neume motif, which at the beginning outlines the letter "V" but is later often transformed; the parallel-chord motif (here it begins with seventh chords); and the ascending motion by thirds in the bass, which is hidden or implicit at the beginning (see Ex. 10.3).

Example 10.2. Debussy, *Préludes*, Bk. 2, no. 7, transformations of actor A (main actor).

Example 10.3. Debussy, *Préludes*, Bk. 2, no. 7, motifs
comprising actor A (main actor).

We call the next two elements: Bx, a chromatic descending scale spanning three octaves, and By, the tritone motif B–F♯–G♯–B. Then comes section C (m. 3), where the chords in parallel motion spatially expand actor A, as we have already noted. As a timbral effect, we find the alternation of chords from sharp and flat regions: the colors change kaleidoscopically because of this alternation, a technique equivalent to that of pointillism in Impressionist painting. Section C is in a simple xxy form: motif, repetition, something new. After that Bx and By, the two motifs of section B, return once again superimposed.

Going on, we again encounter actor A (m. 7), from which we might infer that at least the beginning of the piece is formally symmetrical. But at the same time, actor A is transformed: it has been transferred to the high register and placed in thick chords in parallel motion, now plain major and minor triads, in contrast to the seventh chords of its first appearance. We may interpret the harmony as VI of F♯ major; that is, as a deceptive cadence after the dominant function which has to this point dominated the text. The D♯ minor chord may be interpreted enharmonically as E♭ minor, if we consider the following temporary tonicization of B♭ major in mm. 9–12. All these comments concern the internal spatiality, which is disengaged in relation to the overall tonic of F♯ major.

Moving to the actorial category, it is necessary to note that actor A will return several more times, always with new traits. We might be tempted to say that its transformations are due to the influence of interpolated sections; as if the interpolated sections, by their action and 'doing', cause the transformation. Thus we might see how actor A becomes modalized thanks to these transitional sections.

In the following section, D (mm. 10–12), B♭ major becomes the temporary tonal center. Even this section has a certain formal property: the motif, its repetition, and something else (though the last part is of shorter duration). It is characterized by the change of atmosphere to a modality of capriciousness, joyous excitement, and impatience. Here we do not feel thematic consistency; that is, we cannot derive the phemes directly from actor A. The general tone is "a bit animated and carefree"; it is born of a momentary impulsiveness and illogical caprice. The external spatiality is characterized by ascending motion toward E♭6, even though at the end of m. 10 the upper melodic line is interrupted by displacement into a lower register (E♭5). What also holds our attention is that the tonic chord of B♭ major appears in second (six-four) inversion. This inversion becomes important near the end of the piece (mm. 39–41); it is thus prepared iconically here. Further, the indexical motion toward the E♭ (transformed into D♯ at the end of m. 12) is thwarted by the displacement of the upper line into different registers.

In the latter half of m. 12 there is an arpeggiated dominant ninth chord of F♯ major; thus we interpret the F♮ as E♯ and proceed by enharmonic change of color to section E (mm. 13–15). E is a section of 'becoming', and the succeeding transition (mm. 16–19) prepares for the return of actor A. In semiotic terms, actor A˝ is premodalized by section E. Nonetheless, in m. 13 we first hear an entirely new motif, which is evidently an intertext in the "tonosphere" of Debussy; that is, it is a citation of typical chromatic, symmetrical, languid, and dreamlike themes. It is a self-reflective theme that Debussy uses elsewhere to describe the syrinx and the afternoon of a faune. By these modalities Debussy represents a relaxed energy, the principle of 'not-willing'.

Then comes the premodalization of actor A˝, in the undulating rhythmic figure of mm. 16–19. There is a development of the appoggiatura motif over the low C♯ pedal, which is again doubled in higher registers. As a third line, we have the chromatic ascending motion in the tenor line (upper line of the bass clef). Finally, it is a matter of pluri-isotopies, very complex and superimposed. We can at least speak of a tri-isotopy, in which each isotopy or level has its own modal content: 1. The pedal point emphasizes 'being' and stasis. 2. The chromatic appoggiaturas, very indexical and actorial, represent a sort of lamentation, even though we cannot consider this a signification of "plaint." Nevertheless the seme contains nostalgia or longing. 3. The ascending chromatic motion in the tenor depicts the modality of 'will'.

Next, the interoceptivity of the piece and the external and internal indexicality unite and reinforce each other by means of a waltz variant of actor A (m. 20). The ascending bass motion by minor thirds is underlined by the bass notes on the strong parts of the measure. The melody itself is a transformation of the appoggiatura motif and the neume motif of the principal actor, in which movement by seconds dominates. The momentary dance section of m. 20 comes to mind suddenly, like an episode from a story already told, and it postmodalizes the following transitional section (mm. 21–24). The musical substance of this transition is neutral; although an ascending chromatic line reemerges in the tenor part of the middle bass clef. In the upper part (among others), the neume motif is inverted and figuration of actor A's appoggiaturas occurs.

This episode prepares the listener for the return in m. 25 of a new transformation: actor A‴, where the parallel motion by six-four chords is placed simultaneously in extreme registers, in contrast to the opening occurrence of parallel-motion chords in the central register. From another angle, we hear the new tonic, E♭ major, in the central register and in root position, containing an appoggiatura that alternates between a major and a minor second. This motif is an extreme condensation of the appoggiatura motif of the principal actor. The global form of this section (mm. 25–27) is symmetrical: xyx. Note that the principal actor now returns very disengaged with regard to both outer spatiality (registral extremes) and inner spatiality (E♭ and G), though the G major was prepared by actor A″ in m. 20.

In mm. 28–31 we hear a development of elements from section C. In the background we can discern elements of the seventh chord on G, borrowed from section B (again note the superimposition of levels), in second inversion. Despite the return and development of previous material, in the modal sense we do not feel this section as an iconic evocation of something already heard, but as a premodalization of events to follow. At the same time, the solemn rhythmic figure in the bass is a reference (intertext) to the music of *Pelléas*. This very powerful 'will-to-do' contains strong elements of the modality of 'can'.

The state to which this preparation leads is again a kind of frustration, because for a consequent we have motif E (mm. 32–33), a motif that coils around itself. It is narcissistic and represents 'not-willing', therefore a musical 'lie'. In terms of Greimas's epistemic articulation, it signifies 'appearing/not-being': what we have been waiting for does not appear. The motif is heard only once, after which we encounter a transition comprising a combination of chromatic appoggiaturas, the tritone motif By, and the descending figure of the melodic part. The tritone motif is victorious and almost totally prevails. At the same time, it recalls the beginning of the piece and thereby consists of an allusion to symmetry. When motif Bx, in which the descending chromatic passage also returns (m. 37), joins with the inversion of the neume motif and its first expansion, the idea of cyclic form is clearly seen (Debussy was a pupil of Franck). Then the return of opening sections continues with the expansion of the neume motif C in mm. 37–38, now inverted and joined with motif Bx, which follows directly.

The last occurrence of actor A is in the main key of F♯ (mm. 39–40); but since we await a resolution to the tonic in the upper register, we do not have a definitive resolution of the initial problem. Our expectation has been fooled each time at the occurrence of the principal actor. For always, after having "the passage of action" (in the terminology of Brémond), we end up in incompletion or imperfectivity. Actor A is now rhythmically transformed, and in place of the sevenths, we get six-four chords (m. 39). The idea of rhythmic condensation also returns (m. 41) from section C, while combining the initial neume motif and its inversion in the same figure.

The coda (mm. 32–42) consists of a unique texture in comparison with the rest of the musical substance. We are now in the upper register, which we expected, but without the tonic of F♯ major. In the temporal realm, the dotted-sixteenth-note figure is curiously regular, almost mechanical. The opening parallel fifths create the impression of emptiness, which perhaps evokes the title's "light of the moon" as its musical symbol. In any case, this passage remains somewhat enigmatic. The appoggiatura G for F♯ (m. 44) in the final chords (the tonic six-four), which in no way signifies complete repose (consonance and the principle of 'being'), refers to the fact that the competition between the major and minor second has now been resolved in favor of the latter. The appoggiatura is at the same time a final allusion to the emotional indexes contained in the principal musical actor. Debussy wants to underline this by his directive to "slightly color the small note."

In Debussy's narrative program the complete unification of the subject with its object of value never occurs. In all the passages where the principal actor, A, returns to action, where 'doing' is realized, the material heard is not the object that is sought. This has been reinforced each time by the musical directions of *subito piano* or *pianissimo*.

We may now interpret the global form of this piece as a rondo (see Fig. 10.2), which is extraordinary in the sense that the repeated refrain is a very brief thematic actor that always changes upon repetition. We can easily see, especially toward the end of the piece, that it is typical of Debussy's formal planning to construct superimposed levels (Ernst Kurth called such superimposition "paralinear counterpoint"). The impression persists that this music consists of planes floating one above the other, moved by musical currents, in different tempos and producing asynchronous states.

A (m. 1) Bx,y (m. 2) C (mm. 3–4) Bx,y (mm. 5-6) A′ (mm. 7–9)

premod.→
D,x,x,x (mm. 10–12) E (mm. 13–15) **transition** (mm. 16–19) A″ (m. 20)

← postmod.   premod.→
transition (mm. 21–24) A‴(x,y,x) (mm. 25–27) C/By (mm. 28–30)

← postmod.
E′ (mm. 32–33) By (mm. 34–36) C/B(y),C/B(x) (mm. 37–38) A‴‴
(mm. 39–40)

C (m. 41) F (**coda** mm. 42–45)

Figure 10.2. Debussy, *Préludes*, Bk. 2, no. 7, as rondo form.

We can also present the narrative programs in a formal scheme that takes the variations of actors A through A″″ as its point of departure (refer to Ex. 10.2). Let us remember what was previously said about relations between subject and object of value. They may be either S ∧ O (the subject is joined to or possesses the object) or S ∨ O (the subject is separated from or deprived of the object). For this prelude, we derive the formula shown in Fig. 10.3, where E = 'being' and m = modality, which varies with each utterance of 'doing', symbolized by F. We can distinguish between four modal states in the piece: m1 = neutral, m2 = dysphoric, m3 = apparently euphoric ('appearing/not-being'), m4 = euphoric.

$$\text{Em1 } (A \vee O); \text{Fm2 } [A' \to (A'' \vee O)]; \text{Fm3 } [A'' \to (A''' \vee O)]; \text{Fm4}$$
$$[A''' \to (A'''' \vee O)]$$

Figure 10.3. Debussy, *Préludes*, Bk. 2, no. 7, subject/object activity based on actor A.

A Sketch for a Modal Grammar

It is necessary to discuss the Prelude briefly from a modal point of view, in light of the standard kinetic and energetic types that can be seen in the piece. If we take as our context the grammar of tonal music, the very beginning of the piece is extremely disengaged, outside the center of action, as concerns the inner spatiality. With regard to the external spatiality, actor A is located in the central range of the piano and is therefore engaged. With regard to temporality, the beginning is disengaged by virtue of the "slow" tempo and especially by virtue of the eighth notes, which appear as early as the third bar. Looking at the most actorial modalities ('know', 'will', 'must', 'can'), we notice that even the repeated-note motif expresses a rather strong 'will'. The neume motif, in combination with the parallel-motion chords, necessarily represents a negation of the norms of functional harmony. That is, it exhibits the principle of 'not-must'. This theme is very rich in potential 'knowing', as we have already said. The descending chromatic line in motif Bx creates a vector that pulls us toward the low register and that has a powerful 'will' toward a certain point in tonal space. This point is desirable and indispensable, but in the end it is not the tonic of F♯ major; after the repetition of motif Bx, the deceptive cadence in m. 7 instead brings us to VI of F♯ major.

Another vector emerges in section C, and it proves to be the most important: 'will' toward the high register. This is emphasized by the *crescendo* marks in m. 3 and later. In thymic value, mm. 1–6 are neutral. On the other hand, actor A is clearly dysphoric. In contrast, section D is capricious and urbane, with its euphoric B♭ major. Section D, then, belongs to the category of 'appearing/not-being'; that is, the euphoric state is a disguise, a 'lie', and it does not represent the attainment of the object of value which is implied by the underlying narrative program. Still, the D section manifests a 'will' or desire for the high register, even though this desire has been frustrated each time by octave displacement of the lines, that is, by spatial disengagement into various registers.

Section E clearly represents 'not-will' by its static nature. Yet its value of 'know' is remarkably high, since it introduces new thematic material. Even so, section E represents the category of imperfectivity, or incompletion. The following transition (mm. 16–19), taken as a totality, is a passage of action; but it contains the isotopies of 'being' and 'doing', isotopies which contradict each other. 'Being' arises through the static C♯ pedal. 'Doing' is represented by the indexical figures of the appoggiaturas and the melodic line that rises from the tenor.

Section A″ is dominated by temporal-rhythmic articulation. Though section A″ is carefully prepared, it has little 'knowing', and it affects us only by its simple power of waltz, without having any particular 'will'. Section A″ has no real tendency toward anything, and is nothing other than a waltz written according to the stylistic norms of that genre. This means that section A″ contains very little 'must'. It is nevertheless capable of postmodalizing the transition that follows. As its latent 'will', the transition seeks the high register.

In m. 25, the return of actor A‴ is not a disappointment, since it was not even expected in this place. Instead, A‴ is a surprise, and it effects a counterbalance which emphasizes the temporality of the preceding section. This emphasis is attained by external spatiality, through shifts of register. Its effect of potential 'knowing' is mitigated by the redundancy of musical material; but the loss of 'knowing' is compensated for by a new spatial disengagement and by the *subito pianissimo*.

The combination that follows, C and B♭, contains a very strong value of 'can do' because of its rhythmic articulation and dynamism. The 'will' toward the high register is very intense. The harmonies in this section are totally nonfunctional, and the 'will' culminates on the dominant of F♯ major at m. 32. This section (C/B♭) is indeed an incompletion, a frustration or a lie, when compared to the impassioned desire in the preceding section; nevertheless, the section that follows (mm. 34–36) is postmodalized by this section's 'knowing'. At the same time, the ear begins to understand the effect of a normative 'must' of cyclic form. The element B♭ returns in m. 34, and, soon after, the other motifs from the opening return. We are disengaged from the temporal, spatial, and actorial entropy of the piece's middle sections, where we were almost lost (from the narrative point of view).

Still, the object of value is only partially attained. At m. 39 the principal actor is heard in the same register as the beginning and almost in its opening configuration (which was very disengaged). All the same, we are not in the "proper" register for final resolution to the tonic. The actor has been influenced by the modal activity of the piece and is no longer the same actor that it was at the beginning. Rather, it is now an experienced actor. Thus the end of this piece signifies only a partial victory—the return to the tonic—but at the same time something remains unfinished: resolution in the proper register.

Perhaps Debussy's modernity lies in the fact that his tonosphere is not unequivocally black or white in its modalities. Total heroicness is possible only in the Beethoven tradition. Here values are mixed, and we remain in a state of uncertainty, in the epistemic sense, until the end of the Prelude. Debussy tells no grand story. His universe is basically the contradictory and pluri-isotopic world of the twentieth century. He is a composer of Thirdness, in the sense that everything is well thought-out and filtered through the meta-levels of his musical statements.

10.2 Minimalism and Anti-Narrativity

In the history of Western Classical music, there is a recurring alternation between complexity and simplicity, or, in terms of information theory, between entropy and redundancy. Highly sophisticated complexity and systematizing has always, after reaching a certain stage, suddenly swung to the other extreme–to a very simple principle of articulation. A well-known example is the transition from Dutch polyphony, which emphasized plasticity and linearity, to the quasichordal, uniform textures of Palestrina. Another is the change from Baroque counterpoint to the homophony of Classicism at the same time as a sociological change, when music became public and expanded to new social strata, in a word, when it was popularized. Finally, the rich orchestral colors of late Romanticism were turned to musical aphoristics with the birth of modernism at the turn of the twentieth century, and atonality gave way to Neoclassicism in the 1920s and 30s. Viewed against this historical background, the term "new simplicity" as a general rubric for minimalist music of the 1960s and 70s seems inappropriate, particularly as to the word "new," since it is in fact a phenomenon that has been repeated numerous times. Furthermore, close scrutiny shows this "simplicity" to be a multifaceted phenomenon which dialectically resolves many revolutionary ideas of the post-1945, musical avant-garde.[1]

Composer Wolfgang Rihm (1980: 80) objects to such categorization and suggests that the term "new simplicity" stems from a journalistic urge to classify: this is serial, this post-serial, this aleatory, this Minimalist art, and so on. "When I hate something, I classify it," he said. He opposes the view of himself at the vanguard of the "new simplicity" and says that his only aim is to write music that innocently expressed joy and pain: "When music can come out of itself and convey something, then it tells me something about country, love, and death. This is old and simple."

Rihm's statement might drive some aestheticians, music scholars as well as composers, to despair, especially at a time when postmodernists have given permission to use old, simple musical elements and even to write tonally, but only in aid of irony or parody—one can no longer seriously write tonally, make poems with rhymes, paint representational paintings, or build Gothic houses! Umberto Eco endorses this aspect of the postmodernist attitude, as does the philosopher and prophet of postmodernism, Jean-François Lyotard (1984). Lyotard puts the same idea in a somewhat more complicated way when he says that post-modernism includes two typical "modes." First, it is unable to present anything directly, implying nostalgia for the presence of a human subject; primary emphasis instead goes to the conception itself and its "inhuman" nature.[5] Second, the goal might be the naive pleasure of finding new rules for the game, be it pictorial, musical, artistic, or whatever. Typically, the postmodern artist has no preestablished rules or categories but is instead searching for them. Without such rules, the postmodern artist is eternally seeking and trying to make visible something that cannot be rendered present. For example, Proust surrenders his authorial identity to temporality: he remembers too much and too well. Joyce abandons his identity for the principle of "too many books," as in the verbal acrobatics of *Finnegans Wake* and in his texts about texts. In music, we may think of a post-modern composer as one who replaces self-identity with the principle of "too much music." Such a composer has heard too much music to be able to say anything himself, positively and absolutely, to be himself, with his own voice present in the musical text he creates.

We may add to these reflections two remarks of a semiotic nature. First, as to the idea of excess characteristic of our contemporary culture, we may recall Jean Baudrillard's applied semiotics (1968) as a critique of the culture of "simulacrum" and "multiplicity." Art becomes simple because simple, unsophisticated structures can be endlessly multiplied and reproduced. Second, the absence of a subject is a special narrative device, an actorial disengagement. Rihm's comments are disturbing in their simplistic conception of actoriality. For structuralists and semioticians have demonstrated that no naive, direct expression of any subject exists, but that everything is conditioned by the codes and conventions of particular sign systems.

Simplicity in music is anything but simple. Basically, music is always a dialectic between a present sound phenomenon and absent spiritual or mental structures, such as principles of cognition, significations, aesthetics. Music that is scarcely *in praesentia* may contain sophisticated references *in absentia*. The phenomenon of Erik Satie relies on the positing of an absent meaning. His compositions as well as his verbal texts and his drawings provoke the receiver mentally to create these meanings. *Musique pauvre* turns the listener's attention from sense perception, from the sounding surface, toward metaphysics and meditation.

This leads us to examine some musical phenomena, philosophies, and sound products that typify the new simplicity and Minimalism, whence these latter notions originate. In painting, Minimalism goes by many different names: ABC-art, anti-illusionism, the Art of Bare Bones, Literal Art, Ignorant Nihilism, Idiot Art, Object Art, Reductive Art, Rejective Art, Primary Structures.⁶ Despite the variety in names, Yvonne Rainer (1974) has presented as simple dichotomies the main features of all Minimalist sculpture, what it is against and what it strives for:

Minimalism is opposed to:	*Minimalism strives for:*
representative references	non-referential forms
hierarchic relationships	unidimensional forms or modules
illusionism	literalness
complexity, details	simplicity
monumentality	human dimensions
handicraft art	industrial production
textured surfaces	smooth surfaces

Unlike the Cubists, who still had contact with anthropomorphic forms, Minimalists used simple, immediately recognizable forms, such as cubes. Aesthetic attention shifted from inner to outer relationships, such as the dialectics between the concept of a cube and varied forms of an object realizing this cube, forms which appear as the spectator moves around the object. The interaction between a sculpture and the negative space formed by its architectonic environment became a primary concern. Recognizing the importance of this interaction, many American West Coast artists (such as Larry Bell, Michael Asher, Robert Irwin, Bruce Nauman, and Doug Wheeler) created entire inner spaces that surround the spectator. Works by these artists can be characterized as Minimal because their visual stimulus is so scant that the spectator's own phenomenological experience of light, space, and duration constitutes the work of art. In other words, in artistic communication attention moves away from both the artist and the work, and toward the receiver.

All this fits well with our preliminary statements about musical Minimalism: by the scarcity of musical stimuli the listener is encouraged to shape a musical work. Yet this does not involve a specific message addressed to the listener, Jakobson's "conative" function of communication. Although Minimalist music presupposes a musical listener-subject, such music is basically impersonal and de-actorial, at least in its American manifestations (the European representatives of *musique pauvre*, from Rihm to Pärt, have created their own variant).

The *nouveau roman* cannot be considered a literary enactment of Minimalism. Though some novels without punctuation, such as a "labyrinth" of signifiers by Philippe Sollers, force the reader into active shaping, the text retains its inner grammatical structure. Rather, the forerunners of Minimalism are found among Dadaist poets, who, like the Cubists, aimed to create art that could be enjoyed even if it could not be understood. This led to the elaboration of language as merely phonetic material and to total omission of the semantic level (a phenomenon with parallels in Stravinsky's music). Also, the Dadaists based poems on the idea of repetition. Indeed, one of the definitions of Dada was that it is synonymous with the phrase "Qu'est-ce que beau? Ne connais pas, ne connais pas. . . ." In this sense Lyotard still shows a Dadaist bent, when he argues that a postmodernist cannot even pose the question What is beautiful? but must ask, What can be *said* to be beautiful? A poem in the same vein is "Il y a," by Tristan Tzara, which consists only of a list of all that "there is."

Musical Minimalism, while connected with the modernist trends which preceded it, stands in a polemical relation with the complexity and subtleties of the serial school on the structural level of the work, and with John Cage's aleatory philosophy on the aesthetic level. Small wonder that European composers have a reserved attitude toward Minimalism as an "-ism," since twentieth-century European art is a seemingly endless parade of different manifestations of new music and art.[7]

Unlike Rihm, some composers willingly admit to being Minimalists. La Monte Young, with his Theatre of Eternal Music, Steve Reich, Philip Glass, and some other Americans are the most important names. Yet behind all their work stands the music philosophy of John Cage. Typically, however, Minimalists have not elaborated a music philosophy on a par with that of Cage, but are rather practicing musicians, who speak less and do more.

The serial school (Boulez, early Stockhausen) and the Cagean philosophy of silence and Minimalism represent different attitudes toward the same musical problem, namely, how a musical process is controlled. The serial school wants maximum control over musical process, whereas Cage rejects this idea, believing that the more musical structure is controlled the more it controls the composer. This in turn goes against his philosophy of freedom, which obviously originates from the American transcendentalists Thoreau and Emerson, and for which Daniel Charles has used the suitable terms of "musique du non-vouloir" and "musique indéterminée" (Charles 1978: 66). But the less a composer's will attempts to subordinate the music and the listener, the more space is left for the listener's will (as shown in Fig. 10.4).

non-vouloir   *vouloir*

Composer → →   Music   ← ← Listener

Figure 10.4.

Steve Reich has said that he wants neither listener nor composer to express themselves in a proper sense, but to subordinate themselves to the power of music and to experience ecstasy by merging with it. When listening to or performing Reich's gradual Minimalist processes, one attends an emancipatory, impersonal ritual. Such processes leave no room for mental improvisation; the listener's attention shifts away from "he and she," "you and me," outward toward "it" (Reich 1974: 11).

These three attitudes—serialist, aleatory, Minimalist—toward the control of musical process could easily be typologized with categories invented by George Herbert Mead and later applied by Charles Morris in the visual arts: letting things happen, making things happen, and watching things happen. These mental attitudes crystallize as principles: dependency (permitting the object to influence oneself, as in Reich's Minimalism), detachment (letting the object be what it is, as in Cage), domination (ruling over the object, as do serial composers). Thus in the manipulation of musical material these principles also project different musical aesthetics.

We could continue by analyzing Minimalism according to these semiotic categories, but such a method would be all too "etic," as ethnomusicologists and anthropologists say. Let us instead take an "emic" approach to the problem, employing concepts and expressions used by the Minimalist composers themselves.

Musique pauvre

In many respects, behind Minimalist musical thinking one senses Cage's music philosophy: a blend of Hindu aesthetics, medieval mysticism, and American transcendentalism. Cage even believes that Master Eckhart must have been conscious of the doctrines of oriental philosophers, so great is the similarity between the two. One of the cornerstones of Cage's philosophy is the principle "There is poetry as soon as we realize we possess nothing." For Cage, tones or sounds already exist, independent of a composer's will. "I do not want to force tones to follow me" (Cage in Charles 1981: 87). This idea, a kind of quietism, he transforms into a pedagogical principle: "Permit each person, as well as sound, to be the center of creation."

In the realm of musical art, Cage considers his great prophet to be Erik Satie. The art of both Thoreau and Satie balance each other, to Cage's mind, creating between them a tranquil continuity (Cage in Charles 1981: 185). For Cage, Satie's music expresses completely the composer's aesthetic. Cagean ideas are also reflected, in an astonishing way, in Arvo Pärt's works and in his views on composing. Pärt (1984) tells of an experience that helps explain his background as a composer of meditation music:

> Once in Russia I spoke with a monk and asked him how a man can develop himself as a composer. He answered by saying that he did not know any solution. I told him that I also wrote prayers, that I composed them and texts of psalms, and that perhaps it helped me in being a composer. To this he said: No, you are wrong. All the prayers have already been written. Everything has been prepared. Now you have to prepare yourself.

Pärt continues, saying he believes that sometimes a moment comes when even the greatest artist no longer wants to make art. "Perhaps then we appreciate him even more, since at that moment he has exceeded, transcended his work." Just such an attitude lies behind "scarce music," *musique pauvre*.

The considerably more pragmatic American Minimalists, such as Reich, might, like Pärt, refer to medieval music, but in a purely practical sense; for instance, when Reich borrows the technique of hocket. After all, the philosophies of Pärt's music and Cage's resemble each other: to both composers all music has already been written, it already exists, we only have to open ourselves and listen to it. This calls to mind the difference between *pensée structurale* and *pensée structurelle*. According to the former way of thinking, the structures exist in the human brain. A scholar or artist need only become conscious of them. The latter way of thinking suggests that no abstract structures exist; they have to be made, created, from which it follows that everything is artifice, invention, interpretation, discourse, meta-language, construction—whether they are laws uncovered by a scientist or artistic structures.

In a post-modern, "simple" art, these attitudes or ways of thinking fuse into an inseparable tangle. The Cagean attitude represents the former; the latter represents sophisticated post-modernism in which one borrows styles of earlier periods with a view to irony. In any case, no such irony arises when Pärt quotes medieval or other earlier style periods, Reich African music, and Glass Baroque opera or Viennese-Classical melody with Alberti bass. These composers quote structural forms from an earlier style period not as a specifically historical allusion, but only for the sake of the structure itself, simply because such forms represent musical shapes that please them. No music is more anti-historical than Minimalism. Rather, it is musical information-processing that follows simple Gestaltist theoretical principles, such as similarity, proximity, and good continuation.

In principle Minimalist music should be accessible to anyone, but it is in fact only for a person of the electronic age. Some repetitive compositions resemble psychological tests expanded to Kafkaesque proportions, whose innocent objects the listeners are forced to be. Psychomusicologists have studied the way simple musical shapes are synthesized in the brain, and the way different musical stimuli fed to separate ears are articulated by cognition into one unified figure. At one pole of the scarcity and extremely reduced simplicity of Minimalist music we have medieval and Hindu philosophy, at the other, modern empirical science and cognitive psychology.

A third trait of *musique pauvre*, one which makes it acceptable even in sophisticated avant-garde circles of the world's great artistic centers, is the alternation between presence and absence. The deconstructionist theories of Jacques Derrida stress how changing even the slightest piece of the signifier can call forth extensive reflections on the signified, as do the letters *e* and *a* in the words *différence* and *différance*. Music that is only slightly present leaves abundant space for absent meanings and tempts one to intellectual reflection.

Repetition

The idea of repetition as the dominant principle of composition does not seem to be a new invention. Repetition has in all structural analyses served as the starting point for exploring a work of art and its style. But what happens when this principle, which in Classical art always appears against the background of nonrepetition (entropy), suddenly wrenches itself away from its earlier minority position and becomes a prevailing law? Earlier repetition was expressly the *différance* of a work, a feature breaking automatization of everyday perception, a device of estrangement that made a work artistic.

In their poetics, the Russian Formalists succeeded in describing the principle of repetition fairly exhaustively. To quote Shklovsky: "In poetry blood is never blood but a rhyme for the word flood." In other words, repetition serves as estrangement when it is set against the semantic level of language and when it rejects associations with everyday reality. Juri Tynianov considered repetition in poetry as belonging to the "instrumentation" of a poem, by which he meant the phonological coloring of a verse. Therefore, the rhythmic function of repetition should not be identified with meter. Tynianov's observation also applies to repetition in Minimal music. Of course in music the contrast between a semantic and a phonetic level is not obvious, unless we conceive of familiar melodic figures, chosen from an intonational store and based on earlier styles, as the background for a musical semantics. Examples would include Pärt's use of medieval and renaissance polyphony, and Glass's borrowing of ostinatos from Baroque music, as in his opera *Satyaghara*, which the composer calls a structural composition because repetition of the same chaconne forms the basic organizational principle. Such figures are "made strange" by a surprising repetition not characteristic of the style from which the repeated element has been taken.

In his treatise on versification Tynianov (1977) discusses the following aspects of repetition: 1. the proximity and cohesion of repetitions; 2. their relation to meter; 3. a quantitative factor: the number of phonemes and the nature of their groupings, where one may distinguish complete repetition (*geminatio*) and partial repetition (*reduplicatio*); 4. a qualitative factor: the quality of phonemes; 5. the nature of the repeated word (material or formal); 6. the nature of the words joined with instrumentation.

The above scheme fits well, almost without renovation, the program of repetitive music: The repetitions of repetitive music are situated extremely closely and densely in relation to each other. They form clear isotopic levels, which, according to the principle of gemination, can either continue almost endlessly or gradually become transformed (*reduplicatio*). In the first case repetitive music is a unique phenomenon in music history, unless one looks outside European music to include the rhythmics of African music and *gamelan* ensembles, which have served as one starting point for Steve Reich, whose music contains mostly partial repetitions. Among other pieces, his *Piano Phase* is based on repetition of the same figure by two pianos (see Ex. 10.4). The second piano starts later than the first, then gradually accelerates in tempo, eventually causing the musical figures to become interlaced. The process continues until a return to the initial situation.

One can say that rhythm and meter coincide; the time values of a repeated figure create musical accentuation. The repeated figures themselves are not

Example 10.4. Steve Reich, *Piano Phase*.

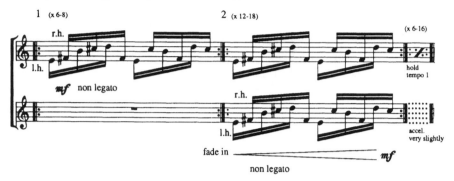

often symmetrical, in contrast to the mechanistic symmetry created by their recurrence. In this sense, for instance, m. 26 of Debussy's *L'isle joyeuse* might be considered a glimpse of that composer's idea of "Minimalism" (Ex. 10.5).

Example 10.5. Debussy, *L'isle joyeuse*, m. 26.

As to the qualitative factor, Minimalists generally employ ordinary instruments and not synthetically produced sounds. When asked about his relationship to electronic music, Glass replied: "I have no interest whatsoever in it. . . . A real goal and challenge for me has always been the language of music and not any effects or tricks. Even when traditional composers have ventured into this area, they have produced works with no interest for me" (Gagne and Caras 1982: 224). Similarly, Steve Reich says: "I have always been disappointed with tape music or so-called concrete music, since it produces uneasily recognizable sounds." It is true that his career as a composer started with tape music, but then Reich exploited speech, to which he added rhythmic structures, without changing the speech timbre or pitch, which only increased the appeal of its significations.

In semiotic terms, a common feature of Minimalism is the desire to maintain the units of the first articulation. (Whether these units exist in music was a problem disputed in the 1960s.) Here one must admit that application of Tynianov's repetitive model to Reich or Glass does violence to the nature of their music insofar as the origin of such music is not linguistic but gestural. Glass says of his opera *Einstein on the Beach*: "I do not know if I want to divide my music into head and body, but if one wants to use these expressions, this music is a very physical expression. . . . The problem is that a good deal of the content of this music, which has for us an immediate biological impact, is the most unknown to us" (Gagne and Caras 1982: 226). Reich in turn says that in his music the idea of repetition relates to dance.

In any case, what is essential in repetitive music is that the principle of repetition has shifted to the position of the dominant idea of a work of art. Thus it no longer performs the task assigned it by the Russian Formalists, that of producing surprise. The crucial artistic device now becomes the slightest *change* in the redundancy created by repetition. We meet therefore in Minimalist art a double *différance*: *différence* as a *différance*.

Atemporality and Anti-Narrativity

What Gianni Vattimo says in *La fine della modernita* (1985) meshes nicely with the Minimalist conception of time: "The crisis of the future, which is characteristic of all postmodern life and social activities, finds in art its privileged channel of expression." Minimalist music rejects temporal segmentation and traditional functions of musical time: in this music one can no longer distinguish among beginning, end, introduction, or other temporal functions of music. Here music really has become a machine that stops time (Lévi-Strauss).

The gradual processes of Reich's music can be experienced as macroscopically expanded objectifications of processes of temporal change, as depicted by Henri Bergson. In general, the influence of musical time, that almost imperceptible *presque-rien*, is present in musical form *in absentia*. It influences from behind the scenes, and a composer can use it as a strategy for the timing of musical events. Nevertheless, in Reich's music this temporal process has been made present. Reich aims for perfect audibility of musical form and is not fascinated by hidden musical structures. In order to meet this demand for audibility with the greatest possible accuracy, it is presupposed that the musical process will unfold extremely slowly. As metaphors of the graduality of music, Reich encourages us to imagine the following events: a moving swing slowly coming to rest, sand running through an hour glass, and burying your feet in the sand at the ocean's edge, then watching and listening as water fills the impressions.

In fact, the Minimalist conception of time is by nature just such a reified reduction of the *temps d'espace* criticized by Henri Bergson. To his mind change and movement are indivisible units. Bergson's thesis is that

> There are changes, but there is no object which would change: a change needs
> no support. There are movements, but there are no unchangeable, discrete, fixed

> objects which would move. . . . Let us listen to a melody: does it not clearly express a movement that does not concern any mobile object, a change in which nothing changes? This change will be sufficient; it is a creature, an object itself. [Bergson 1938]

Bergson means that a change cannot be rendered visible, since if we do so it becomes something unchangeable, the reduction of a movement to a series of immobile points in a space. Minimalist works are therefore objectifications of series of "now" moments. They represent pure durativity in the sense that they have neither beginning nor end, and, in fact, no temporal articulation. In this sense Minimalist music is also anti-narrative.

The problem of musical narrativity is very broad and does not depend merely on temporal organization. Musical narrativity also presupposes both a tonal hierarchy made temporal and an actorial engagement. The anti-narrativity of Minimalism coincides with a post-modern aesthetic which has also rejected narrativity. According to Lyotard, post-modernism is a state in which one no longer believes in grand stories or master narratives. Belief, confidence, and the sacred are absent. Nevertheless, even Pärt's music projects a minimum of narrativity. In a sense his compositions suggest a title such as "the last story": though they contain abundant repetition and stability, his works are basically expanded cadences in which the music seems constantly about to finish. On the other hand, the narrative illusion is kept alive by musical signs, symbols, indexes, and icons, all of which refer to a universe of human meanings: the minor key, bells, the sound of a string ensemble with all its associations, the figurative quality of music as a descending movement, canonic techniques, and so on.

American Minimalists, however, consider their music to be completely subject-less. Reich says, in his 1968 essay "Music as a Gradual Process" (1981), that musical process, in addition to exercising complete control, must bring us into contact with the impersonal. Likewise Glass has declared himself an opponent of narrativity. Yet in their arguments against narrativity in music, they use those concepts by which narrativity can best be elucidated. Namely, narrativity, in music as in other sign systems, is based on spatial, temporal, and actorial categories, and the principle that we have here called the modal character of music. As stated above, modalization enlivens the bare bones of musical structures; it flows, so to speak, into all the musical gaps and makes continuous the musical process. It creates a bridge between two separate tones, two phrases, two sections, two movements, and it provides music with energy. Though Minimalist music does not particularly need such "bridges" because it is already extremely continuous, a music that is structurally impoverished may catalyze and activate a very intense process of modalization in the listener, for whom music without complex organization is the same as completely organized music that leaves no room for modalization.

Through modalization the listener creates an imaginary or virtual region that fills the space left between work and listener, a space that arises even in the most complete musical performance. Then musical form takes shape as a dialogue between listener and the music listened to, which dialogue even Cage requires from an ideal musical event. What impulses, then, does music itself add to this dialogue? The composer, too, can control this dialogue by anticipating the shaping of musical form on the basis of a listener's modalization.

In this connection it is useful to reconsider the conceptual pair engagement/disengagement from Greimas's semiotics, to help clarify why Minimalism is anti-narrative and its relation to the modernism preceding it. In musical discourse, as in general human discourse, a balance obtains between three basic categories, the temporal, spatial, and actorial. Lévi-Strauss was right: music is a sign system that always lacks something. To music we feel an irresistible need to add something that is missing. This absence in turn relates to the important operations of engagement/disengagement in music. In all music the starting point is a situation in which the conditions of "now/here/I" are engaged. This is the fundamental state of music. The moment one departs from this state, moves to a musical action ('doing'), one starts to shift off these conditions and a disengagement occurs. Yet in this dialogue with music the listener reacts so that the more that a disengagement occurs with respect to spatiality, temporality, or actoriality, or with all of them simultaneously, the more one tries with modalities and modalizations to fill the gap, the distanciation, the absence created by this disengagement.

Modernists dreamed of a totally disengaged work of art. This dream also marked a deep change in the epistemes of occidental culture: the shift to a world view in which man as an acting and willing subject has become alienated, *ex-centré* from the center of his being. In atonal music especially, spatial disengagement prevails: there is no longer any fulcrum of tonal space, any center that would be undeniably "here." Yet in the temporal respect both atonal and serial music often use models quite like those of tonal music. Similarly, such music retains the actorial category; that is, it keeps icons, indexes, and symbols referring to a human subject. Also, the lengths of phrases and the indexical connections, i.e., the logic of musical progression, remain the same.

Yet considering reactions to atonality in our post-modern age, one wonders if we have now returned from modernism, with its situation of a "fallen subject," to a safe engagement of *hic/nunc/ego*. Not entirely: modernists created works whose particular goal was to activate people as destinatees of art. This is why the *nouveau roman*, a novel without punctuation and segmentation, was invented: so that readers would shape the text by determining its centers and principles of formation. As a musical counterpart we have John Cage's extremely scanty pieces, among others, his *Music of Changes*, which consists only of a series of chords and knocks, separated from each other by long pauses. During the pauses, listeners and interpreters forget the ways in which they modalized the previous musical point, and they change modalizations. In this case the listener must push his or her modalizing ability to the extreme, not at all knowing how the player will modalize or approach the next "point." Here we have shifted to a Heideggerian discourse in which each concept refers

to everything that has been said and will be said, in which thought does n
stop for a moment, and where a phobia of stagnation dominates. Thus Mir
malist music can take place on the level of continuous isotopies in whic
changes can be gradual, as in Reich, or abrupt and contrasting, as in tl
changes between piano and wind sections in the first movement of Glass
Glassworks.[8]

In sum, Minimalism presents itself as a multifaceted and paradoxical ph
nomenon connected to the general development of aesthetics and philosopl
of art in recent decades. Here it has also been investigated as a possible fie
for application of a semiotic theory. I hope that I have not overly exploite
Minimalism as a pretext for introducing ideas of musical semiotics. Still, or
should bear in mind that structuralism and semiotics are also phenomena th
arose during the same time period.

CONCLUSION

Now it is time to put together the results of our inquiry and try to make a synthesis of all that was said above. In Part One, in which "the theory itself" was supposed to be established, the reader may have noticed that we did not go straight to the generative trajectory, but first offered a panorama of the field of musical semiotics. This did not pretend to be an exhaustive history of musical semiotics,[1] but rather as preparation of the soil from which the theory would grow. The background of the theory was manifold, drawing from so-called classical semiotics, from Peirce to Greimas, and from some great thinkers in the tradition of musicology, from Ernst Kurth to Boris Asafiev.

A cornerstone of the whole generative model—the level of the modalities—was approached not only through Greimas, but also via the modal logic of the Finnish philosopher Georg Henry von Wright. It is through this crucial phase of modalities that the semiotic approach has gained a more "cognitive" nature. Yet I hope not too much so, since a common counterargument against the modalities, especially as a tool for music analysis, is that they are too subjective. Nevertheless, let us repeat that modalities are not invented or introduced unexpectedly, without objective, empirical bases in the text itself. It is the temporal, spatial, and actorial articulations on the previous level of the generative course, that, so to speak, produce the modalities or allow them to emerge. It might be tempting to try studying the prefigurements of modalities on a concrete and detailed level in the musical discourse, e.g., by attempting to determine accurate modal values for different intervals, rhythms, chords, timbres, and so on. But such an enterprise might lead to a "dictionary" of modalities whose validity would certainly be questionable, because the modalities are first and foremost of a contextual nature.

Another criticism concerning the universality of modal concepts was expressed by anthropologist Elli-Kaija Köngäs-Maranda, who is well known for her studies in North American Indian mythology. In a conversation with me she wondered whether the old German modal verbs (*dürfen, wollen, können*) might have a legitimacy in a broader, non-European cultural framework. Naturally, it might be very hard for a cultural outsider even to speak of the inner modalities of a text whose codes and isotopies are unknown to her- or himself. Therefore modalities obviously exist only within a certain competency. But this is not proof against their existence or their decisive role in many a sign process.

Let us not be too positivistic, and reject something only on the grounds that we cannot yet quantify it (albeit the analysis of Chopin's Ballade in G minor was perhaps a first step in that direction). In any case, the modalities are linked with previous observations on musical time, space, and actors.

Musical time was conceived as an encounter of two paradigms: that of memory, which increases as a musical piece moves toward its end, and that of expectation, which diminishes in the course of a composition, since according to information theory our expectations are naturally greatest at the beginning and decrease as we know about the style and grammar of the piece, and can thus infer how it will probably end.

The most important finding regarding musical space was perhaps the distinction between its inner and outer aspects. It was also shown how the musical space, too, is *per se* of a modal nature and not just an indifferent, physical coordinate of "high" and "low" pitches and other sound materials.

The discussion of musical actors makes one ponder the nature of musical subjects. We took into account the fact that the subject can be situated either on the levels of enunciate (the text itself) or of enunciation (the process of text production, the act of enunciating or uttering). In the former case we suggested that a musical actor can be an entity that carries various activities, effectuates them, and serves as a ground for different modalities. It would be difficult to speak about any musical action or 'doing' without noticing who or what is acting or doing. The same holds true for modalities. A musical subject is an entity that supports the modalities. It would be oversophisticated to talk about 'will', 'can', or 'must' if there were no one who wants to, can, or must do something. Therefore, ultimately actoriality is the principle that makes (often otherwise abstract) musical discourse to some extent anthropomorphic in nature.

In spite of the centrality of Greimasian reasoning in our theory, there is also room for other methods, such as that of Charles S. Peirce. A theory of musical semiotics might have been built exclusively on the Peircean basis. Nevertheless, and without committing eclecticism, as a musicologist I felt entitled to use many of Peirce's concepts alongside those of Greimas, when they are called for by the musical facts under investigation. Being fully aware of the discrepancies of the epistemological choices of these two great semioticians, I still think it possible to use them side by side, though without mixing the two.

Part Two sought to demonstrate how the theory works in practice, showing how the theory can apply to musical works from extremely different style periods, from Viennese Classicism to Minimalism. In order to avoid reductionism, which is often committed by structuralist models of analysis, in each analysis the method is somewhat different, reflecting the varying characters of the musical pieces themselves.

In the analysis of the first movement of Beethoven's "Waldstein," the most pertinent level was taken to be that of musical actors. Here it may be appropriate to clarify the difference between the concepts of actor and actant. Actants are functional roles into which musical themes (actors) can be situated. Just as in folk tales, as analyzed by Vladimir Propp, one actantial role can manifest itself in several different actors. Greimas's actantial model of mythical communication consists in actants such as subject and object, sender and receiver, helper and opponent, each of which may appear through various actors. Likewise in a musical piece, let us say in a sonata, the role of the principal theme-actant can be taken over by various musical actors. Also in the "Waldstein" analysis, we experimented with a special method of measuring the tensions inherent in musical space and with relating the inner and outer space with each other.

In the two studies of Chopin, the semiotic analysis became narrative in the proper sense. By narrativity in music we understood two things: Narrativity is a music-historical fact conveyed by compositions that, either by their special style and *topos* or by their literary programs, evoke the area of narration; and narrativity is a structural phenomenon wherein almost any musical piece unfolding in time and making something become something else is narrative.

In this study, narrativity in the former sense was approached in the analyses of Liszt and Fauré in Chap. 7. In the latter sense, the Chopin studies focused on semantic structures of the pieces in question. One may say of the *Polonaise-Fantaisie* as well as of G minor Ballade that they are narrative without telling a specific story. My main interest has therefore been in those purely musical structures that enable those pieces to tell some story to a listener.

The study of the *Polonaise-Fantaisie* was based on the simple idea of first segmenting the piece into what I called narrative programs, and then of using the semiotic square as the deep structure that generates the narrative arch and tension of the whole piece. Besides a systematic working through of all the levels of the generative course, the main achievement in the analysis of G minor Ballade was the modal grammar. Therein the various modalities—which by nature are continuous, dynamic, and tensional—were digitalized with five different degrees, ranging from extremely positive (++) to extremely negative (--). This made it possible to formalize the modal content of the whole piece, which might prove useful for a computer analysis. Nevertheless there remained questions or gaps to be filled by subsequent studies. Namely, in the desire to pursue a complete analysis of the piece, I mostly moved on the textual level of macrosyntagms without determining the modalities on the microlevel. In the same way as in cognitive musicology there has been talk of a subsemantic phase (particularly by Marc Leman); one might speak about submodalities, that is, smaller articulations of 'will', 'can' , 'must', and the rest. We may need to establish a vocabulary or repertory of these sub-units in order to analyze, say, pieces by Giacinto Scelsi, Kaija Saariaho, Tristan Murail, Magnus Lindberg, or other composers of so-called spectral music, which apparently consists of one, incessant 'being' but which also contains interesting variations on the micro- or sublevel of this main modality.

With the study of Liszt's *Vallée d'Obermann*, inspired by Étienne de Sénancour's novel, and of the Fauré/Bussine song, "Après un rêve," I entered the area of intertextuality. Moreover, in Fauré's case I also moved from examination of the enunciate (the score and its inherent isotopies and modalities) to the study of the enunciation (performance or interpretation). In the latter case I no longer spoke about modalities but about modalizations. In the Appendix I tried to elucidate twenty-two different modalizations of the Fauré song, by singers, cellists, and violinists. I considered this elucidation possible only after a careful study of the musical text itself. It is very hard, to my mind, to separate the research of musical performance from the music itself—enunciation from enunciate, to put it in semiotic terms.

In the chapter dealing with Musorgsky's *Pictures at an Exhibition*, I made an excursion into the use of Peirce's semiotics, especially his concepts of Firstness, Secondness, and Thirdness. I tried to show that the musical form of different "pictures" does not seem to follow the inherent musical logic itself, but emerges from the inner subject, the spectator or listener whose modalizing attitude decides, among other things, when a piece closes or begins. The analysis also aimed to demonstrate that some Greimasian and Peircean concepts could be employed side by side without any contradiction and without a strictly axiomatic generative procedure.

With the Sibelius analysis in Chap. 9 I tried to reach a level of reflection that would lead us beyond traditional and often fixed national meanings, such as the "landscape tradition" of interpreting Sibelius's music. In this sense the study could be called deconstructionist as well as narrativistic.

With certain key concepts of our method, Debussy's Impressionism was investigated in the next chapter. It was revealed that Prelude no. 7 from Book 2 (". . . La terrasse des audiences du clair de lune") was not so much a realistic-impressionistic portrayal—as are many of his other preludes—as a special transformation of narrative elements that were already organized in an anti-narrative way.

With Minimalism (Chap. 10.2) we are faced with a music that is not narrative in the Classical sense but nonetheless semiotic in nature. The role of repetition in Minimalism was clarified by means of theories by the Russian Formalist Yuri Tynianov. "Absent" meanings were examined in the so-called *musique pauvre* of Arvo Pärt. In the end, we concluded that the power of modalization still seems to play a crucial role in the cognition of music such as John Cage's *Changes*.

Despite the variety of these illustrations of the theory, it seems to me that it provides a "method," a procedure that can be repeated and used in different musical situations. Now seeing my "method" as a single entity, I can also see how to continue its development. On one hand, the basic theoretical concepts of the method must be continuously reconsidered and sharpened. On the other, totally new paths may open up from concepts such as *subject* and lead us to observations that enter the domain of what I should like to call "existential semiotics."

APPENDIX

Analysis of Recorded Performances of "Après un rêve" from Chap. 7.2

Vocal Interpretations

Pierre Bernac

The old rule that "to move other people, the artist himself must not be moved" seems to hold true for Bernac's interpretation. It is characterized by accurate following of the text, with only small nuances added. In a word, it is a well-balanced, classical interpretation.

The tempo is moderate, with metronome marking of $\flat$ = 134. The voice tries to bring out the phonetic values of the words, not so much the semantic ones. Vibrato is used in such a way that it does not disturb the normal, basic quality of the voice. Breathing and phrasing strictly follow the instructions in the text. Only in two places ("je t'appelle, ô nuit" and "reviens, ô nuit" before the exclamation) does Bernac break the phrase, by adding an extra breath. In terms of dynamics, the only deviation from the text is the *pianissimo* repetition of the word "hélas." The fact that Bernac separates the *crescendo* which precedes the climax from the *accelerando*—which many other performers, particularly instrumentalists, combine at precisely this place—illustrates his control of musical techniques. *Glissandi* are typical, especially for long notes ("l'auro-o-o-re").

The semantic gesture of the interpretation emphasizes the *topos* "after the dream," where the performer as the subject of the enunciation situates himself. Modally, there prevails a combination of 'not will' (no strong energetic moment), 'knowing' (the cognitive moment dominates), 'can' (vocal techniques are in the foreground, because of the high degree of control), and 'must' (an interpretation that follows certain norms). The basic modality is 'being', the striving for balance or relative stability.

Kiri Te Kanawa

In this interpretation the semantic value of the words is the least important aspect; the instrumentality of the voice projects above all else. The voice seems to become suspended on long notes and to expand from them into an object of admiration for the listeners. The singing subject places herself outside all *topoi* of the poem. The tempo, $\flat$ = 98, is slower than Bernac's, which increases the possibilities of creating more vocal nuances. The words are not easily discerned, because of the instrumentality of the voice; likewise, little meaning seems to be given to the phonetic values of the text. Much vibrato is used. Generally, the breathing departs from the marks in the text, in favor of longer slurs. The breath pauses, which Bernac respects as norms, are here almost unnoticeable. The voice attempts to create a perfect illusion of immateriality; in this interpretation there is very little of Roland Barthes's "phenotext" (1977: 179–89). Maximal indexicality and contiguity prevail. The climactic "Hélas" is thus performed without abandon, and the dotted rhythms are not stressed ("Je t'appelle"). There are many *glissandi* in the scale passages, particularly in descending ones ("vers la lumière"), but none at all in the larger intervallic leaps—all quite different from Bernac's performance. The basic modality is 'being', along with 'not-will' and 'not-must' (no obedience to the style is essential here), while 'can' and 'knowing', complete control and knowledge, are strongly emphasized.

Claire Croiza

Throughout, the paradigm of this performance seems to be the most historically accurate. The restless alternation of tempos and the deficiencies in vocal technique are particularly striking features. The interpretation is based on the imitation of speech, as in a chanson. Although Paul Valéry apparently considered Croiza's voice the most beautiful in the world (Cooper 1978), it belongs to spoken theatre not to the art of singing. The tempo at the beginning is ♪ = 132–34, but the basic pulsation varies so much that it cannot be determined precisely. There is relatively little vibrato, and the breathing is very obvious, since the singer must cut short the longer notes, add breaths, and start the triplet figure, among others, almost always too early. The very first phrase, "Dans un sommeil," is divided into three discrete quarter notes instead of a conjunct movement. Since the tempo is very fast, the words on short notes have to be performed as in a recitative, *quasi parlando*. Other phenomenal qualities of the voice are exploited, too, like *glissandi* and the thick, open sound at "splendeurs." The most important stylistic devices are the retardations and accelerations throughout the piece, which create the dramatic structure. The sharpness of the dotted notes is stressed ("Je t'appelle").

The basic modality is 'doing' (*faire*). Techniques are not controlled, which produces 'cannot'. The 'knowing' of the singer focuses on displaying the dramatic content of the text. The moment of 'willing' is likewise great in this interpretation. The singer functions as a subject who puts herself into the events and who experiences all three states of the poem; yet she does not relate them in an elegiac or balladic way, but keeps to the light style of a salon concert. Thus the listener is not much moved by the realistic illusion of the tune itself. Rather, the interpretation distances itself from the listener's modalities.

Nan Merrimam

The most important interpretational means for Merrimam is retardation. This is why the basic tempo is relatively fast, ♪ = 120. Nevertheless, she does not make *ritardandi* in order to extend the words, but to provide the song with a "languido" tinge. That is also why the interpretation as a whole is not dramatic. In some places the retardation gives certain words an emphasis (like "triste reveil") which justifies the relation of the interpretation to the semiotic content and its textual topos. The "awakening" is the most conspicuous of all these.

Throughout the piece the voice has a thin quality, with much vibrato. Breathing follows the breaks marked in the text, but without any underlining. This is an objective interpretation that inclines toward the instrumentality of the voice. *Ritardandi* can be heard as attempts to escape the action, i.e., as 'not-doing'. The performance is likewise characterized by 'not-willing' (no strong energetic charge) and by neutral usage of both 'can' and 'knowing'. The constantly vibrating voice serves as a unifying style feature.

Regine Crespin

The semantic gesture of Crespin's interpretation is heaviness and abandonment to the dream *topos*. The listener can hardly believe that any awakening could occur in the song, so prevalent is the sinking into the isotopy of the dream. In particular, the emphasis on the descending scale passages with *glissandi*, retardation, and small *crescendos* creates the impression of the heaviness of the dream. The overall flavor is one of repressed passion.

The basic tempo is relatively slow, ♪ = 100, and as an almost harmful mannerism, the singer slows down at the end of almost every phrase. The longer and more stressed notes are, as it were, grasped from below with a glissando. On the other hand, the triplet melismas are always performed with retardation, and clearly, the last time ("mystérieuse"), as in a vocalise, thin, as if played by an instrument—almost like an allusion to plain chant. As regards dynamics, the climax ("hélas") is sung *fortissimo* and followed by *subito pianissimo*, not however with a repetition of that word, but as late as the word "songes." In the French tradition, the breaths carefully follow the slurs marked in the text, except toward the end, where in favor of a conjunct, ascending line Crespin sacrifices one breath pause ("reviens, radieuse"); the same happens in the fifth bar from the end.

The dominant modal value of the singing is its dramatic quality, which emerges from the contrasts between the 'being' of the dream and the 'doing' of the awakening and recollection of the dream. There is 'can' in Crespin's interpretation, a superb 'knowing', and some 'must' (in the phrasing). Although the abundant use of *ritardandi* determines the modality as that of 'being,' it also manifests a very strong tendency to *non-être*, toward drama and action. The subjects of enunciate and enunciation tend to fuse, because of the abandonment of the latter.

Elly Ameling

The first point to be made here concerns tempo. The basic tempo can be characterized as mobile: ♪ = 116, which is rigorously maintained until the end. What is this *devoir* of the tempo supposed to convey? Ameling's most important devices are slight glissandi and the careful, subtle phrasing of the melismas. In the triplet figure she has time to make two *crescendos* and to allow longer tones to blossom forth and die away, most typically in the first "reviens" call. Yet these subtle nuances do not seem to be determined by the dramatic-narrative structure of the song. Rather, this case represents a variant of interpretations based on the instrumentality of the voice. In any case, the general flavor is narrative, while at the same time distant and objective. The basic quality of the voice is light and wafting.

The fundamental modality is an active 'doing', but on the purely musical level of the voice. In fact, the whole interpretation is far from the dream *topos*, not to speak of the awakening. 'Knowing' and 'can' are rather strong, along with kinetic 'will'. In the phrasing at the end, some breath pauses are eliminated; this occurs in other interpretations where a sufficiently fast tempo and a firm control of vocal techniques make it possible.

Gerard Friedmann

The choice of tempo, ♪ = 120, supports the general mood of the interpretation, which is light, lyrical, and *bel canto*. The Italian style is suggested by accentuated breathing, the aspirant quality, and *crescendos* on individual tones that end in a pathetic and sudden way (for example, on "radieuse"). On the other hand, in the first half of the song there are strong *crescendos*, even marked in the text ("Tu rayonnais" and "Tu m'appelais"), which can be interpreted as a decrease of the role of the actant "tu." In other regards, too, the interpretation stresses the actant "je" and his state after the dream, which is neither dramatized nor transformed into a particularly dysphoric longing for the state of the dream. A contrast to the fairly abundant use of vibrato is formed by the speechlike recitation of short notes (for example, "ta voix pure et sonore"), i.e., with articulation in the front of the mouth. There are few glissandi, and the phrasing is remarkably free, hardly following the original text. As a whole, this interpretation stresses 'being', while the cognitive ('knowing'), normative ('must'), and energetic ('willing') moments are inessential.

Ian Partridge

The basic modality of this interpretation is demanding, begging, moaning, emphasized by descending glissandi, even on consecutive notes of a scale. Vibrato is used in a very controlled way in order to increase the modality of begging. The basic tempo is the same as with Friedmann but varies greatly. A special mannerism is a strong retardation on the melismatic triplet figure ("mirage," etc.). The overall flavor supports Fauré's performance instruction of *dolce*; accordingly, all the consonants are extremely soft, even on fast notes (as on "éclairé par l'aurore"), unlike the interpretations of singers who insist on a speechlike articulation of these passages. The phrasing is free and omits some breath marks. An archetypal figure of the interpretation here is the linking of *glis-sandi, crescendo/diminuendo,* and vibrato, as shown in Ex. 1.

Appendix Example 1. Fauré, "Après un rêve."

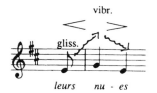

In terms of its modal values this represents the category of 'not-being' or the striv-ing for action. In this sense it realizes the figure of begging, a very common figure in French music. One can even distinguish the /e/ "muette," a mute and unheard /e/ vowel at the end of a motif. Teachers of instrumental music use this linguistic metaphor in order to illustrate the rounding of light phrase endings. (Jules Gentil, at the École Nor-male de Musique in Paris, used to advise students to play the phrase in Ex. 2 by imagining the words "je vous prie.")

Appendix Example 2. Franck: Prelude, Chorale, and
Fugue, m. 25.

Nikolai Gedda

This performance is not characterized by the instrumentality or speech-likeness of the voice, but by its own voice-likeness; i.e., the foregrounding of the voice itself seems to neglect all other aspects of interpretation and to make the singer rather indifferent and insensitive regarding the semantic structure of the music and text. The vibrato comes to be an entirely dominant style feature, omnipresent in the interpretation. The basic dynamic is *forte,* which tends to make the triplet melismas sound harsh. As to the tempo, the starting point is the same as with the preceding singers. Instead of *dolce* the performance advice seems to be *giusto.* Glissandi are not used at the beginning, only just before the climax, the "hélas," which is raised in the heroic tenor style and not as a sign or symbol of the awakening. The very frequent use of vibrato combined with *crescendos* in the final section emphasizes the brilliance of the voice, but does not at all fit with the *topos* and the inner modalities of the song itself.

The whole interpretation is therefore characterized by a strong 'can do', but with a complete blindness to 'knowing', particularly regarding the poetic content of the song. This also illustrates how the 'must' in the act of enunciation—in this case the Italian *bel canto*, with its norms and clichés—can entirely mask the 'must' of the enunciate (text) itself and the norms set by the composer. The modality of 'will' also receives a positive value exclusively on the level of musical enunciation, in this case that of the singing.

A semiotic analysis of interpretation cannot be a norm-setting process, but some critical conclusions may follow from the analysis. As to this interpretation: even a great singer can be wrong!

Frederica von Stade

The slower the tempo, the easier it is for an interpreter to add his or her own surmodalizations to the text itself; while on the other hand its coherence and tension—what semiotics calls its indexicality—become more difficult. This performance is the slowest of all ($\flat$ = 84), but von Stade exploits the slowness as a resource for a repressed passion, with a dreamlike state and dramaticism emerging from it. Of all the *topoi* of the song, the state of the dream is the most striking. Momentarily the tempo seems to stop altogether, as if sleep-walking.

The interpreter is also fascinated by the phonetic values of the text ("le bonheur," etc.); she alternates the roles of open and closed long vowels. Vibrato is not very open; glissandi occur almost everywhere, especially at the beginning. Dynamic differences are used to build the form: the first section is *pianissimo* and the second *forte*. This becomes dramatically manifest at the beginning of the second section ("je quittais la terre"), which suddenly becomes very passionate.

Modally, the most outstanding feature is the combination 'will not-to-be', or the will to escape from 'being', which intention, however, remains almost obscured, since the temporal dimension is so conspicuously ruled by 'cannot', or the inability to act. As to the cognitive content, the phonetic level is particularly stressed, as is the semantic structure of the poetic text. Otherwise the interpretation in many regards goes against the 'must' of the text as well as that of the interpretive tradition.

Barbra Streisand

Surprisingly, Streisand's interpretation, generally speaking, may sound amazingly faithful to the instructions given by Fauré. Nevertheless, some traits, such as the re-orchestration typical of Hollywood film music, place the whole performance in a quite different isotopy, a sphere of style norms, or 'must', that differs from the preceding *lied* interpretations. In comparison with the tradition of the *lied* or *mélodie*, this interpretation comes across as *kitsch* because features of the musical text are stressed that are not relevant to the musical logic. Of course a *kitsch* interpretation also has its own semantic universe of values: in this case the dream *topos* and its spatial metaphors ("je quittais la terre," "lumière," "ciel," etc.) are foregrounded, as a release from the force of gravity. Echo effects are produced by recording techniques and additional ascending lines for the violins. Yet here the interpreter is evidently not aiming to reveal a semantic structure hidden in the poem, since she is captivated by the semantic content of individual words, giving them an exaggerated, almost banal stress ("je t'appelle," "rends-moi tes mensonges," "mystérieuse"). The emphasizing of the French /r/ consonant ("pure") serves this same goal. This text-bound starting point makes her violate the musical logic, for instance, she gives too much stress to the weak tones at the ends of bars ("que charmait ton . . ."). There are many places where Streisand also performs quite contrarily to what is written in the music, for no apparent artistic reason (for example, the *diminuendo pro crescendo* on "tu rayonnais," the change of the triplets into dotted notes on "je quittais la," *calando diminuendo* at the word "radieuse" *pro forte*, etc.).

The general modality of the interpretation is a languishing 'not-will' combined with detailed attention to the 'knowing', 'can', and 'must' appropriate to entertainment music.

What is felt as excessive liberty and arbitrariness regarding the performance of Classical music is here quite deliberate and subject to the norms of a different musical style.

Katia Ricciarelli

The most operatic interpretation is undoubtedly that of Ricciarelli. The basic tempo is hard to define because of great liberties, but its average metronome value is $\flat$ = 116. Ricciarelli uses a strong aspirant quality and interrupts long lines, albeit following Fauré's marks, where most other performers tend to create longer phrases. Sudden accelerations and retardations break the global form of the song, or rather prevent that form from emerging. The interpreter abandons herself to the poetic content of the text, not focusing so fragmentarily on separate words as Streisand does, but nevertheless taking such short units that the semantic structure of the background does not become explicit. Her aim is to create contrasts on the surface level of the text (*crescendo/diminuendo, accelerando/ ritardando, forte/subito piano*; see, for example, the section of "hélas, hélas"). Breaths are heard very strongly, which appears to be part of her style and not some overindulgence to be fought against. Carrying on the notion of contrast, the modalizations also take place as quick alternations of contrary modalities: 'will/will not', 'doing/not doing'. As to the norms of the *lied* tradition, Ricciarelli transforms the instructions of the text quite freely, thus representing the principle of 'not-must'. Instead she follows the rules of operatic interpretation, whereas Streisand subordinates the song to the conventions of entertainment music.

Instrumental Interpretations

Entirely different problems naturally arise in the instrumental arrangements for violoncello by Pablo Casals and for violin by A. Bachmann. Still, some dimensions concerning singing—tempo, vibrato, dynamics, phrasing, glissandi, and construction of the global form—remain valid. On the other hand, it is impossible to know whether cellists and violinists are conscious of the musical-poetic semantics of the song, which the models of *topos* and actants discussed above make explicit. There is rather a secondary semantics in a more abstract sense. For example, the plot which the interpretation (enunciation) provides for the musical text (enunciate) can well be manifested as a narrative program, according to which the climax of the work means the attainment of or conjunction with the valued object. The preceding phases, then, express separation or disjunction from the valued object and efforts of varying success to attain it. From the perspective of the semantics of instrumental music, it is undecidable as to which concrete figure of the poetic text, which actant, would be joined to this sought-for object of value ("tu" or "nuit mysterieuse").

Sasha Vectomov

The Casals arrangement is already a modalization of Fauré's melody. The line has been made more continuous by eliminating some rhythmic figures given by the text. The second section has been placed an octave higher, which in itself modalizes that section with a stronger 'will' and 'can'. On the other hand, the piece contains two climaxes, in the places corresponding to the words "hélas" (m. 31) and "radieuse" (m. 41), on the tones F5 and E♭5 (this arrangement is in the key of C minor). Casals orders the octave leap after the F5 (m. 31) to be played without glissando. The cello enables one to realize a longer melodic line, or *Bewegungsphase* (Kurth 1922: 21–25) than does singing, which is subordinated to the demands of breathing.

One problem in the piece is the transition from the symmetrical, repeated sections to the culmination of the end and the attainment of the object of value. Many cellists start to accelerate as early as the end of the second section, as if beginning another piece. This happens in Vectomov's interpretation. The tones where the climax is, or should be, are not played here with the greatest possible *forte*; rather, the dynamic climax precedes attainment of the sought-for tone. In both cases the main stress is on the action, not on the object of the action.

Modally, in this interpretation the piece is divided, more clearly than with the singers, into one section of 'being' (the two sections of the beginning) and one of 'doing' (the final section). This syntagmatic division of the fundamental modalities is also supported by the change of tempo, from $\flat$ = 104 of the beginning, to a remarkably faster tempo in the final section. The soloist does not particularly display his technical skills, thus the 'can' degree is not so great in this interpretation.

Janos Starker

This interpretation divides the piece abruptly into two segments: an inexpressive and "distant" initial part (mm. 1–16) and a more nuanced latter part. In the first half Starker omits almost all dynamic signs and thus creates a modalization of 'know'/ 'not-will'/ 'do'. Correspondingly, in the latter half he neglects all performance instructions that would obstruct the forward motion, the 'will do' of the music. He provides the climactic F5 and E♭5 with a euphoric value: they become musical objects of value which are sought-for and attained, so that the musical subject is conjuncted to its object (which can be formulated with the symbols S1 ∧ O1 and S1 ∧ O2). The average tempo is $\flat$ = 108, becoming faster before the climaxes and slowing at the end. The whole interpretation is characterized by discretion, which demands a technical 'can' and 'knowing' of its own.

Pablo Casals

The most outstanding feature in the Casals performance is very frequent use of glissandi. He also divides the piece into two parts: the beginning, with a slow tempo—but unlike in Starker, with an extremely nuanced expressivity—and then the action in the proper sense in the latter half. Here again the tempo becomes more agitated and in m. 24 seems to begin an entirely new piece. Since Casals uses glissando as a continuous stylistic device (as Nikolai Gedda uses his vibrato), it is no wonder that he marks at least one moment where glissando must *not* be used, namely, in the climax after the F1. It is also amusing that he does not follow his own arrangement but, e.g., twice plays the notes of the triplet figure differently from what is written in the score, in mm. 7 and 22.

After the climax, when the object formed by the F1 has been attained, the renunciation and withdrawal occur so quickly that one almost believes the piece is ending with mm. 32–33, but they make the next culmination only the more surprising with its *molto accelerando*. Casals builds a small drama within this brief composition. In particular, the expressive possibilities, 'can', of the cello are here efficiently exploited, as well as rather straightforward alternations between 'being' and 'doing'. Casals's basic tempo is $\flat$ = c. 98.

Antonio Janigro

A semiotician should not advance his own evaluations as axiological units. In this case, however, one has to say that the structures of the musical enunciation fit splendidly with the structure of the enunciate itself, as interpreted above. Among the vocal interpretations one might be tempted to compare this with Crespin's, with the controlled formation and coloring of each individual tone. Glissando is used very moderately, mostly in the smaller intervals, not in the great leaps. The isotopies of the original song are transparent in this interpretation: the dream (mm. 1–28), the awakening (mm. 29–32), and after the dream, or the demand of the return of the night (mm. 33–47).

The tempo throughout is remarkably slow, $\flat$ = 86. The dream of the beginning is described with a light, suspending, retarding procedure. The triplet figures are played exactly, without manneristic nuances, as strong-weak-weak (in other respects, the interpretation is also ideally instrumental). Otherwise Janigro builds his interpretation completely contrary to the dynamic marks suggested by Casals: where there should be *crescendo poco a poco* (m. 27), there is *subito piano*; instead of *diminuendo* in

m. 33, one hears a strong *crescendo*. Moreover, with an understatement technique, Janigro has the rare capacity for changing the single-line melody into a polyphonic texture by creating abrupt changes of levels (especially at m. 37). He constructs three climaxes in his interpretation: the F5 in m. 31, E♭5 in m. 35, and E♭5 again in m. 41. An ideal balance of all the modalities prevails in this performance.

Mstislav Rostropovitch

A very strong intensity of sound is typical of this interpretation. The awakening occurs right after the first section, when the muted *tranquillo* flavor changes into a passionate and demanding 'will to-do'. Whereas all the previous interpretations give up the sought-for value object immediately after the climax, this interpretation maintains and revels in the victories achieved.

Temporally, the performance is audacious and follows the old rule according to which one can slow down as much as one likes *before* the first beat of the bar, but on the strong beat of the next bar the tempo must be resumed. By this means Rostropovitch changes the texture at the end into an expressive recitative. Vibrato is frequently and brilliantly used, and perhaps because of this the element of 'can' rules over 'knowing', the intellectual, cognitive category. The focus is in any case on 'doing', action, on the *Diesseitigkeit*.

Paul Tortelier

Tortelier's interpretation might be considered "Cartesian," in the sense that it respects the requirements ('must') of the temporal category faithfully and systematically, and has expelled the mystic night altogether: after the first two lines, the performance moves directly into the daylight of *mezzo forte*. As a mannerism, Tortelier gives an additional accentuation to the first, strong beats of the bars, which, coupled with the relatively fast tempo ($\flat$ = 112) naturally gives the interpretation a sturdy movement. The attainment of the climax, the F5 and E♭5, occurs in a triumphant way, not demanding or begging, as with other interpreters. At the end of m. 34, Tortelier adds one sixteenth note in order to increase the effect of the upbeat. The whole modalization of the piece differs in a strange way from the hidden modalities of the musical enunciation itself. The entire tune has been placed into a fairly monotonous category of 'can do'. No epistemic dimensions of truth or lie are evoked in the listener, but the playing represents the category of a "naked truth."

André Navarra

The general mood of this performance is light and unsentimental, trying to avoid all touching gestures. This is mainly brought about by the rather fast tempo, $\flat$ = 124. There are neither glissandi, those direct signs of emotion in the musical enunciation, nor vibrato as a kinetic or thymic device. In fact, this performance is also far from the aesthetic of the original song. Its modalizing impact has been consciously alienated; its starting point seems to be an unsentimental performance of a salon piece, a *Charakterstück*.

Arthur Grumiaux

In Bachmann's violin arrangement the modal values of different registers of the instrument are employed very efficiently. Because the main section of the piece, beginning with the repetition of m. 1 at m. 17, is placed in the upper register, one surprisingly experiences this section as belonging to the isotopy of the dream, as if it were phantasmagoria. This impression would be even stronger if the relatively fast tempo, $\flat$ = 108, and the exaggerated accentuation of the beginnings of the bars did not make the piece as a whole more energetic and disciplined. The most pertinent stylistic means used by Grumiaux are the accentuation of separate tones and relatively large dynamic differences.

Aleksandr Knjazev

This interpretation is a "normal" case, as far as that can be defined, and it shows how there is more and more recurrence as the paradigm becomes more and more extensive. After all, the possibilities of musical enunciation are limited. The tempo is average, ♪ = 102. The most important factor making the music a narration is perhaps that, after the first culmination on F5, the performer still plays *forte* for four bars, and after the next climax, on E♭5, this *forte* is given up with a languishing gesture that underlines the surprise of yet a third climax on the second E♭5, in m. 41.

Andrew Lloyd Webber

The last of our last sample intonations only adds the idea that the change of register in m. 17 can also be made as unnoticeable as possible. In this case the dynamics are fairly uniform (*mezzo forte*) throughout the piece, except for the *forte* at the end. Against this background, some nuances of *subito piano* appear as interesting deviations. The choice of tempo is ♪ = 96. The modalizations emphasize 'being', despite the overall loud dynamics. There is no obvious attempt to escape from this state of 'being', which is securely established in the very first bars. Therefore, even the modality of 'will' remains weak.

GLOSSARY

Actant, actantial role, actor: Actants are syntactic units, in the form of binary oppositions, that precede semantic investment. Developed temporally as actantial pairs, actants become a story. Actantial roles are defined in terms of their modal content and function in a narrative. Several actors may embody a single actant, or one actor may fulfil a variety of actantial roles. Actors emerge through semes of individuation and so become points of convergence between syntax and semantics.

Agent/patient: Actantial pair consisting of doer of an action (agent) and receiver of that action (patient). See actant.

Aspectual categories: Qualitative terms for processes. We can for example understand inchoativity/durativity/terminativity as qualitative aspects of the beginning/middle/end paradigm typical of traditional (Western) narrative plots. These categories also appear as binary oppositions; e.g., *achèvement/inachèvement* or completion/incompletion.

Destinatee: Receiver half of the actantial pair, sender/receiver (see **actant**).

Engagement/disengagement (*embrayage/débrayage*): **Spatial** disengagement occurs upon moving away from any text's norm of location—its "here." **Temporal** disengagement is a proceeding into the past or future in relation to a textual "now." **Actorial** disengagement draws attention away from a central "ego" by focusing on other actors. Engagement reverses disengagement.

Enunciation/enunciate: **Enunciation** is the act of producing a phrase or an entire "text"; in music, the act of writing, performing, listening, and interpreting a musical work. The **enunciate** is the result of this act, a fixed object or the "text" itself; in music, a composition, musical message, the score itself. Narrative theories distinguish subjects of enunciation and enunciate, for example, a composer as a real person and as a fictive "hero" in a musical text (as in a symphonic poem).

Euphoria/dysphoria: wellness/unwellness; in Greimas, aspects of the thymic category, which derives from human sensory perception. Plato (in the *Republic*) opposed the thymic or animalistic to the rational side of human nature.

Generative course: Moving from simplest to most complex, from abstract to concrete, Greimas's generative course, unlike Chomsky's generative grammar, aims to account for both semantics and syntax at every level, and ultimately for all semiotic systems.

Greimas, A. J. (1917–1992): Lithuanian-born founder of the so-called Parisian school of semioticians. Current narratology originated in the work of Greimas, T. Todorov, G. Genette, and R. Barthes. Greimas's work, taking its point of departure from the linguistics of Saussure, Hjelmslev, and Jakobson and from the narrative theory of Russian formalist Vladimir Propp, represents the most sustained attempt to deal with semantic as well as formal structures of signifying systems.

Index, icon, symbol/legisign, sinsign, qualisign: Philosopher-logician C. S. Peirce divided signs into three broad categories. *Icons* resemble their object (e.g., photographs are iconic signs). *Indexes* derive from an existential or metonymic relation (e.g., smoke is an index of fire). *Symbols* are stipulated by rule or convention (e.g., national flags). For Peirce, a *legisign* serves as a rule for the production of subsequent signs, i.e., *sinsigns* ("single signs"), which are perceived as *qualisigns*.

Interpretant: According to Peirce, semiosis (the action of signs) involves three coordinates: the sign (something that stands for or represents something else) addresses somebody and creates in that person's mind another sign, the interpretant. The object is that for which a sign stands. See C. S. Peirce, Collected Papers (Cambridge: Harvard University Press, 1931–58), 2.228.

Intonations: In Russian musicologist Boris Asafiev's theory, *intonazia* are phonic manifestations that correlate with the phenomenal world. Musical intonations result when sounds from life experiences, which include inner psychic experiences, are transmuted into musical elements (e.g., a melody) and processes (e.g., growth of musical phrases).

Isotopy: A set of semantic categories whose redundancy guarantees the coherence of a sign-complex and makes possible the uniform reading of any text. Musical isotopies can be formed by deep structure, thematicity, genre features, texture alone, and general text strategies (e.g., plot arrangement).

Langue/parole: In Saussurian linguistics, *langue* is the abstract system by which natural language (*langage*) operates. *Paroles* are non-abstract, concrete realizations of that system in, e.g., speech acts. For example, "cat" may be a noun according to *langue*. In real usage, however, it gains its meaning not from the system, but from its immediate import; e.g., "the cat is on the mat."

Modalities: Modalities are general human ways of evaluation; in language, for example, the subjunctive tense colors speech with wishes and beliefs. As a series of emotional states, modalities account for the way the listener unites a musical text with human values. 'Being' and 'Doing' are the primary modalities, which may combine with other, relatively subordinate modalities such as 'must', 'can', and so on.

Musemes: See **phemes** and **semes**.

Narrative function: In his groundbreaking work during the 1920s, Vladimir Propp conceived of narrative functions as formal roles that operate apart from their particular characterizations. One of Greimas's achievements was to generalize further Propp's functions.

Narrative program (*programme narratif*): Narrative segments, linked causally, that operate at surface levels of a discourse. The minimal narrative program consists in a change of state effected by an actor on any other actor.

Object, conjunction: The object is half of the actantial pair subject/object. Many narratives center on a basic subject/object relationship in which a subject is separated from (disjunction) and struggles for union with (conjunction) its sought-for-object. See **actant**.

Opponent: Half of the actantial pair helper/opponent. See **actant**.

Pheme, seme, lexeme: Of the generic class **musemes**, phemes are distinctive features of the signifier or acoustic substance that, when invested with meaning, become semes or features of the signified (the latter roughly equivalent to "concept"). Several semes may combine into a larger unit, called a lexeme.

Semiotic square: For Greimas, the "elementary structure of signification." Known in philosophical logic as the "square of oppositions," it represents visually the logical articulations of any semantic category. Developing the traditional logical concepts of contradictory (diagonal arrows) and contrary (horizontal arrows), the square diagrams the ways in which, starting from any given term, a complete meaning system can be derived through exhaustion of logical possibilities.

Signifier/signified (Saussure); **expression/content** (Hjelmslev): Unlike Peirce, who viewed signs as trichotomies, Saussure and Hjelmslev view them as two-sided. Very roughly, the signifier is the material (sounding or written) side of the sign; the signified is the thought or concept for which it stands. In music, the signified may be a modality; e.g., a rapid ascending chromatic line can arouse a positive value of 'will'.

Spatial, temporal, actorial categories: See **engagement/disengagement**.

Syntagm/paradigm: In Saussurian linguistics, *langue* functions along two axes. The syntagmatic, or "horizontal," axis unfolds as process (thus a syntagm is a processive element) and the paradigmatic, or "vertical," axis as system.

Uttering/utterance: See **enunciation/enunciate**.

NOTES

1. In Search of a Theory

1. Andre Schaeffner (1968) calls this the "materiality" of music, in the sense of being bound to specific instruments.

2. Investigation of these questions has already begun. Norwegian composer Lasse Thoresen (1987) has developed a method for temporal analysis of musical isotopies (called "time field analysis") which distinguishes three main phases: beginning, developing, and terminating. Boris Asafiev (1977) speaks of *impetus, motus,* and *terminus* as three main phases.

3. Except for the final phrase, where Beethoven, probably deliberately, violates the stylistic norm of a sarabande (Uhde 1974: 470).

4. For a more recent version of this idea see Alexandra and Roger Pierce (1989 and 1991).

5. Wittgenstein called this kind of relational system "family resemblances" (*Familieähnlichkeit*).

6. In Umberto Eco's semiotics, the ideological and the technical represent the external conditions for communication.

7. The concept of musical kinesis is important in the musical semiotics of Ivanka Stoianova (1978), which in turn relies on Ernst Kurth (1922, 1947) and Boris Asafiev (1977).

8. On the other hand, some music cultures are so homogeneous that their rules can be made explicit with such simple dichotomies. See, for example, the generative models developed for Swedish children's songs, in Sundberg et al. (1983).

9. For more on models of discourse about music, see Chap. 2.2, on musical macrotime.

10. In Schumann we find a good example of "absolute" music in Busoni's sense, namely, the beginning of the last movement of his C major Fantasy. It is perhaps the only music that forms a musical counterpart to the extremely abstract and spiritualized "absolute" poetry represented by the chorus of the spirits at the end of Goethe's *Faust* II. But this is only my personal opinion, which would naturally need more argumentation to be semiotically justified as an intertextual comparison.

11. To Busoni's examples one might add works by Chopin, among others, particularly as regards the cadences and endings of his later works, and the tendency toward dissolution of musical form, as in the coda of the F minor Ballade or in the last movement of the Sonata in B♭ minor. Such pieces come very close to the music that Busoni mentioned as freed from conventional form; their goal is to attain something unknown and to break the symmetrical conception of form.

12. The concept of isotopy also comes close to that of "time-span" by Lerdahl and Jackendoff or "time-field" by Lasse Thoresen. The dominant unit of an isotopy is called a "head" by Lerdahl and Jackendoff, a "dominant" by Russian formalists, a "nuclear lexeme" by linguists.

13. To use David Lidov's terms, it is not so much a principle of musical "design" as that of "grammar" (1980: 55–59).

14. In one sense, Asafiev's (1977) notion of intonation concerns just this anthropomorphic level of music, insofar as intonations are modalized or perhaps axiologized musical units which remain in human musical memory and form the store of intonations of a given period.

15. Talk of "intuition" may well sound naive from the viewpoint of semiotics, which aims at precision, but intuition can nevertheless serve as the starting point for semiotic work. One may take as a methodological principle, à la Henri Bergson, the argument that intuition always precedes analysis. The problem is how to transform this intuition into a communicable model.

16. In these scenes one may almost speak of the semiotics of silence in the same sense as Jankélévitch speaks about pauses in music: "Music emerges from silence; music is interrupted or temporarily disturbed silence" (1961: 170). The fact that even silence speaks in opera and that the above-mentioned scenes are, in spite of everything, experienced as unflaggingly intensive, is due to the continuity that the deep modal level gives to the events onstage. The muteness of Wagner's protagonists, as Adorno says, only underlines this modal level, which is hidden but present at every moment.

17. Arnold Schoenberg, *Theory of Harmony*, trans. Roy E. Carter (Los Angeles: University of California Press, 1978).

18. This point of view recalls the problem of *pensée structurale* and *pensée structurelle*, i.e., whether musical structures exist *a priori* when the composer/musicologist/listener merely finds them, or whether the composer/musicologist/listener always creates a new structure, his or her own version based on personal intellect and fantasy.

19. In speaking of 'will' in music, we refer not only to Schopenhauer but also to Swiss music psychologist Ernst Kurth, who considered all music a manifestation of the 'will' (*Willenerscheinung*).

20. This process of comparison is not far removed from Peirce's idea of "correspectiveness" between a sign and its *interpretant*. Only here it is done in purely musical terms as opposed to any literary, visual, or other intertextual interpretations of music.

21. Negation through silence can be a real negation only in very rare cases. Whether John Cage's philosophy of silence meets this requirement is difficult to say.

22. For example, Lerdahl and Jackendoff (1985), Baroni and Jacoboni (1978), Camilleri (1987), Pelinski (1981), Sundberg et al. (1983), and Pekkilä (1987).

23. I am slightly transforming Peirce's theory and its epistemological "realism," bringing it closer to Greimas's "nominalism."

2. Musical Time

1. It is interesting that many years later, discussing Beethoven's poetical ideas, Arnold Schering mentions the same sonata as an early form of program music.

2. For example, at times our models of "music" have excluded/included bird song, noises, and so on. Moreover, within the limits of what is considered music in the purely material sense, there is a constant oscillation between two spheres. One represents order and redundancy, and at the level of the signified, pleasure and harmony. The other represents disorder, chaos and entropy, displeasure. This oscillation may be illustrated by the concepts of dissonance and consonance. In music history the sphere of consonance has gradually enlarged so as to include the sphere reserved for dissonances, which transforms everything into musical order. Though we now speak of the distinction and dialectic between music and anti-music, we are still moving within music, whereas the more radical distinction of consonance/dissonance meant a separation between music and non-music (Uspenski et al. 1973: 2), as shown in Fig. 2.6.

3. Musical Space

1. We exclude such cases as medieval *musica speculativa* and some modern avant-garde music like Dieter Schnebel's *Musik zum Lesen*.

2. This goes for the study of almost any sign system. For instance, following Greimas (1987: 38) one can say that, in their worship of stones and trees, the ancient Finns were not so stupid as positivist nineteenth-century ethnographers believed, since what the

Finns were worshiping, and still worship, was the *spirit* of these stones and trees.

3. On metaphorical spatiality in linguistics, see Plöger 1990.

4. This interpretation of Greimas's disengagement/engagement is not "orthodox," but it has proved useful for music analysis.

5. Hatten illustrates markedness with the motion of the bass line from an augmented to a perfect fourth in m. 4 of the Adagio of Beethoven's Piano Sonata in E♭ major, Op.7 no. 4.

6. It is no coincidence that the three main categories of musical space—point, line, and field—are the same as in Wassily Kandinsky's theory of the plastic arts (1970).

4. Musical Actors

1. Renewed interest in Kurth is beginning to appear. See, for instance, Lee Rothfarb, *Ernst Kurth as Theorist and Analyst* (Philadelphia: University of Pennsylvania Press, 1988). Yet such studies overlook the semiotical nature of Kurth's work.

2. Likewise, Gino Stefani has distinguished between beats or accents—rhythmic units at the surface level—and pulsations (1982: 94–97). Another music semiotician, Alexandra Pierce (1982: 1–12), takes this deeper phenomenon into account when she speaks of the "junctures" of melody, musical movement, and segmentation. Even the implication model of Meyer (1973) may be considered an application of Kurth's view: the abductive reasoning in Meyer's model is possible only if one posits underlying phases of motion against which our expectations play.

3. Persichetti (1961: 14), among others, has developed a means of gauging and symbolizing such consonance/dissonance.

4. What is actoriality, for instance, in Japanese *gagaku* music? Or in Buddhist *shomyo* singing? In the flute orchestra music of the Suya Indians? In computer and electronic tape music? A musical-semiotic theory must also be able to deal with such phenomena, but to what extent this is possible on the basis of Kurth's theory remains unanswered.

5. This conception of actoriality comes close to that of "proto-intonations" in Asafiev's theories (1977). Among others, Medushewsky (forthcoming) has modified Asafiev's concepts toward a narratological model.

6. By "infer" I do not necessarily mean complex inductive-deductive reasoning on the levels of Secondness or Thirdness, but an event that might take place extremely rapidly—as when we turn on the radio and instantly recognize what kind of music is playing; i.e., we make a primitive taxonomy. Similarly, in the socio-semiotic respect, it used to take only a second to identify whether the English news reporter was the Voice of America or Radio Moscow. In the case of Western art music, we apply all our modal competence and reconstruct in a moment the musical subject who "speaks" in that music. On the other hand, what captivates us in music like traditional Japanese *gagaku* is perhaps the fact that the intentional subject remains unknown and enigmatic to us. In the music of the *Noh* theatre or *Kabuki* performance we can distinguish, with spatial-temporal-actorial criteria, musical units which we might suppose, on the basis of our Western competence, to carry musical subjects, but we cannot be sure of this.

7. Greimas and Fontanille (1991) discusses modulations of passions, which one may take as a form or a result of incompatibility.

8. When Medushewsky (forthcoming) speaks of a "motoric," "exalted," or "meditative I," he evidently means just this kind of inner narrator, the intentional subject that is not actually heard or seen but is nonetheless present at any moment. Yet this might be an exaggeration: we do not always need to suppose a specific "I" behind the narration; a text may merely 'be'. This no doubt holds true in music in the sense that there is "subjectless" music which is by nature "objectal," i.e., a representative object without subject.

5. Semiosis of the Classical Style: Beethoven's "Waldstein"

1. We stop short here of a modal grammar, which will have to wait until Chap. 6.2, where we shall explore Chopin.

2. Such actorial terminology also plays an important role in the musical concepts of the American religious sect described by Thomas Mann at the beginning of *Doktor Faust*. Notes are classified as "lords" and "servants."

3. This model for measuring musical tension in terms of distance from the tonic was developed by Johan Sundberg, Lars Fryden, and Anders Askenfelt, in their essay "What Tells You the Player is Musical?" (1983).

4. In his essay "On the Moods of a Music-Logic" (1960), Charles Seeger created a musical-analytical model based on *musemes*, in which he divided rhythmic units into their smaller parts and examined those parts in terms of decrease/increase of tension. We must consider Seeger our precursor despite the fact that he never went beyond the taxonomic phase in his method and did not show in a concrete analysis how his musical "logic" might function in analytic practice.

5. A weakness of this descriptive method is that even though a rhythmic *débrayage* might occur in only one part, the values represent the phenomenon as if it were taking place in all parts simultaneously. In mm. 10–11, for example, the value +1 accounts only for the appearance of sixteenth notes in the upper part, while the lower part remains at the basic time unit of 0.

6. Boris Asafiev's analysis (1977) of Bach's C♯ minor Fugue, *Well-Tempered Clavier* I, pays special attention to inner temporality, as does Kurth's (1922: 209–12).

7. Though we shall not do so here, the inner temporality could be digitized and measured with numeric time units similar to those used in measuring the inner spatiality. Temporal comparison is always realized according to two semiotic principles: similarity or iconicity, and contiguity or indexicality. Contiguous musical elements invite stronger comparison than elements separated by temporal distance, unless similarity in the form of a recurring motif effects a powerful association or memory bridge between two sections. So one might digitize the principles of similarity and contiguity according to their relative force in the memory.

8. We should again point out that modalities can be mutually incompatible, as with *vouloir/savoir-faire* and *devoir faire*. The situation of *savoir devoir* would be rare, however, because an element that provides new information rarely meets the obligations of a preestablished norm.

9. On "innovation," see Mäkelä 1989: 162.

10. This condition suggests that *pouvoir* alone cannot form a proper musical action but requires support from other modalities.

6. Narrativity in Chopin

1. In general, +disengagement also increases the modality of 'will', whereas -disengagement would evoke 'not-will'; or on the level of fundamental modalities, +disengagement = 'doing', -disengagement = 'being'.

2. Even within the modality of 'can' there can exist an instrumental innovation, as Mäkelä (1989) has shown; that is, in some cases 'know' and 'can' are not mutually exclusive.

3. Moreover, a careful Schenkerian analysis of the entire piece would precisely determine the 'must' of the pitch organization.

4. On the spatial level, Schenkerians would of course like to see here the normative end point (scale degree $\hat{1}$) of a *Linienzug*.

5. "Aveugler" (to blind), the French lexicalization by Zilberberg (1985) is too visual for music; the term "mislead" is better.

6. The sign ~ means the modality of 'appearing'.

7. Music and Literature

1. In this sense the idea of a musical "actor" comes rather close to a concept in the generative theory of Lerdahl and Jackendoff, namely, that of a "head"—the main unit or element of a phrase: "a single structurally most important event is chosen as head" (1985: 124) from among a phrase's pitch events; other pitches are said to be subordinated to it (1985: 120).

2. In this regard, see the analysis by George Sand in her preface to *Obermann*.

3. For the tonal tensions, Schenker analysis might best reveal the internal tonal space. Without making an "orthodox" Schenkerian reduction at all levels, one could make what some American music theoreticians call a "bass line sketch," which charts the movements of the bass and its most important tonal functions. Such a sketch can reveal the most important tonal tensions of the song, which undoubtedly also serve as the basis for the tensions in its interpretation. In addition, one should remember that Schenker developed his method expressly as a tool for performing musicians. This is sometimes hard to believe, because it is so far removed from the aural structures of music perception; it is rather in the realm of abstract theoretical organization.

4. The method is intended for the analysis of relatively simple tonal tunes, particularly for an extensive corpus of melodies, such as the Swedish children's songs studied by Sundberg and his colleagues (1983: 65).

5. Our numbering does not indicate whether the chords are pure triads or have added notes, such as sevenths, ninths, and so on. When a modulation takes place, should we count the values starting from the new tonic? If so, how do those values relate to the original tonic, to which the music may return? Should one first assign values (indicating degrees of tension) to larger spatial-temporal sections, and only later assign the values for individual chords, according to the section or isotopy in which they occur?

6. The recordings used in this analysis are by Pierre Bernac, accompanied by Francis Poulenc; Kiri Te Kanawa, accompanied by Richard Amner, CB 331.76868 (London, 1979); Claire Croiza, accompanied by Georg Reeves, EMI, ALP 2115 (1E 063, 11639); Nan Merrimam, accompanied by Gerald Moore, Columbia 33cx, 1213; Regine Crespin, accompanied by John Wustmann, EMI 290446 1 PM 375 (Paris, 1966); Elly Ameling, accompanied by Dalton Baldwin, EMI ASD 2902 0C 063 02375; Gerard Friedmann, accompanied by Franz Zubal, Da Camera Magna, SM 90 004; Ian Partridge, accompanied by Jennifer Partridge, Pearl SHE 524; Nikolai Gedda, accompanied by Aldo Ciccolini, Pathé Marconi, 2C 063 10.000; Frederica von Stade, accompanied by Jean-Philippe Collard, EMI 0C 067–73 099T; Barbra Streisand, Columbia Symphony Orchestra, conducted by Claus Ogerman, CBS 74484; Sasha Vectomov, accompanied by Alfred Holecek, Supraphon LPM 448; Janos Starker, accompanied by Leon Pommers, Nixa PLP 708; Pablo Casals, accompanied by Nicolai Mednikoff, HR 214; Antonio Janigro, accompanied by Eugenio Bagnoli, Westminster 1956, XWN 18004; Mstislav Rostropovitch, accompanied by Vladimir Jampolski, CPPP 015567–68 (1966); Paul Tortelier, accompanied by Shuku Iwasaki, HQS 1289 (1972); André Navarra, accompanied by Erika Kilcher, Calliope, WE 681 (1980); Arthur Grumiaux, accompanied by Istvan Hajdu, Philips 6599373; Aleksandr Knjazev, accompanied by Tatjana Matjunina, Melodija 10–11371–2; Andrew Lloyd Webber, accompanied by Yitkin Seow, ACM 2202. The results of this investigation are given in the Appendix, below.

8. Music and Visual Arts

1. This overview of the piece raises several questions related to the problem of musical realism, namely, how various places, times, and actors are musically depicted. To put this more radically, if the titles of movements were changed, would the musical portrayal maintain its validity? For example, could the music of the Unhatched Chicks just as well describe the French market women quarreling at Limoges, and vice versa? In

other words, to what extent is the musical realism really *musical* and not just dictated by the programmatic texts?

2. This too much/little is a special musical-aesthetic device which the Russian Formalists called a *priem*.

3. The disappearance of borders is a trait which must have pleased Debussy, in whose music one sees the first germs of modernism and *oeuvre desoeuvrée*.

4. There is a similar technique in the scene with the entrance of guests to Wartburg in Wagner's *Tannhäuser*.

5. Kielian-Gilbert shows how this scheme functions in many works from Schubert to Satie. It is the famous scheme of Lévi-Strauss's algebra of mythical thought in his *Structural Anthropology*.

6. See also the use of the Dorian mode in Albéniz's *Cordoba* and at the end of Sibelius's Sixth Symphony.

7. See Bakhtin's semiotics of "dispute" (1970).

8. The painting shows the artist and his friend V. A. Kenel.

9. The Semiotics of Symphonism

1. This aspect of musical temporality has been stressed by the conductor George Schneevoigt, in his historic recording of the Fourth Symphony. I heard it for the first time during a seminar on music philosophy held by Professor Daniel Charles at Paris University VIII. The experience of hearing Sibelius's music in a totally different musical and cultural context prompted this semiotic analysis of the Fourth Symphony.

2. See the analyses made of Ilmari Krohn (1945/1946) and Eino Roiha (1941), who also aimed to demonstrate that the whole symphony could be reduced to the structures of communication, in the aforementioned meaning, of the symphonic genre in Western erudite music, i.e., to that genre's *devoir*, or stylistic norms.

3. This has been most coherently stated by Veijo Murtomaki (1990), who has been able to classify the essential events of the inner spatiality as the different means of filling the interval of a fifth, and the neighboring-tone movement around it.

4. This is an implication of the type "gap-fill," which is created by the piece itself (see Meyer 1973).

5. Such a typology of subjects is done by Viatscheslav Medushewsky in his narrative theory (forthcoming).

6. It is for good reason that Boulez advises us to pay attention in analysis to the conjunction points of twelve-tone serial matrixes, where rows might overlap in pitch content.

7. Such seemingly interruptive devices no doubt diminished the interest in Sibelius's music in the German area, for Adorno, among others, because of Germany's heritage of composers in the tradition of musical "organicism."

8. In addition, Tawaststjerna sees the central idea of the piece as actorial: "Growth of A Theme: An Improvisation in Three Phases" (in 1972).

10. Toward the Modern Scene

1. The importance of repetition in Debussy's music has already been noted by Nicolas Ruwet, among others.

2. Exactly as a narrative scheme in Claude Brémond's *Logique du récit* (1973).

3. One might think that Debussy learned this technique of harmonic coloration from the Russians, such as Musorgsky and Rimsky-Korsakov; but, in fact, the Russians learned it from none other than Berlioz.

4. At a congress held in Austria in 1979 on the theme "Zur neuen Einfachheit in der Musik" (On the New Simplicity in Music), subtitled "An Aesthetic Innovation or Concession to the Audience?", almost all the speakers criticized the very concept of

minimalism; and most of the European composers in attendance, whose works were studied at the symposium, strongly refused to be identified with this trend, which originated in the United States. Though almost all of them viewed Erik Satie as the precursor of the "new simplicity" (think of his *Socrate*, or *Vexations*, a piece in which the same phrase repeats 840 times), the European and especially the German scholars had difficulty locating this movement within traditional music-aesthetic categories.

5. Lyotard refers to Apollinaire in this context.

6. It has been argued that the term itself was an invention of the philosopher Richard Wollheim and that the whole movement is mostly American—the only truly significant and genuine contribution of Americans to world art. The first important exposition of Minimal art, entitled "Primary Structures," took place in 1966 at the Jewish Museum, in New York.

7. Helmut Kirchmeyer, a German pedagogue and Stravinsky scholar, has listed "isms" of the twentieth century: "atonalism, bruitism, chromaticism, dadaism, Debussyism, eroticism, exoticism, expressionism, folklorism, formalism, futurism, impressionism, intellectualism, classicism, conservatorism, constructivism, cubism, lyricism, machinism, mechanism, modernism, motorism, mysticism, naturalism, neoclassicism, neoprimitivism, neoromanticism, orientalism, Orfism, primitivism, progressism, provincialism, purism, realism, revolutionism, romanticism, Scriabinism, Stravinskyism, superchromaticism, symbolism, vitalism, Wagnerism . . ." (1958: 222). His list itself reads like a Dadaist poem of the "Il y a" type, consisting of all that can be found in the cellar stores of art history.

8. As such, the idea of applying isotopies to musical composition may have been first noticed by Costin Miereanu, a "minimalist" himself in works such as *Piano miroirs*.

Conclusion

1. For a recent overview of music semiotics and other relevant topics, I refer the reader to Raymond Monelle's *Linguistics and Semiotics in Music* (New York: Harwood Academic Publishers, 1992).

BIBLIOGRAPHY

Abbate, Carolyn (1991). *Unsung Voices: Opera and Musical Narrative in the Nine-teenth Century.* Princeton: Princeton University Press.
Abraham, Gerald (1960). *Chopin's Musical Style.* London: Oxford University Press.
_____ (1975). *The Music of Sibelius.* New York: Da Capo.
Adler, Guido (1911). *Der Stil in der Musik.* Leipzig: Breitkopf & Härtel.
Adorno, Theodor W. (1952). *Versuch über Wagner.* Berlin: Suhrkampf.
Agawu, Kofi V. (1991). *Playing with Signs: A Semiotic Interpretation of Classic Music.* Princeton: Princeton University Press.
Ahonen, Pertti (1984). "A. J. Greimasin Pariisin koulukunnan semiotiikka: Sosi-aaliantropologiasta ja kansansatujen tutkimuksesta yleiseen ihmistieteeseen" [The semiotics of A. J. Greimas' Paris school. From social anthropology and study of folklore to general human sciences]. *Suomen Antropologi* 4.
d'Alembert, Jean le Rond (1821). *Oeuvres.* Vol. 1, part 1. Paris: Belin.
Appia, Adolphe (1899). *Die Musik und Inszenierung.* Munich: Bruckmann.
Asafiev, Boris (1977). "Musical Form as a Process." 3 vols. Translation and commentary by J. R. Tull. Diss., Ohio State University.
[Asafiev] Assafjew-Glebow, B. W. (n.d.). *Tschaikowskys "Eugen Onegin": Versuch einer Analyse des Stils und der musikalischen Dramaturgie.* Potsdam: Athenaion.
Attali, Jacques (1977). *Bruits: Essai sur l'économie politique de la musique.* Vendome: Presses Universitaires de France.
Bakhtin, Mikhail (1970). *La poétique de Dostoievski.* Paris: Seuil.
Ballantine, Christopher (1983). *Twentieth Century Symphony.* London: Dennis Dobson.
Ballif, Claude (1979). *Voyage de mon oreille.* Paris: Union Générale.
Baroni, Mario (1979). *Il declino del patriarca: Verdi e le contraddizioni della famiglia borghese.* Bologna: Antiquae Musicae Italicae Studiosi, Universita degli Studi di Bologna.
_____ (1987). "Accompaniment Formulas in Verdi's *Ernani.*" *Semiotica* 66 (1/3), 129–40.
_____ (1992). "The Concept of Hierarchy: A Theoretical Approach." In Tarasti, ed. (forthcoming).
Baroni, Mario, and Carlo Jacoboni (1978). *Proposals for a Grammar of Melody: The Bach Chorales.* Montreal: Presses de l'Université de Montréal.
Barthes, Roland (1964). *Essais critiques.* Paris: Seuil.
_____ (1975). "Rasch." In *Langue, discours, société.* Paris: Seuil.
_____ (1977). *Image Music Text.* Trans. Stephen Heath. New York: Hill and Wang.
Baudrillard, Jean (1968). *Système des objets.* Paris: Gallimard.
Baur, John (1985). *Music Theory through Literature,* vol. 2. Englewood Cliffs, NJ: Prentice Hall.
Bengtsson, Ingmar (1977). *Musikvetenskap: En översikt.* Stockholm: Esselte Studium.
Benoist-Mechin, Jacques (1926). *La musique et l'immortalité dans l'oeuvre de Marcel Proust.* Paris: Simon Kra.
Bergson, Henri (1938). *La pensée et le mouvant.* Paris: Presses Universitaires de France.
Berio, Luciano (1974). "Une question à Luciano Berio." In *Sessions IRCAM du 19 au 23 octobre.* Paris: Renaud-Barrault.

Berlioz, Hector, and Richard Strauss (1904). *Instrumentationslehre I-II*. Leipzig: Peters.
Bernac, Pierre (1978). *The Interpretation of French Song*. New York: Norton.
Besseler, Heinrich (1957). "Spielfiguren in der Instrumentalmusik." *Deutsches Jahrbuch der Musikwissenschaft*, ed. Walter Vetter. Leipzig: Peters. Pp. 12–38.
Blacking, John (1974). *How Musical Is Man?* Seattle: University of Washington Press.
Boiles, Charles (1973). "Les chants instrumentaux des Tepehuas." *Musique en jeu* 12:81–99.
Bouissac, Paul (1976). *Circus and Culture: A Semiotic Approach*. Bloomington: Indiana University Press.
Bouissac, Paul; Michael Herzfeld; and Roland Posner, eds. (1986). *Iconicity: Essays on the Nature of Culture. Festschrift for Thomas A. Sebeok on his Sixty-Fifth Birthday*. Tübingen: Stauffenburg.
Boulez, Pierre (1971). *On Music Today*. Cambridge: Harvard University Press.
Brelet, Gisèle (1949). *Le temps musical*, Vols. 1–2. Paris: Presses Universitaires de France.
Brémond, Claude (1973). *Logique du récit*. Paris: Seuil.
Broms, Henri, and Rebecca Kaufmann (1988). *Semiotics of Culture: Proceedings of the Twenty-Fifth Symposium of the Tartu-Moscow School of Semiotics, Imatra, Finland, 27–29 July 1987*. Helsinki: Arator.
Busoni, Ferruccio (1916). *Entwurf einer neuen Aesthetik der Tonkunst*. Leipzig: Insel.
Cage, John (1981). *For the Birds: John Cage in Conversation with Daniel Charles*. Boston: Marion Boyars.
Calvocoressi, M.D. (1946). *Mussorgsky*. London: Dent and Sons.
Camilleri, Lelio (1987). "Towards a Computational Theory of Music." In *The Semiotic Web 1986*, ed. Thomas A. Sebeok and Jean Umiker-Sebeok. Berlin: Mouton.
Cardine, Dom Eugene (1982). *Gregorian Semiology*. Trans. Robert M. Fowels. Sablé-sur-Sarthe: Solesmes.
Castellana, Marcello (1990). "Entre imaginaire et symbolique: Sciences du langage et sciences des arts musicaux." Doctoral thesis, Université de Paris.
Chailley, Jacques (1977). *Traité historique d'analyse harmonique*. Paris: Leduc.
Charbonnières, Georges (1970). *Conversations with Claude Lévi-Strauss*. London: Cape.
Charles, Daniel (1978a). *Gloses sur John Cage*. Paris: Union Générale.
––––––– (1978b). *Le temps de la voix*. Paris: Delarge.
––––––– (1984). *Musik und Vergessen*. Berlin: Merve.
––––––– (1987). "Son et temps." *Semiotica* 66 (1/3):171–80.
––––––– (1989). *Zeitspielräume: Performance Musik Aesthetik*. Berlin: Merve.
––––––– (forthcoming). "Music and Antimetaphor." In Tarasti, ed. (forthcoming).
Chatwin, Bruce (1988). *Songlines*. New York: Pan.
Chiarucci, Henri (1973). "Essai d'analyse structurale d'oeuvres musicales." *Musique en jeu* 12.
Cholopowa, Valentina, and Juri Cholopov (1989). *Anton Webern: Leben und Werk*. Berlin: Henschel.
Christensen, Otto (forthcoming). "Interpretation and Meaning in Music." In Tarasti, ed. (forthcoming).
Clynes, Manfred (1978). *Sentics: The Touch of Emotions*. New York: Anchor.
Cocteau, Jean (1918/1979). *Le coq et l'arlequin: Notes autour de la musique*. Paris: Stock.
Cogan, Robert, and Pozzi Escot (1976). *Sonic Design: The Nature of Sound and Music*. Englewood Cliffs, NJ: Prentice Hall.
Coker, Wilson (1972). *Music and Meaning: A Theoretical Introduction to Musical Aesthetics*. New York: Free Press.

Cooke, Deryck (1959). *The Language of Music*. London: Oxford University Press.
Cooper, Grosvenor, and Leonard B. Meyer (1959). *The Rhythmic Structure of Music*. Chicago: University of Chicago Press.
Cooper, Martin (1979). Liner notes for *A Recital of French Songs: Claire Crozza (1882–1946), Mezzo-soprano*. EMI Records, ALP 2115.
Dahlhaus, Carl (1977). *Grundlagen der Musikgeschichte*. Köln: Hans Gerig.
_____ (1988). *Ludwig von Beethoven und seine Zeit*. Regensburg: Laaber.
Dalmonte, Rossana (1983). *Franz Liszt: La vita, l'opera, i testi musicali*. Milan: Feltirelli.
Delalande, François (1987). "The Concept of Expansion in Theories concerning the Relationships between Music and Poetry." *Semiotica* 66 (1/3):111–28.
_____ (forthcoming). "Meaning and Behaviour Patterns: The Creation of Sense in Interpreting and Listening to Music." In Tarasti, ed. (forthcoming).
Deliège, Celestin (1984). *Les fondements de la musique tonale*. Paris: Lattes.
Derrida, Jacques (1982). *Margins of Philosophy*. Trans. Alan Bass. Chicago: University of Chicago Press.
Descartes, René (1654/1970). *Les passions de l'âme*. Paris: Librairie Philosophique J. Vrin.
Desquilbé, Fabienne (1988/89). "La narrativité chez Claudio Monteverdi: Les isotopies sémantiques dans 'L'Orfeo.'" Masters thesis, Aix-en-Provence, Université de Provence.
Doubravova, Jarmila (1982). *Hudba a vytvarné umeni* [Music and Fine Arts]. Prague: Academia.
_____ (forthcoming). "The Symbol of the Tree in Musical *Art nouveau* Style." In Tarasti, ed. (forthcoming).
Dufourt, Hugues (1991). *Musique, pouvoir, écriture*. Herissey-Evreux: Bourgois.
Eco, Umberto (1968/1971). *La struttura assente*. Milan: Pompiani.
_____ (1976). *A Theory of Semiotics*. Bloomington: Indiana University Press.
_____ (1987). "Fakes and Forgeries." *Versus* 46:3–29.
Eigeldinger, Jean-Jacques (1979). *Chopin vu par ses élèves*. Neuchatel: Baconnière.
Einstein, Alfred (1951). *Grösse in der Musik*. Zürich: Pan.
Ekman, Karl (1935). *Jean Sibelius: Taiteilijan elämä ja persoonallisuus*. Helsinki: Otava.
Escal, Françoise (1979). *Espaces sociaux, espaces musicaux*. Paris: Payot.
_____ (1984). *Le compositeur et ses modèles*. Paris: Presses Universitaires de France.
_____ (1987). "Roland Barthes: Fragment d'un discours sur la musique." *Semiotica* 66 (1/3):57–68.
Evans, Jonathan D., and André Helbo, eds. (1986). *Semiotics and International Scholarship: Towards a Language of Theory*. NATO ASI Series D: Behavioural and Social Sciences 33. Dordrecht: Nijhoff.
Fontanille, Jacques (1980). "Le désespoir." Documents de recherche 16, Groupe de recherches sémio-linguistiques. Paris: CNRS.
_____ (1987). *Le savoir partagé: Sémiotique et théorie de la connaissance chez Marcel Proust*. Paris: Hades-Benjamins.
Foucault, Michel (1970). *The Order of Things: An Archaeology of the Human Sciences*. London: Tavistock.
Fourier, Charles (1848). *Oeuvres complètes*. 6 vols. Paris: Librairie Sociétaire.
Gagné, Cole, and Tracey Caras (1982). *Soundpieces: Interviews with American Composers*. London: Scarecrow.
Goodman, Nelson (1976). *Languages of Art: An Approach to a Theory of Symbols*. Indianapolis: Hackett.
Grabócz, Márta (1986). *Morphologie des oeuvres pour piano de Liszt: L'influence du programme sur l'évolution des formes instrumentales*. Budapest: MTA Zenetudomanyi Intezet.

Gray, Cecil (1935). *Sibelius: The Symphonies*. London: Oxford University Press.
Gray, Cecil, and Jussi Jalas (1945). *Sibeliuksen sinfoniat* [Sibelius's Symphonies]. Helsinki: Fazer.
Greimas, Algirdas Julien (1967). *Sémantique structurale: Recherche de méthode*. Paris: Larousse.
_____ (1976). "Pour une théorie des modalités." *Langages* 3.
_____ (1979). *Du sens I: Essais sémiotiques*. Paris: Seuil.
_____ (1983). *Du sens II: Essais sémiotiques*. Paris: Seuil.
Greimas, A. J., and Joseph Courtés (1979). *Sémiotique: Dictionnaire raisonné de la théorie du langage*. Paris: Hachette.
Greimas, A. J., and Jacques Fontanille (1991). *Sémiotique des passions: Des états de choses aux états d'âme*. Paris: Seuil.
Grund, Cynthia (forthcoming). "How Philosophical Characteristics of a Musical Work Lose Sight of the 'Music' and How It Might Be Put Back." In Tarasti, ed. (forthcoming).
Guilhot, J., et al. (1979). *La musico-thérapie et les méthodes nouvelles d'association des techniques*. Paris: ESF.
Halm, August (1916). *Von zwei Kulturen der Musik*. Munich: Georg Müller.
Hatten, Robert S. (1982). "Toward a Semiotic Model of Style in Music: Epistemological and Methodological Bases." Diss., Indiana University, Bloomington.
_____ (1987a). "Aspects of Dramatic Closure in Beethoven: A Semiotic Perspective on Music Analysis via Strategies of Dramatic Conflict." *Semiotica* 66 (1/3):197–210.
_____ (1987b). "Style, Motivation, and Markedness." In *The Semiotic Web 1986*, eds. Thomas A. Sebeok and Jean Umiker-Sebeok. Berlin: Mouton. Pp. 408–28.
_____ (forthcoming). "The Troping of Meaning in Music." In Tarasti, ed. (forthcoming).
Hawkins, Sir John (1776/1963). *A General History of the Science and Practice of Music*. New York: Dover.
Hegel, Georg Friedrich (1969). *Wissenschaft der Logik*. 20 vols. Frankfurt am Main: Suhrkamp.
Heidegger, Martin (1967). *Sein und Zeit*. Tübingen: Max Niemeyer.
Helbo, André (1987). *Theory of Performing Arts*. Amsterdam: Benjamins.
Hénault, Anne (1983). *Narratologie, sémiotique générale: Les enjeux de la sémiotique 2*. Paris: Presses Universitaires de France.
Henze, Hans Werner, ed. (1981). *Neue Aspekte der musikalischen Ästhetik II*. Frankfurt am Main: Fischer.
Hildesheimer, Wolfgang (1980). *Mozart*. Frankfurt am Main: Suhrkamp.
Hjelmslev, Louis (1961). *Prolegomena to a Theory of Language*. Madison: University of Wisconsin Press.
Hosokawa, Shubei (1987a). "L'effet lyrique." *Semiotica* 66 (1/3):141–54.
_____ (1987b). *Der Walkman-Effekt*. Berlin: Merve.
_____ (1987c). "Technique/Technology of Reproduction in Music." In *Basic Concepts of Studies in Musical Signification*, ed. Eero Tarasti. Special issue of *The Semiotic Web 1986*, ed. Thomas A. Sebeok and Jean Umiker-Sebeok. Berlin: Mouton.
Howell, Timothy (1985). "Jean Sibelius: Progressive Techniques in the Symphonies and Tone Poems." Diss., University of Southhampton.
Imberty, Michel (1981). *Les écritures du temps: Sémantique psychologique de la musique*. Vol. 2. Paris: Dunod.
d'Indy, Vincent (1897–1898; 1899–1900). *Cours de composition musicale*. Paris: Durand.
Jakobson, Roman (1963). *Essais de linguistique générale*. Paris: Minuit.
Jankélévitch, Vladimir (1961). *La musique et l'ineffable*. Paris: Colin.
_____ (1974). *L'irreversible et la nostalgie*. Paris: Flammarion.

_____ (1980). *Le je-ne-sais-quoi et le presque-rien 1: La manière et l'occasion.* Paris: Seuil.

Jiránek, Jároslav (1967). *Asafjevova teorie intonace* [Asafiev's Theory of Intonation]. Prague: Academia.

_____ (1985). *Zu Grundfragen der musikalischen Semiotik.* Berlin: Neue Musik.

_____ (1987). "On the Nature of Musical Signs." In *Basic Concepts of Musical Signification,* ed. Eero Tarasti. Special issue of *The Semiotic Web 1986.* Berlin: Mouton.

_____ (forthcoming). "Intonation as a Specific Form of Musical Semiosis." In Tarasti, ed. (forthcoming).

Jordan, Alan T. (1984). "Harmonic Style in Selected Sibelius Symphonies." Diss., Indiana University, Bloomington.

Karbusicky, Vladimir (1979). *Systematische Musikwissenschaft.* Munich: Wilhelm Fink.

_____ (1986). *Grundriss der musikalischen Semantik.* Darmstadt: Wissenschaftliche Buchgesellschaft.

_____ (1987a). "The Index Sign in Music." *Semiotica* 66 (1/3):23–36.

_____ (1987b). " 'Signification' in Music: A Metaphor?" In *Basic Concepts of Studies in Musical Signification,* ed. Eero Tarasti. Special issue of *The Semiotic Web 1986.* Berlin: Mouton.

_____ (1987c). "Zeichen und Musik." Special issue of *Zeitschrift für Semiotik* 9 (3/4), ed. Karbusicky. Tübingen: Stauffenberg Verlag.

_____ (forthcoming). "On the Genesis of the Musical Sign." In Tarasti, ed. (forthcoming).

Kerman, Joseph (1985). *Contemplating Music: Challenges to Musicology.* Cambridge: Harvard University Press.

Kielian-Gilbert, Marianne (1990). "Interpreting Musical Analogy: From Rhetorical Device to Perceptual Process." *Music Perception* 8 (1):63–94.

Kirchmeyer, Helmut (1958). *Igor Strawinsky: Zeitgeschichte im Persönlichkeitsbild.* Regensburg: Bosse.

Kivy, Peter (1984). *Sound and Semblance: Reflections on Musical Representation.* Princeton, NJ: Princeton University Press.

Klotins, Arnold (1987). *Muzika un idejas* [Music and Ideas]. Riga: Liesma.

Kolleritsch, Otto (1981). *Zur "Neuen Einfachheit" in der Musik.* Studien zur Wertungsforschung 14. Wien: Universal.

Kon, Joseph (forthcoming). "Asafiev and Tynianov." In Tarasti, ed. (forthcoming).

Koury, Daniel J. (1986). *Orchestral Performance Practice in the Nineteenth Century: Size, Proportions, and Seating.* Ann Arbor, MI: UMI Research Press.

Kowzan, Tadeusz (1975). *Littérature et spectacle.* Approaches to Semiotics 58 (Berlin: Mouton). Warsaw: PWN Scientific Editions of Poland.

Krohn, Ilmari (1945/1946). *Der Stimmungsgehalt der Symphonien von Jean Sibelius I-II.* Annales academiae scientiarum fennica 17–18. Helsinki: Suomalaisen kirjallisuuden seuran kirjapaino.

Kulka, Jiri (forthcoming). "A Semiopsychological Theory of Communication in Music." In Tarasti, ed. (forthcoming).

Kurkela, Kari (1986). *Note and Tone: A Semantic Analysis of Conventional Music Notation.* Helsinki: Finnish Musicological Society.

_____ (1992). "Tempo Deviations and Musical Signification." In *Basic Concepts of Musical Signification,* ed. Eero Tarasti. Special issue of *The Semiotic Web,* ed. Thomas A. Sebeok and Jean Umiker-Sebeok. Berlin: Mouton.

Kurth, Ernst (1922). *Grundlagen des linearen Kontrapunktes.* Berlin: Max Hesse.

_____ (1947 [1992]). *Musikpsychologie.* Hildesheim: Georg Olms.

Laloy, Louis (1974). *La musique retrouvée 1902–1907.* Poitiers: Desclée de Brouwer.

Langer, Susanne K. (1951). *Philosophy in a New Key.* New York: Mentor.
LaRue, Jan (1970). *Guidelines for Style Analysis.* New York: Norton.
Layton, Robert (1978). *Sibelius.* New York: Viking.
Leichtentritt, Hugo (1921). *Analyse der Chopin'schen Klavierwerke.* Berlin: Hesse.
Lerdahl, Fred, and Ray Jackendoff (1985). *A Generative Theory of Tonal Music.* Cambridge: MIT Press.
Lévi-Strauss, Claude (1958). *Anthropologie structurale.* Paris: Plon.
———— (1964). *Mythologiques I: Le cru et le cuit.* Paris: Plon.
———— (1971). *Mythologiques IV: L'homme nu.* Paris: Plon.
Lidov, David (1980). "Musical Structure and Musical Significance: Part I." Working paper. Toronto: Victoria University, Toronto Semiotic Circle.
———— (1987). "Mind and Body in Music." *Semiotica* 66 (1/3):69–98.
———— (forthcoming). "Toward a Reinterpretation of Compositional Theory." In Tarasti, ed. (forthcoming).
Ligabue, Marco (1988/1989). "Mezzo espressivo e segni di memoria musicali nel loro divenire." Manuscript. Universita studi di Firenze.
Ligabue, Marco, and Francesco Giomi (forthcoming). "Some Relationships between Terminology: Analytic Strategies and Computational Grammar." In Tarasti, ed. (forthcoming).
Lissa, Zofia (1963). Essay in *Book of the First International Congress Devoted to the Works of Chopin,* ed. Lissa. Warsaw: PNW.
Littlefield, Richard, and David Neumeyer (1992). "Rewriting Schenker: Narrative-History-Ideology. *Music Theory Spectrum* 14 (1):37–65.
Lotman, Juri (1973). *La structure du texte artistique.* Paris: Gallimard.
———— (1989). *Merkkien maailma: Kirjoitelmia semiotikasta.* Helsinki: SN-kirjat Oy.
Lyotard, Jean-François (1984). *The Postmodern Condition: A Report on Knowledge.* Theory and History of Literature 10. Minneapolis: University of Minnesota Press.
Mâche, François-Bernard (1971). "Méthodes linguistiques et musicologie." *Musique en jeu* 5:75–91.
———— (1983). *Musique, mythe, nature; ou, les dauphins d'Arion.* Paris: Klincksieck.
———— (forthcoming). "Method and System." In Tarasti, ed. (forthcoming).
Mäkelä, Tomi (1987). "Instrumental Figures as Iconic Signs." In *Basic Concepts of Signification,* ed. Eero Tarasti. Special issue of *The Semiotic Web,* ed. Thomas A. Sebeok and Jean Umiker-Sebeok. Berlin: Mouton.
———— (1989). *Virtuosität und Werkcharakter: Eine analytische und theoretische Untersuchung zur Virtuosität in den Klavierkonzerten der Hochromantik.* Munich: Emil Katzbichler.
Marconi, Luca (forthcoming). "Pertinence in Music." In Tarasti, ed. (forthcoming).
Marsden, Alan (forthcoming). "Musical Pragmatics and Computer Modelling." In Tarasti, ed. (forthcoming).
Martinez, José Luiz (1991). *Musica a semiotica: Um estudo sobre a questao da representaçao na linguagem musical.* São Paulo: Pontifica Universidade Catolica.
Mead, George Herbert (1948). *The Philosophy of Act.* Chicago: University of Chicago Press.
Medushewsky, Viatcheslav (forthcoming). "Musical Intonation: The Language of Intuition and Logic." In Tarasti, ed. (forthcoming).
Meyer, Leonard B. (1973). *Explaining Music.* Chicago: University of Chicago Press.
———— (1989). *Style and Music: Theory, History, and Ideology.* Philadelphia: University of Pennsylvania Press.
Miereanu, Costin (1987). "Structures profondes, structures superficielles, structures de la manifestation en musique." *Semiotica* 66 (1/3):37–56.
Mirigliano, Rosario (forthcoming). "The Sign in Music: A Reflection on the Theoretical

Bases of Musical Signification." In Tarasti, ed. (forthcoming).
Monelle, Raymond (1992). *Linguistics and Semiotics in Music.* New York: Harwood Academic Publishers.
―――― (forthcoming). "Music and Semantics." In Tarasti, ed. (forthcoming).
Morris, Charles (1956). *Varieties of Human Values.* Chicago: University of Chicago Press.
Mosley, David L. (1992). *Gesture, Sign, and Song: An Interdisciplinary Approach to Schumann's "Liederkreis" Opus 39.* New York: Peter Lang.
―――― (forthcoming). "Peirce's 'Ground' and the Phenomenon of Nineteenth-Century Lieder." In Tarasti, ed. (forthcoming).
Mukařovsky, Jan (1977). *Structure, Sign, and Function.* Trans. and ed. John Burbank and Peter Steiner. New Haven: Yale University Press.
Murtomäki, Veijo (1990). *Symphonic Unity: The Development of Formal Thinking in the Symphonies of Sibelius.* Acta Musicologica Universitatis Helsingiensis V. Helsinki: University of Helsinki.
Narmour, Eugene (1977). *Beyond Schenkerism: The Need for Alternatives in Music Analysis.* Chicago: University of Chicago Press.
Nattiez, Jean-Jacques (1975). *Fondements d'une sémiologie de la musique.* Paris: Union Générale.
―――― (1984). *Proust musicien.* Paris: Bourgois.
―――― (1985). *Points de repère.* Paris: Seuil.
―――― (1987a). "Sémiologie des jeux vocaux Inuit." *Semiotica* 66 (1/3):259–78.
―――― (1987b). *Musicologie générale et sémiologie.* Paris: Bourgois.
―――― (1990). *Music and Discourse: Toward a Semiology of Music.* Trans. Carolyn Abbate. Princeton, NJ: Princeton University Press.
Neumeyer, David, and Susan Tepping (1988 [1992]). *A Guide to Schenkerian Analysis.* Englewood Cliffs, NJ: Prentice Hall.
Nielsen, Frede V. (1983). *Oplevelse af musikalsk spaending* [Experience of Musical Tension]. Copenhagen: Akademisk Forlag.
―――― (1989). "Musical 'Tension' and Related Concepts." In *Basic Concepts of Musical Signification.* Special issue of *The Semiotic Web*, ed. Thomas A. Sebeok and Jean Umiker-Sebeok. Berlin: Mouton.
Normet, Leo (1970). "Vielä Sibeliuksen Neljännestä" [On Sibelius's Fourth Symphony]. In *Suomen Musiikin Vuosikirja 1968–1969.* Helsinki: Otava. Pp. 28–43.
―――― (1989). "Länsimaisen taidemusiikin tärkeimmät suuntaukset 1900-luvulla" [The Most Important Trends of Twentieth-Century Art Music]. *Synteesi* 1–2.
―――― (forthcoming). "On the Synthetic Style in Music in the Years of the European Art nouveau." In Tarasti, ed. (forthcoming).
Noske, Frits (1977). *The Signifier and the Signified: Studies in the Operas of Mozart and Verdi.* The Hague: Martinus Nijhoff.
Osmond-Smith, David (1975). "L'iconisme formel: Pour une typologie des transformations dans l'analyse musicale." *Semiotica* 15 (11).
Osolsobe, Ivo (1980). "Cours de théâtristique générale." *Études littéraires* 13 (3).
Pallasmaa, Juhani (1989). "Rakennustaiteen runous [The poetry of architecture]." *Synteesi* 3:26–28.
Parland, Oscar (1966). *Muuttumisia* [Changes]. Porvoo: Werner Söderström.
Parret, Herman (1982). "Elements pour une typologie raisonnée des passions." *Documents de recherche IV,* 37 (Groupe de recherche sémio-linguistiques). Paris: CNRS.
Pärt, Arvo (1984). Liner notes for recording of *Tabula rasa.* EGM Records, New Series. ECM 1275.
Peirce, Charles S. (1977). *Semiotic and Significs: The Correspondence between Charles S. Peirce and Victoria Lady Welby,* ed. Charles S. Hardwick. Bloomington: Indiana University Press.

Pekkilä, Erkki (1987). "Ideal Patterns in the Finnish *juoksuvalssi*: A Paradigmatic Segment Analysis." *Semiotica* 66 (1/3): 299–314.

———— (1988). *Musiikki tekstinä: Kuulonvaraisen musiikkikulttuurrin analyysiteoria ja-metodi* [Music as Text: A Theory and Method for the Study of Oral Music Culture]. Acta Musicologica Fennica 17. Helsinki: Suomen Musiikkitieteellinen Seura.

Pelinski, Ramon (1981). *La musique des Inuit du Caribou: Cinq perspectives méthodologiques*. Montreal: Presses de l'Université de Montréal.

Persichetti, Vincent (1961). *Twentieth-Century Harmony*. New York: Norton.

Petrov, Vladimir (1991). "Emotional Impact of Art: Social Aspect." In *Art and Emotions: Proceedings of the International Symposium, September 17–21, 1991*. Perm: Perm State Institute of Culture.

———— (forthcoming). "Art Evolution in the Light of Brain Asymmetry: A Review of Empirical Investigations." In Tarasti, ed. (forthcoming).

Pierce, Alexandra (1982). *Essays on Music Theory, Performance, and Movement*. Redlands, CA: University of Redlands Press.

———— (1987). "Music and Movement." In *Basic Concepts of Musical Signification*. Special issue of *The Semiotic Web*, ed. Thomas A. Sebeok and Jean Umiker-Sebeok. Berlin: Mouton.

———— (forthcoming). "Character and Characterization in Musical Performance: Effects of Sensory Experience upon Meaning." In Tarasti, ed. (forthcoming).

Pike, Lionel (1978). *Beethoven, Sibelius, and the "Profound Logic": Studies in Symphonic Analysis*. London: Athlone.

Ploger, Willi (1990). *Beiträge zu einem Klanggestaltlich motivierten Kommunikationsmodell*. Helsinki: Institut für Allgemeine Sprachwissenschaft.

Posner, Roland (1981). *Rational Discourse and Poetic Communication: Methods of Linguistic, Literary, and Philosophical Analysis*. The Hague: Mouton.

Pozzi, Raffaele, ed. (1989). *La musica come linguaggio universale*. Florence: Olschki.

Propp, Vladimir (1958). *Morphology of the Folktale*. Trans. L. Scott. Bloomington: Indiana University Press.

Rainer, Yvonne (1973). *Work 1961–1973*. New York: New York University Press.

Rantala, Veikko; Lewis Rowell; and Eero Tarasti, eds. (1988). *Essays on the Philosophy of Music*. Acta Philosophica Fennica 43. Helsinki: Societas Philosophica Fennica.

Ratner, Leonard (1980). *Classic Music: Expression, Form, and Style*. New York: Schirmer.

Rector, Monica (1985). "Towards a Classification of Gestures in Orchestra Conducting." In *Exigences et perspectives de la sémiotique: Recueil d'hommages pour Algirdas Julien Greimas*. Amsterdam: Benjamins. Pp. 625–30.

Reich, Steve (1981). *Writings about Music*. Halifax: Nova Scotia College of Art and Design.

Réti, Rudolph (1951). *The Thematic Process in Music*. New York: MacMillan.

Reznikoff, Igor (1981). "Intonation and Modality in the Music of Oral Tradition and Antiquity." In *Basic Concepts of Musical Signification*. Special issue of *The Semiotic Web*, ed. Thomas A. Sebeok and Jean Umiker-Sebeok. Berlin: Mouton.

Ricoeur, Paul (1983). *Temps et récit*. Vol. 1. Paris: Seuil.

Rimsky-Korsakov, Nikolai (1914). *Principes d'orchestration*. Paris: Max Eschig.

Ringbom, Nils-Erik (1948). *Sibelius*. Helsinki: Otava.

Roiha, Eino (1741). *Die Symphonien von Jean Sibelius. Eine form-analytische Studie*. Jyväskylä: Gummerus.

Rolland, Romain (1921). *Vie de Beethoven*. Paris: Hachette.

Rosen, Charles (1976). *The Classical Style*. London: Faber and Faber.

———— (1980). *Sonata Forms*. New York: Norton.

Rowell, Lewis (1979). "The Subconscious Language of Musical Time." *Music Theory Spectrum* 1:96–106.

———— (1983). *Thinking about Music: An Introduction to the Philosophy of Music.* Amherst: University of Massachusetts Press.

———— (1987). "Stasis in Music." *Semiotica* 66 (1/3):181–96.

Ruskin, John (1987). *Modern Painters*, ed. David Barrie. London: Deutsch.

Ruwet, Nicolas (1972). *Langage, musique, poésie*. Paris: Seuil.

Rydman, Kari (1963). "Sibeliuksen neljännen sinfonian rakenneongelmista" [On the Structural Problems of Sibelius's Fourth Symphony]. In *Suomen Musiikin Vuosikirja 1962–1963*. Helsinki: Otava. Pp. 17–32.

Salmenhaara, Erkki (1984). *Jean Sibelius*. Helsinki: Tammi.

Salosaari, Kari (1989). *Perusteita näyttelijäntyön semiotiikkaan* [Fundamentals in the Semiotics of the Player's Craft]. Tampere, Finland: University of Tampere.

Salzer, Felix (1960). *Strukturelles Hören*. 2 vols. Wilhelmshaven: Otto Heinrich Noetzel.

Schaeffer, Pierre (1966). *Traité des objets musicaux*. Paris: Seuil.

Schaeffner, André (1968). *Les origines des instruments de musique*. The Hague: Mouton.

Schenker, Heinrich (1954). *Harmony*, ed. Oswald Jonas. Chicago: University of Chicago Press.

———— (1956). *Neue musikalische Theorien und Phantasien 3: Der freie Satz.* Vienna: Universal.

Schering, Arnold (1936). *Beethoven und die Dichtung*. Berlin: Junker und Dünnhaupt.

Schoenberg, Arnold (1911). *Harmonielehre*. Leipzig: Universal.

———— (1975). *Style and Idea*, ed. Leonard Stein. London: Faber and Faber.

Seashore, Carl (1932). *The Vibrato in Voice and Instruments*. Iowa City: University of Iowa Press.

Sebeok, Thomas A. (1976). *Contributions to the Doctrine of Signs*. Bloomington: Indiana University Press.

———— (1977). *A Perfusion of Signs*. Bloomington: Indiana University Press.

———— (1979). *The Sign and Its Masters*. Austin: University of Texas Press.

———— (1986). *I Think I Am a Verb*. New York: Plenum.

———— (1991a). *Semiotics in the United States*. Bloomington: Indiana University Press.

———— (1991b). *A Sign Is Just a Sign*. Bloomington: Indiana University Press.

Seeger, Charles (1960). "On the Moods of a Music-Logic." *Journal of the American Musicological Society* 13:224–61.

Sénancour, Étienne de (1833). *Obermann*. Paris: Ledoux.

Sloboda, John (1987). *The Musical Mind: The Cognitive Psychology of Music*. Oxford: Oxford University Press.

Souriau, Étienne (1969). *Correspondence des arts*. Paris: Flammarion.

Stefani, Gino (1976). *Introduzione alla semiotica della musica*. Palermo: Sellerio.

———— (1979). *Perché la musica*. Brescia: La Scuola.

———— (1982). *La competenza musicale*. Bologna: CLUEB.

———— (1987a). "A Theory of Musical Competence." *Semiotica* 66 (1/3).

———— (1987b). *Il segno della musica: Saggi di semiotica musicale*. Palermo: Sellerio.

Stoianova, Ivanka (1978). *Geste, texte, musique*. Paris: Union Générale.

———— (1981). "Die 'Neue Einfachheit' in der heutigen Praxis." In *Zur "Neuen Einfachheit" in der Musik*, ed. Otto Kolleritsch. Vienna: Universal.

Sundberg, Johan; Lars Fryden; and Anders Askenfelt (1983). "What Tells You the Player Is Musical?" In *Studies of Performance*, ed. Sundberg. Stockholm: Royal Swedish Music Academy.

Szalbocsi, Bence (1965). *A History of Melody*. Budapest: Corvina.

Tagg, Philip (1979). "Kojak," *Fifty Seconds of Television Music: Towards the Analysis of* Affekt *in Popular Music*. Gothenburg: Musikvetenskapliga Institutionen.
⸻ (1987). "Musicology and the Semiotics of Popular Music." *Semiotica* 66 (1/3): 279–98.
Tarasti, Eero (1979). *Myth and Music*. The Hague: Mouton.
⸻ (1983a). "Sur les structures élémentaires du discours musical." In *Actes sémiotiques* 4: 6–13. Paris: EHESS, Groupe de recherches sémio-linguistiques.
⸻ (1983b). "De l'interpretation musicale." In *Actes sémiotiques, Documents* 5. Paris: EHESS.
⸻ (1984). "Pour une narratologie de Chopin." *International Review of the Aesthetics and Sociology of Music* 15 (1): 53–75.
⸻ (1985a). "Music as Sign and Process." In *Analytica: Studies in the Description and Analysis of Music in Honour of Ingmar Bengtsson*. Stockholm: Royal Swedish Academy of Music.
⸻ (1985b). "A la recherche des 'modalités musicales'." In *Exigences et perspectives de la sémiotique: Recueil d'hommages pour A. J. Greimas*. Amsterdam: Benjamins.
⸻ (1986a). "Ferrucio Busoni o dell'ambiguita strutturale: Aspetti mitici e strutturali di *Doktor Faust*." *Il flusso del tempo* 11, 311–28.
⸻ (1986b). "Music Models through Ages: A Semiotic Interpretation." *International Review of the Aesthetics and Sociology of Music* 17 (1): 22–32.
⸻ (1987a). "On the Modalities of Opera." *Semiotica* 66 (1/3): 155–68.
⸻ (1987b). "Vers une grammaire narrative de la musique." *Degrés* 52: d1–d24.
⸻ (1987c). "Le role du temps dans le discours musical." In *Sémiotique en jeu*. Actes Sémiotiques 5. Paris: EHESS.
⸻ (1987d). "Cage et la modalité du non-vouloir." In *John Cage*, ed. Daniel Charles. Special issues of *Revue d'esthétique* 13–15.
⸻ (1988a). "Le minimalisme du point de vue sémiotique." *Degrés* 53, i1–i22.
⸻ (1988b). "On the Modalities and Narrativity in Music." In Rantala et al., eds.
⸻ (1989). "L'analyse sémiotique d'un prélude de Debussy: 'La terrasse des audiences du clair de lune': La mise en évidence d'un parcours génératif." *Analyse musicale* 16: 67–74.
⸻ (1991a). *Johdatusta semiotiikkaan: Esseitä taiteen ja kulttuurin merkkijärjestelmistä* [Introduction to Semiotics: Essays in the Sign Systems of Art and Culture]. Helsinki: Gaudeamus.
⸻ (forthcoming). *Heitor Villa-Lobos*. Jefferson, NC: McFarland Publishers.
⸻, ed. (1987). *Basic Concepts of Studies in Musical Signification*. Special issue of *The Semiotic Web 1986*. Berlin: Mouton.
⸻, ed. (1991b). *Merkkien kronikka* [Chronicle of Signs]. Imatra: International Semiotics Institute.
⸻, ed. (1991c). "Semiotics of Finland." Special issue of *Semiotica*. Berlin: Mouton.
⸻, ed. (1991d). "La *sémiotique* finlandaise." Special issue of *Degrés*. Brussels.
⸻, ed. (forthcoming). *Musical Signification: Proceedings from the Second International Congress on Musical Signification held at the University of Helsinki in 1988*. Berlin: Mouton.
Tawaststjerna, Erik (1972). *Jean Sibelius III*. Helsinki: Otava.
⸻ (1976). *Sibelius I*. Trans. Robert Layton. London: Faber and Faber.
Thoresen, Lasse (1987). "An Auditive Analysis of Schubert's Piano Sonata Op. 42." *Semiotica* 66 (1/3): 211–37.
Tynianov, Juri (1977). *Le vers lui-même: Les problèmes du vers*. Paris: Union Générale.
Uhde, Jürgen (1974). *Beethovens Klaviermusik* 3. Stuttgart: Reclam.
Uspenski, B. A., et al. (1973). "Theses on the Semiotic Study of Culture." In *Structures*

of Texts and Semiotics of Culture. Ed. J. van der Eng and Mojmir Grygar. The Hague: Mouton.

Vattimo, Gianni (1985). *La fine della modernita: Nihilismo ed ermeneutica nella cultura postmoderna*. Rome: Garganzi.

Walker, John A. (1977). *Glossary of Art, Architecture, and Design since 1945*. London: Faber and Faber.

Wright, Georg Henrik von (1963). *Norm and Action: A Logical Enquiry*. London: Routledge and Kegan Paul.

Zilberberg, Claude (1985). *L'essor du poème: Information rhythmique*. Vol. 2. Saint-Maurdes-Fosses: Phoriques.

Zuckerkandl, Victor (1959). *The Sense of Music*. Princeton, NJ: Princeton University Press.

INDEX

EERO TARASTI is Professor of Musicology at the University of Helsinki. One of the world's leading semioticians, he is author of Myth and Music, a study of Heitor Villa-Lobos, and many articles published in journals of musicology and semiotics.